UNHOLY

An Almost Complete Hagiography of Gay Saints

Illustrations by F.G. BORGHI
Texts by BJÖRN KOLL

SALZGEBER

VORBEMERKUNG

Was Sie in diesem Buch lesen, gehört in die Kategorie *Historische Fiktion*, einige würden vielleicht auch von *Historischem Blödsinn* sprechen. Will sagen: Keiner der hier beschriebenen Heiligen hat je gelebt und nichts von dem, was über sie behauptet wird, stimmt. Ähnlichkeiten mit lebenden oder verstorbenen Menschen und Heiligen wären rein zufällig und völlig unbeabsichtigt, aber selbstverständlich kollidieren unsere schwulen Heiligen zuweilen mit dem Zeit- und Kulturgeschehen. Keinesfalls sollen religiöse Gefühle verletzt werden. Wenn Sie in diesem Punkt sensibel oder humorfrei sind, stellen Sie die schwulen Heiligen also bitte zurück in den Bücherschrank.

Alle Namenstage unserer Heiligen werden im Format des Schwulen Kalenders verzeichnet. Auf Nennungen im Römisch-Katholischen, Äthiopischen, Gregorianischen, Griechisch-Orthodoxen, Julianischen, Koptischen, Schwedischen, Berberischen, Chuch'e, Rumi, Gengō, Suriyakati, Minguo, Badi, Bengalischen, Diskordianischen, Französisch- oder Sowjetisch-Revolutionären, Georgischen, Hinduistischen, Indischen, Iranischen, Irischen, Altisländischen, Malayalam, Maliye, Megalithischen, Nakaiiy, Orissa, Porhalaan, Sikh, Tamilischen oder Zoroastrischen Kalenderformat wurde *aus gutem Grund* verzichtet.

PREFACE

Everything you are about to read in this book falls under the category of *historical fiction* — some might even say *historical nonsense*. In other words, none of the saints described here actually existed and none of the claims made about them are true. While any resemblance to actual saints or persons, either living or dead, is purely coincidental and completely unintentional, our gay saints do occasionally cross paths with certain historical and cultural trends. Under no circumstances do we intend to offend anyone's religious sensibilities. So please, if you are sensitive or lacking in humor in this regard, this book is not for you.

All the name days of our saints are listed in the Gay Calendar format. We have opted not to include any entries in the Roman Catholic, Ethiopian, Gregorian, Greek Orthodox, Julian, Coptic, Swedish, Berber, Juche, Rumi, Gengō, Suriyakhati, Minguo, Badi, Bengali, Discordian, Revolutionary French or Soviet, Georgian, Hindu, Indian, Iranian, Irish, Old Icelandic, Malayalam, Maliyya, Megalithic, Nakaiy, Orissa, Porhalaan, Sikh, Tamil or Zoroastrian calendar formats. *For good reason.*

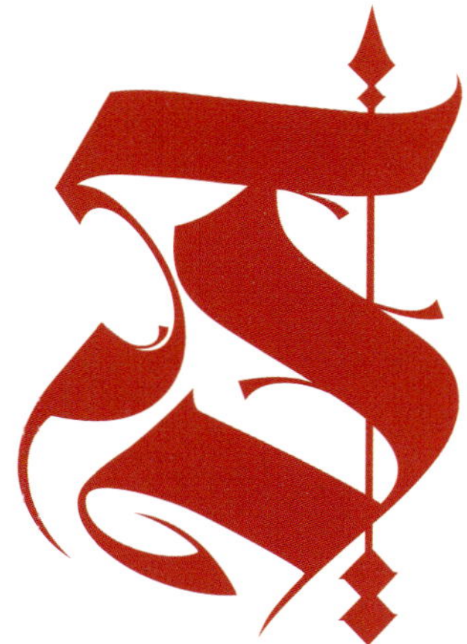

elbstverständlich gab es schon immer schwule Heilige. Bis 1891 wurden diese auch in der Kirche prominent gefeiert und hatten gerade im Volksglauben eine große Popularität. So war über Jahrhunderte der 28. Juni als *Tag der schwulen Heiligen* ein ganz besonderer Feiertag unter Christen, der zwischenzeitlich in Vergessenheit geriet, um erst 1969 in der New Yorker Christopher Street unter ganz anderen Vorzeichen wiederbelebt zu werden. Es ist noch nicht genau erforscht, was gerade Papst Leo XIII. veranlasste, seine Enzyklika *Rerum Novarum* um ein geheimes Kapitel zu ergänzen, das kategorisch und ohne Begründung anordnete, alle schwulen Heiligen mit sofortiger Wirkung aus den offiziellen Hagiographien, insbesondere aus dem *Martyrologium Romanum*, zu entfernen und jegliche weitere Anbetung, Anrufung und sogar Erwähnung unter Strafe stellte. Die Enzyklika und das geheime Zusatzprotokoll erschienen am 15. Mai 1891 und wurden radikal umgesetzt. Nicht nur das Drucken der beliebten Heiligenbilder wurde sofort untersagt, sie wurden auch von den Pfarrern eingesammelt, vernichtet und sämtlich durch Marienbilder ersetzt.

Dies alles steht möglicherweise im direkten Zusammenhang mit der Marienverehrung durch Leo XIII. In seiner *Augustissimae virginis mariae (Erhabene Jungfrau Maria)* bestätigte er nicht nur das Dogma der Unbefleckten Empfängnis, sondern forderte auch, jeder Gläubige solle die „Marienverehrung zu seiner liebsten und teuersten Angelegenheit machen". Durch sein langes Pontifikat von über 25 Jahren und 5 Monaten hatte Leo XIII. ausreichend Zeit, für eine wirklich vollständige Tilgung aller Spuren der schwulen Heiligen zu sorgen. Gemälde, deren Reproduktionen, aber auch Fresken wurden unter Beaufsichtigung der Kongregation für die Glaubenslehre zerstört oder übermalt. Spuren lassen sich aber häufig von aufmerksamen Betrachtern immer noch entdecken.

In den 85 Regalkilometern des Vatikanischen Apostolischen Archivs wurde — direkt neben dem Brief Heinrichs VIII. mit der Bitte um Annullierung einer seiner Ehen — je ein Exemplar verschiedener Bildnisse schwuler Heiliger aufbewahrt. Die Lagerung erfolgte in einem von Mario Prada und seinem Bruder Martino gefertigten Koffer, den Pius XII. 1939 erworben hatte, der ihm dann aber nicht mehr gefiel. Im Mai 1944 — kurz vor der Befreiung der Stadt Rom — wurde der Koffer von einem Beauftragten Heinrich Himmlers geklaut, und bis 1959 verlor sich seine Spur. Dann tauchte der Koffer samt Inhalt am 25. August 1959 bei einer Tagung im Institut für Marxismus-Leninismus in Bukarest wieder auf. Elena Ceaușescu („Ich war doch wie eine Mutter zu euch."), offenbar mit Sinn für gute Qualität ausgestattet, eignete sich den Koffer an und behielt ihn bis zu ihrer Erschießung am 25. Dezember 1989. Bei der am 21. Juli 2010 durchgeführten Exhumierung der Ceaușescus wurden Spuren des Koffers gefunden, die die Gewissheit brachten, dass es sich wirklich um die verscharrten Eheleute handelte.

Die Heiligenbilder selbst wurden auf der Bukarester Konferenz 1959 (sie trug den internationalen Titel *Sozialismus First!* oder auch *First Sozialismus!* und das wird je nach Übersetzendem unterschiedlich gesehen) mit der Fragestellung, ob sie sich für antireligiöse Propaganda eignen könnten, ausführlich und kritisch diskutiert. Letztendlich waren es die Vertreter von Nikita Sergejewitsch Chruschtschow und Walter Ulbricht, also aus der Sowjetunion und der DDR, die sich dagegen aussprachen. Gerade in der DDR war man damals dabei, *Zehn Gebote der sozialistischen Moral und Ethik* (auch: *10 Gebote für den neuen sozialistischen Menschen*) zu etablieren, die kirchliche Traditionen durch staatliche Ideologie ersetzen sollten. Ein Anliegen, bei dem die schwulen Heiligen in den Augen der Funktionäre nur gestört hätten. Darüber hinaus war der heilige Emil (siehe Seite 42) den versammelten Spießern auch besonders peinlich.

Die Heiligenbilder wurden in das Berliner Institut für Marxismus-Leninismus beim Zentralkomitee der Sozialistischen Einheitspartei Deutschlands verbracht und interessierten dort erstmal niemanden mehr — zumal sie versteckt und nicht katalogisiert in einer rumänischen Gesamtausgabe der Werke von Karl Marx (Band 1 bis 42) verteilt wurden. Der Koffer war schließlich in Rumänien verblieben. Der chinesische Diplomat Ki Peng (andere sprechen auch von Ai Peng) erwarb 2024 diese Gesamtausgabe bei einem Berliner Trödler. Ihm verdanken wir auch die wertvollen Recherchen zu den einzelnen Heiligen, die er in mühevoller Detailarbeit aus ganz verschiedenen Archiven zusammensammelte. Ki konnte sich dabei nicht nur auf weltweite Sympathien verlassen, sondern wurde auch großzügig vom *Institut für Informationswiederbeschaffung* (I.F.I. oder auch Wikipedia) unterstützt.

Und noch kurz zur zahlenmäßigen Einordnung: In seinem *Ökumenischen Heiligenlexikon* (Stand Sommer 2024, zuletzt aktualisiert am 24.06.2024) führt Autor Joachim Schäfer 8.490 Personen und rund 8.200 namenlose Märtyrer, also rund 16.700 Heilige und Selige auf. Grundlage seiner Untersuchungen ist das seit 1584 erscheinende *Martyrologium Romanum* in der jeweils aktuellen Ausgabe. Außerdem sei der Korrektheit halber dazugesagt: Papst Leo XIII. war nicht der erste Papst, der Heilige wieder aus dem Programm warf. Schon Benedikt XIV. tilgte 1748 zum Beispiel Clemens von Alexandria, den wir auf Seite 24 wieder zu seinem guten Recht kommen lassen. In diesem Kosmos der 16.700 Heiligen und Seligen fallen unsere wiederentdeckten 109 schwulen Kandidaten also nicht weiter auf, aber sie sorgen für ein bisschen Farbe und Abwechslung. Kurz vor Redaktionsschluss meldete sich Ki Peng übrigens unerwartet, um zu fragen, warum dieses Buch noch nicht im Druck sei. Dabei kündigte er einen weiteren Fund bei dem gleichen Berliner Trödler an. Bleiben wir also gespannt, was noch so alles ans Tageslicht kommt.

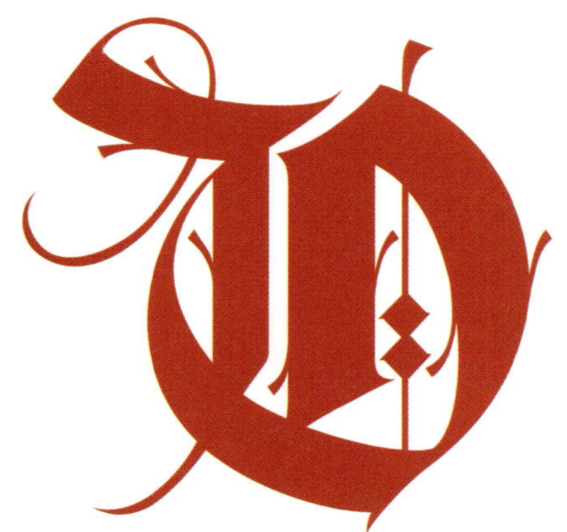bviously, there have always been gay saints. Until 1891, they were also widely celebrated in the church and were especially popular in folk traditions. *Gay Saints' Day* on June 28 was a very special holiday celebrated by Christians for centuries and then forgotten, only to be revived in 1969 on Christopher Street in New York under entirely different auspices. Scholars are still not entirely sure what prompted Pope Leo XIII to add a secret chapter to his encyclical *Rerum Novarum*, which categorically (and groundlessly) ordered all gay saints to be removed from the official hagiographies, especially the *Martyrologium Romanum*, with immediate effect and made all further worship, invocation and even mention of them a punishable offense. The encyclical and its secret supplemental protocol were published on May 15, 1891 and were rigorously implemented. Not only was there an immediate ban on printing holy cards with the popular portraits of gay saints, all the existing images were seized by the priests, destroyed, and replaced with images of the Virgin Mary.

This may be directly linked to the Marian views espoused by Pope Leo XIII who, in his *Augustissimae virginis mariae (The Most August Virgin Mary)*, not only confirmed the dogma of the Immaculate Conception, but also exhorted the faithful to "hold nothing dearer than devotion to Mary." Leo XIII's long pontificate of over twenty-five years and five months gave him plenty of time to ensure that all traces of the gay saints had been completely eradicated. Paintings (originals and reproductions alike) and frescoes were destroyed or painted over under the supervision of the Congregation for the Doctrine of the Faith. The observant viewer will, however, often still be able to discover traces.

A copy of each of the various portraits of the gay saints was stored somewhere in the eighty-five kilometers of shelves in the Vatican Apostolic Archives — right next to a letter from Henry VIII requesting the annulment of one of his marriages. They were kept in a suitcase made by Mario Prada and his brother Martino, which Pius XII had acquired in 1939 but then decided he no longer liked. In May 1944 — shortly before the Liberation of Rome — the suitcase was stolen by an agent of Heinrich Himmler, and until 1959 all trace of it was lost. Then, on August 25, 1959, the suitcase and its contents resurfaced at a conference at the Institute for Marxism-Leninism in Bucharest. Elena "I was like a mother to you" Ceaușescu, clearly blessed with a keen eye for quality, appropriated the suitcase and kept it until she was shot on December 25, 1989. The exhumation of Elena and her husband on July 21, 2010 revealed traces of the suitcase, which confirmed that the bodies were indeed those of the unlucky couple.

The portraits of the saints themselves were discussed critically and at length at the Bucharest conference in 1959 (which bore the international title *Socialism First!* or *First Socialism!* depending on which translation you prefer) as to whether they might be suitable for use in anti-religious propaganda. Ultimately, this plan was prevented by the representatives of Nikita Sergeyevich Khrushchev and Walter Ulbricht, i.e., the Soviet Union and the GDR. At the time, the GDR in particular was in the process of establishing its own *Ten Commandments of Socialist Morality and Ethics* (also known as the *Ten Commandments for the New Socialist Man*), which were intended to replace the traditions of the church with an ideology of the state. In the eyes of the party officials, the gay saints would only have been a hindrance. St. Emil (see page 42) was a particular source of embarrassment to the assembled philistines.

The pictures were taken to the Berlin Institute for Marxism-Leninism at the Central Committee of the Socialist Unity Party of Germany, where they were no longer of interest to anyone — especially since they were not catalogued and instead hidden away in a Romanian edition of the complete works of Karl Marx (volumes 1 to 42). The suitcase itself remained in Romania. In 2024, the Chinese diplomat Ai Peng acquired the edition from a junk dealer in Berlin. We also have him to thank for the valuable research on the individual saints, which he painstakingly compiled from a host of different archives. Not only did Ai enjoy the goodwill of an international community, he also received generous support from the *Institute for Information Retrieval* (I.I.R. or Wikipedia).

Finally, a brief look at the numbers: In his *Ecumenical Dictionary of Saints* (as of summer 2024, last updated on June 24, 2024), Joachim Schäfer lists 8,490 named individuals and around 8,200 nameless martyrs, i.e., around 16,700 saints and blesseds. His research is based on the latest edition of the *Martyrologium Romanum*, which has been in circulation since 1584. For the sake of accuracy, it should also be noted that Pope Leo XIII was not the first pope to drop saints from the calendar. In 1748, for example, Clement of Alexandria was removed by Benedict XIV and we have duly reinstated him on page 24. In this vast cosmos of 16,700 saints and blesseds, our newly rediscovered 109 gay contenders are barely noticeable, but they do provide a bit of color and variety. Shortly before this book went to press, we were unexpectedly contacted by Ai Peng to ask why it was not yet in print. He then announced that he had made yet another find at the same Berlin junk dealer. We will be following his story with interest to see what else comes to light.

DER HEILIGE AFRIEL

Afriel (544 bis 599) war ein Westgote und arbeitete in Toledo als Barkeeper in einer Nachtbar. Wie bei kaum einem anderen Heiligen gehen die Geschichten über ihn kreuz und quer und völlig durcheinander. Manche beschreiben ihn als Engel, was er keinesfalls war. Als Engel der Jugend soll er mit seinen Energien aber für Vitalität und innere Stärke sorgen. Bei den Deutschen wird seine Geschichte als Sage von Siegfried erzählt, der im Drachenblut gebadet hat. Hier spielt das Lindenblatt auf der Schulter eine entscheidende Rolle. Angeblich war die Stelle, wo das Blatt beim Baden im Blut gelegen hatte, seine einzige verwundbare Stelle. Unsere historisch korrekte Abbildung zeigt eindeutig kein Lindenblatt, und auch die Engelsflügel sehen eher angeklebt aus. Das hat alles seine Richtigkeit, denn Afriel war schlichtweg ein kiffender Teenager, der sich gerne verkleidete und in seinem Job wahnsinnig viel Spaß hatte. Seine *Muchacho-Bar* in Toledo war der Hotspot der Stadt, zumal es damals noch kein Internet gab und die Menschen noch vor die Tür gingen. Legendäre Mottopartys und die liebevolle Gestaltung des Raums zogen Jung und Alt an, und der Darkroom war immer gut besucht. Cannabis bezog Afriel aus Marokko, und es mag sein, dass er sich mit dem Verkauf unter dem Tresen illegal etwas dazuverdiente. Afriel steht aber nicht nur für hedonistische Feierkultur, er war auch der Erfinder des therapeutischen Spiels *Ich sehe was, was du nicht siehst*, bei dem in der damaligen Form die Menschen am Tresen im berauschten oder nüchternen Zustand von ihren Sorgen, Ängsten, Träumen und Hoffnungen oder auch schlicht von ihrer Kindheit erzählen durften. Es gab keinen besseren Zuhörer als Afriel. Damit war er der Erfinder der Psychoanalyse, mit der er dann in späteren, ruhigeren Jahren auch sein Geld verdiente. Zu seinen Kunden — erst in der Bar und dann auf der Couch — gehörte übrigens auch Rekkared I., König der Westgoten von April/Mai 586 bis Dezember 601. Rekkared verwendete viel Energie auf den Wechsel vom arianischen zum katholischen Glauben und hatte einen jüngeren Bruder: Hermenegild (übrigens ein katholischer Heiliger), der möglicherweise vom eigenen Vater ermordet wurde. Auch Rekkareds unehelicher Sohn und Nachfolger Liuva II. — mehrere Ehen von Rekkared blieben kinderlos oder wurden nicht vollzogen — starb eines gewaltsamen Todes. Ihm wurde die Hand abgeschlagen. Umso verdienstvoller, dass Afriel in diesem ganzen Gemetzel seine gute Laune nicht verlor. Zugleich zeigt der Fall Rekkared deutlich die Grenzen der Psychoanalyse auf, sodass die moderne Forschung fragt, ob vielleicht eine Familienaufstellung besser geholfen hätte.

Afriel ist der Heilige der Psychoanalytiker und kann, wann immer es kompliziert wird, angerufen werden. Ob er dann allerdings hilft oder anderweitig beschäftigt ist, ist eine andere Frage. Wir gedenken Afriels am 17. Mai.

SAINT AFRIEL

Afriel (544 to 599) was a Visigoth and worked as a barkeeper in a nightclub in Toledo. More than almost any other saint, he is the subject of countless varied and often contradictory stories. Sometimes described as angelic, he was certainly no angel. As an emblem of youth, however, he is said to use his powers to restore vitality and inner strength. The Germans tell his story as the tale of Siegfried, who bathed in the blood of a dragon. A leaf fell from a lime tree onto his shoulder while he was submerged in the bloody bath, leaving an untouched spot, the only spot where he was vulnerable. Our historically accurate illustration clearly does not show a leaf, and the angel's wings appear to be tacked on. This is perfectly correct, because Afriel was nothing more than a pot-smoking teenager who liked to dress up and have a crazy amount of fun at the bar where he worked. The *Muchacho Bar* in Toledo was the city's hottest hangout, especially as there was no internet back then and people still regularly left the house. Legendary theme parties and the beautifully designed space attracted visitors of all ages, and the darkroom was always packed. Afriel sourced his cannabis from Morocco, and he may have earned a little extra illicit cash by selling it under the bar. But Afriel is not only associated with hedonistic party culture, he was also the inventor of the therapeutic game *I spy with my little eye* which, in its original form, gave people at the bar the opportunity to talk about their worries, anxieties, hopes and dreams, or simply about their childhoods, regardless of whether they were drunk or sober. Nobody was a better listener than Afriel. This made him the inventor of psychoanalysis, with which he was to earn his living in his later, somewhat mellower years. One of his clients — first in the bar and then on the couch — was Visigoth King Reccared I (April/May 586 to December 601). Reccared wasted a lot of energy on converting from Arianism to the Catholic faith and had a younger brother called Hermenegild (a Catholic saint, by the way), who may have been murdered by his own father. Reccared's illegitimate son and successor Liuva II — several of Reccared's marriages remained childless or were not consummated — also died a violent death: he had his hand cut off. In light of this carnage, it is all the more commendable that Afriel managed to maintain his cheerful disposition. At the same time, the story of Reccared clearly demonstrates the limitations of psychoanalysis, prompting modern researchers to ask whether family therapy might have been more helpful.

Afriel is the patron saint of psychoanalysts and may be invoked whenever things get complicated. Whether he will actually provide any help or be otherwise occupied is another question entirely. May 17 is dedicated to the memory of St. Afriel.

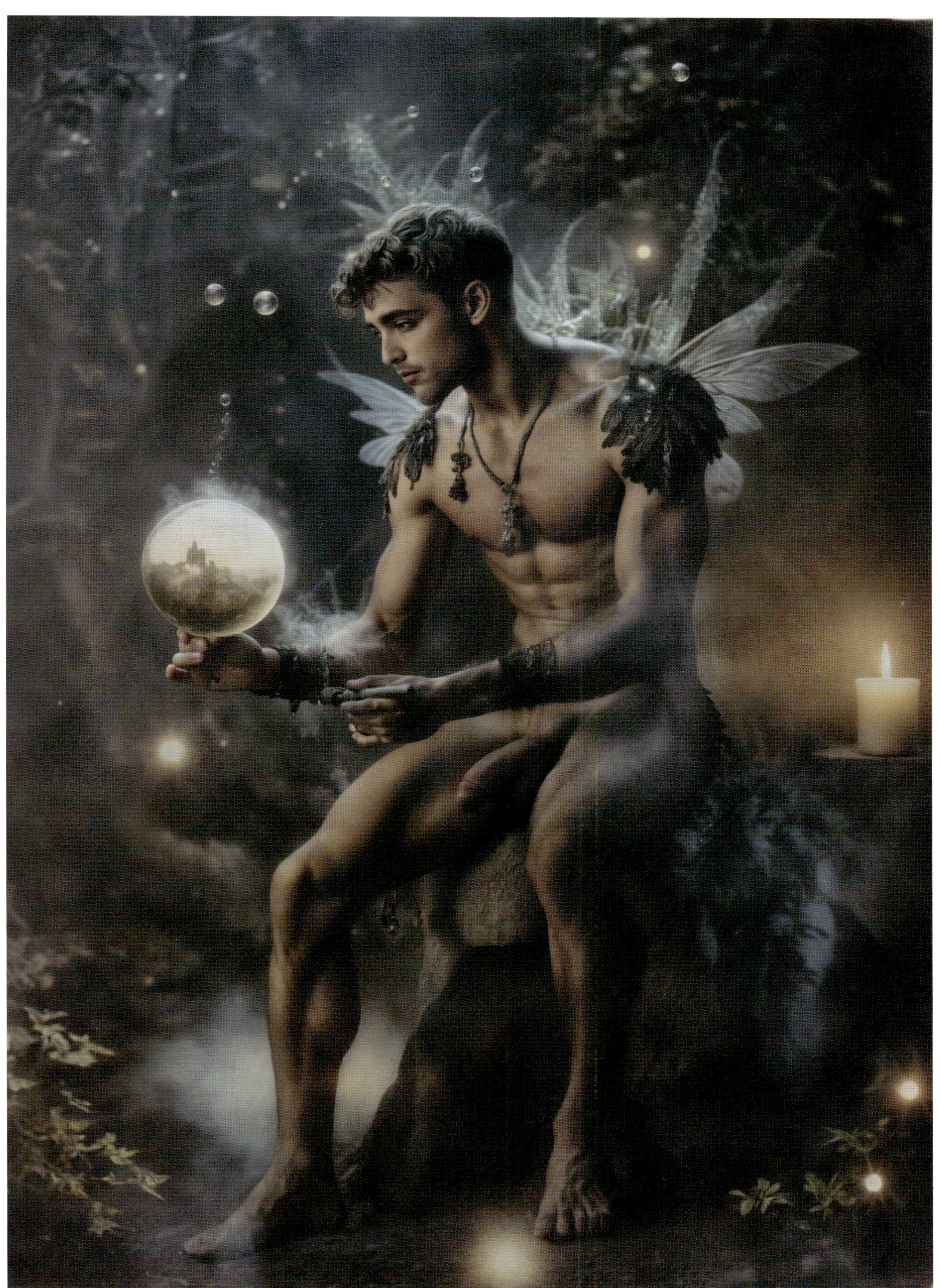

DER HEILIGE AFRIEL · SAINT AFRIEL

DER HEILIGE AINSLEY

Der heilige Ainsley wurde 1001 in Strontian auf der schottischen Halbinsel Ardnamurchan (schottisch-gälisch: Àird nam Murchan) geboren. Entsprechend seinem Vornamen, der sowohl weiblich als auch männlich ist, entwickelte Ainsley sich zu einem fröhlichen, aufgeweckten und neugierigen Kind. Er entdeckte das chemische Element Strontium (Elementsymbol Sr; Ordnungszahl 38), das er auf dem Leuchtturm nahe dem Point of Ardnamurchan dafür verwendete, besonders schöne rote Feuer zu entfachen. Damit lockte Ainsley regelmäßig Wikingerschiffe an und hatte bald auf jedem Schiff einen Liebhaber, häufig auch mehrere. Dies wurde als *Ainsley-* oder *Love-Not-Hate-Verfahren* an vielen anderen schottischen Küstenorten und später auch in Irland kopiert, was schnell zu einer Aussöhnung zwischen den räuberischen Nordmännern und der lokalen Bevölkerung führte. Man sagt, dass diese Entwicklung dem lieben Gott so gut gefiel, dass er in der Kentra Bay den Sand singen ließ und immer noch lässt. Beim Betreten des Strandabschnitts der sogenannten *Singing Sands* ertönen tiefe, wohlige Töne, die an glücklichen Sex erinnern. Darüber hinaus entwickelte der aufgeweckte und sehr feierfreudige Ainsley auch das Verfahren zur Whisky-Herstellung. Er wollte sich bei seinen Wikingerfreunden, die ihn gerne mit Met versorgten, erkenntlich zeigen und ihnen zum Dank seinerseits eine Freude machen. Das Wissen um die Whisky-Herstellung wurde über die Jahrhunderte weitergegeben, während das Strontium in Vergessenheit geriet und erst 1790 wiederentdeckt wurde. Der Heilige Ainsley wurde im hohen Alter gemeinsam mit seinem letzten Liebhaber Erik Kjempe Pikk unter dem Hügel Rickys Cairn beerdigt.

Ein Heiligenbild des heiligen Ainsley fehlte in keiner schottischen Brauerei. Die Bilder mussten häufig ausgewechselt werden, weil es zur Tradition wurde, dass jeder Mensch beim Vorbeilaufen einmal zärtlich an einer bestimmten Stelle über das Bild streichelte. Der heilige Ainsley wird (auch) am 13. Dezember gefeiert.

SAINT AINSLEY

St. Ainsley was born in Strontian on the Scottish peninsula of Ardnamurchan (Scottish Gaelic: Àird nam Murchan) in 1001. In keeping with his given name, which can be both male and female, Ainsley was a lively, bright and curious child. He discovered the chemical element strontium (symbol Sr; atomic number 38), which he used to light exceptionally beautiful red fires at the lighthouse near the Point of Ardnamurchan. This regularly attracted Viking ships, and Ainsley soon had a lover — often more than one — on every ship. This practice (known as the *Ainsley* or *Love-Not-Hate method*) was adopted in many other Scottish coastal towns and later in Ireland, and quickly brought about a reconciliation between the rapacious Norsemen and the local population. It is said that this development pleased the Lord so much that He made the sands sing in Kentra Bay. Which they do to this day. Just step onto the stretch of beach known as the *Singing Sands*, and you will hear deep, melodious sounds reminiscent of blissful sex. The bright and party-loving Ainsley was also responsible for the development of whisky making. This was to show his gratitude to his Viking friends, who were always more than happy to provide him with mead, by offering them a wee dram in return. While knowledge about whisky production was passed down through the centuries, strontium was completely forgotten and only rediscovered in 1790. Saint Ainsley died at a very ripe old age and was buried under Rickys Cairn mound together with his last lover, Erik Kjempe Pikk.

A portrait of St. Ainsley used to hang on the wall of every Scottish brewery. The pictures had to be replaced frequently because it became a tradition for visitors to stroke a certain part of the portrait tenderly as they walked by. The feast of St. Ainsley is celebrated on December 13.

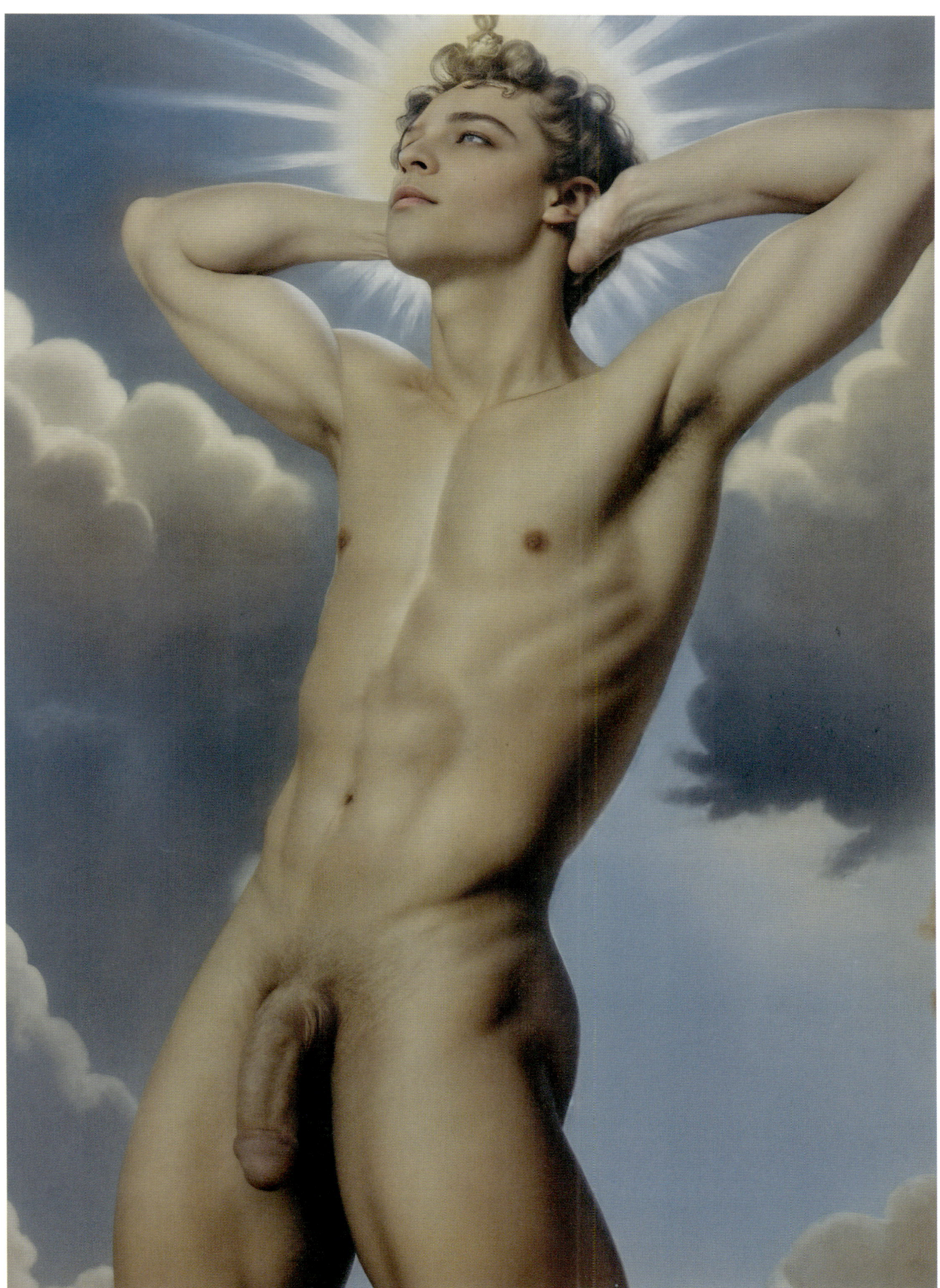

DER HEILIGE AINSLEY · SAINT AINSLEY

DIE HEILIGEN BAKCHOS, SERGIOS UND VISSARÍON

Sergios und Bakchos, auch Sergius und Bacchus (altgriechisch Σέργιος και Βάκχος, angeblich † um 303 in Resafa, Syrien) waren *erastai* (altgriechisch *Liebende*) und durch den Ritus der Adelphopoiesis (*Bruderschaft*) miteinander verbunden. Sie sind als frühchristliche Märtyrer bestens bekannt. Aber wir kennen auch Vissaríon, und damit die ganze Wahrheit. Vissaríon war der Dritte im Bunde, auf den Sergios und Bakchos einfach nicht verzichten wollten, weil er ihre Beziehung aufpeppte. Eine ganz moderne Ehe zu dritt sozusagen. Die drei schoben langweilige Wachdienste in Resafa, das an der Strata Diocletiana (Diokletianische Straße) im Norden Syriens in der Wüste lag. Es standen die in der römischen Armee üblichen Versetzungen an: Sergios sollte nach Colonia Claudia Ara Agrippinensium (Köln), Bakchos nach Lutetia Parisiorum (Paris) und Vissaríon sogar nach Londinium (London), also an den Arsch der Welt, versetzt werden. Weil darauf keiner von ihnen Lust hatte, beschlossen sie — angestiftet von Vissaríon, der ein kleiner Rebell war — zu desertieren. In Frauenkleidern marschierten sie die Strata Diocletiana über Damaskus bis nach Bostra hinunter, dann weiter nach Petra, wo ihnen Beduinen zur Flucht nach Ägypten verhalfen. Dort tauchten sie unter und gründete unter falschem Namen in Assuan ein sehr schönes Hotel mit breiten Betten, weicher Bettwäsche, einem Spa, freundlichen Mitarbeitenden, einem tollen Blick auf die Katarakte im Nil und allem, was sonst noch so dazugehört. Die römische Armeeführung war sauer, und damit das Beispiel nicht Schule machte, wurde eine wilde Geschichte erfunden. Darin ging es um Auspeitschen bis zum Tode, Enthauptung, Frauenkleider als Strafe, eine goldene Hellebarde, die irgendwo in Italien vom Himmel fiel, und Leichen, die in den Euphrat geworfen und nun von Adler und Löwe bewacht würden … Nun ja. Vissaríon, als der vermeintliche Hauptschuldige, wurde in diesen Geschichten einfach gecancelt. Sergios und Bakchos machten derweil in den ostorthodoxen und orientalisch-orthodoxen Zweigen der katholischen Kirchen Karriere, wurden aber dann ausgerechnet 1969, parallel zu Stonewall, aus dem *Martyrologium* gestrichen.

Bakchos, Sergios und Vissaríon kümmern sich um kluge Soldaten, vertreiben Langeweile und helfen Hoteliers, ganz besonders an ihrem Gedenktag, dem 8. Januar.

SAINTS BACCHUS, SERGIUS AND VISSARÍON

Sergius and Bacchus (Ancient Greek Σέργιος και Βάκχος, allegedly † around 303 in Resafa, Syria) were *erastai* (Ancient Greek: *lovers*) and were bound together by the rite of adelphopoiesis (*brotherhood*). They are already well known as early Christian martyrs. Today, however, we know the whole truth: there was a third man called Vissaríon. Three is company — at least according to Sergius and Bacchus, who refused to live without Vissaríon because he spiced up their relationship. A modern throuple, so to speak. The three of them were assigned to monotonous guard duties in Resafa, which was situated in the desert on the Strata Diocletiana (Diocletian's Road) in northern Syria. As was customary in the Roman army, the three officers were due to be transferred: Sergius was to be sent to Colonia Claudia Ara Agrippinensium (Cologne), Bacchus to Lutetia Parisiorum (Paris) and Vissaríon as far away as Londinium (London), i.e., the sticks. None of them were enthusiastic about this move, and so — under the instigation of Vissaríon, who was a bit of a rebel — they decided to desert. Donning women's clothing, they set out along the Strata Diocletiana via Damascus to Bostra, then on to Petra, where they escaped to Egypt with the assistance of some Bedouins. In Egypt, they went into hiding and, taking on an assumed name, set up a very nice hotel in Aswan with spacious beds, soft bedding, a spa, friendly staff, a great view of the cataracts in the Nile and anything else your heart might desire. The Roman army leadership was furious and made up a bizarre story to prevent this from setting a precedent. The story involved its protagonists being flogged to death, beheaded, forced to wear women's clothing as a punishment, as well as a golden halberd falling from the sky somewhere in Italy, and corpses being thrown into the Euphrates, where they are now guarded by eagles and lions … Go figure. Vissaríon, supposedly the main culprit, was simply dropped from these stories. Sergius and Bacchus enjoyed great popularity in the Eastern Orthodox and Oriental Orthodox branches of the Catholic Church, but were then struck from the *Martyrologium* in 1969, ironically enough, the same year as Stonewall.

Bacchus, Sergius and Vissaríon take care of clever soldiers, banish boredom and help hoteliers, especially on their feast day, January 8th.

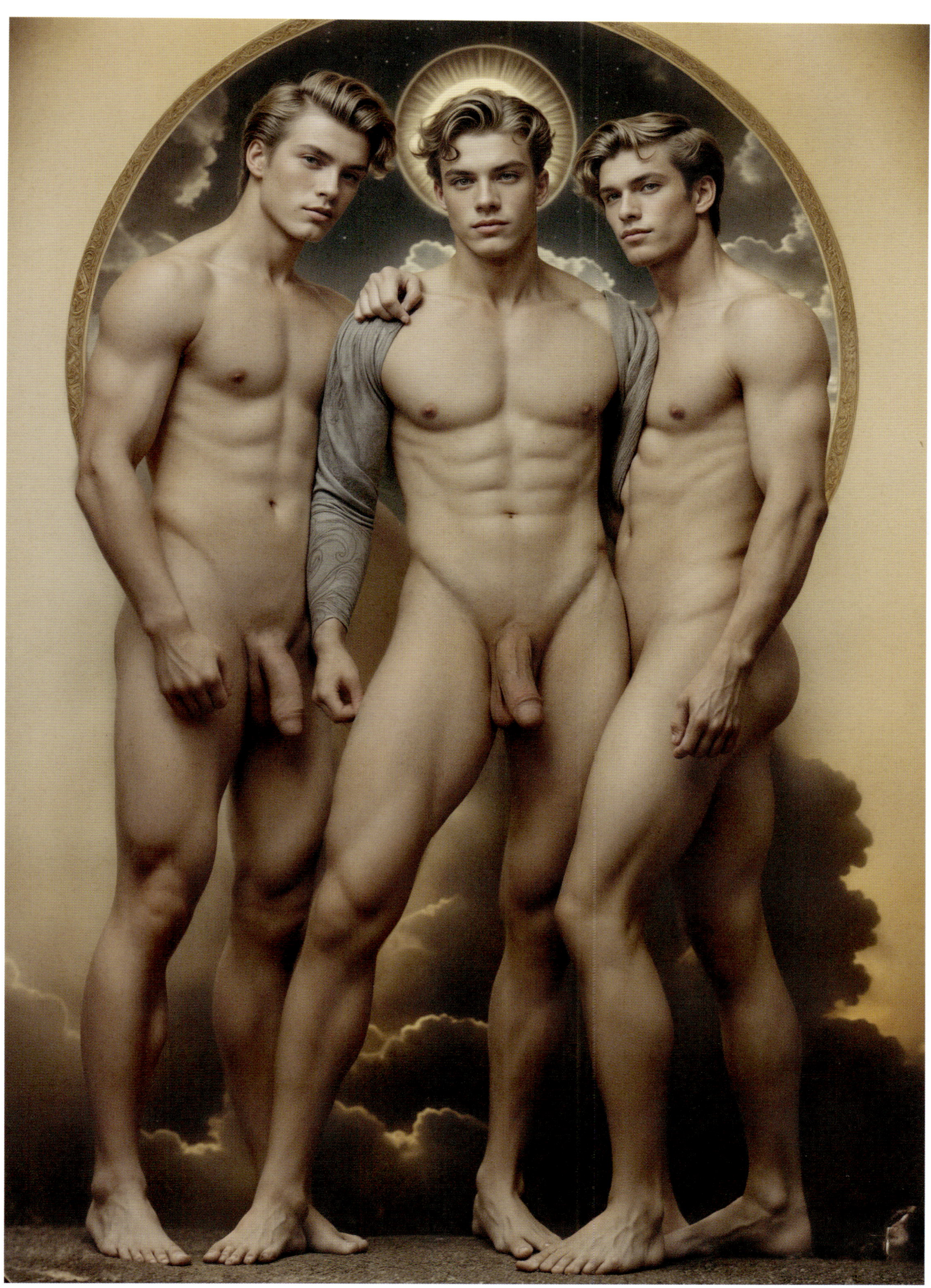

DIE HEILIGEN BAKCHOS, SERGIOS UND VISSARÍON
SAINT BAKCHOS, SERGIOS AND VISSARÍON

BENT

Bent Braderup wurde 1763 in Kopenhagen geboren und ging 1779 nach Philadelphia, wo er zum Mitarbeiter von Alexander Hamilton, dem späteren ersten Finanzminister der USA wurde. Schon vor der Unterzeichnung der Unabhängigkeitserklärung am 4. Juli 1776 hatten die ehemaligen Kolonien jede Menge Papiergeld ausgegeben, das sehr schnell an Wert verlor. Es kam zu Protesten gegen das wertlose Geld und wütende Amerikaner prägten den Ausdruck *not worth a Continental*. Bent ging mit dem Problem flexibel um. Das hatte er schon auf der Schiffsreise nach Amerika gelernt, denn immer, wenn er sich mit „Hi, I'm Bent" vorstellte, fingen alle an zu lachen, weil in Großbritannien *bent* ein umgangssprachlicher Ausdruck für homosexuell ist. Er stellte sich dann korrekt mit „Hi, I'm Bent and I'm gay…" vor, was er später im Finanzministerium durch den Zusatz „… and we all have to be honest" ergänzte. Dank Bent und zur Überraschung vieler übernahm der neugegründete Staat 1789 die Kriegsschulden und zahlte die unglaubliche Summe von 75 Millionen Dollar tatsächlich zurück. Damit verdanken wir Bent, dass der Dollar ein Erfolg wurde und die Staatsfinanzen der USA zumindest bis heute irgendwie funktionieren.

Bent wird von Haushaltspolitikern und anderen ehrlichen Menschen geschätzt. Er wird am 25. Februar verehrt.

BENT

Bent Braderup was born in Copenhagen in 1763. In 1779 he emigrated to Philadelphia, where he became an employee of Alexander Hamilton, who was later to become the first US Secretary of the Treasury. The former colonies had already issued a lot of paper money before the Declaration of Independence was signed on July 4, 1776, and it quickly lost value. There were protests against the worthless money and an irate American public coined the phrase *not worth a Continental*. Bent took a flexible approach to the problem. This was something he had learned on the voyage to America: whenever he introduced himself there as "Hi, I'm Bent," everyone burst out laughing (in the UK, bent is a slang term for gay) and so he took to introducing himself by saying "Hi, I'm Bent and I'm gay," to which he later, at the Ministry of Finance, added "… and we all have to be honest." Thanks to Bent and to the surprise of many, the newly founded state took over the war debt in 1789 and actually paid back the staggering sum of 75 million dollars. So we have Bent to thank for the success of the dollar and the fact that US public finances are still functional, at least until now.

Bent is held in high regard by fiscal policymakers and other honest folk. His feast day is celebrated on February 25.

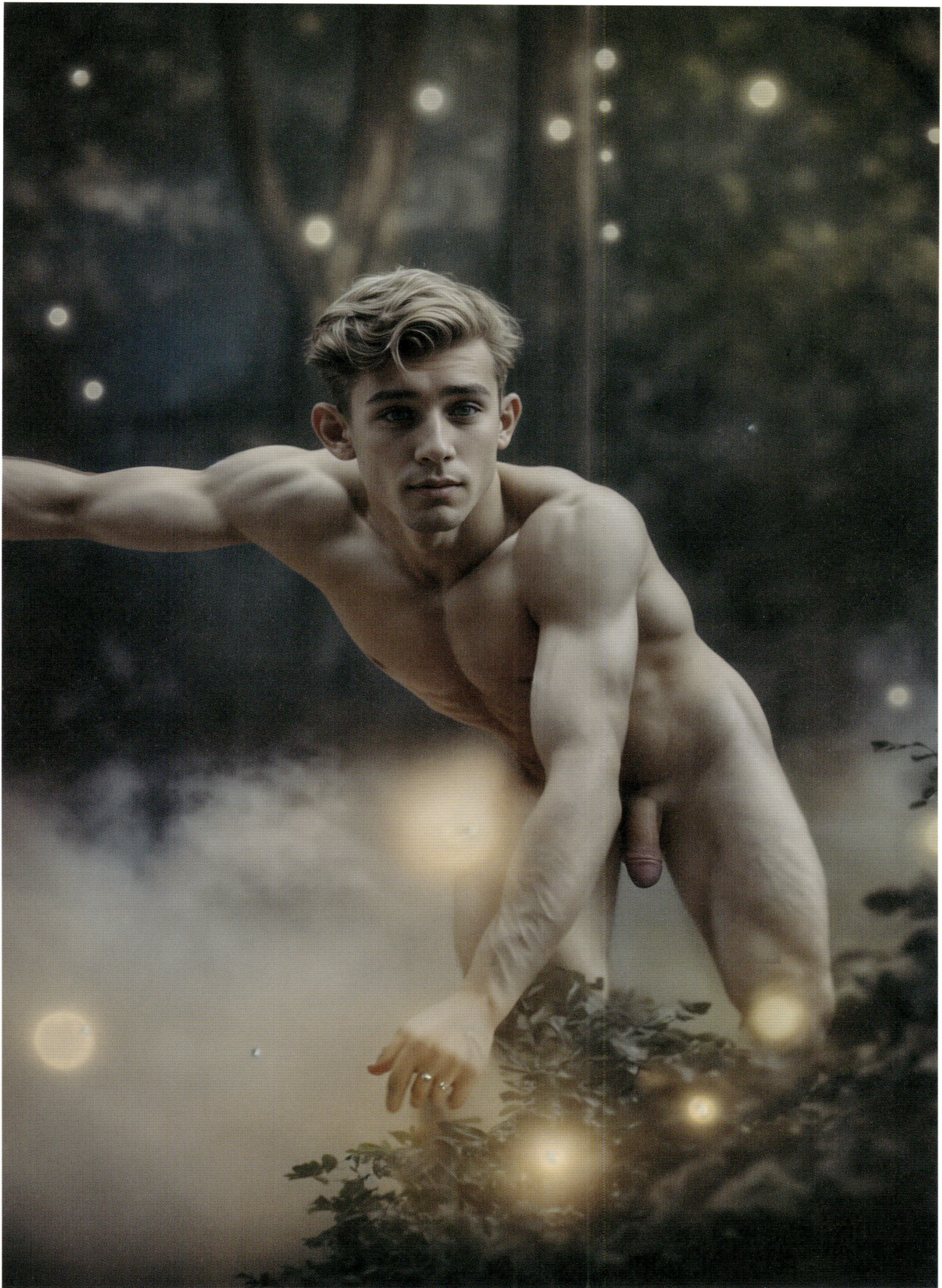

BENT

DER HEILIGE BORIS

An der Abbildung des russischen heiligen Boris lässt sich vieles ablesen: Boris kann fliegen, was bei der Größe Russlands von Vorteil ist, er hat ein großes strahlendes Herz, was ihn die triste Realität besser ertragen lässt, und selbstverständlich hat er immer ein paar Birkenzweige dabei, um Spaß in der Banja zu haben. Boris ist in Nischnewartowsk im Autonomen Kreis der Chanten und Mansen/Jugra, in Balakowo in der Oblast Saratow, in Archangelsk oder Tscheljabinsk genauso zuhause wie in Petropawlowsk-Kamtschatski. Und Sie haben richtig vermutet: Boris lebt noch. Er kann als Iwan, Anatolij, Andrej, Danilo, Fedor, Feodor, Fjodor, Alexej, Pjotr, Wladislaw, Jurij, Lew, Michail, Mischa, Nikolaj, Sascha, Sergej, Igor, Wladimir, Anton, Artjom in Erscheinung treten — oder eben unter den Namen all der anderen wunderbaren Menschen, denen wir im weiten Russland alles Gute wünschen. Ein Land übrigens, das mit seinen 17.075.020 Quadratkilometern sehr viel Platz für die nur 145 Millionen dort lebenden Menschen bietet. Es wäre schön, wenn das mit den *Grenzen* und *die Nachbarn einfach mal in Ruhe zu lassen* in Zukunft besser klappen würde.

Aktuell befindet sich der heilige Boris in einer schwierigen Phase. Bleiben wir optimistisch, dass er seinen Beitrag zur Heilung einer toxischen Gesellschaft leisten wird. Der Gedenktag des heiligen Boris ist der 5. Januar, aber ihn täglich anzurufen kann kaum schaden.

SAINT BORIS

The portrait of the Russian Saint Boris reveals several of his wonderful qualities: Boris can fly, which is a great asset, given the size of Russia, he has a big radiant heart, which helps him bear the bleakness of reality, and of course he always carries a couple of birch twigs for fun in the banya. Boris is equally at home in Nizhnevartovsk in Khanty-Mansi Autonomous Okrug, in Balakovo in Saratov Oblast, in Arkhangelsk, in Chelyabinsk and in Petropavlovsk-Kamchatsky. And you guessed it right: Boris is still very much alive. He can appear to us as Ivan, Anatoly, Andrei, Danilo, Fedor, Feodor, Fyodor, Alexei, Pyotr, Vladislav, Yuri, Lev, Mikhail, Misha, Nikolai, Sasha, Sergei, Igor, Vladimir, Anton, Artyom — or under the name of one of the many other wonderful people in the vast country of Russia to whom we wish all the best. A country that covers a total of 6,601,665 square miles: plenty of space for the only 145 million people who live there. If only they had less trouble with the whole *borders thing* and *leaving your neighbors alone*. Perhaps they will in future.

St. Boris is currently going through a difficult phase. Let's hope that he will soon be able to contribute to healing a toxic society. St. Boris' feast day is January 5, but it can't hurt to invoke him every day.

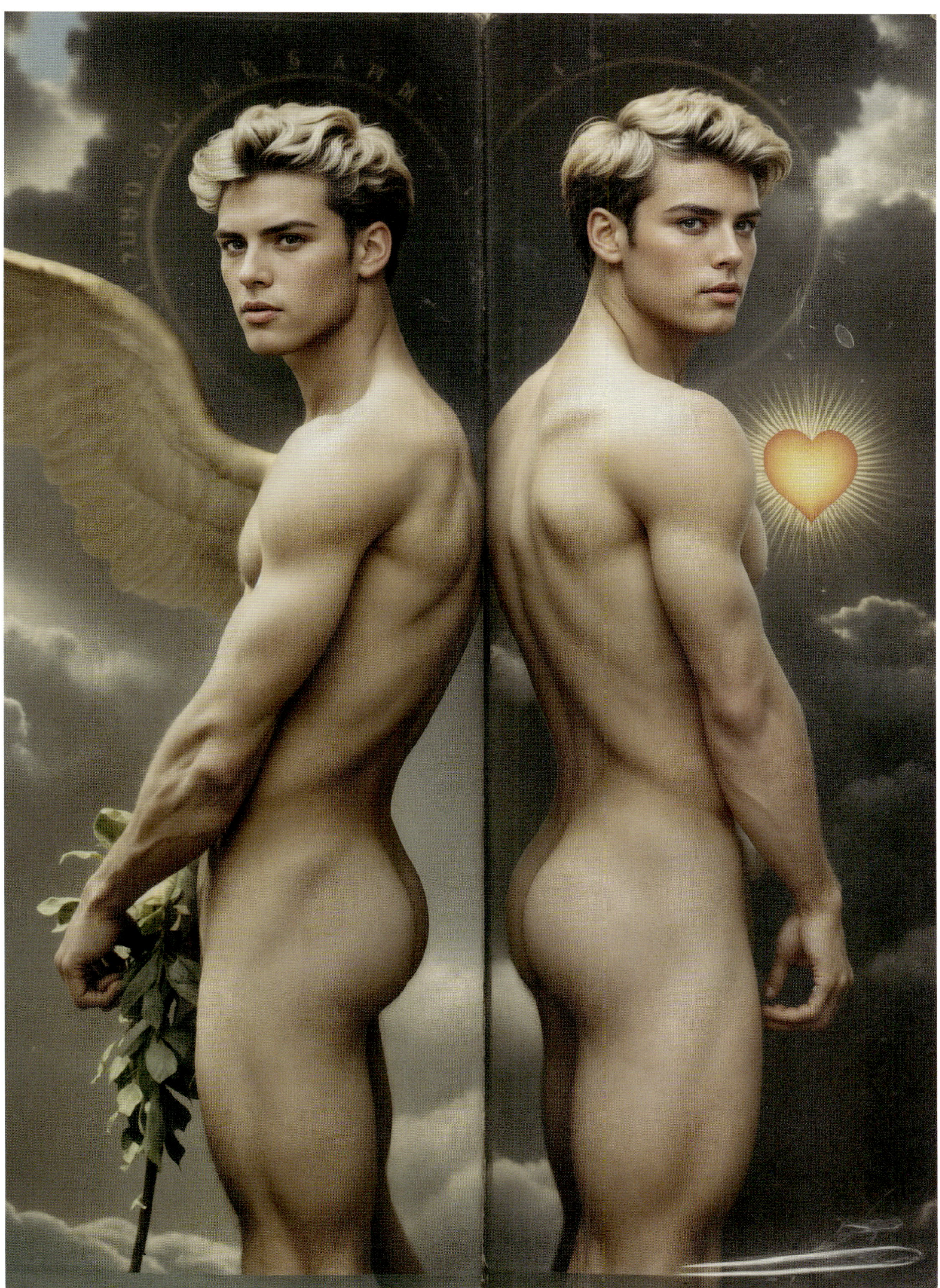

DER HEILIGE BORIS · SAINT BORIS

DER HEILIGE CANDIDUS

Candidus war Offizier in der berühmten Thebaischen (auch: Thebäischen) Legion, die aus 6.600 christlichen Soldaten bestand und im Jahre 303 von Kaiser Maximian irgendwo in der Schweiz im Kanton Wallis angeblich vollständig ausgelöscht wurde. Es wird behauptet, dass die Soldaten nicht an einem heidnischen Opfer teilnehmen wollten und sich geweigert hatten, gegen christliche Glaubensbrüder zu kämpfen. Das kann so natürlich nicht ganz stimmen, denn Christen hatten noch nie ein Problem, aufeinander einzuschlagen. Und Kaiser Maximian war vielleicht ein wenig schlicht und ungebildet, aber 6.600 gut ausgebildete Kämpfer einfach umzubringen, dürfte selbst für ihn zu dumm gewesen sein. Die tatsächliche Geschichte verlief ganz anders: Candidus — er wird übrigens wie seine Heiligenkollegen Achatius von Byzanz, Demetrios von Saloniki, Emmeram von Regensburg, Florian, Knud, Thomas und Wenzeslaus immer mit Lanze dargestellt — organisierte in der Thebaischen Legion die Soldatenfreizeit und war demzufolge sehr beliebt in der Truppe. Ihm unterstanden die (Dampf-) Bäder, er organisierte Wanderungen in die Schweizer Bergwelt und er verantwortete auch die Unterbringungen in den Schlafstätten, sodass jeder bei seinem Liebsten liegen konnte. Ein umfangreiches Sportprogramm und Spiele wie Flaschendrehen sorgten dafür, dass die Soldaten nicht dick wurden und immer ihren Spaß hatten. So verbrachte man die Zeit friedlich und entspannt in Octodurum (heute: Martigny), denn die Armee war von der Verwaltung in Rom schlicht vergessen worden. Als die Bürokraten den Fehler entdeckten, entschieden sie sich fürs Vertuschen und behaupteten kurzerhand, Maximian hätte alle umgebracht. In Wahrheit löste sich die Legion einfach auf und die Soldaten zogen nach Solothurn, Zürich, Genf, Basel und andere schöne Orte. Manche kamen sogar bis nach Köln und Paris.

Candidus ist ein leuchtendes Beispiel dafür, wie anregend und inspirierend das friedliche Zusammenleben von Männern organisiert werden kann. Candidus' Farben Orange und Hellgelb wurden später in Rot und Weiß geändert und bilden die Schweizer Nationalfarben. Der 27. Januar ist der Gedenktag für Candidus und seine Männer.

SAINT CANDIDUS

Candidus was an officer in the famous Theban Legion, which consisted of 6,600 Christian soldiers and was supposedly completely wiped out by Emperor Maximian in the canton of Valais somewhere in Switzerland in 303. The story goes that the soldiers did not want to take part in a pagan sacrifice and refused to fight against their fellow Christians. Obviously that can't be entirely true — after all, Christians have never had a problem with beating each other up. And Emperor Maximian may have been a bit simple and lacking in education, but even he would not have been stupid enough to slaughter 6,600 of his own well-trained fighters. The real story was entirely different: Candidus — who, like his fellow saints Agathius of Byzantium, Demetrius of Thessaloniki, Emmeram of Regensburg, Florian, Canute, Thomas and Wenceslaus, is always depicted with a lance — was responsible for organizing the rest and recreation activities for the soldiers in the Theban Legion, which made him very popular among the troops. He was in charge of the (steam) baths, organized hikes in the Swiss mountains and was also responsible for the sleeping arrangements and ensuring that everyone could sleep with their lovers. He organized an extensive sports program and games like spin the bottle to ensure that the soldiers had fun and didn't get fat. Time passed peacefully and comfortably in Octodurum (now known as Martigny) in this way, as the army had simply been forgotten by the authorities in Rome. When the bureaucrats spotted their error, they decided to cover it up by claiming that Maximian had had everyone killed. In actual fact, the legion simply disbanded and the soldiers relocated to Solothurn, Zurich, Geneva, Basel and other beautiful spots. Some even made it as far as Cologne and Paris.

Candidus is a shining example of how to organize a peaceful, stimulating and even inspiring community of men. Candidus' colors orange and light yellow were later changed to red and white and became the Swiss national colors. January 27 is dedicated to Candidus and his men.

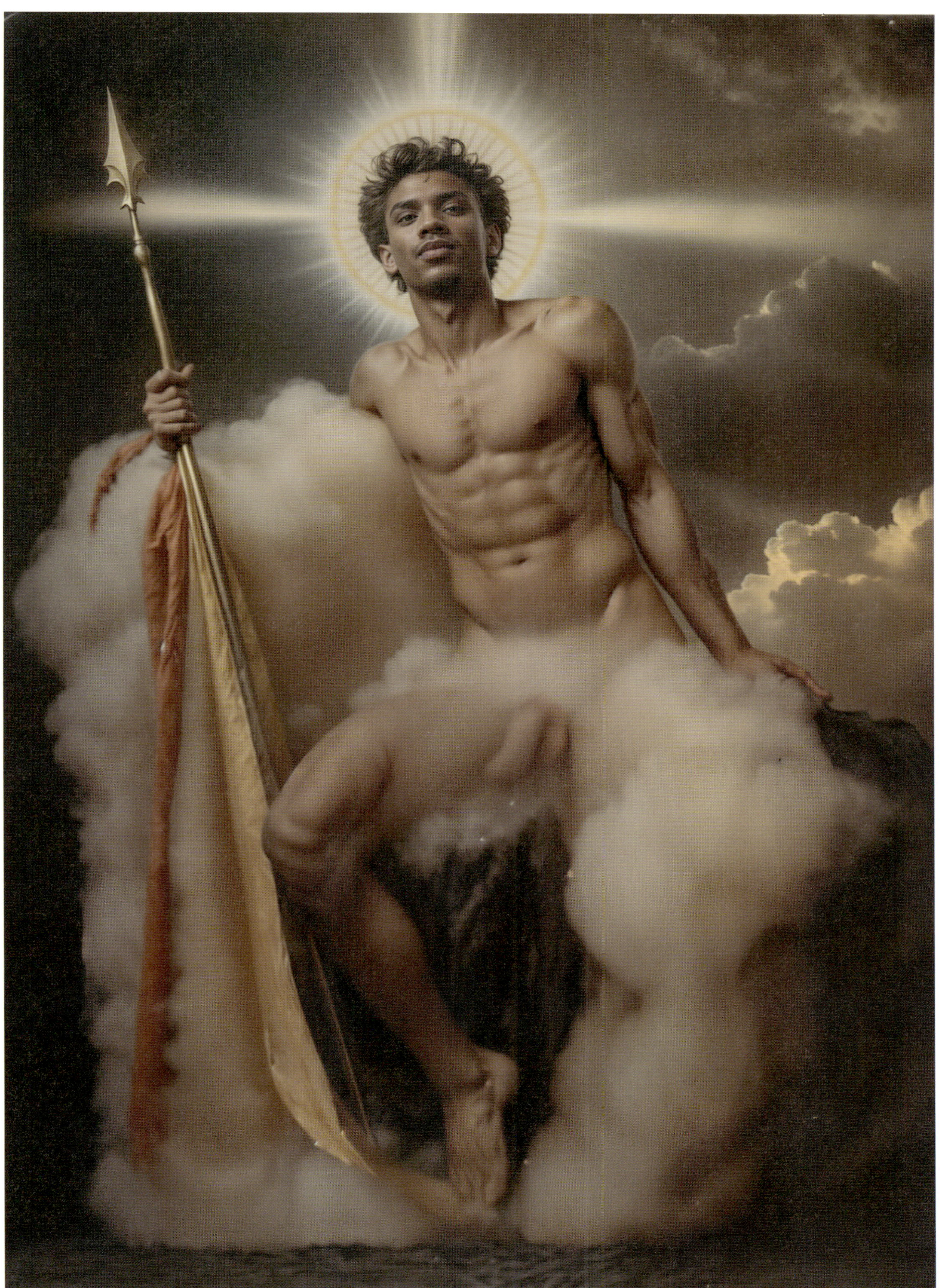

DER HEILIGE CANDIDUS · SAINT CANDIDUS

DER HEILIGE CÉDRIC UND FRANÇOIS

Cédric gehörte zu einer Gruppe junger Männer, die 1820 gemeinsam durch die Lande zogen und untereinander sehr vertraut waren. Gerne hielten sie sich an der französischen Mittelmeerküste auf. Da war es angenehm warm, nachts glitzerten die Sterne so schön und man konnte unter freiem Himmel schlafen. Natürlich hatte Cédric (zu Deutsch *Der Liebenswürdige*) seinen besonderen Liebling: François (zu Deutsch *Der kleine Franzose*). Die beiden taten das, was junge Männer so tun. So konnten sie ihren Alltag vergessen und sich vom Herumwandern erholen. Am Strand von Agay hatten Cédric und die Jungs ihr Hauptquartier. Von dort aus zogen sie in völlig unbekannte und abgeschiedene Ort wie Cannes, Antibes oder Saint-Tropez. Damit gilt Cédric als Entdecker jenes schönen Landstrichs im Süden Frankreichs, und ihm zu Ehren (beziehungsweise, um an seine blauen Augen zu erinnern) wurde dieser Teil der provenzalischen Küste später *Côte d'Azur* genannt. Natürlich ist die Menschheitsgeschichte voll von Männergruppen, die mehr oder weniger ohne Ziel durch die Gegend ziehen. In der Regel stürzten sie sich aber auf Gegenden wie Galiläa oder auch Berlin, also Landstriche, die schon bekannt und entdeckt waren. Sich dagegen mal in eine wirklich komplett unbekannte Gegend ohne touristische Infrastruktur vorzuwagen, war eine Pioniertat — und wäre es auch heute noch.

Der heilige Cédric kann bei Überfüllungen an Stränden oder Poolanlagen angerufen werden, insbesondere auch an seinem Feiertag, dem 6. Juni.

SAINT CÉDRIC AND FRANÇOIS

Cédric belonged to a group of young men who roamed the country together in 1820 and were very familiar with each other. They liked to hang out on the French Mediterranean coast, because it was pleasantly warm there and they could sleep out in the open, under the stars twinkling brightly in the night sky. Naturally, Cédric (which literally means *Lovable*) had his own special favorite: François (*The Little Frenchman*). At night, the two of them did what young men do, which helped them recover from all the roaming they did in the daytime. Cédric and the boys set up headquarters on Agay beach. From there, they ventured out to totally unknown and secluded places such as Cannes, Antibes and Saint-Tropez. As a result, Cédric is credited with discovering this beautiful stretch of land in the south of France, and this part of the Provençal coast was later called the *Côte d'Azur* in his honor (or rather, in memory of his beautiful blue eyes). Of course, human history is peppered with groups of men roaming around without any particular destination. Generally speaking, however, they tended to flock to areas like Galilee or Berlin, i.e., down well-trodden paths to regions that had already been explored. By contrast, to venture into a completely unknown area with no tourist infrastructure was a pioneering move — and still is today.

St. Cédric can be invoked against crowded beaches and pools, especially on his feast day, June 6.

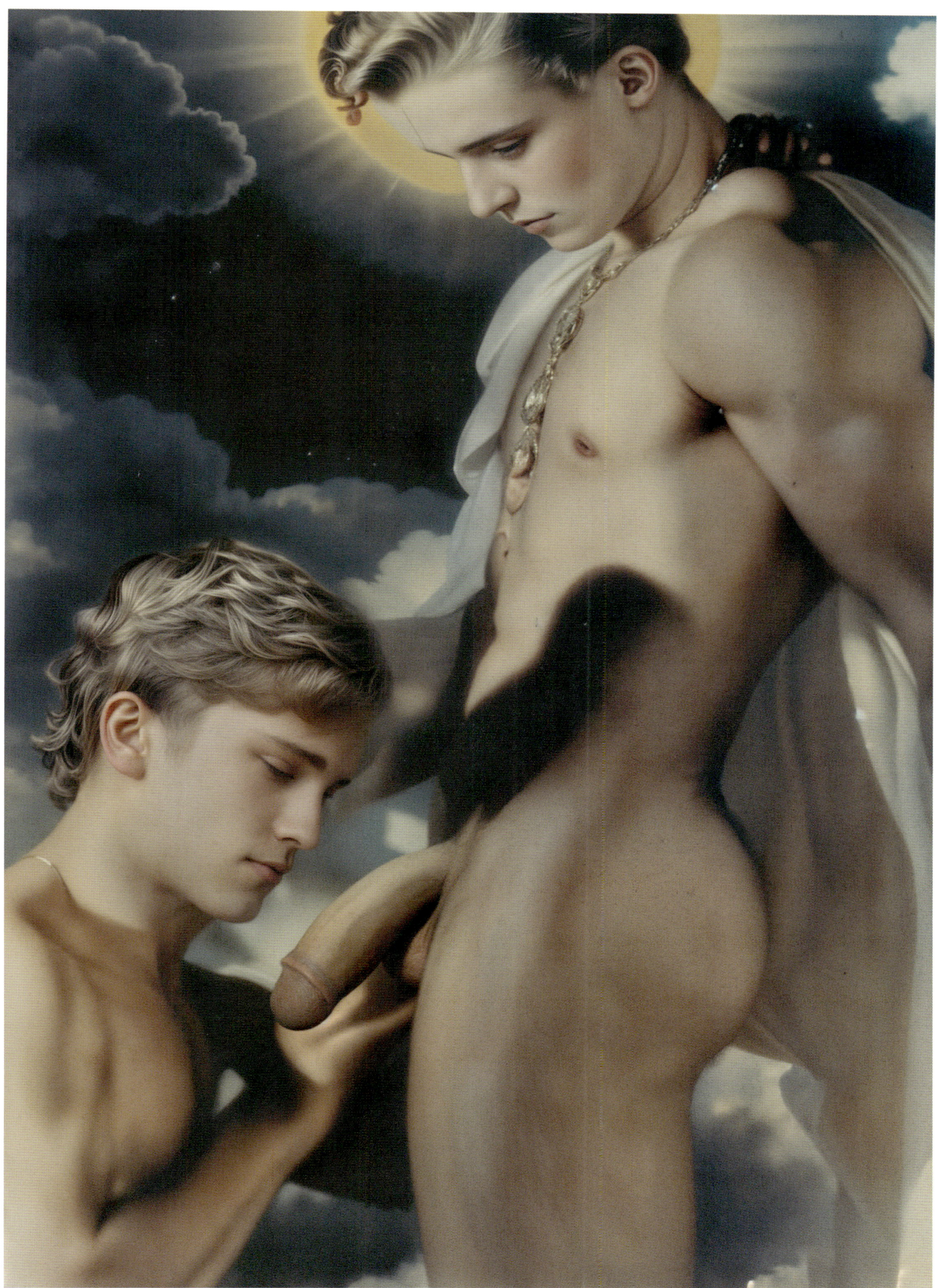

DER HEILIGE CÉDRIC UND FRANÇOIS · SAINT CÉDRIC AND FRANÇOIS

DER HEILIGE CHARLES

Charles Ryder wurde am 1. Juni 1335 in Helions Bumpstead (bei Steeple Bumpstead) als Sohn eines Landadligen geboren und am 11. Februar 1355 während des Aufruhrs am Sankt-Scholastika-Tag (St Scholastica Day riot) an der University of Oxford schwer verletzt. Hintergrund war, dass mittelalterliche Universitäten eine Vielzahl an königlichen und päpstlichen Privilegien genossen, zu denen natürlich auch freier und ausschweifender schwuler Sex gehörte, wenn auch nur untereinander, also im Kreis der Akademiker, denn Bürger hatten dieses Privileg damals leider nicht. In der Swindlestock Tavern, einer Bar im Stadtzentrum von Oxford an der Kreuzung von St Aldate's, Cornmarket Street, Queen Street und High Street, nahe dem Carfax Tower, hatte Charles den Sohn eines Schuhmachers mit dem Namen Sebastian kennengelernt und sich mit ihm auf die Toilette zurückgezogen. Charles und Sebastians Vergnügen war kaum zu überhören und dank der Form der Toilettentür, die gerade mal den Blick auf die Körpermitte verwehrte, auch nicht zu übersehen. Neidische Bürger wollten das auch, und nicht wenige Studenten waren sauer auf Charles, weil sie ihn lieber für sich allein gehabt hätten. Es kam zu dem, was auch als *Das große Gemetzel* (englisch *Great Slaughter*) bezeichnet wurde. Nur dem beherzten Einschreiten von Charles, der sich trotz eines blauen Auges und eines gebrochenen Ellenbogens zwischen die Parteien stellte, ist es zu verdanken, dass es keine Toten gab. Neuere Forschungen konnten belegen, dass ohne sein Zutun bis zu 63 Studenten und 30 Bürger ihr Leben hätten verlieren können. Als direkte Folge erließ Edward III. eine Charta zugunsten der Universität, die die Privilegien zwar festschrieb, aber die Studenten zu mehr Diskretion verpflichtete. Sie hat bis heute so an den Universitäten im Vereinigten Königreich Gültigkeit. Evelyn Waugh setzte Charles und Sebastian 1945 mit seinem Roman *Brideshead Revisited* ein Denkmal. Darin verhandelt er insbesondere das ewige Dilemma von Schuld und Sühne, ohne allerdings das Kernanliegen des heiligen Charles wirklich zu durchdringen: die komplette Freiheit bei der Auswahl von Sexualpartnern im gegenseitigen Einverständnis hätte nicht nur im Roman viel Leid ersparen können.

Charles und Sebastian verließen Oxford und arbeiteten als Gärtner in Castle Howard, wo sie insbesondere den Woodland Garden und den Walled Garden neu gestalteten. Passenderweise ist der Apollo auf dem Belvedere nach Charles Ryder gestaltet. War es doch Apollo, der für das Gedeihen der Früchte sorgte, Hirten und Weidevieh beschützte und die männliche Jugend pflegte. Der heilige Charles gehört zum Spätsommer und wird am 22. August gefeiert.

SAINT CHARLES

Charles Ryder was born on June 1, 1335 in Helions Bumpstead (near Steeple Bumpstead), the son of a country nobleman. On February 11, 1355, he sustained serious injuries at the St Scholastica Day riot at the University of Oxford. The background to this was the following: In the Middle Ages, universities enjoyed a number of royal and papal privileges, which of course included unrestricted and debauched gay sex, albeit only among themselves, i.e., academics, as the common townsfolk sadly did not have this privilege. One day, Charles met a man called Sebastian, the son of a shoemaker, in the Swindlestock Tavern, which was located in the center of Oxford at the corner of St Aldate's, Cornmarket Street, Queen Street and High Street, near Carfax Tower, and repaired to the gentlemen's lavatory with him. It was impossible not to overhear Charles and Sebastian's shenanigans and, thanks to the shape of the toilet door which blocked only the view of their midriffs, impossible not to see them. This excited the envy of quite a few townsfolk, as well as several students, who were angry with Charles because they would have rather kept him to themselves. This led to what was also referred to as the *Great Slaughter*. It was only thanks to the courageous intervention of Charles, who stepped in to separate the two warring parties despite incurring a black eye and a broken elbow, that there were no fatalities. Recent research findings have shown that as many as 63 students and 30 townspeople might have lost their lives without his intervention. In direct response to this, Edward III issued a charter in favor of the university, which secured the university's privileges but obliged the students to be more discreet. It is still in force today at universities in the United Kingdom. Evelyn Waugh memorialized Charles and Sebastian in his novel *Brideshead Revisited* in 1945. The novel wrestles with the eternal dilemma of guilt and atonement without really getting to the heart of St. Charles' core message: total freedom to choose sexual partners by mutual consent might have prevented a great deal of suffering — not just in the novel.

Charles and Sebastian left Oxford and took up work as gardeners at Castle Howard, where they redesigned the Woodland Garden and the Walled Garden. Appropriately enough, the statue of Apollo on the Belvedere is modeled on Charles Ryder. After all, it was Apollo who made the fruit ripen, protected shepherds and grazing animals, and took care of young men. St. Charles is celebrated in late summer on August 22.

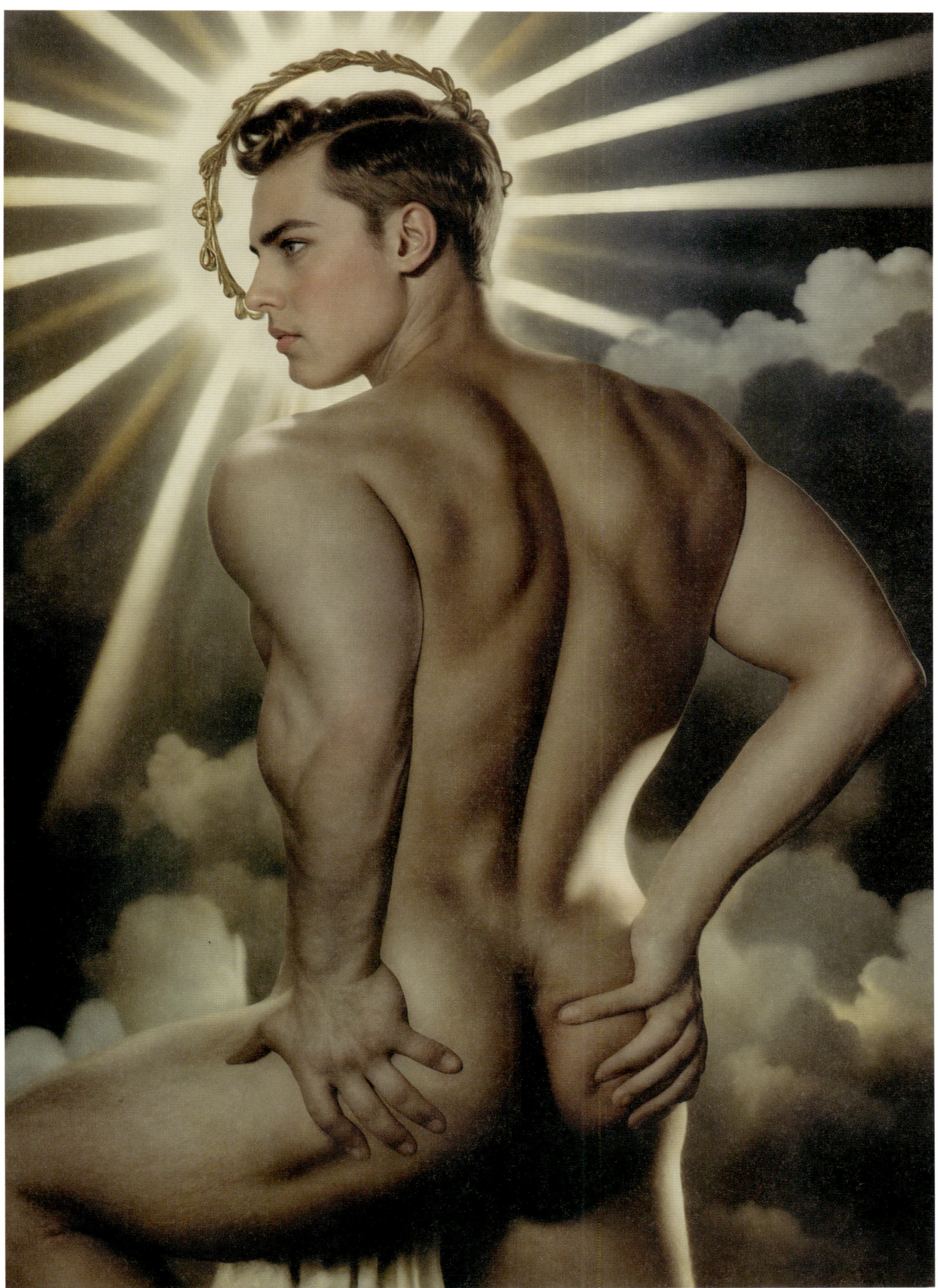

DER HEILIGE CHARLES · SAINT CHARLES

DER HEILIGE CLEMENS

Clemens von Alexandria (*um 150 vielleicht in Athen; †um 215 vielleicht in Kappadokien) war ein auf Griechisch schreibender Philosoph und Autor. Lange war er heilig, wurde aber 1748 von Papst Benedikt XIV. aus dem *Martyrologium Romanum* getilgt. Sein Hauptwerk trägt den schönen Titel *Stromateis* (Plural von στρωματεύς strōmateús, Teppich, Flickwerk) und besteht aus acht Büchern, von denen nur sieben erhalten sind. Seine Themen waren *Nutzen der griechischen Kultur für Christen; Glauben, Buße, Tugenden; Maßvolle Enthaltsamkeit; Martyrium, Askese und Emotionslosigkeit; Allegorische Schriftauslegung* und mit gleich zwei Bänden *Der Christ als wahrer Intellektueller.* Der achte Band hatte *Wahre Liebe, wahre Freundschaft* zum Inhalt und widmete sich der Frage, „warum guter Sex" — bei allem Maßhalten — „wichtig ist", schließlich war Clemens Grieche. Er bemühte sich, das Christentum mit der Philosophie des Altertums und dem wahren Leben unter einen Hut zu bekommen. Kritisiert wurde Clemens unter anderem für seine Erkenntnis, dass Christi Heilversprechen allen zugänglich sei, eine im Prinzip universalistische Lehre. Das größte Problem war aber sicherlich, dass unser Heiliger in Besitz des Geheimen Markusevangeliums gelangte und hieraus freimütig zitierte: „Und sie kamen nach Bethanien, und eine gewisse Frau, deren Bruder gestorben war, war dort. Und herzu kommend, warf sie sich vor Jesus nieder und sagte zu ihm: ‚Sohn Davids, habe Erbarmen mit mir'. Aber die Jünger wiesen sie zurück. Und Jesus, der in Wut geriet, ging mit ihr in den Garten, wo das Grab war, und sogleich wurde ein lauter Schrei aus dem Grab gehört. Und näher tretend, rollte Jesus den Stein vom Eingang des Grabes weg. Und sogleich ging er hinein, wo der Jüngling war, streckte seine Hand aus und zog ihn hoch, indem er dessen Hand ergriff. Aber der Jüngling, als er ihn ansah, liebte ihn und fing an, ihn anzuflehen, dass er bei ihm sein möge. Und sie gingen aus dem Grab heraus und kamen in das Haus des Jünglings, denn er war reich. Und nach sechs Tagen sagte ihm Jesus, was er tun solle, und am Abend kam der Jüngling zu ihm, ein leinenes Tuch über seinem nackten Körper tragend. Und er blieb diese Nacht bei ihm, denn Jesus lehrte ihn das Geheimnis des Reiches Gottes. Und von da erhob er sich und ging auf die andere Seite des Jordans zurück." Für Clemens war das alles kein Problem, aber Papst Benedikt XIV. scheint der Text nicht gefallen zu haben.

Alles Wahre muss allen Menschen gesagt werden. Dafür verehren wir den heiligen Clemens, ganz besonders an seinem Gedenktag, dem 9. November.

SAINT CLEMENT

Clement of Alexandria (*around 150, possibly in Athens; †around 215, possibly in Cappadocia) was a philosopher whose works were written in Ancient Greek. He was a saint until 1748, when Pope Benedict XIV kicked him out of the *Martyrologium Romanum*. His magnum opus bears the delightful title *Stromateis* (the plural of στρωματεύς or strōmateús — carpet or patchwork) and consists of eight books, of which only seven have survived. The seven extant volumes covered topics such as *The benefits of Greek culture for Christians, Faith, penance and virtues, Moderate abstinence, Martyrdom, asceticism and emotionlessness, Allegorical interpretation of the scripture* as well as two volumes on *The Christian as true intellectual.* The eighth volume was devoted to *True love, true friendship* and addressed the question of "why good sex" — in moderation — "is important." After all, Clement was Greek. His work was an attempt to reconcile Christianity with both classical philosophy and real life. One thing Clement's critics vilified him for was his assertion that the promise of salvation in Christ was available to everyone, an essentially universalist doctrine. The greatest problem, however, lay in the fact that our saint was in possession of the Secret Gospel of St. Mark, from which he freely quoted: "And they came to Bethany. And there was a certain woman there whose brother had died. And approaching, she prostrated before Jesus and said to him, 'Son of David have mercy on me.' But the disciples rebuked her. And having become angry Jesus went away with her into the garden where the tomb was. And immediately a great cry was heard from the tomb. And approaching, Jesus rolled the stone from the door of the tomb, and going in immediately to where the young man was, he stretched out his hand and raised him, taking hold of his hand. But the young man, having looked upon him, loved him and began to entreat him to be with him. And going out from the tomb they went into the house of the young man; for he was rich. And after six days Jesus commanded him; and when it was evening the young man came to him wearing a linen sheet about his naked body, and he remained with him that night; for Jesus was teaching him the mystery of the kingdom of God. Then arising, he returned from there to the other side of the Jordan." None of this was a problem for Clement, but Pope Benedict XIV clearly did not approve.

All humankind must be told the truth, which is why we venerate St. Clement, especially on his feast day, November 9.

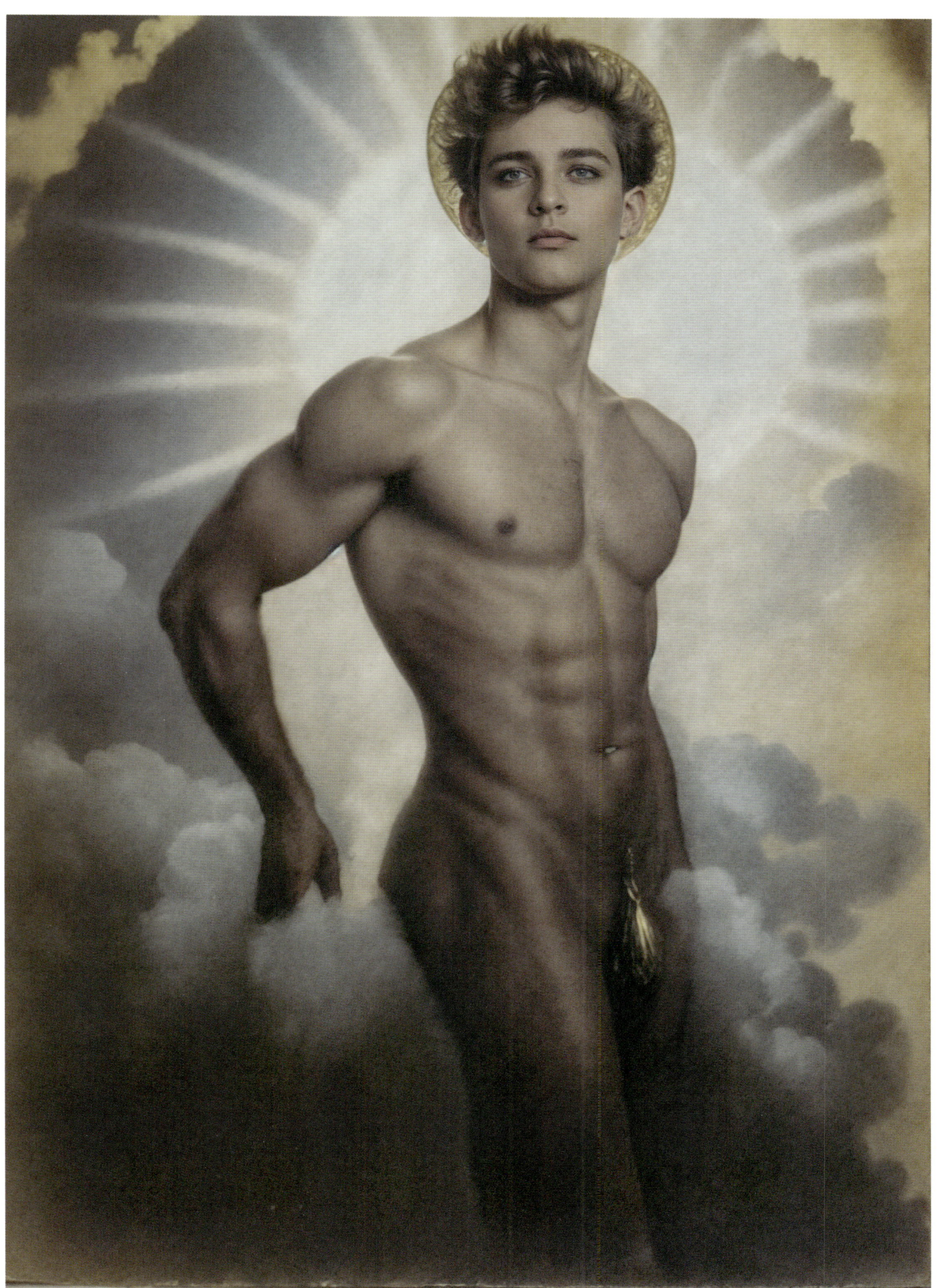

DER HEILIGE CLEMENS · SAINT CLEMENS

CONNOR UND CARSON

Connor Miller und Carson Smith, beide Hafenarbeiter, waren richtige New Yorker Jungs aus Greenwich Village. Sie lernten sich 1841 durch Zufall an der Straßenkreuzung Hudson und Barrow kennen. Connor teilte sich in der Bedford Street einen Schlafplatz mit anderen Hafenarbeitern, und da man untereinander solidarisch war, konnten Connor und Carson dort ungestört Sex haben. Dann geschah ein Wunder: Beim Ficken (entschuldigen Sie die derbe Wortwahl) fingen die beiden an zu schweben und hoben ab Richtung Himmel. Nur die Zimmerdecke konnte sie aufhalten. Wenn Sie jetzt einwenden, dass es sich dabei nur um eine klassische Levitation, also eine von Zauberkünstlern vorgeführte Illusion, gehandelt haben kann, sind Sie im Unrecht. Oder Ihnen fehlt der Glaube, was bedauerlich wäre. Alle Hafenarbeiter waren begeistert. Immer wieder und vor immer größerem Publikum mussten Connor und Carson das Wunder vollbringen. Endlich lag ein Beweis für so viele ungeklärte Fragen der Menschheit vor. Auch New Yorks Bischof John Dubois war entzückt und meldete das Ganze nach Rom. Aber Papst Gregor XVI. wollte davon nichts hören. Das lag höchstwahrscheinlich daran, dass der gute Mann schlecht gelaunt war und schon 1832 in seiner ersten Enzyklika *Mirari vos* (Deutsch: *Ihr wundert euch*) Naturalismus, Rationalismus, religiöse Indifferenz sowie Gewissens- und Meinungsfreiheit verurteilt hatte — also eigentlich alles, was Connor und Carson zum Abheben gebracht hatte.

Wir wundern uns über das Wunder von Connor und Carson nicht. Wir glauben nur an das Wunder der Liebe, das wir am 19. Februar feiern. Jedes Jahr, immer wieder.

CONNOR AND CARSON

Connor Miller and Carson Smith were both dockworkers, real New York lads from Greenwich Village. They met by chance at the crossing between Hudson and Barrow in 1841. Connor shared a berth with other dockworkers on Bedford Street and, thanks to the bonds of solidarity between them, Connor's fellow workers never bothered him when he and Carson had sex there. Then a miracle happened: one day, the two of them were busy fucking (pardon my French) when they were suddenly lifted off the ground and floated up into the air. They didn't stop until they hit the ceiling. Now you might argue that this could only have been a classic case of levitation, i.e., an illusion performed by magicians, but you would be wrong. Or simply lacking in faith, which would be a pity. The dockworkers were thrilled. Connor and Carson had to perform their miracle over and over again in front of a growing audience. Here at last was the answer to so many of humanity's unanswered questions. The Bishop of New York, John Dubois, was equally delighted and sent a report to Rome. But Pope Gregory XVI just didn't want to know. This was because the good pope was most likely in a bad mood and had already condemned naturalism, rationalism, religious indifference, liberty of conscience and freedom of speech in his first encyclical *Mirari vos (That you wonder)* — in other words, everything that had boosted Connor and Carson into the air — in 1832.

We do not wonder at the miracle of Connor and Carson. For we believe in the miracle of love which we celebrate on February 19th. Year after year.

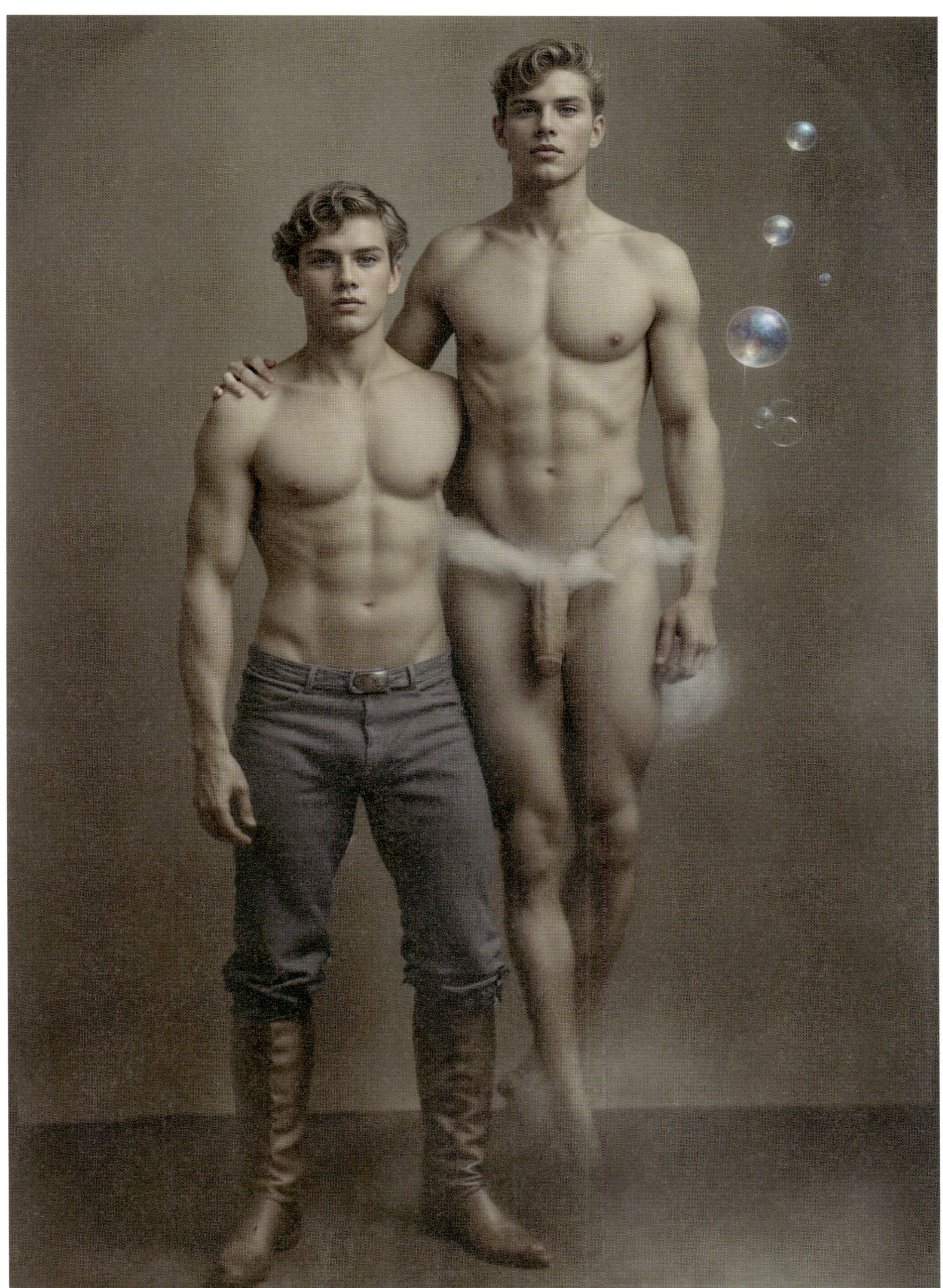

CONNOR & CARSON

DER HEILIGE CUBA

Kolumbus landete am 27. Oktober 1492 auf einer Insel in der Karibik. Dort war seine erste Tat, einen freundlichen nackten Mann, der sich ihm fröhlich näherte, zu erschlagen. Dieser Mann hieß *Cuba*, aber Kolumbus nannte die Insel trotzdem *Juana*, nach dem Prinzen Don Juan. Dessen Vater Fernando II., König von Spanien, ordnete im Jahr 1515 die Umbenennung in *Fernandina* an. Die Gründe dafür können wir nur erahnen, über die Ursprünge des Namens Cuba lässt sich dagegen sehr viel mehr erzählen. Er stammt aus der Sprache der Kariben oder der Taíno und lässt sich mit *coa* (= Schwanz, Schwert, Penis, Flöte, Glied, Zipfel, Pinsel, Rute, Lümmel, Pimmel, Ködel, Schniedel, Pullermann oder allen anderen Worten, die Sie für das männliche Glied kennen) und *bana* (= groß) übersetzen. Ein wirklich treffender Name, den die Eltern ihrem da Sohn gegeben haben, denn was Sie im Bild sehen ist noch nicht mal seine Erektion. Die traurige Geschichte von Cubas Ermordung wurde überall erzählt. Infolgedessen berichteten immer mehr Männer, dass Cuba ihnen noch zu Lebzeiten seinen üppigen Segen geschenkt habe, oder er ihnen nach der Kolumbus-Bluttat des Nachts als Engel erschienen sei. Irgendwann war die Bewegung so stark, dass die genervten Spanier aufgaben und die Insel endlich korrekt in Cuba umbenannten.

Cuba wirkt immer noch auf Kuba, kann sich aber nicht wirklich entscheiden, in welche Richtung er die Geschicke des Landes lenken soll. Cubas Feiertag ist der 26. Juli.

SAINT CUBA

On October 27, 1492, Columbus landed on an island in the Caribbean. The first thing he did there was to kill a friendly naked man who had cheerfully walked up to him. This man's name was *Cuba*, but despite this, Columbus named the island *Juana*, after the prince Don Juan. In 1515, the prince's father Fernando II, King of Spain, ordered it to be changed to *Fernandina*. We can only speculate on his reasons for this, but there is much more to say about the origins of the name Cuba. It derives from the Carib or Taíno language and can be translated as *coa* (= cock, sword, penis, flute, member, tip, brush, pole, wiener, dong, dick, pecker, schlong or any other word used for the male appendage) and *bana* (= big). The name Cuba's parents gave their son is absolutely spot-on, given that what you see in the picture is not even its erect state. The sad story of the murder of Cuba spread far and wide. As a result, more and more men reported that Cuba had — while still alive — bestowed his lavish blessing upon them, or that he had appeared to them as an angel at night following Columbus' bloody deed. At some point, the groundswell of support was so strong that the exasperated Spaniards finally gave up and renamed the island Cuba.

Cuba still has an impact on Cuba but cannot make up his mind as to which direction the country's fortunes should take. Cuba's feast day is on July 26.

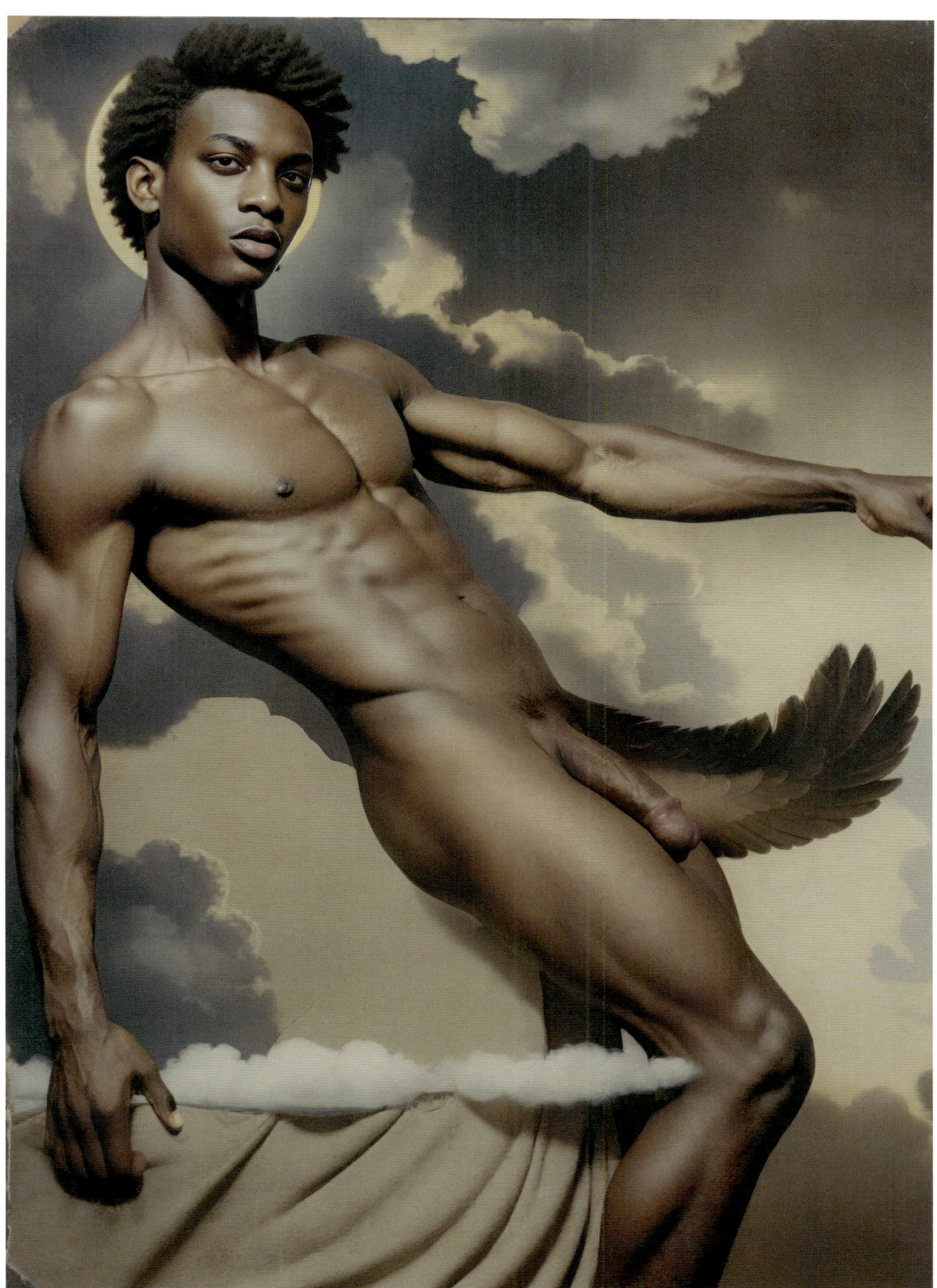

DER HEILIGE CUBA · SAINT CUBA

DER HEILIGE DAMIAN

Unser Damian hat mit den heiligen Zwillingsbrüdern Kosmas und Damian nichts zu tun. Zum Thema Zwillingsinzest werden Sie beim → HEILIGEN PETER (Seite 144) und dem → HEILIGEN EDMUND (ebenfalls Seite 144) fündig. Unser Damian war auch kein Apotheker, sondern Architekt. Er lebte im 8. Jahrhundert in Antwerpen und dürfte bei der Verwüstung der Stadt durch die Normannen im Jahre 836 so um die 20 Jahre alt gewesen sein. Viel steckt drin in dem Namen Damian: das griechische Wort *daman* (mächtig), vielleicht auch *demos* (Volk) oder *damázein* (bezwingen). So war Damian mächtig gebaut, ließ sich vom Volk der gutaussehenden Nordmänner jedoch gerne bezwingen. Die Zerstörung der Stadt war für ihn ein Glücksfall. Als Architekt plante er den Wiederaufbau im Zeichen von Ästhetik, Schönheit, Harmonie und Sinn für menschliche Dimensionen, wie sie noch heute in vielen mittelalterlichen europäischen Stadtkernen erlebbar sind. Wenn alles ein wenig wie organisch oder zufällig entstanden wirkt, dabei aber hochfunktional ist, ist Damians Segen in der Regel nicht weit. Und wenn Sie sich zuweilen wundern, dass es nur so selten gerade Straßen gibt, können Sie sicher sein, dass dafür die hier abgebildete Körperhaltung des Heiligen Pate stand. Auch diese ist gleichermaßen organisch wie funktional.

Der heilige Damian ist für Architekten zuständig, bei ihnen allerdings oft erfolglos. Wirkmächtiger ist er bei Menschen, die Rückschläge als Chance verstehen und diese ergreifen. Der Gedenktag des heiligen Damian ist der 8. April.

SAINT DAMIAN

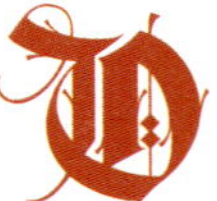

Our Damian has nothing to do with the saintly twins Cosmas and Damian. If it's tales of twin incest you're looking for, turn to → SAINT PETER (page 144) or → SAINT EDMUND (page 144 as well). Nor was our Damian a pharmacist, he was an architect. He lived in Antwerp in the eighth century and was probably around twenty years old when the city was sacked by the Normans in 836. The name Damian contains multiple meanings: the Greek word *daman* (powerful), perhaps also *demos* (people) or *damázein* (to conquer). Damian was powerfully built but was more than happy to be conquered by the handsome Norsemen. The destruction of the city was a stroke of luck for him. As an architect, he designed the new city in a spirit of aesthetics, beauty, harmony and a feeling for human dimensions that can still be experienced in many medieval European city centers today. And if you occasionally wonder why there are so few straight roads, you can be sure that this was inspired by the posture of the saint depicted here. This too, is both organic and functional.

St. Damian is the patron saint of architects but has never had much success with them. He is more effective when interceding on behalf of people for whom every setback is an opportunity. The feast day of St. Damian is April 8.

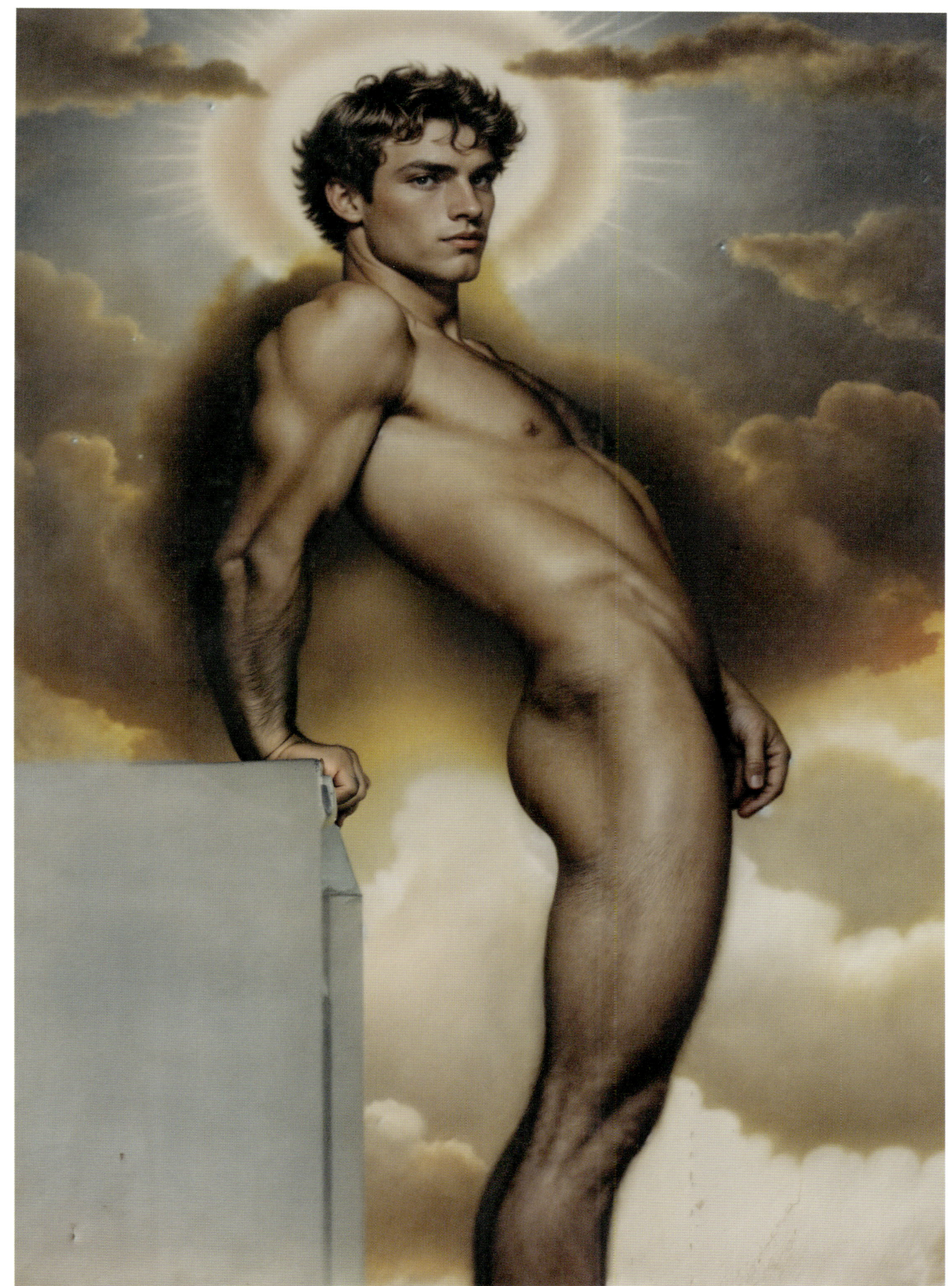

DER HEILIGE DAMIAN · SAINT DAMIAN

DER HEILIGE DONATUS

Unser Donatus (* um 200 in Brundisium, heute Brindisi; † 262 Rom) ist bitte nicht mit Donatus von Arezzo, Donatus von Besançon, Donatus von Evorea oder gar Donatus von Münstereifel zu verwechseln. Die sind zwar auch alle Heilige, kümmerten sich aber eher um Missionierung, Exorzismus oder kamen aus Albanien. Unser Donatus (deutsch: *der von Gott Geschenkte*) liebte Männer genauso wie Verstecktes und Verborgenes, und erforschte beide neben seiner Arbeit als Fischer eingehend. Sei es bei entspannenden Besuchen der Thermen von Rom oder in den kleinen Gassen am Hafen seiner Heimatstadt Brundisium. Er folgte dabei allen Grundsätzen, mit denen heute das Unbewusste beschrieben wird, und nannte sie *Abditum mentis* (*Versteck des Geistes* oder *das Verborgene des Geistes*). Menschliches Denken, Fühlen und Handeln wird nicht nur von bewussten Entscheidungen, sondern zum größten Teil von Intuition, Trieben und verborgenen, nicht zu kontrollierenden Strukturen bestimmt. Sigmund Freud, Carl Gustav Jung, Alfred Adler, Erich Fromm und viele andere machten diesen Umstand später unnötig kompliziert. Donatus jedoch lebte überaus glücklich im völligen Einklang mit seinem Unbewussten. Unsere historische korrekte Darstellung vereint *Ich* und *Über-Ich* des Donatus in einem Bild. Es ist unverkennbar, dass die beiden hervorragend zusammenpassen und sicherlich gleich viel Spaß miteinander haben werden. Nur die schiefe Hauskante symbolisiert, dass die Welt aus den Fugen geraten ist und von Donatus gestützt werden muss.

Der heilige Donatus kann jederzeit und von jedem angesprochen werden, aber eigentlich gilt: Erkenne dich selbst. Der Feiertag des heiligen Donatus ist der 2. August.

SAINT DONATUS

Our Donatus (* around 200 in Brundisium, present-day Brindisi; † 262 Rome) should not be confused with Donatus of Arezzo, Donatus of Besançon, Donatus of Evorea or even Donatus of Münstereifel. Whilst they are also all saints, they were more concerned with missionary work or exorcism — or were from Albania. Our Donatus (*given by God*) loved men as much as he loved the hidden and unseen and explored both of these in depth while also working as a fisherman. His explorations took him all over the country, from leisurely visits to the thermal baths of Rome to the narrow streets of the harbor in his hometown of Brundisium. He adopted all the principles that are used to describe the unconscious today, which he termed the *abditum mentis* (*hiding place* or *the hidden part of the mind*). Human thoughts, feelings and actions are governed not only by conscious decisions, but to a large extent by intuition, instinct and hidden structures outside our control. This circumstance was later made unnecessarily complicated by Sigmund Freud, Carl Gustav Jung, Alfred Adler, Erich Fromm and many others. Donatus, however, led a very happy life in complete harmony with his unconscious. Our historically accurate portrayal combines Donatus' *ego* and *superego* in a single image. Clearly, the two are a perfect match and probably have a lot of fun together. The only thing out of place is the crooked wall, representing a world that is out of joint. It clearly needs Donatus to prop it up.

Saint Donatus can be invoked by anyone at any time, but the most important thing is: know thyself. The feast day of St. Donatus is August 2.

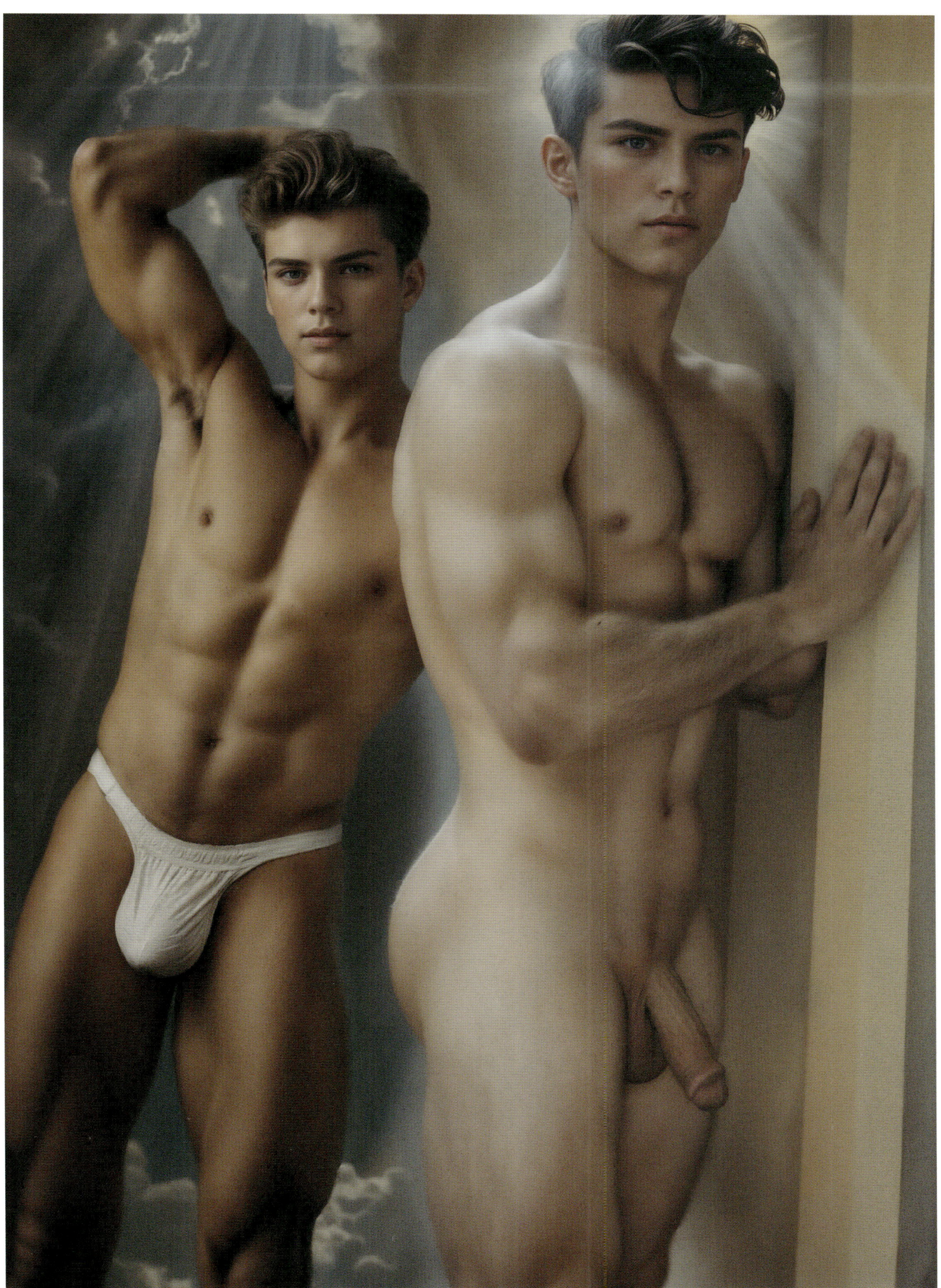

DER HEILIGE DONATUS · SAINT DONATUS

DER HEILIGE DIHYA

Dihya (tamazight ⴷⵉⵀⵢⴰ, arabisch ديهيا, *schöne Gazelle*) war ein Berberkönig, der den Widerstand der nordafrikanischen Ureinwohner gegen die arabischen Eroberer organisierte. Interessanterweise wurde er nach seinem Tod 701 häufig als Frau dargestellt, was oft auf die orale Tradition der Berber oder feministische Propaganda zurückgeführt wird, in Wahrheit aber wohl damit zusammenhing, dass Dihya selbst gerne von sich in weiblicher Form sprach. Sie kennen das. Es kursieren unterschiedlichste Berichte, die Dihya mal jüdisch, mal christlich und mal muslimisch verorten, aber tatsächlich war ihm Religion schlicht egal. Berber sehen in Dihya derweil einen anti-arabischen Nationalisten, während Araber ihn als bösartige Hexe beschreiben. Nichts von alledem stimmt. Dihya hatte ein sehr lebhaftes Temperament, war manchmal aufbrausend, zickig, despotisch und auch ziemlich affektiert und effeminiert und ließ sich von niemandem etwas sagen. Er hatte ein supergutes Netzwerk und ein äußerst ausschweifendes Sexualleben. Als die Araber ins Land kamen, hatten sie von Juba (siehe → DER HEILIGE JUBA, Seite 102) noch nichts gehört und taten sich schwer mit einem gesunden Sexualverhalten. Das ärgerte Dihya und sie drohte, alles in Trümmer zu legen, was ihr auf Seiten der Berber große Unterstützung einbrachte. Man organisierte Workshops, Sexpartys, Teach-ins und erprobte mannigfaltige Strategien des zivilen Ungehorsams. Am Ende konnte die sexuelle Rebellion durch einen Kompromiss, der eigentlich ein Sieg für alle Beteiligten war, beigelegt werden. Die Araber übernahmen Jubas Vorbild und Dihya wurde Agnostikerin. Damit waren alle glücklich. Dihyas politischer Gestaltungswille, ihr selbstbewusstes Schwulsein und ihre emanzipatorische Arbeit sind ein leuchtendes Vorbild. Leider verstarb er viel zu früh, als er völlig besoffen mit hochhackigen Schuhen auf einem Tresen in Kairo einen Cancan tanzen wollte und unglücklich mit seinem Hinterkopf auf eine Marmorplatte knallte.

Bei jeglichen Problemen mit der Vereinbarung von weiblichen und männlichen Seiten kann Dihya helfen. Er wird am 11. März gefeiert.

SAINT DIHYA

Dihya (Tamazight ⴷⵉⵀⵢⴰ, Arabic ديهيا, *beautiful gazelle*) was a Berber king who orchestrated the resistance of indigenous North Africans against the Arab conquerors. Curiously enough, after his death in 701, he was often referred to as a woman — something that is commonly attributed to either Berber oral tradition or feminist propaganda, but in reality was probably due to the fact that Dihya himself sometimes liked to use female pronouns for himself. Dihya is sometimes said to have been Jewish, sometimes Christian and sometimes Muslim, but in actual fact he simply didn't care about religion. While Berbers see Dihya as an anti-Arab nationalist, Arabs describe her as an evil witch. None of this is true. Mercurial and volatile in temperament, Dihya was sometimes quick-tempered, bitchy, and despotic as well as affected and effeminate, and nobody could tell him what to do. She was supremely well-connected and enjoyed an extremely profligate sex life. When the Arabs arrived in the country, they had not yet heard of Juba (see → SAINT JUBA, page 102) and had a hard time accepting healthy sexual behavior. This infuriated Dihya and she threatened to lay waste to everything, which garnered him enormous support from the Berbers. They organized workshops, sex parties, teach-ins and experimented with a variety of civil disobedience strategies. In the end, the sexual rebellion was settled with a compromise that was actually a victory for everyone involved. The Arabs followed Juba's example and Dihya became an agnostic. Everyone was happy. Dihya is a shining example of political determination, self-confident queerness and emancipatory activism. He sadly died far too young while trying to dance the cancan on top of a bar in Cairo, blind drunk and wearing high-heeled shoes, and fell, hitting the back of his head on a marble slab.

Dihya helps all people who have trouble reconciling their feminine and masculine sides. His feast day is March 11.

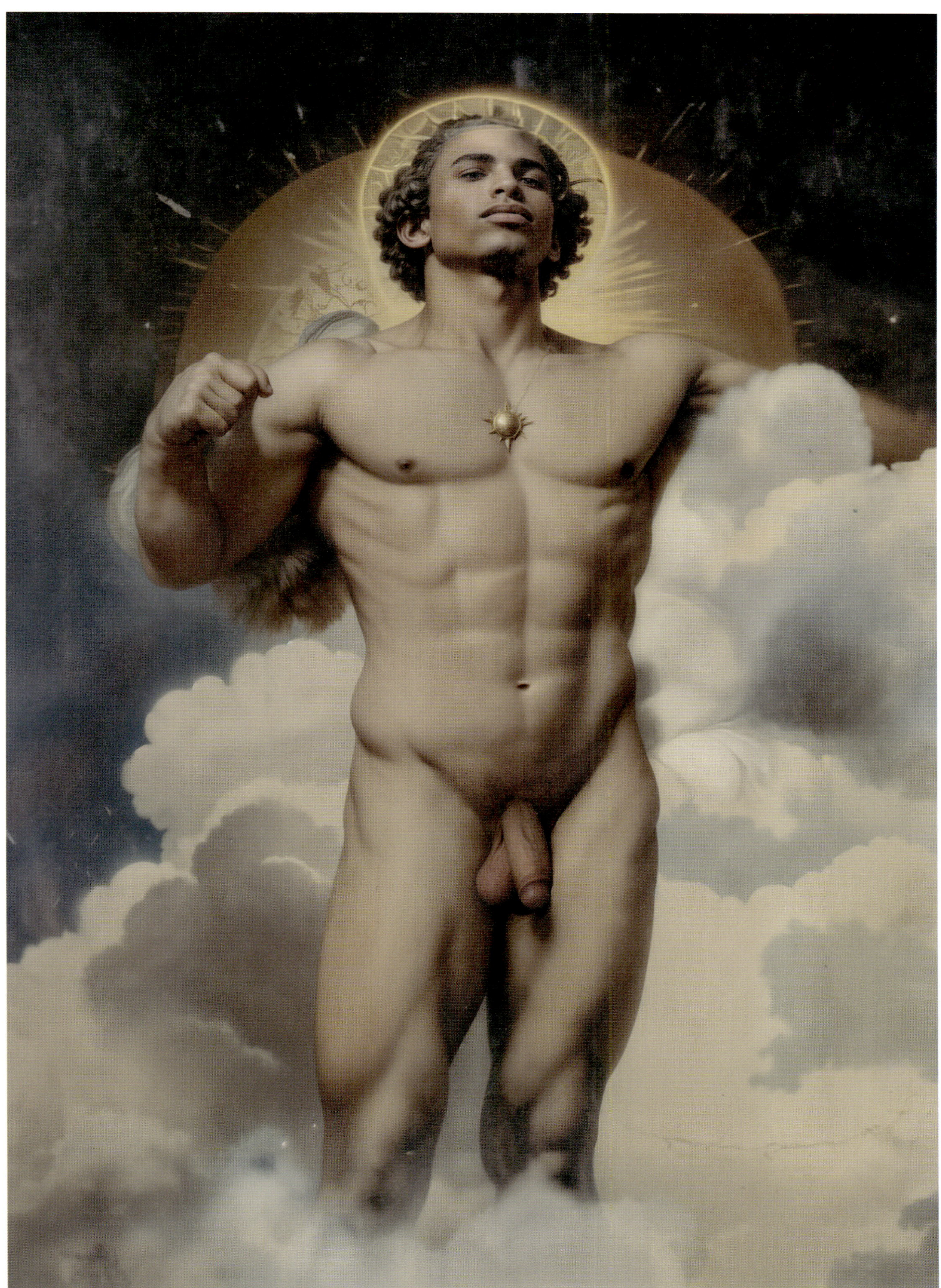

DER HEILIGE DIHYA · SAINT DIHYA

DER HEILIGE DYLAN AUS MONTREAL

Bevor wir Dylans Geschichte erzählen, erinnern wir uns kurz an den heiligen Sebastian. Wegen seines *guten Benehmens* wurde er Offizier der Leibwache der Römischen Kaiser Diokletian und Maximian, und weil er Christ war, wurde er von numidischen Bogenschützen erschossen. Er war dann aber gar nicht tot und wurde ausgerechnet von einer Witwe mit dem Namen Irene gesund gepflegt. Der Kaiser war sauer und ließ ihn mit Keulen erschlagen und in die Cloaca Maxima werfen, den Abflussgraben, der in den Tiber mündete. Es folgte die Pest, was bei den gegebenen hygienischen Bedingungen und nicht korrekter Bestattung nicht weiter verwunderlich war. Bis zur großen Stunde des heiligen Dylan dauerte es danach noch mal knapp 1.600 Jahre. Dylan Parker wurde 1852 nach dem großen Brand von Montreal, der 1.200 Häuser zerstörte, zum Gesundheitsbeauftragten der Stadt und räumte dort mal so richtig auf. Er sorgte für sauberes Trinkwasser und ein funktionierendes Abwassersystem (ohne Leichen), und schon flogen die Pfeile, die ja für Krankheiten wie Pest, Cholera, Typhus und so weiter stehen, an ihm und den Bewohnern der Stadt vorbei. Dylans Gatte Moise Tellier gründete übrigens 1869 einen Apfel- und Kuchenladen, der als erstes urkundlich erwähntes Schwulenlokal in Nordamerika gilt. So weit zu den Fakten. Warum allerdings ein von Pfeilen durchbohrter Mensch einer der Lieblingsheiligen der katholischen und auch orthodoxen Kirche ist, bleibt zu diskutieren.

Der heilige Dylan sorgt für Gesundheit. Sein Gedenktag wird traditionell am 14. Juni begangen.

SAINT DYLAN OF MONTREAL

Before we start with Dylan's story, let's take a moment to remember Saint Sebastian. He was made an officer in the Praetorian Guard — bodyguards to the Roman emperors Diocletian and Maximian — as a reward for *good behavior* and was shot full of arrows by Numidian archers for being a Christian. This did not kill him, however, and he was nursed back to health by a widow with the unlikely name of Irene. The emperor was furious and had him beaten to death with clubs before being thrown into the Cloaca Maxima, the Roman sewer that carried effluent to the River Tiber. This was followed by the plague, which was hardly surprising in light of the poor hygiene and dodgy burial practices. Another 1,600 years passed before the coming of Saint Dylan. Dylan Parker became the municipal health officer in 1852 after the Great Fire of Montreal, which destroyed 1,200 buildings, and immediately got to work cleaning up the city. He made sure there was clean drinking water and a functioning sewage system (without any corpses), and the arrows that represent diseases such as the plague, cholera, typhoid and so on flew past him and the city's inhabitants without hitting a single one. Dylan's husband Moise Tellier founded an apple pie store in 1869, which is believed to be the first documented gay bar in North America. So much for the facts. Why a man pierced by arrows should be one of the favorite saints of the Catholic and Orthodox churches, however, is another question.

Saint Dylan is the patron saint of health. His feast day is traditionally celebrated on June 14.

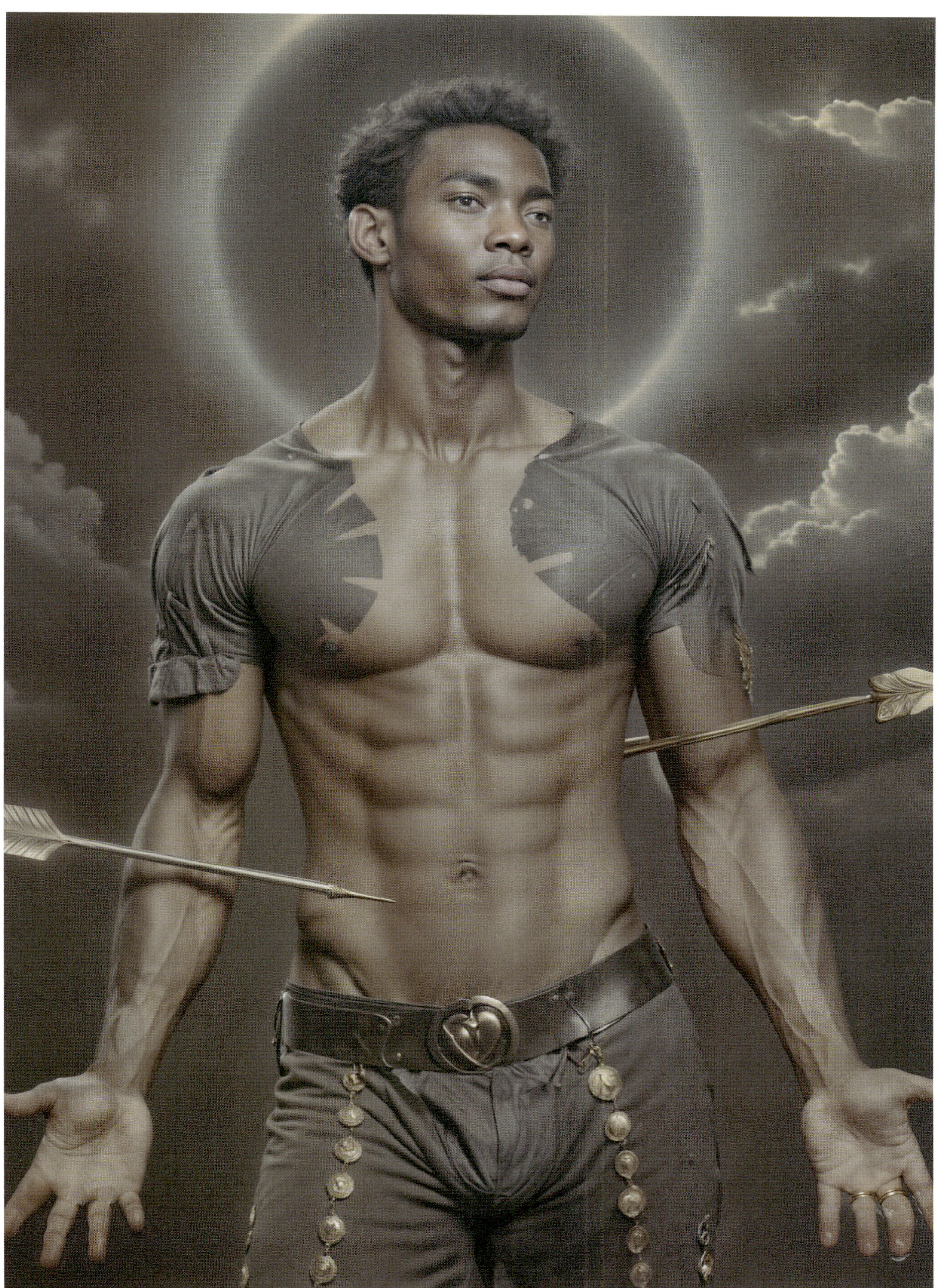

DER HEILIGE DYLAN AUS MONTREAL · SAINT DYLAN FROM MONTREAL

DER HEILIGE EDWARD

Edward Nigma (auch *E. Nigma*) gibt Rätsel auf und wir wissen in der Regel nichts über ihn. Er steht in den Büschen, Dünen, öffentlichen Toiletten, der Dampfsauna, dem Darkroom oder jedem anderen Ort dieser Welt. Bei Tag und Nacht. Mal führt seine Hand mit sanfter Kraft, mal lässt er sich selbst leiten, aber immer riecht er verführerisch. Und ist das Ziel erst mal erreicht, winkt große Belohnung. Sein Zauber liegt im Unbekannten.

Der heilige Edward freut sich über stille oder laute Gebete. Hauptsache, man kümmert sich um ihn. Möglicherweise fällt der Gedenktag von E. Nigma auf den 15. Januar.

SAINT EDWARD

Edward Nigma (aka *E. Nigma*) is a mystery and we don't really know anything about him. You will find him in the bushes, sand dunes, public toilets, the steam sauna, the darkroom or just about anywhere else. Night or day. Sometimes his strong and gentle hand will guide you, sometimes he will let you take the lead, but he always smells seductive. And once you've reached the finish line, you can expect a generous reward. He casts the spell of the unknown.

Saint Edward listens to all prayers, however loud or soft. Pay attention to him and he'll take care of you. The feast day of E. Nigma is said to fall on January 15.

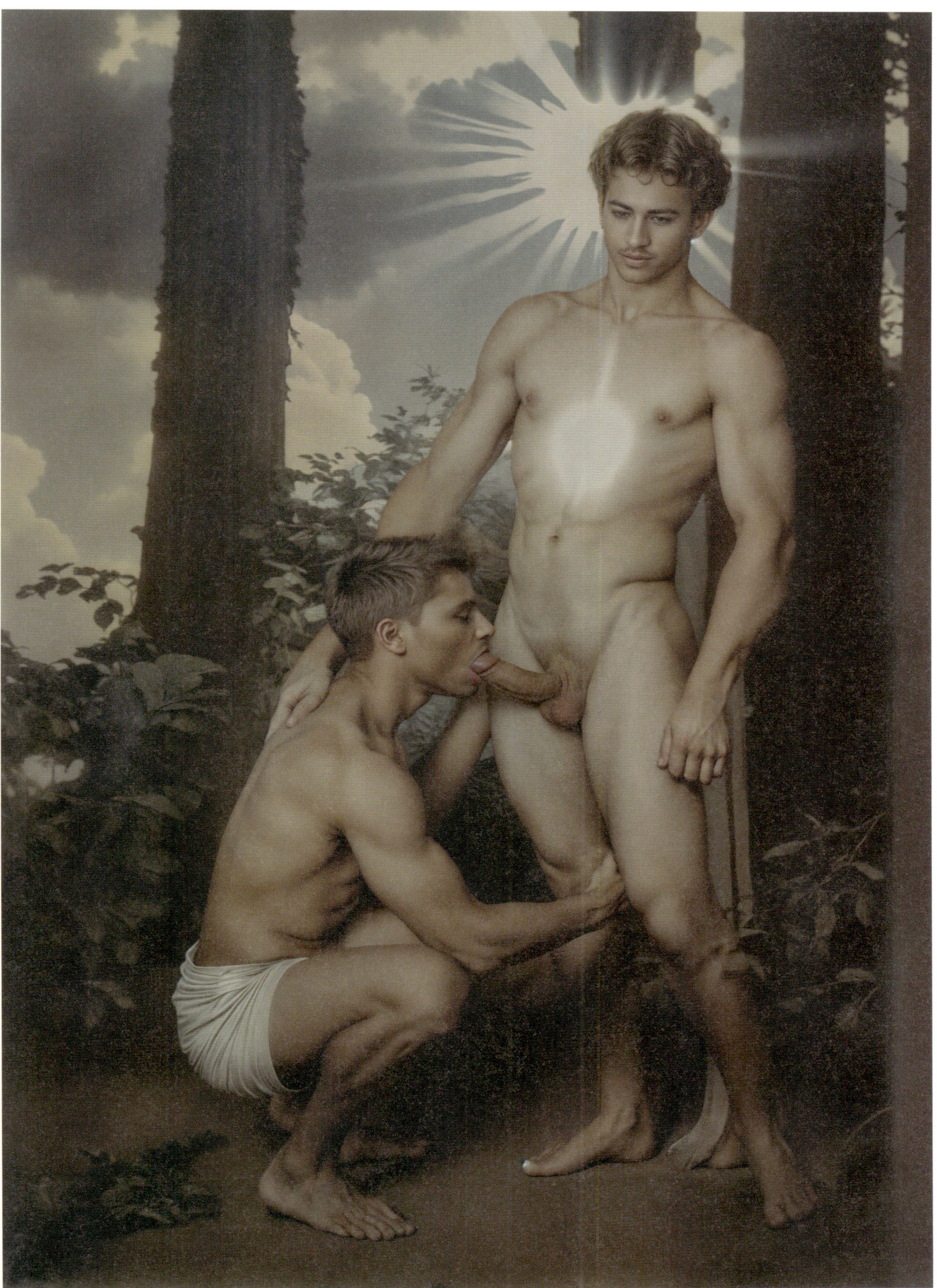

DER HEILIGE EDWARD · SAINT EDWARD

DER HEILIGE ELNATAN UND DER HEILIGE BERHANE

Der Tanach (die Bibel) der Juden kennt 24 Bücher und das frühe Christentum versammelte im Alten Testament 54 Bücher, um es im Mittelalter auf 46 Bücher zu kürzen. Den armen Protestanten müssen gar 39 Bücher genügen. Äthiopisch-orthodoxe Christen wurden dahingehend besonders reich beschenkt, denn ihre Bibel besteht aus 81 Büchern. Eigentlich müssten es sogar 82 sein, denn *Das Buch Elnatan und Berhane* fehlt hier mittlerweile genauso wie in den zuvor genannten heiligen Schriften. Es erzählt etwas ausschweifend und umständlich und mit blumiger Sprache die Geschichte von zwei Prinzen aus Aksum, ist im Prinzip aber eine Handlungsanweisung, wie zwei schwule Männer am besten ihr Zusammenleben organisieren sollten. Lange Passagen erläutern, was wie am besten gewaschen und gereinigt wird, welche Speisen für den Verkehr geeignet sind, wann man einfach mal sagen sollte *Ja, du hast selbstverständlich recht!* und wann man die Klappe halten sollte. Etwas poppiger formuliert, ist das Buch eine Mischung aus Sex- und Lebensratgeber und hätte noch heute das Zeug zum Bestseller.

Die heilige Elnatan und Berhane werden beide am 30. März gefeiert und von angehenden Bestsellerautoren auf der Suche nach einem Verleger um Hilfe gebeten.

SAINT ELNATAN AND SAINT BERHANE

The Hebrew bible, or Tanakh, has twenty-four books, whereas the early Christians compiled the Old Testament into fifty-four books, only to shorten it to forty-six in the Middle Ages. And the poor Protestants only have thirty-nine. Ethiopian Orthodox Christians are especially richly endowed in this respect, as their Bible consists of eighty-one books. There should in fact be eighty-two, but these and the other aforementioned holy Scriptures are all missing *The Book of Elnatan and Berhane*. This book — in a somewhat rambling and long-winded fashion and rather florid prose — tells the story of two princes from Aksum but is basically an instruction manual on how two gay men might best organize their life together. There are long passages explaining what parts to wash and how, which foods are most suitable for consumption during intercourse, when to say *Yes, of course you're right!* and when to shut the hell up. In other words, the book is a blend of sex and life advice that could easily have become a bestseller even today.

St. Elnatan and St. Berhane are both celebrated on March 30 and invoked by aspiring bestselling authors in search of a publisher.

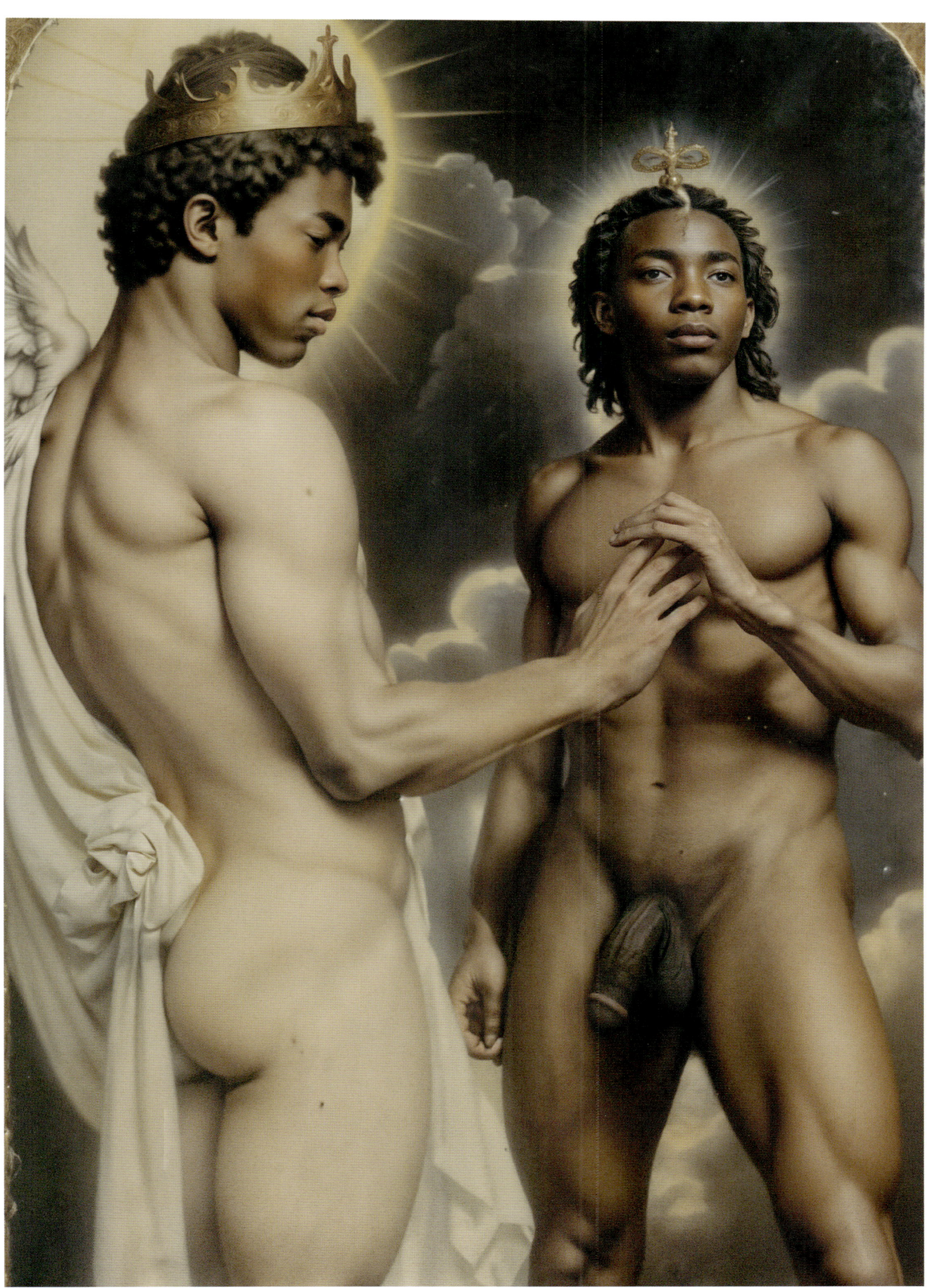

DER HEILIGE ELNATAN UND DER HEILIGE BERHANE
SAINT ELNATAN AND SAINT BERHANE

DER HEILIGE EMIL

Emil Engels (* 16. April 1818 in Trier, † 30. Oktober 1864 bei Eckernförde) war ein Jugendfreund von Karl Marx. Er wuchs, anders als Karl, in ärmlichen Verhältnissen auf. Immerhin hatte er das Glück, nicht ab seinem vierten Lebensjahr bis zu 18 Stunden am Tag arbeiten zu müssen, sondern bis zu seinem 12. Lebensjahr zur Schule gehen zu können. Danach fand er eine Lehrstelle bei einem freundlichen jüdischen Fahrradmechaniker. So war Emil ein fröhlicher, aufgeweckter und sehr aktiver junger Mann. Er lernte den gleichaltrigen Karl im Stadtpark von Trier kennen und führte bis 1835 eine Beziehung mit ihm. In dieser Zeit schrieb Karl auch das verschollene Frühwerk *Der Sex*, in dem er alles, was er mit Emil gelernt hatte, zu seinen wesentlichen Thesen verarbeitete: „Radikal sein ist die Sache an der Wurzel fassen"; „Das Sein bestimmt das Bewusstsein"; „Ihre Hosentaschen zu öffnen, keine Fragen zu stellen und an die allgemeine Tugend der Menschheit zu glauben — das dient ihren Absichten am allerbesten"; „Jeder nach seinen Fähigkeiten, jedem nach seinen Bedürfnissen"; „Homosexuelle aller Länder vereinigt euch" und so weiter. Die Beziehung von Emil und Karl musste scheitern, denn Emil wollte sich mit einer guten Idee selbstständig machen (es ging darum, Fahrräder mittels Gummireifen bequemer zu machen), aber Karl verweigerte ihm das bisschen benötigte Startkapital, weil er meinte, dass ein Proletarier aus systemimmanenten Gründen auch ein Proletarier bleiben müsse und keinesfalls Kapitalist werden könne. Zudem wollte Karl selbst Karriere machen, wurde ein bisschen dick und ließ sich einen scheußlichen Bart stehen. Er heiratete dann Jenny von Westphalen. Dennoch steht fest, dass Karl alles, was er über das Leben wusste, aus den Erfahrungen der Beziehung mit Emil schöpfte, was er diesem aber nie dankte. Noch kurz vor Ende des Deutsch-Dänischen Kriegs wurde Emil eingezogen und bei Eckernförde von einer verirrten Kugel getroffen. Karl wurde dann ein typischer Bestsellerautor, der seine Werke nach einem einzigen Grundsatz verfasste: „Ich dehne diesen Band aus, da die deutschen Hunde den Wert der Bücher nach dem Kubikinhalt schätzen." Alles, was er durch Emil gelernt hatte, wurde also wieder und wieder ausgewalzt. Es gibt Gerüchte, dass ein Exemplar von *Der Sex* noch in Moskauer Archiven lagert. Es bleibt also spannend.

Ungeachtet der Tatsache, dass Karl ihn daran hinderte, die Idee mit den Gummireifen umzusetzen, hilft Emil interessanterweise bis heute allen Fahrradfahrern. Zusammen mit Karl feiert er seinen Geburts- und Ehrentag am 16. April.

SAINT EMIL

Emil Engels (* April 16, 1818 in Trier, † October 30, 1864 near Eckernförde) was a childhood friend of Karl Marx. Unlike Karl, he grew up in humble circumstances. Nevertheless, he was lucky enough not to have to work up to eighteen hours a day from the age of four but was instead allowed to attend school until the age of twelve. He then landed an apprenticeship with a friendly Jewish bicycle mechanic. Emil was a bright, cheerful and very active young man. He met Karl, who was the same age, in the city park in Trier and the two of them were a couple until 1835. It was during this period that Karl also wrote his now-lost early work *Sex*, in which he incorporated everything he and Emil had learned about the subject into his key theses: "To be radical is to go to the root of the matter"; "Being determines consciousness"; "To open their breeches' pockets, ask no questions, and believe in the general virtue of mankind, serves best their purpose"; "From each according to his ability, to each according to his needs"; "Homosexuals of the world, unite" and so on. The relationship between Emil and Karl was doomed because Emil had a great business idea (it involved using rubber tires to make bicycles more comfortable), but Karl refused to give him the minimal start-up capital he needed to start his own business because he believed that a proletarian had to remain a proletarian for reasons inherent in the system and could never become a capitalist. And Karl wanted to make a career for himself. Besides which, he put on weight and grew a hideous beard. Then he married Jenny von Westphalen. Nevertheless, it is clear that everything Karl knew about life stemmed from his relationship with Emil, although he never thanked him. Emil was drafted into the army shortly before the end of the German-Danish War and was hit by a stray bullet near Eckernförde. Karl subsequently became a typical bestselling author who wrote his works in line with a single principle: "I am stretching out this volume, since those German dogs estimate the value of books by their cubic contents." So he continued to regurgitate everything he had learned from Emil over and over again. Rumor has it that a copy of *Sex* is still preserved in the Moscow archives.

Interestingly enough, despite the fact that Karl prevented him from implementing the idea of rubber tires, Emil continues to come to the aid of cyclists to this day. His birthday (and feast day) is the same as Karl's on April 16.

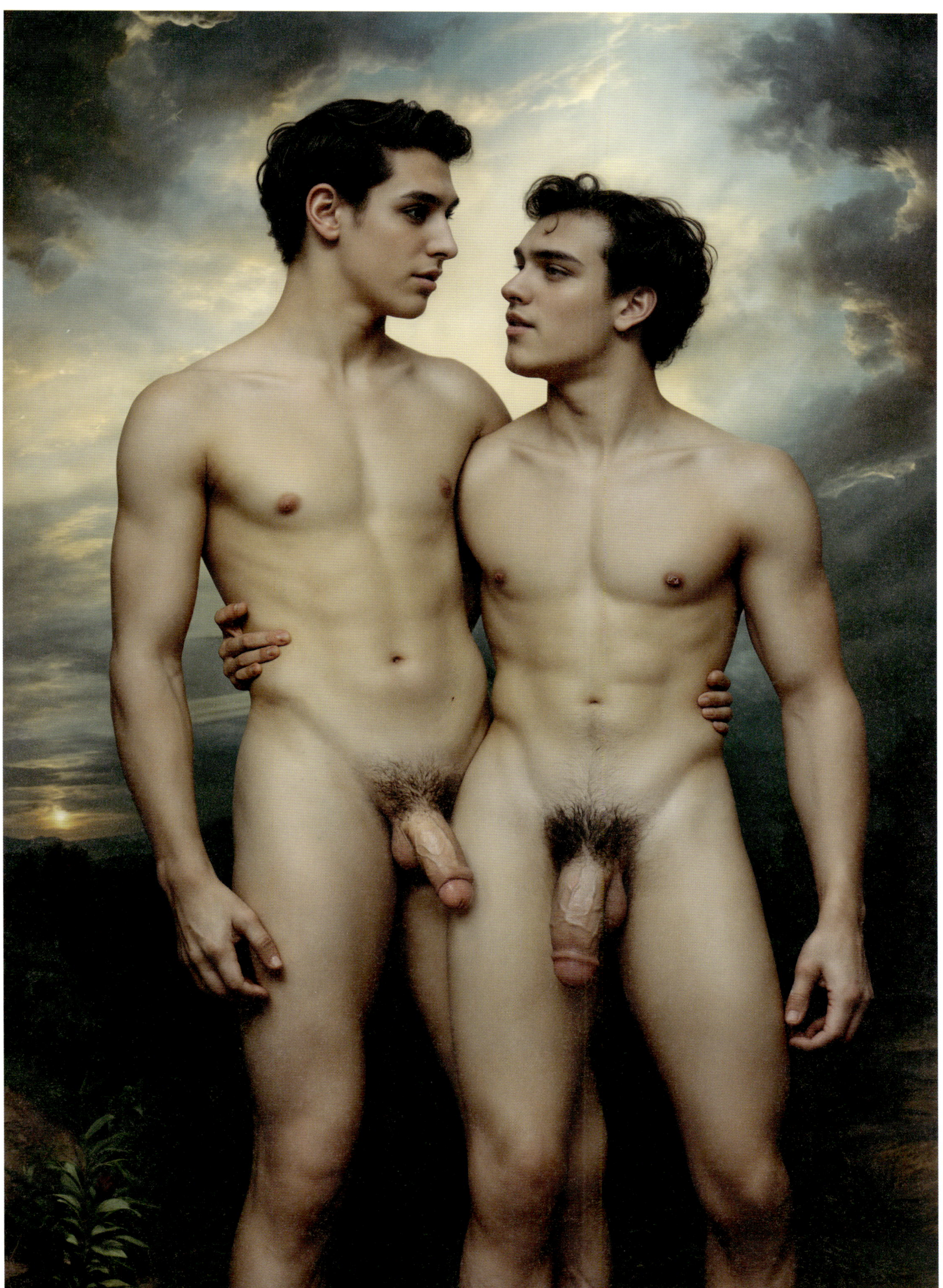

DER HEILIGE EMIL · SAINT EMIL

DER HEILIGE ENRIQUE

Enrique Camarena (genannt *Kiki*) war Student der Wirtschaftswissenschaften in Madrid und ein erbitterter Gegner der Eroberer Hernán Cortés und Francisco Pizarro. Zwischen 1532 und 1535 organisierte Kiki jeden Tag auf der Plaza Mayor eine Demo, bei der er unbekleidet auf das Schicksal der Inkas und Azteken hinwies. In erster Linie ging es ihm natürlich um die empörenden und sinnlosen Massaker in Gottes Namen, die in Mexiko und Peru Millionen Opfer forderten und blühende Zivilisationen zerstörten. Parallel wurden bis 1660 ganze 3,5 Millionen Kilogramm Silber und ähnlich viel Gold nach Spanien verschifft. Allerdings waren die Spanier zu blöde — so beklagte es jedenfalls Enrique —, damit auch nur etwas halbwegs Sinnvolles anzustellen. Zwar zahlte man Schulden und Zinsen und baute Paläste, aber das frühkapitalistische Finanzsystem entwickelte sich in Mitteleuropa und nicht in Spanien. Aber niemand hörte auf Enrique. Der Literaturnobelpreisträger Octavio Paz brachte es später folgendermaßen auf den Punkt: „Während in Europa nach 1500 die Kritik zur Grundlage des neuen Zeitalters wurde, verschloss sich Spanien ihr.“ Stattdessen habe das Land „seine besten Geister“ zensiert und kritisches Denken verboten. So wurde der nackte Enrique am Weihnachtsabend 1535 auf der Plaza Mayor erschlagen. Die kirchliche Zensur führte dann auch noch dazu, dass er mit Gold und obendrein vor der Inkafestung Machu Picchu dargestellt wurde. Alle, die sich der Ruinenstadt nach Tagen des Wanderns schon mal zu Fuß genähert haben, erkennen das sofort. Sie wissen allerdings auch, dass Machu Picchu erst sehr viel später entdeckt wurde. Ob wir es bei der Darstellung also mit der Vision eines hellsichtigen Malers oder einem Zeugnis des geheimen Wissens im Vatikan zu tun haben, weiß wohl nur Kiki selbst.

Der heilige Enrique wird am 23. April insbesondere von Studenten und Volkswirten gefeiert. Der Trinkspruch *Auf Enrique!* drückt dabei allgemeine Hoffnungslosigkeit aus.

SAINT ENRIQUE

Enrique Camarena (also known as *Kiki*) was a student of economics in Madrid and a fierce opponent of the conquistadors Hernán Cortés and Francisco Pizarro. From 1532 to 1535, Kiki organized daily demonstrations in the Plaza Mayor, where he stood naked in the square every day and drew the public's attention to the fate of the Incas and Aztecs. His primary concern was of course the appalling and senseless massacres perpetrated in the name of God, which claimed millions of victims in Mexico and Peru and destroyed entire vibrant civilizations. At the same time, a staggering 3.5 million kilograms of silver and a similar amount of gold had been shipped to Spain by 1660, but the Spaniards were too stupid — or so Enrique claimed — to do anything halfway useful with it. Debts and interest were paid and palaces were built, but the early capitalist financial system originated in Central Europe, not in Spain. But nobody listened to Enrique. Octavio Paz, winner of the Nobel Prize for Literature, would later summarize the issue as follows: "While criticism became the foundation of the new age in Europe after 1500, Spain closed itself off to it." Instead, the country censored "its best minds" and outlawed critical thinking. And so, in 1535, Enrique was killed in the Plaza Mayor on Christmas Eve. The church censors insisted that his portrait not only feature him in gold trappings, but also standing in front of the Inca fortress of Machu Picchu. Everyone who has ever explored the ruined city on foot after days of hiking will recognize it straight away. However, they will also be aware that Machu Picchu was not discovered until much later. Only Kiki himself can say whether we are witnessing the vision of a clairvoyant painter or evidence of secret knowledge hidden away in the Vatican.

St. Enrique is celebrated on April 23, especially by students and economists. Their traditional toast *To Enrique!* is an expression of general hopelessness.

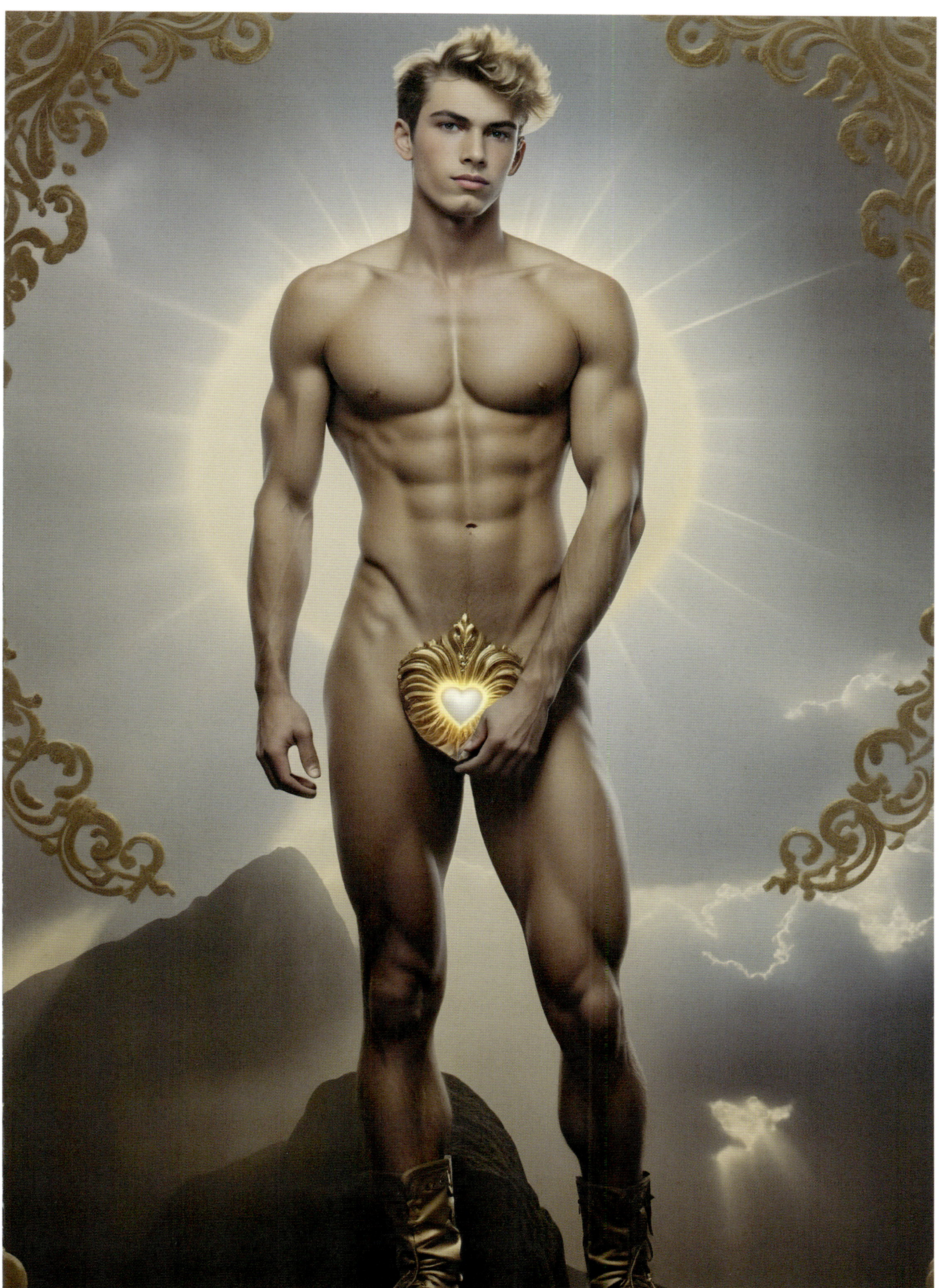

DER HEILIGE ENRIQUE · SAINT ENRIQUE

ERICK ODER ERIK ODER ERIC

Von Anat, Aphrodite, Astarte, Azacca über Freya, Frigg und Hathor bis zu Tanit, Turan, Venus und Voluptas: Die Mehrheit der Liebesgottheiten ist weiblich. Männer sind hier mit Amor, Bes, Eros und Kamadeva nur sehr dürftig vertreten. Das wundert natürlich bei einer Gesellschaft, die Liebe und Sex immer mit Fruchtbarkeit und Reproduktion verbinden möchte, kaum. So wurde auch unser Held Erick einfach aus dem *Martyrologium Romanum* und auch der *Nordischen Götterwelt* gestrichen. Er stammte aus der Ehe von Odin mit Frija, und seine Brüder hießen Balder, Hödur, Hermod und Bragi. Allerdings konnte nur Erick den ganzen ewigen Kampf zwischen Gut und Böse in den Asen und Wanen und dem Ragnarök, also den Weltuntergang, ad absurdum führen. Er besiegte einfach alle mit dem simplen Trick der Ekstase und hebelte damit die sich diametral gegenüberstehenden Notwendigkeiten aus und rettete bekanntermaßen so die Welt. Sehr schön sind in unserer historischen Darstellung das Nordlicht und auch die Phalli zu sehen, die seit Urzeit in den nordischen Ländern in der Landschaft stehen. Menschen, die irgendwelchen abstrusen Träumen von Blut und Ehre nachhängen, könnten durch Erick zweifelsohne geheilt werden. Wenn man ihn denn ließe.

Der Geburtstag von Erick ist leider komplett unbekannt und Sie dürfen ihn feiern, wann immer sie möchten.

ERICK, ALSO KNOWN AS ERIK OR ERIC

From Anat, Aphrodite, Astarte, Azacca, Freya, Frigg and Hathor to Tanit, Turan, Venus and Voluptas: most deities of love are female. The men are only very scantily represented here with Cupid, Bes, Eros and Kamadeva. Of course, this is hardly surprising in a society that constantly strives to link love and sex with fertility and reproduction. Our hero Erick, for example, was dropped from both the *Martyrologium Romanum* and the *Norse pantheon*. He was born of the marriage between Odin and Frija, and his brothers' names were Balder, Hodur, Hermod and Bragi. However, only Erick managed to reduce the eternal battle between good and evil, the Æsir and Vanir, and Ragnarök, i.e., the end of the world, to the point of absurdity. He defeated everyone with one simple trick, namely ecstasy, thereby neutralizing the diametric opposition between the two and — as we all know — saving the world. The Northern Lights and the phalli, which have graced the Nordic countryside since prehistoric times, are beautifully depicted in our historical illustration. People who indulge in bizarre fantasies of blood and honor could undoubtedly be cured by Erick. If only they would let him.

Nobody knows what day Erick's birthday falls on, so you can celebrate it whenever you like.

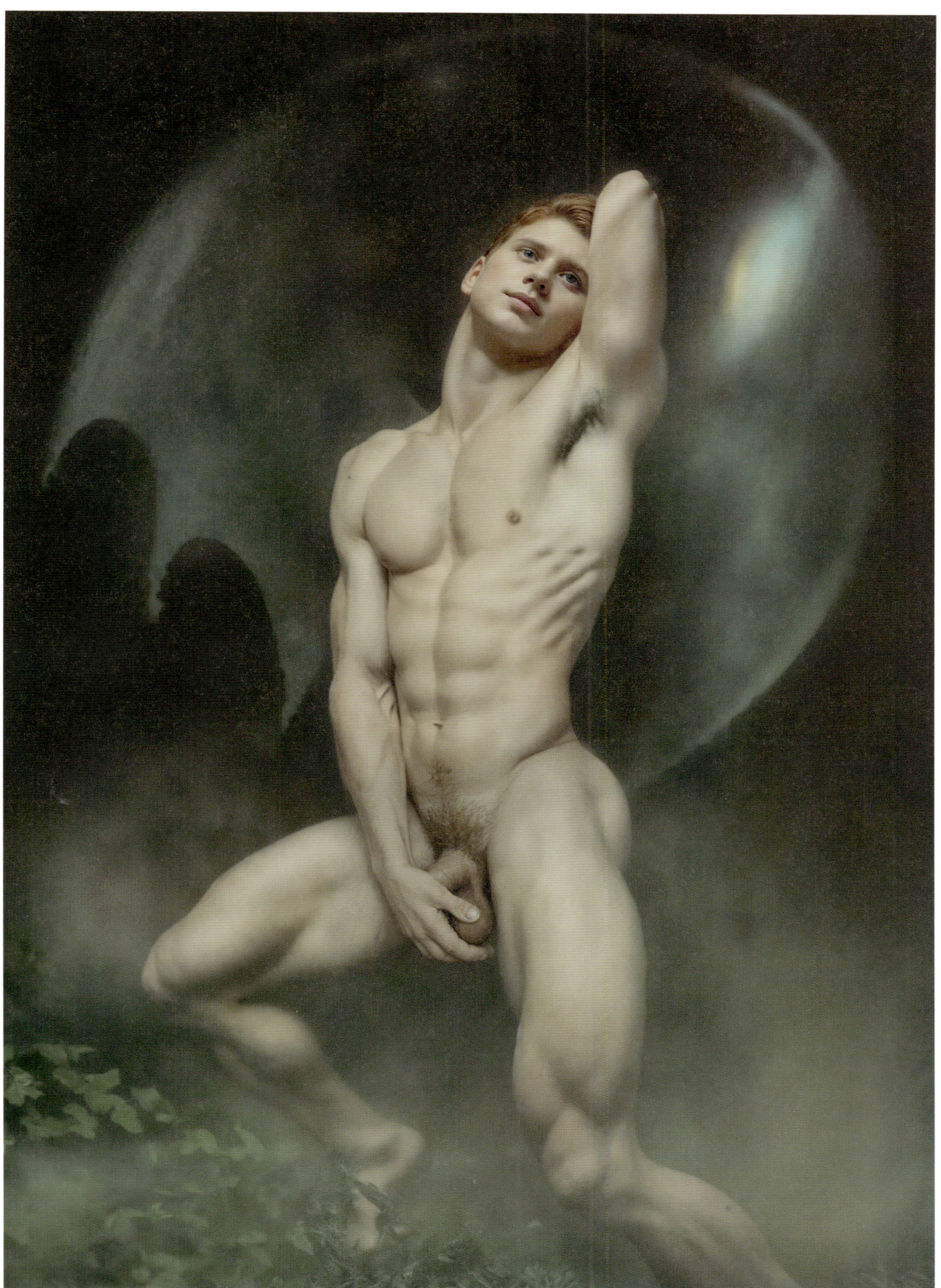

ERICK ODER ERIK ODER ERIC · ERICK, ALSO KNOWN AS ERIK OR ERIC

CAPTAIN FAGGOTRON

Die Lage in Westeros, Essos, Ulthos und Sothoryos ist hoffnungslos verfahren. Die Alten Götter des Waldes, die Sieben, der Ertrunkene Gott, der Herr des Lichts, der Vielgesichtige Gott, der Große Hengst und die Schwarze Ziege von Qohor: Alle haben versagt und keiner kann das von George R.R. Martin und den wildgewordenen HBO-Autoren angerichtete Chaos noch bändigen. Geliebte und nicht so geliebte Helden sterben wie die Fliegen und werden von den Toten auferweckt, nur noch Drogon atomarisiert die Welt. Und können wir wirklich sicher sein, dass nicht auch die Weißen Wanderer wieder auftauchen? Wir danken Harvey Rabbit für den einzig richtigen Vorschlag: Schickt Captain Faggotron! Der wird den Drachen schon reiten und den vier Kontinenten Frieden bringen. Der Captain ist dabei keine reine Erfindung der Neuzeit, sondern wurde immer wieder rangenommen, wenn es kompliziert wurde.

Der Captain kann und weiß alles und teilt seine Vorzüge super gerne. Einfach anrufen! Zum Beispiel am 23. Februar, dem Internationalen Captain-Faggotron-Gedenktag.

CAPTAIN FAGGOTRON

Westeros, Essos, Ulthos and Sothoryos are all in a hopeless state of disarray. The Old Gods of the Forest, the Seven, the Drowned God, the Lord of Light, the Many-Faced God, the Great Stallion and the Black Goat of Qohor: all have failed and none can tame the chaos wrought by George R.R. Martin and the crazed writers at HBO. Heroes, beloved and less beloved, die like flies and are raised from the dead, leaving only Drogon to atomize the world. And can we really be sure that the White Walkers won't show up again? Many thanks to Harvey Rabbit for the only sensible suggestion: send in Captain Faggotron! He will surely ride the dragon and bring peace to the four continents. The Captain is not purely a modern invention but has been invoked since time immemorial whenever things get complicated.

The Captain knows best, there is nothing he can't do, and he loves to share his assets. Just ask him! On February 23, for example, the International Captain Faggotron Memorial Day.

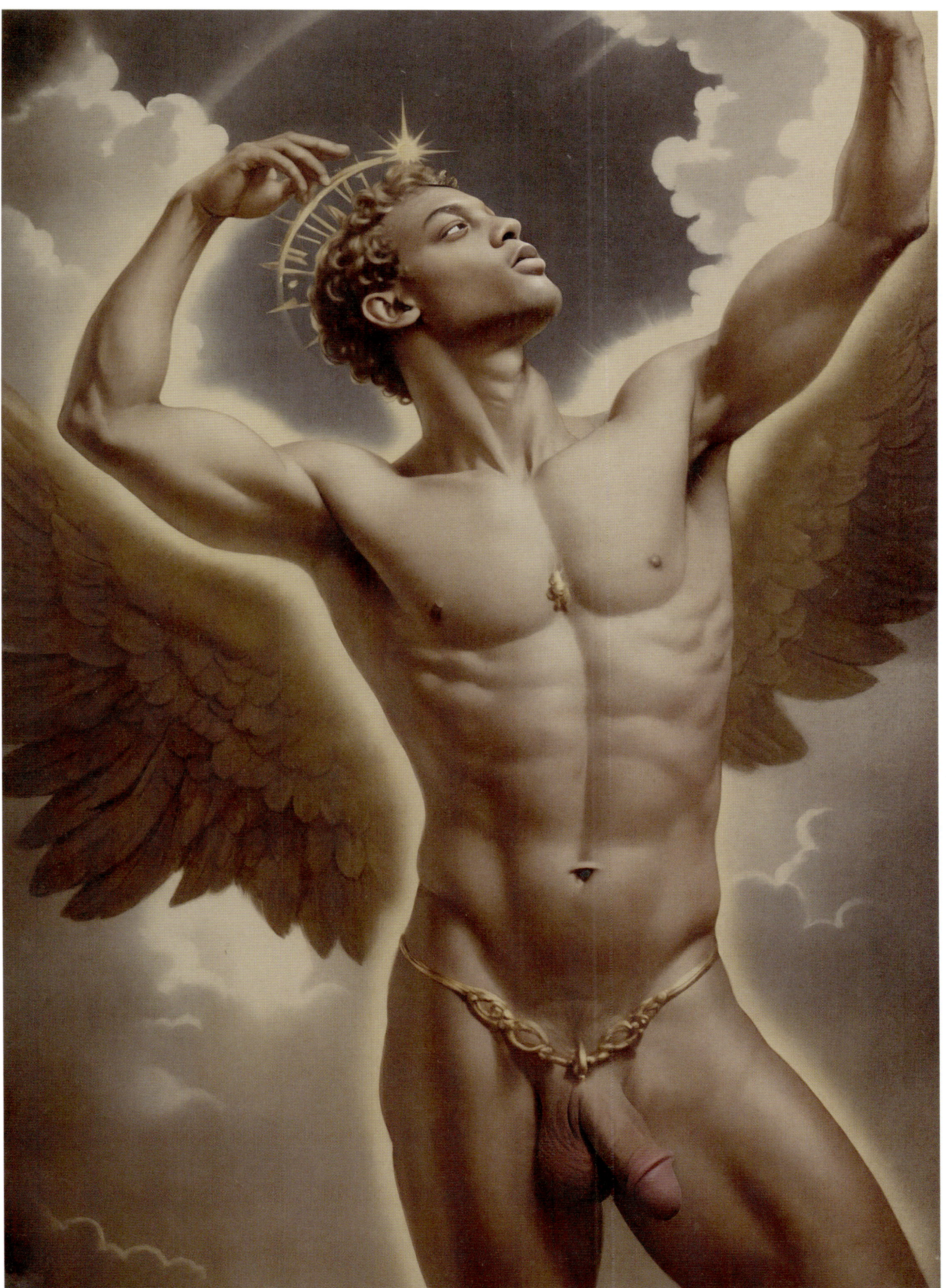

CAPTAIN FAGGOTRON

DER HEILIGE FELIX UND SEINE GEFÄHRTEN

Offizielle Hagiographien verzeichnen zu Felix und seinen *Gefährten* lapidar, dass diese *wohl in Afrika* verstorben seien. Korrekt ist, dass Felix' Freunde Namen hatten, nämlich Euphraxius, Lucian, Hippolytus und Sempronius. Außerdem gab es noch die beste Freundin Felicitas, doch von ihr ist leider keine Abbildung erhalten. Das schwammige „wohl in Afrika" lässt sich ebenfalls präzisieren, denn das Haus der sechs Menschen stand in Karthago, heute ein Villenvorort von Tunis. Wer es ganz genau wissen will, schaut in der Rue Sophonisbe vorbei, schräg gegenüber des Eingangs der Antonius-Pius-Thermen, ungefähr auf Höhe der nicht zu empfehlenden öffentlichen Toilette. Hier lebten die fünf schwulen Männer ungefähr von 150 bis 220 nach Christus und hatten von der oberen Terrasse direkten Meerblick. Die Stadt war zu diesem Zeitpunkt schon mehr oder weniger wiederhergestellt, nur die Antonius-Pius-Thermen befanden sich noch im Bau, was den relativ günstigen Kaufpreis des Grundstücks erklärt. Felix hatte frühzeitig erkannt, dass er für eine monogame Beziehung völlig ungeeignet ist, wollte aber gleichzeitig auf so etwas wie Familie nicht verzichten. So versammelte er seine guten Freunde und Felicitas, sie kauften gemeinsam das Haus und richteten es her, um zusammen alt zu werden — die erste nachweisbare schwule Wohngruppe und spätere Alters-WG. Bei der Darstellung von Felix wurde häufig das Herz verwendet. Es steht für sein duldsames und liebevolles Wesen. Euphraxius, Lucian, Hippolytus und Sempronius ließen sich so abbilden, wie sie sich selbst am besten gefielen. Lucian und Sempronius stritten sich dabei immer um ein elegantes blaues Tuch, das sie allerdings völlig unterschiedlich zu tragen pflegten.

Die Daten der Gedenktage für den heiligen Felix und seine Gefährten sind genauso vielfältig wie die Mitglieder der Wohngemeinschaft selbst. So feiern wir Felix am 16. April, Lucian am 6. April, Sempronius am 9. Juli, Euphraxius am 27. Mai und Hippolytus am 27. Juni. Gelegenheiten, sich bei Problemen mit dem häuslichen Zusammenleben vertrauensvoll an einen der Herren zu wenden, gibt es also gleich fünf.

SAINT FELIX AND HIS COMPANIONS

With regard to Felix and his *companions*, the official hagiographies simply include a terse note to the effect that they *probably died in Africa*. In fact, however, Felix's friends all had names, namely Euphraxius, Lucian, Hippolytus and Sempronius. He also had a best gal pal called Felicitas, but sadly no picture of her has survived. We can also elaborate on the vague "probably in Africa," because the six companions' house was in Carthage, now a residential suburb of Tunis. If you want to see for yourself, head to Rue Sophonisbe, opposite the entrance to the Antonius Pius thermal baths, roughly at the level of the public toilet, which we do not recommend. This is where the five gay men lived from around 150 to 220 AD and enjoyed an unobstructed view of the sea from the upper terrace. The city had already been more or less rebuilt by this time, only the Antonius Pius thermal baths were still under construction, which explains why they managed to purchase the land at a relatively low price. Felix realized early on that he was completely unsuited to a monogamous relationship, but at the same time he didn't want to give up on having a family. That's why he called on his good friends and Felicitas and they all bought the house and set it up so that they would be able to grow old there together — the first verifiable gay co-living group and senior intentional community. Depictions of Felix often feature a heart. It symbolizes his tolerant and loving nature. Euphraxius, Lucian, Hippolytus and Sempronius had their portraits painted any way they liked. Lucian and Sempronius used to constantly fight over an elegant blue shawl, which they wore in completely different ways.

The dates of the feast days of St. Felix and his companions are as varied as the members of the community itself. We celebrate Felix on April 16, Lucian on April 6, Sempronius on July 9, Euphraxius on May 27 and Hippolytus on June 27. So you have five opportunities to confide your domestic problems to one of these gentlemen.

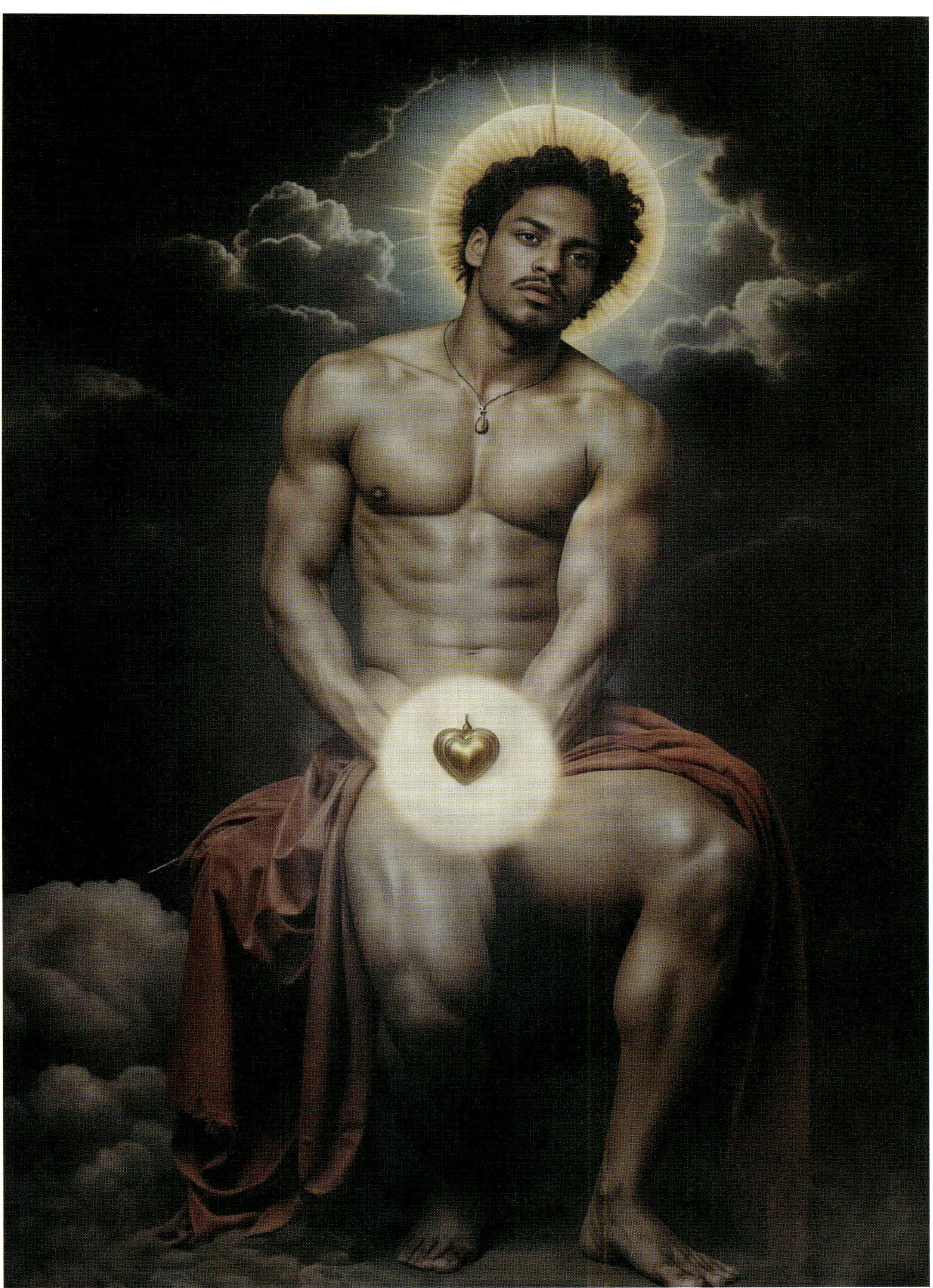

DER HEILIGE FELIX · SAINT FELIX

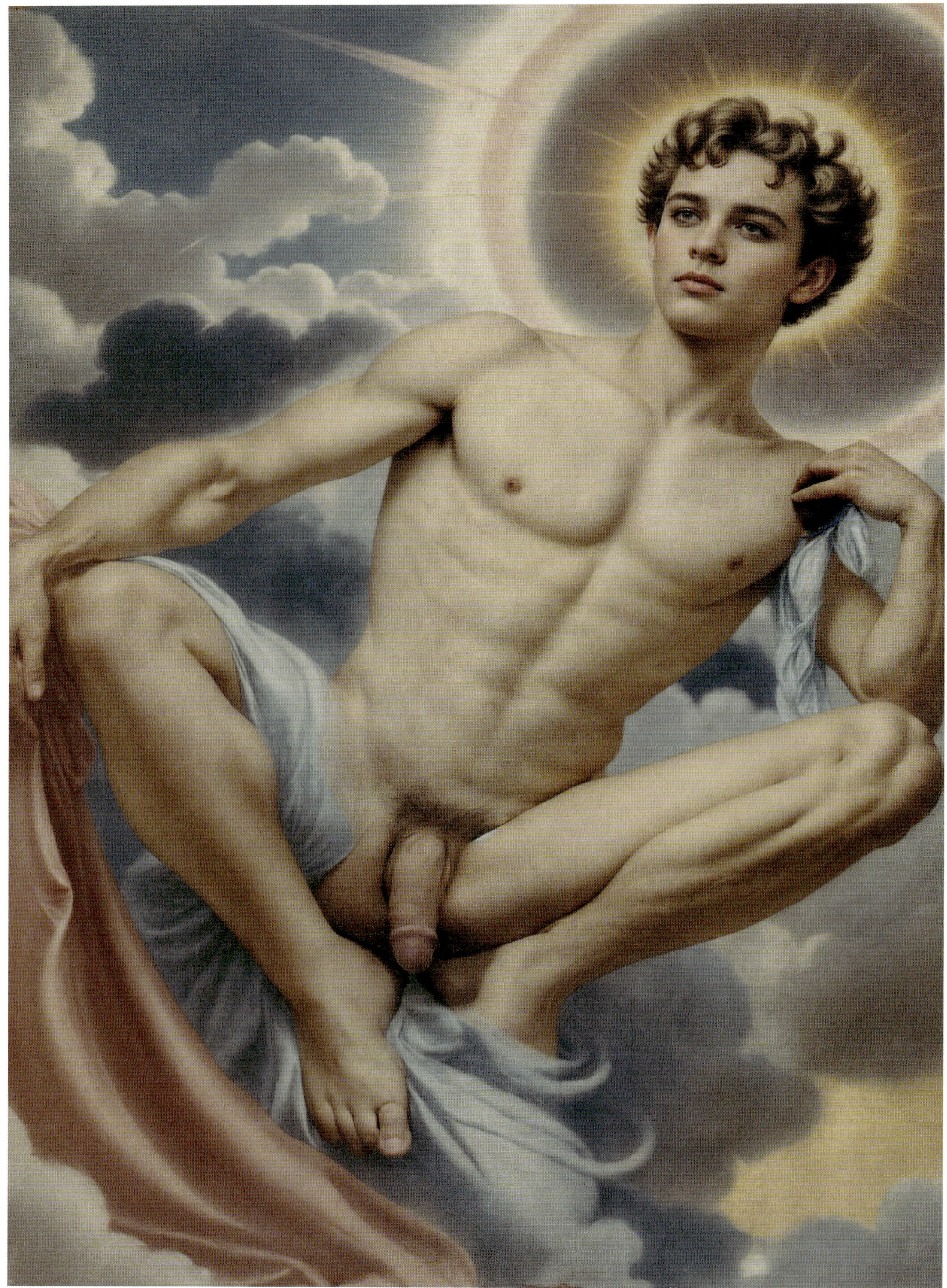

LUCIAN

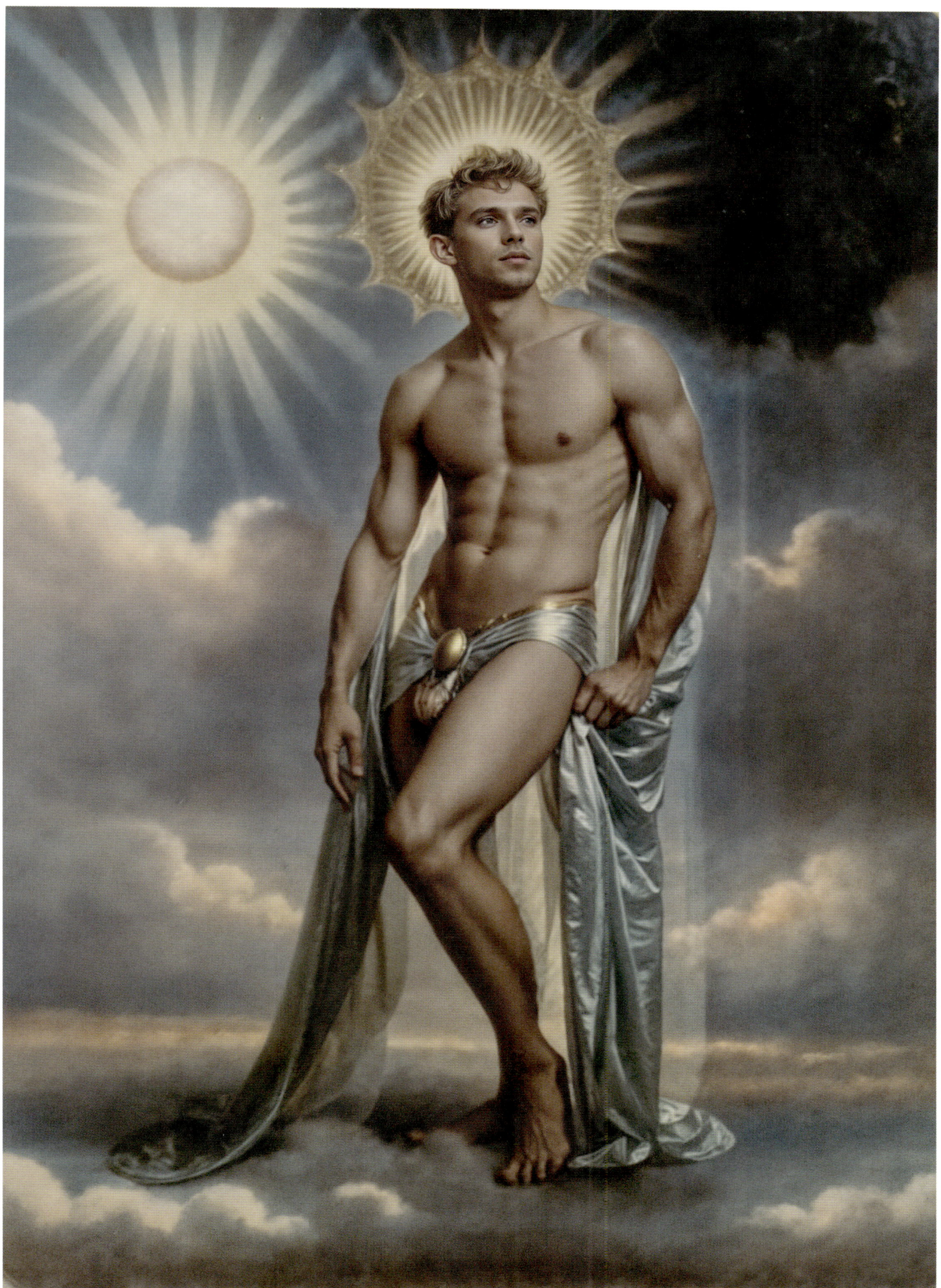

SEMPRONIUS

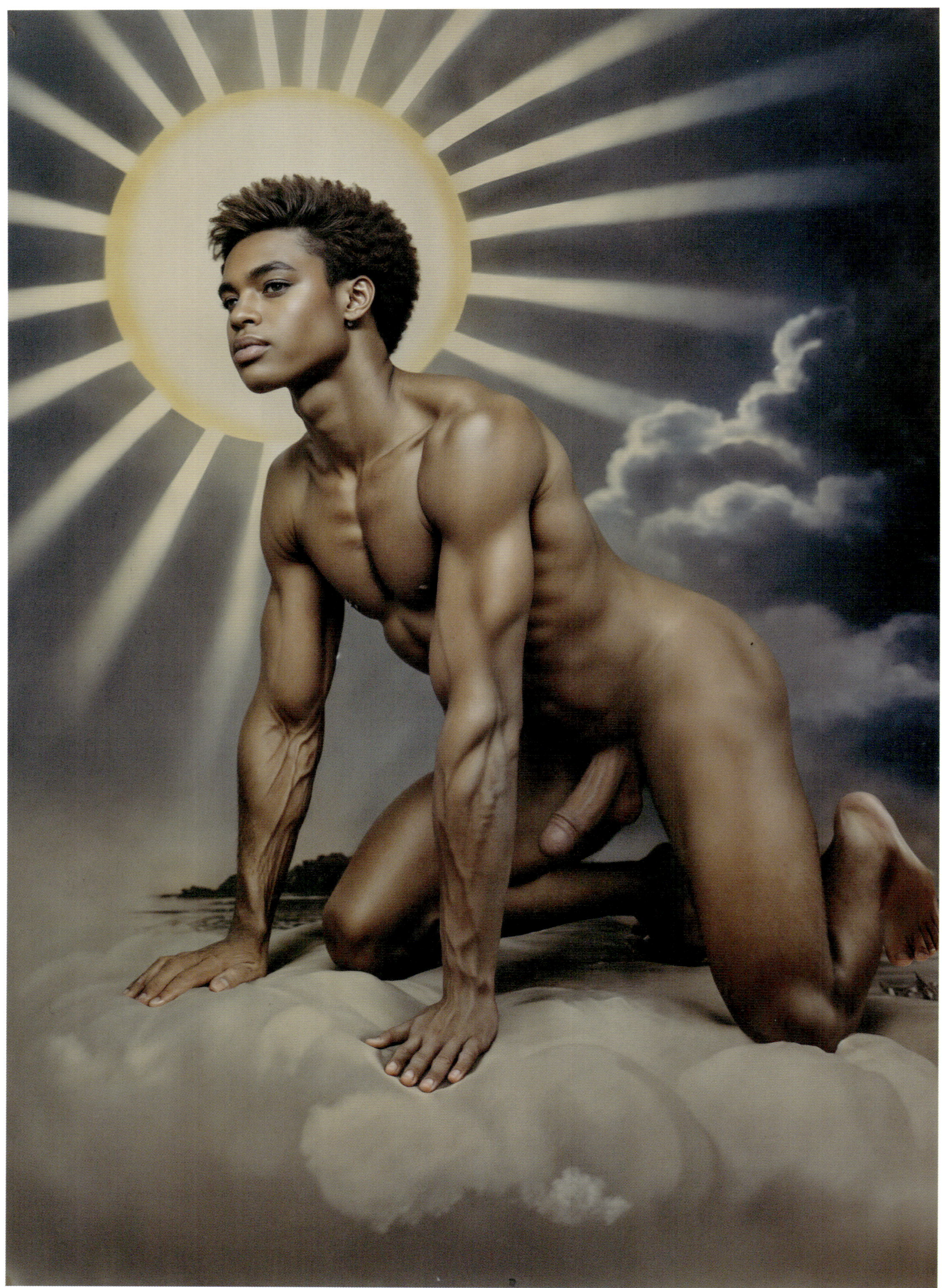

EUPHRAXIUS

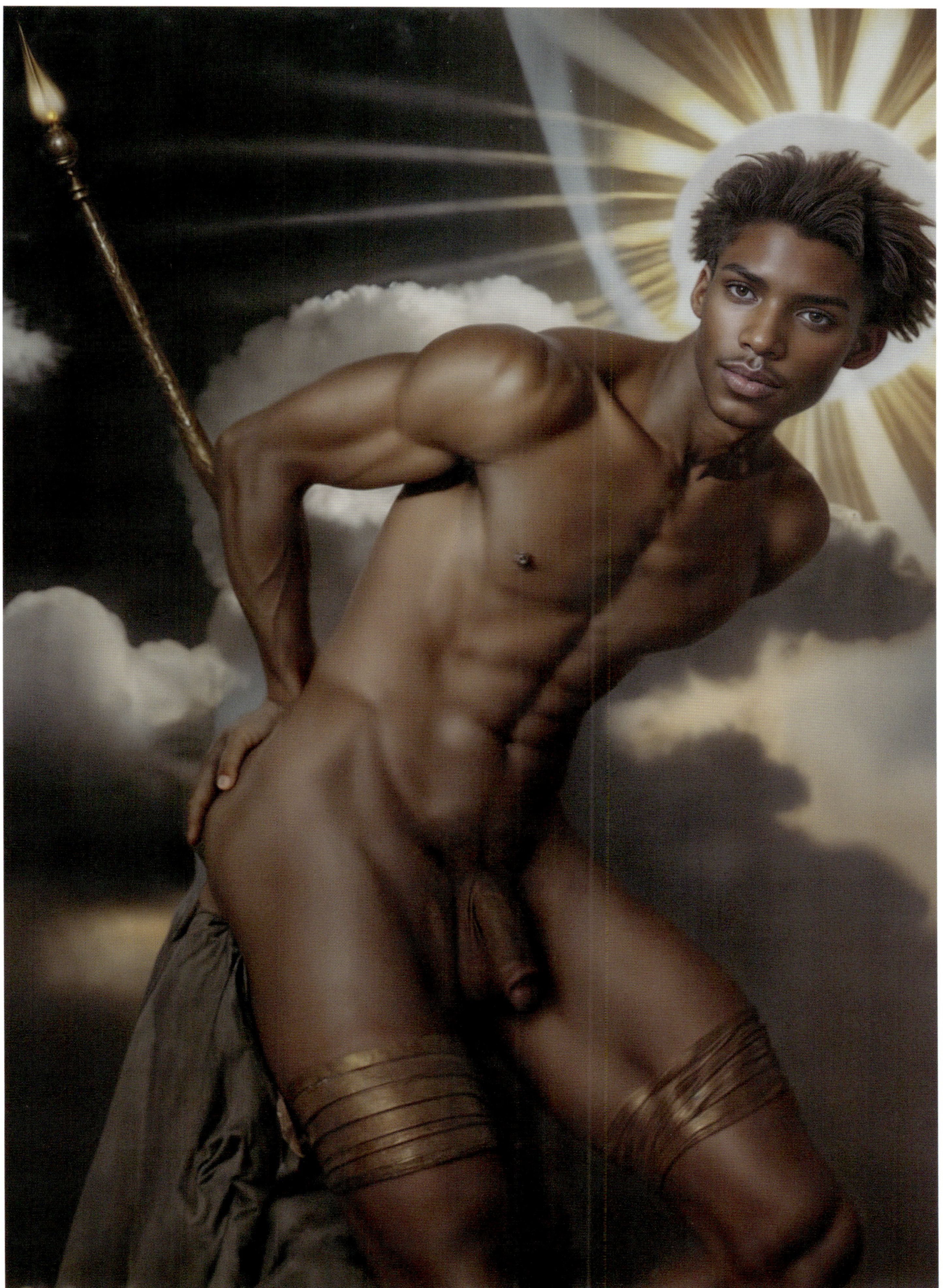

HIPPOLYTUS

DER HEILIGE FINN AUS PORTLAND

Finn Smith wurde 1842 in der damals frisch gegründeten Stadt Portland geboren und verstarb dort 1921 nach einem bunten Seemannsleben, in dem er mehrfach um die Welt reiste. Sein Geburtshaus (eher eine schnell zusammengezimmerte Holzhütte) stand ziemlich genau zwischen den beiden Siedlungsteilen *The Clearing (Die Lichtung)* und *Stumptown (Baumstumpfstadt)*. Letzterer hieß so, weil Bäume einfach nur gefällt und die Stümpfe stehen gelassen wurden. Nach Auskunft seiner Lehrerin, Anna Trump *(selbstverständlich nicht verwandt!)*, war Finn zwar charmant, klug und aufgeweckt, aber ein Rumtreiber, der sich vor allem bei Matrosen und in den Hafenkneipen des umfangreichen Nachtlebens der Stadt wohlfühlte. Wir wissen ja, was das bedeutet. So wurde Finn, kaum dass er 18 Jahre alt war, auch schon schanghait, also entführt, und in die Seefahrt gepresst. Die Anwerber nutzten dabei erstens seinen stark alkoholisierten, also willigen Zustand aus, und zweitens ein Tunnelsystem, das von den Kneipen direkt zum Hafen führte und heute immer noch besichtigt werden kann. Finn landete auf einem Klipper und wurde zu einem sehr beliebten Mitglied der Mannschaft, die oft Wochen oder gar Monate auf See verbrachte. Seine Reisen führten ihn mehrfach ums Kap Horn, nach Australien, China, Westeros, Afrika und Indien — also um die ganze Welt. Finns großes Verdienst war die Erkenntnis, dass Sexualität und deren eifrige Ausübung zu einem gesunden Leben auf See dazugehörten. Genau wie die tägliche Dosis Zitronensaft gegen Skorbut führte Finn später als Kapitän Regeln ein, die den Beischlaf zum Wachwechsel (und wenn es langweilig wurde, manchmal auch während der Wache) organisierten und von den Marinen weltweit übernommen wurden. Dies führte zu großer Zufriedenheit der Mannschaften, sprich zu gesunden, glücklichen und ausgeglichenen Menschen. Papst Pius IX. war bei der Heiligsprechung von Finn aus unerfindlichen Gründen etwas zögerlich, wurde dann aber daran erinnert, dass es die katholische Kirche war, die über Jahrzehnte Zitronen für die Matrosen verboten hatte, weil zu saure Nahrung angeblich nicht einer ausgeglichenen Lebensform entsprach. Das Verbot wurde erst zurückgenommen, als die katholische Kirche auf den Westindischen Inseln große Limettenplantagen erwarb und Sorgen um den Absatz der Ernte hatte. Die Caipirinha war zu diesem Zeitpunkt zwar schon erfunden (siehe → DIE GLORREICHEN UND HEILIGEN SIEBEN ab Seite 158), aber noch nicht international verbreitet. Mit der Begründung, dass man sich ja nicht immer bei Dingen, von denen man schlicht keine Ahnung hat, einmischen muss, ließ Pius IX. seine Vorbehalte bezüglich der Heiligsprechung von Finn schließlich fallen.

Der heilige Finn ist immer noch ein beliebter Ansprechpartner für Matrosen in aller Welt. Seiner wird am 11. Mai gedacht.

SAINT FINN OF PORTLAND

Finn Smith was born in 1842 in the newly founded city of Portland and died there in 1921 after a colorful life as a sailor, during which he traveled around the world several times over. The house (or rather hastily assembled wooden hut) in which he was born stood pretty much exactly between two parts of the settlement called *The Clearing* and *Stumptown*. The latter got its name from the fact that the stumps were left standing after the trees had been felled. According to his teacher, Anna Trump *(no relation!)*, Finn was charming, clever and bright, but he was a night owl who felt most at home with sailors and in the harbor bars of the city's vibrant nightlife. We all know what that means. And so it came to pass that when Finn was barely eighteen years old, he was abducted and forced into service at sea. The recruiters took advantage of both his heavily intoxicated, i.e., docile, state, and of a tunnel system that ran from the bars straight down to the harbor and can still be visited today. Finn wound up on a clipper ship where he became a very popular member of the crew, often spending weeks or even months at sea. His travels took him around Cape Horn, Australia, China, Westeros, Africa and India — in short, around the entire world. Finn's greatest achievement was realizing that sexuality and its vigorous pursuit were part of a healthy life at sea. Later on, when Finn became a captain, he introduced a set of rules, just like the daily dose of lemon juice against scurvy, which provided for sexual intercourse at every change of watch (and sometimes even during the watch if it got boring) and were adopted by navies all over the world. This resulted in a high degree of job satisfaction amongst the crews, i.e., healthy, happy and balanced seamen. For some inexplicable reason, Pope Pius IX was somewhat reluctant to canonize Finn but was then reminded that it was the Catholic Church that had banned lemons for sailors for decades because an overly acidic diet was supposedly not in keeping with a healthy lifestyle. The ban was only lifted when the Catholic Church acquired large lime plantations in the West Indies and was unsure whether it would be able to sell its crops. Whilst the caipirinha had already been invented by this time (see → THE MAGNIFICENT AND SAINTLY SEVEN from page 158), it had not yet gained international popularity. Pius IX finally dropped his reservations with regard to the canonization of Finn on the grounds that one need not always interfere in things one simply doesn't understand.

Saint Finn is still a favorite among sailors all over the world. His feast day is on May 11.

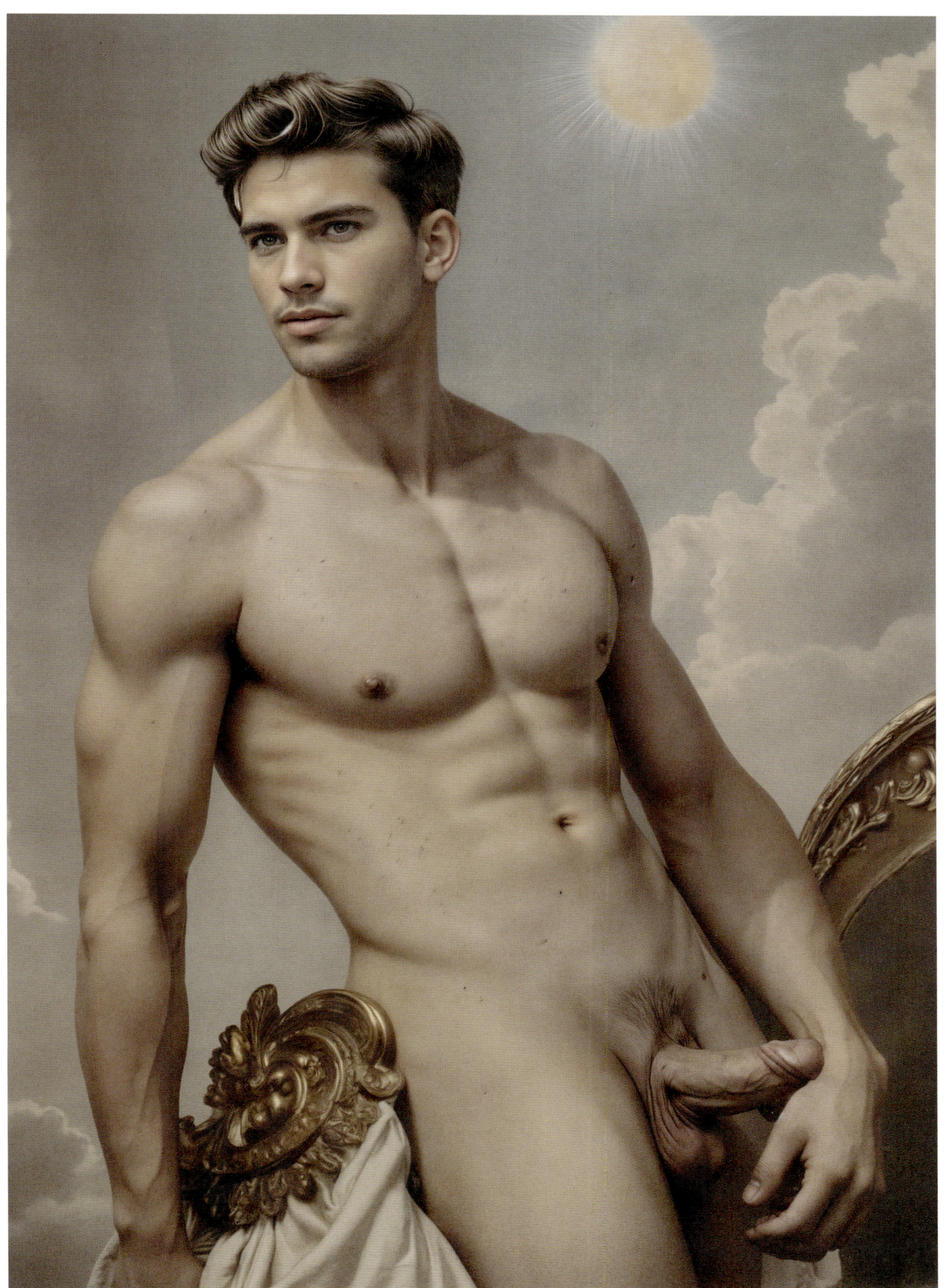

DER HEILIGE FINN AUS PORTLAND · SAINT FINN OF PORTLAND

GAEL UND LEON

Bekanntermaßen besiegte Gaius Julius Caesar 56 v. Chr. Aremorica (auch Armorica, von keltisch *are mori, vor dem Meer*). Der schöne Landstrich ganz im Nordwesten Frankreichs — heute als Bretagne bekannt — sollte bis 409 römisch bleiben. In den Wirren des Abzugs der römischen Armee trug sich dann die schöne Liebesgeschichte des Veneters Gael mit dem Römer Leon zu. Gael war Bagaude, kämpfte also gegen die Besatzer, und Leon war in Aletum (nahe dem heutigen St. Malo) zur Küstenbewachung eingeteilt. Wie sie sich kennengelernt haben, ist nicht genau bekannt, aber ihr Treffpunkt in einer Ruine an der *Plage des Bas Sablons* (wo heute noch gecruist wird) ist überliefert. Ihre Liebe zueinander war so stark, dass Leon desertierte und zu den Bagauden überlief. Hier also doch noch ein paar erklärende Worte zu den Bagauden: Der Begriff bezeichnet verschiedene Gruppen wie Deserteure, entlaufene Sklaven, verarmte Bauern, sozial Deklassierte, kurzum Verlierer des Systems. Gael und Leon wurden später zu den Anführern der streitbaren Truppe gewählt. Sie führten auch die Parole *Freiheit, Gleichheit und Brüderlichkeit* ein, die später in der Weltgeschichte noch mal auftauchen sollte. Der Ursprungsort ihrer Liebe, die Ruine an der *Plage des Bas Sablons*, wurde leider 1942 von deutschen Besatzern abgerissen und mit einem Bunker überbaut, der heute noch steht. Ob er eine Besichtigung wert ist, möge jeder für sich selbst entscheiden.

Gael und Leon sind bretonische Nationalheilige. Sie stehen für Aussöhnung zwischen Besatzern und Besetzten und natürlich für Veränderung, die eigentlich immer eine gute Idee ist. Gael und Leon werden am 2. Dezember gefeiert.

GAEL AND LEON

As we all know, Gaius Julius Caesar defeated Aremorica (or Armorica, from the Gaelic *are mori, before the sea*) in 56 BC. The attractive region in the far north-west of France — now known as Brittany — was to remain under Roman rule until 409. The tale of the love between the Venetian Gael and the Roman Leon unfolded in the chaos that ensued in the wake of the retreat of the Roman army. Gael was a member of the Bagaudae who fought against the occupying forces, while Leon was assigned to guard the coast in Aletum (near present-day St. Malo). It is not known exactly how they met, but we do know where they met: inside a ruin at the *Plage des Bas Sablons* (which is still a cruising area today). Their love for one another was so strong that Leon defected and went to join the Bagaudae. The Bagaudae encampassed a variety of groups including deserters, runaway slaves, impoverished peasants, social outcasts, in short, the losers of the system. Gael and Leon were later elected leaders of the fierce squad. They also introduced the slogan *Liberty, Equality and Fraternity*, which would crop up again later in history. The birthplace of their love, the ruin on the *Plage des Bas Sablons*, was unfortunately destroyed by the German occupying forces in 1942 and a bunker was built on top, which still stands today. Whether it is worth a visit is up to you to decide.

Gael and Leon are Breton national saints. They stand for reconciliation between the occupiers and the occupied and, of course, for change, which is always a good idea. The feast day of Gael and Leon is on December 2.

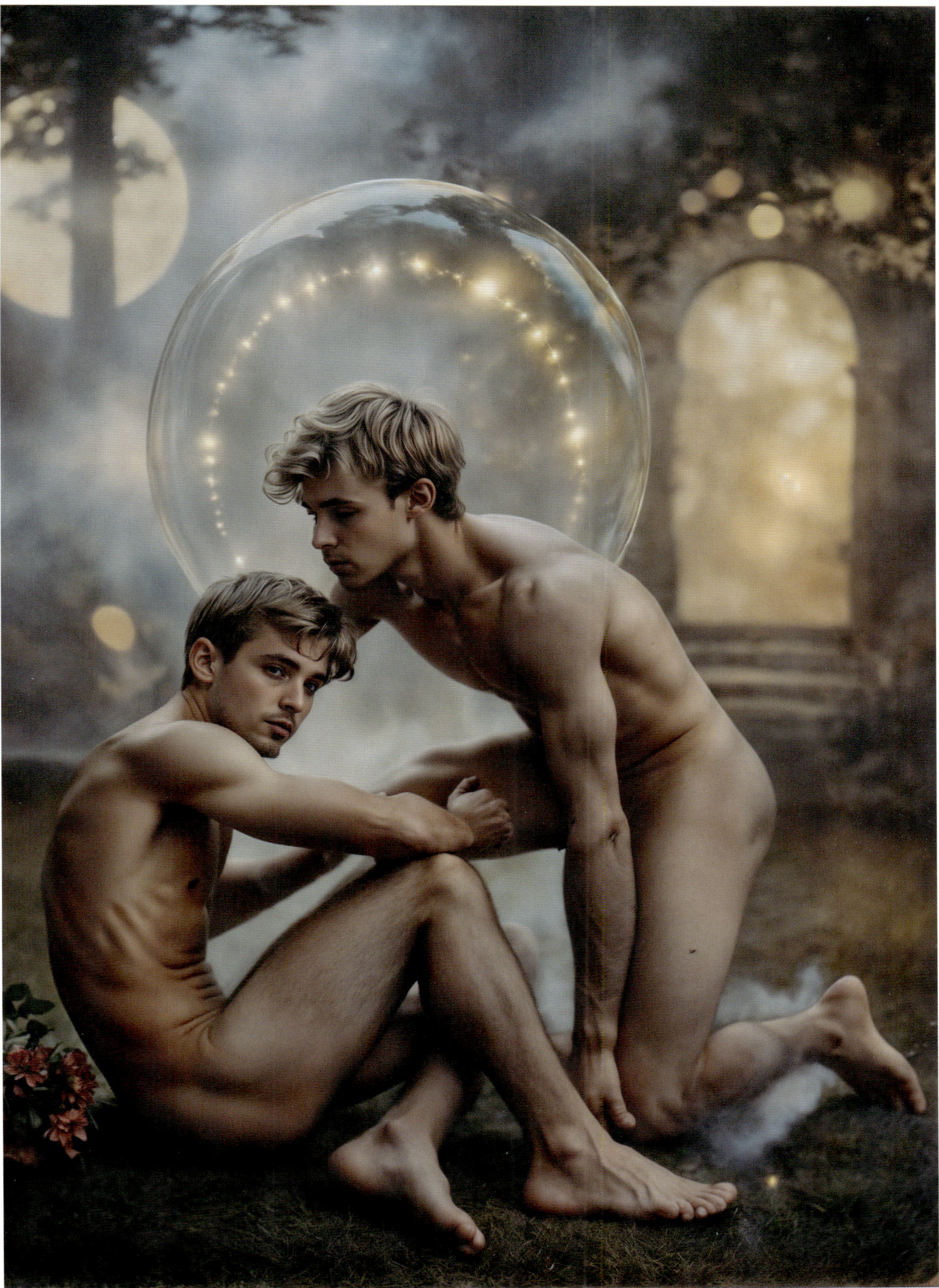

GAEL & LEON

DER HEILIGE GEISERICH

Der heilige Geiserich war Vandale und gilt als Mörder des → HEILIGEN HANNO (siehe Seite 70), weil er sich im öffentlichen Bad von Karthago zu ihm gesetzt und ihm unter Wasser einen geblasen haben soll (so berichten Augenzeugen). Geiserichs Liebeskünste sollen bei Hanno zu einem Herzinfarkt geführt haben, sodass dieser mit einem Lächeln auf den Lippen starb. Der arme Geiserich hingegen war durch den Vorfall schwer traumatisiert, gelobte Enthaltsamkeit und trug fortan einen vergoldeten Keuschheitsgürtel, der Unfälle dieser Art verhindern sollte. Zum Glück konnte er schon bald darauf von Freunden des heiligen Hanno, nämlich seinen Gefährten aus dem ehemaligen *Männer-lieben-Männer-Tempel*, erfolgreich therapiert werden. So legte er den Keuschheitsgürtel schon nach drei Wochen wieder ab, beziehungsweise trug ihn nur noch zum Spaß. Geiserich wurde ein überaus produktives Mitglied der karthagischen Gesellschaft. Im Lukasevangelium, Kapitel 24, Vers 32, wurde er mit folgenden Worten verewigt: „Brannte nicht unser Herz in uns, da er mit uns redete auf dem Wege und uns die Schrift öffnete?" Gemeint war damit natürlich der heilige Hanno und dessen unerschütterliche Gewissheit, dass immer wieder eine neue Liebe, eine neue Hoffnung entzündet wird. Ein bisschen kitschig, aber so war Geiserich nun mal. Wir verdanken ihm nicht nur die posthum veröffentlichte Biographie des heiligen Hanno, sondern auch die Bewahrung und Weitergabe von dessen Herz-Symbol als Mittel, um Zeugnis abzulegen.

Der heilige Geiserich führt die Dinge weiter und entwickelt dabei unglaubliche Kreativität. Sein Gedenktag ist der 26. Juni.

SAINT GAISERIC

St. Gaiseric was a Vandal and is reputed to have murdered → SAINT HANNO (see page 70) because he allegedly sat down next to him in the public baths of Carthage and gave him a blow-job under water (according to eyewitnesses). Gaiseric's amorous skills are said to have given Hanno a heart attack, and he died with a smile on his face. Poor Gaiseric, on the other hand, was severely traumatized by the incident, took an oath of celibacy and took to wearing a gilded chastity belt to prevent accidents of this kind. Luckily, he soon received effective therapy from friends of St. Hanno, namely his former associates from the *Temple of Men Who Love Men*. So after only three weeks, he took the chastity belt off again, and only put it on for fun and games. Geiseric went on to become an extremely productive member of Carthaginian society. He was immortalized with the following words in the Gospel of Luke, chapter 24, verse 32: "Did not our hearts burn within us while he talked to us on the road, while he opened to us the Scriptures?" This was of course a reference to St. Hanno and his unshakeable conviction that there is always a new love, a new hope to be kindled. A bit cheesy, but that's Gaiseric for you. We have him to thank not only for the posthumously published biography of St. Hanno, but also for preserving and passing on the saint's favorite symbol: a heart.

St. Gaiseric adopts and refines other people's ideas, developing incredible creativity in the process. His feast day is June 26.

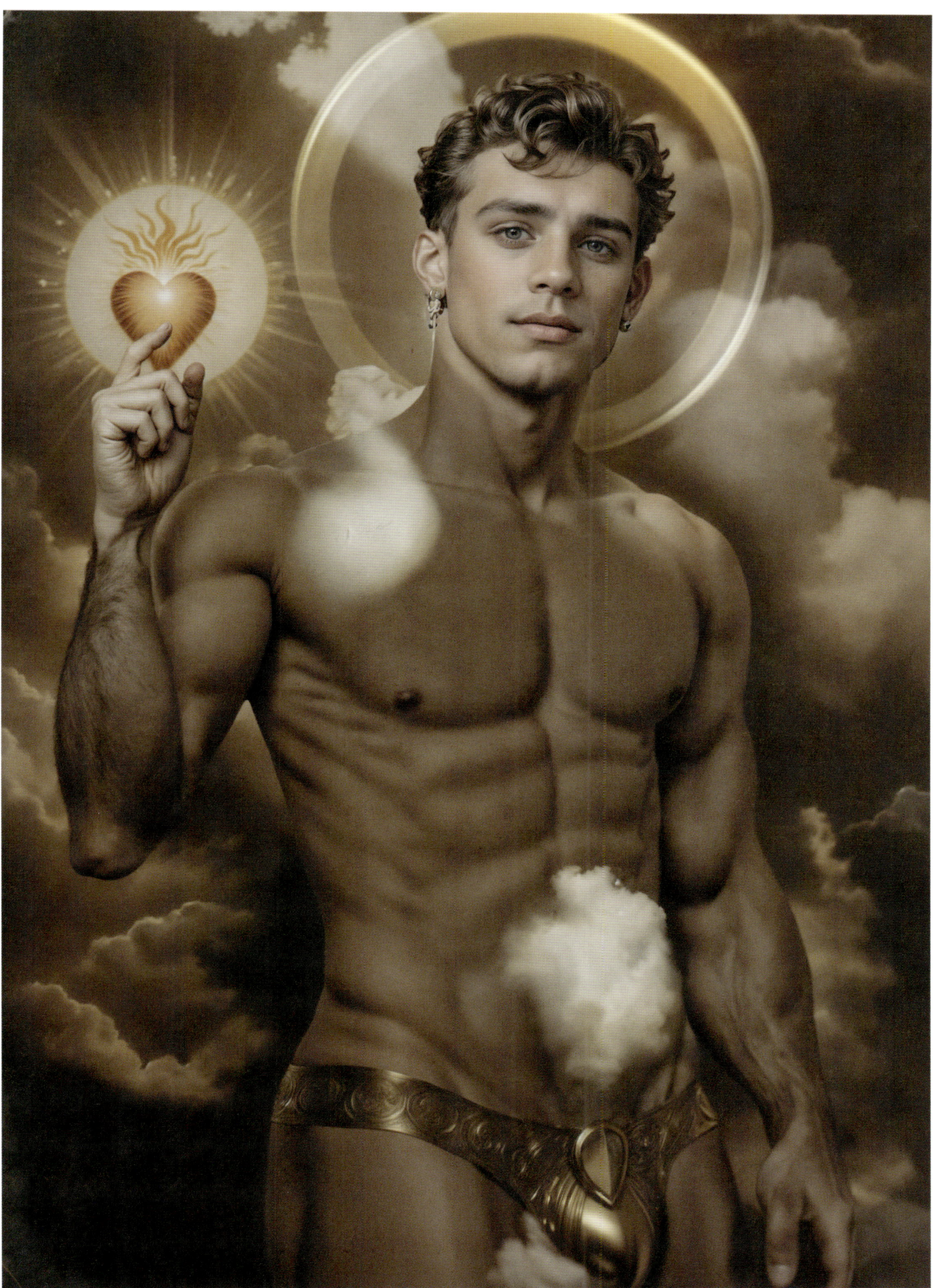

DER HEILIGE GEISERICH · SAINT GAISERIC

DER HEILIGE GIANBATTISTA

Gianbattista Cardano (* 1. Oktober 1500 in Pavia; † 3. Juni 1579 in Porto Venere) war der Bruder von Gerolamo Cardano und ein weiterer unehelicher Sohn des Juristen und Mathematikers Fazio Cardano. Sein Taufpate war Leonardo da Vinci, ein langjähriger Freund des Vaters. Von Gianbattista stammen brillante Erkenntnisse wie die einfache syntaktische Definition für Dualität, also dass zwei Aussagen genau dann dual sind, wenn jedes Vorkommnis des Junktors $\wedge$ (Konjunktion) durch $\vee$ (Disjunktion) und jedes Vorkommnis des Junktors $\vee$ durch $\wedge$ ersetzt wird. Dann geht es irgendwie weiter mit Negationsnormalformen (NNF) und sogar *atomaren Aussagen*, aber um das zu vertiefen, empfehlen wir den Besuch eines Volkshochschulkurses. An dieser Stelle zählt nur, dass Gianbattista nicht nur als Renaissance-Humanist Wichtiges geleistet hat, sondern auch mit so ziemlich jedem Mann in Pavia und Umgebung im Bett war. Es versteht sich von selbst, dass er immer dual, also von vorne und hinten, dargestellt wird. Da sein Geschlechtsteil dagegen ziemlich singulär war, aber auch um den Betrachter nicht zu erschrecken, hält Gianbattista stets schützend eine Hand davor. Er verunglückte 1579 bei einem Badeunfall in Porto Venere im Ligurischen Meer. Bemerkenswerterweise fast an der gleichen Stelle, die Lord Byron immer durchschwamm und an der Percy Bysshe Shelley am 8. Juli 1822 ebenfalls ertrank.

> Gianbattista ist der Heilige für alle Nerds, die man in der Regel zwar leider nicht versteht, mit denen man aber sehr guten Sex haben kann. Probieren Sie es aus. Zum Beispiel am 6. Februar, dem Feiertag des heiligen Gianbattista.

SAINT GIANBATTISTA

Gianbattista Cardano (*October 1, 1500 in Pavia; †June3, 1579 in Porto Venere) was the brother of Gerolamo Cardano and yet another illegitimate son of the jurist and mathematician Fazio Cardano. Leonardo da Vinci, a long-time friend of his father, was his godfather. Gianbattista was the source of such brilliant insights as the simple syntactic definition of duality, i.e., the idea that two statements are dual precisely when every occurrence of the operator $\wedge$ (conjunction) is replaced by $\vee$ (disjunction) and every occurrence of the operator $\vee$ is replaced by $\wedge$. Next, we have negation normal forms (NNF) and even *atomic sentences*, but for a more in-depth explanation, we recommend that you find out if your local community college is offering a course in higher mathematics. The only relevant point here is that Gianbattista was not only a highly accomplished Renaissance polymath but had also slept with pretty much every man in Pavia and the surrounding area. It goes without saying that he is always depicted in dual form, i.e., from the front and behind. As his penis, on the other hand, was rather singular, but also so as not to frighten the viewer, Gianbattista always holds a protective hand in front of it. He died in a bathing accident in Porto Venere in the Ligurian Sea in 1579. Strangely enough, this was almost the same place frequented by Lord Byron and the spot where Percy Bysshe Shelley drowned on July 8, 1822.

> Gianbattista is the patron saint of all nerds — you rarely understand what they're saying, but that doesn't stop you from having really good sex. Give it the old college try. On February 6, for example, the feast day of St. Gianbattista.

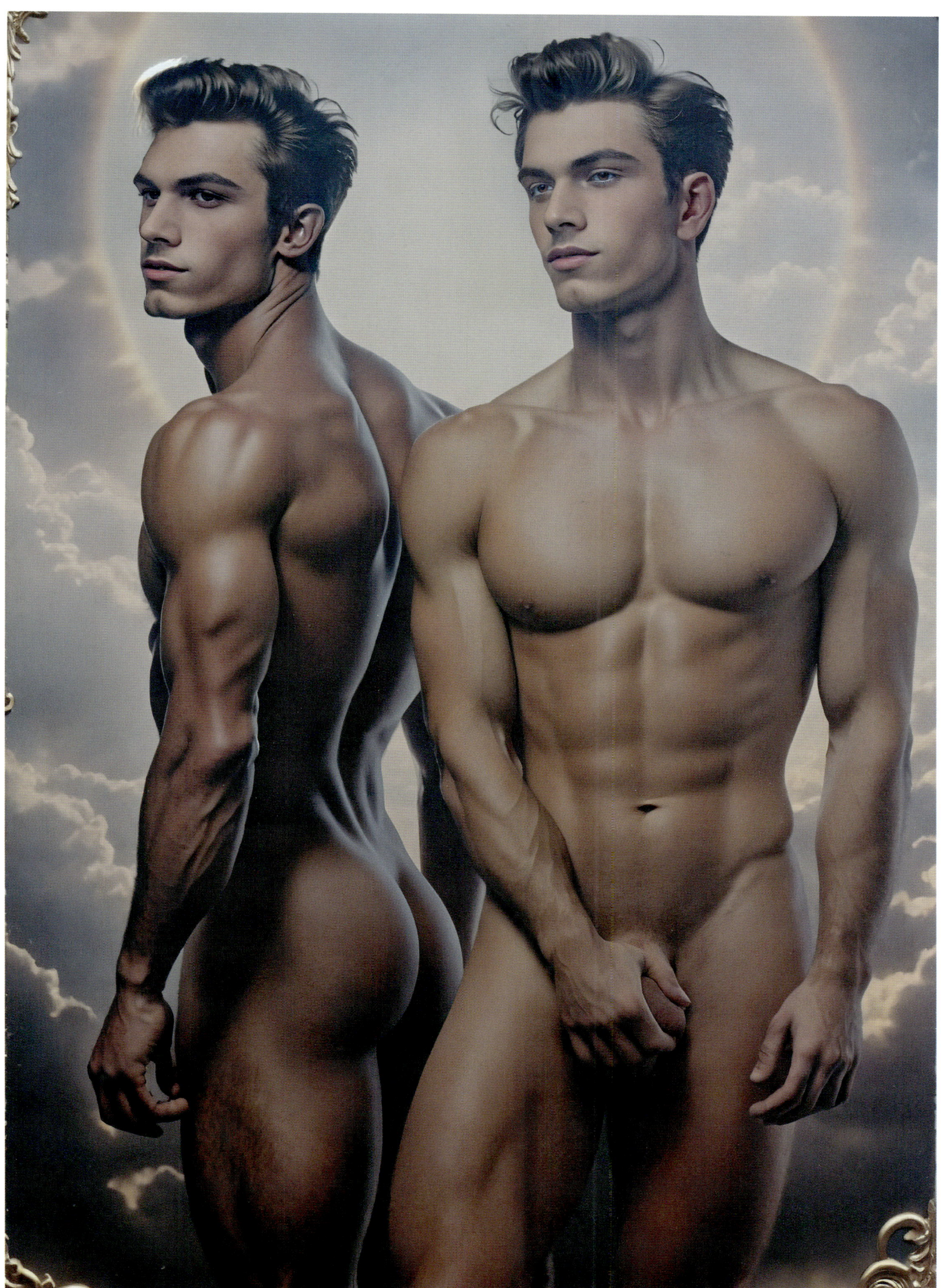

DER HEILIGE GIANBATTISTA · SAINT GIANBATTISTA

DAS HEILIGE GLÖCKCHEN

Glöckchen wurde 1822 als Tom Smith in dem kleinen Ort Climax in Kentucky geboren und verstarb 1849 ebenda. Wenn Sie die Abzweigung zwischen Bighill und Clover Bottom nehmen und bis zur Kürbisfarm in der Sexton Road fahren, sehen Sie sein Geburtshaus sofort. Schon als Kind kleidete Glöckchen sich gerne — zumindest für die ländliche Gegend in Kentucky — auffällig mit Rock und Flügeln und schminkte sich. Zunächst erfreuten sich nur seine Eltern — typische Hillbillies, beziehungsweise Rednecks — und die acht Geschwister daran, als Glöckchen älter wurde, zog er größere Kreise in der Appalachenregion, wobei er Männer und Frauen gleichermaßen bezauberte. Glöckchen brachte der armen Landbevölkerung, die nicht nur bei Bildung und medizinischer Versorgung abgehängt war, das stolze Motto: *Sei, wer du bist, und scher dich nicht drum, was andere darüber denken!* Auch den Begriff *White Trash* für Menschen, denen man Sittenlosigkeit und Unmoral unterstellte, konnte Glöckchen positiv besetzen. Glöckchen trank seinen Whiskey übrigens als Likör, aromatisiert mit Pfirsich, Orange, Vanille, Zimt und dunkler Schokolade. Ein irischer Barkeeper sollte das Rezept später klauen und als *Southern Comfort* vermarkten. Die Bewohner Kentuckys wollten Glöckchen am liebsten zu ihrem Gouverneur wählen, und das wäre für die Politik sicher auch eine große Bereicherung gewesen. Doch leider, leider stieß Glöckchen bei einer seiner häufigen nächtlichen Eskapaden auf einen *großen hungrigen Bären* und wurde von ihm verspeist. In den Wäldern der Appalachen kann man deshalb nachts immer noch häufig kleine Glöckchen klingeln hören.

Glöckchen ist der Held aller Rednecks und kann angerufen werden, wenn man sich auf der Flucht vor einem Bären befindet. Weiterhin steht der Heilige für Lebensfreude, Individualismus und alkoholische Mixgetränke. Glöckchens großer Tag ist der 4. Juli.

SAINT TINKER BELL

Tinker Bell was born as Tom Smith in the small town of Climax in Kentucky in 1822 and died there in 1849. If you turn off at the junction between Bighill and Clover Bottom and drive all the way down to the pumpkin farm on Sexton Road, you will be able to see the house where he was born. Even as a child, Tinker Bell liked to dress flamboyantly — at least for rural Kentucky — wearing a skirt, wings and make-up. In the beginning, only his parents — typical hillbillies or rednecks — and his eight siblings benefitted from these efforts, but as Tink grew older, he began to travel more widely throughout the Appalachian region, charming men and women alike. Tinker Bell brought the impoverished rural population, who had been left behind in terms of education and medical care, the proud motto: *Be who you are and don't worry about what other people think!* Tink also helped reclaim the term *white trash*, which was used to describe people who were suspected of lacking decency and moral fiber. Tinker Bell drank his whiskey as a liqueur, flavored with peach, orange, vanilla, cinnamon and dark chocolate. An Irish bartender later stole the recipe and marketed it as *Southern Comfort*. The people of Kentucky would have liked to elect Tinker Bell as governor, and he would certainly have been a great asset to politics. Alas, during one of his frequent nightly escapades, Tink chanced upon a *large, hungry bear* and was eaten up. If you visit the Appalachian woods at night, you can still hear little bells ringing.

Tinker Bell is the hero of all rednecks and can be called upon for aid when you're being pursued by a bear. He is also the patron saint of joie de vivre, individualism and cocktails. Tinker Bell's big day is July 4th.

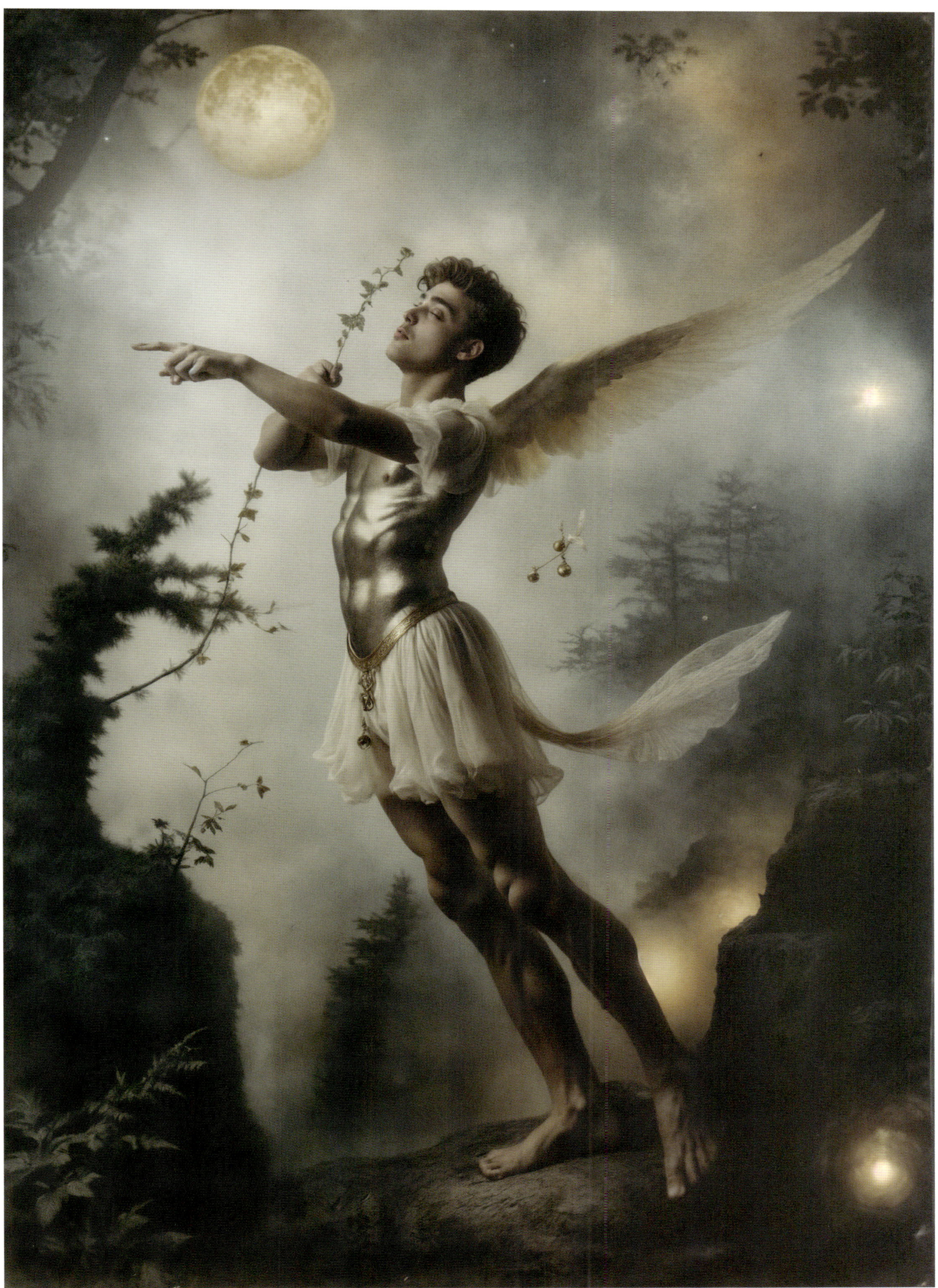

DAS HEILIGE GLÖCKCHEN · SAINT TINKER BELL

GOTTFRIED UND WALDEMAR

Als Kenner der Wagner-Oper *Lohengrin* haben Sie sich sicherlich immer sehr für den bei einem Waldspaziergang verschwundenen Gottfried interessiert, den seine Schwester Elsa angeblich ermordet haben soll. In Wahrheit ist Gottfried einfach weggelaufen, um mit seinem Freund Waldemar ein paar Abenteuer zu erleben. Daheim in Brabant nimmt das Unglück seinen Lauf. Ortrud intrigiert, Elsa wird angeklagt, ein Ritter erscheint, es wird gekämpft und gesiegt, und dann heiratet Elsa den Ritter. Sie darf alles, nur ihn nicht nach seinem Namen befragen. Hierzu ein aufschlussreicher Blick ins Libretto: *Nie sollst du mich befragen, noch Wissens Sorge tragen, woher ich kam der Fahrt, noch wie mein Nam' und Art!* Natürlich tut sie es trotzdem, der Ritter (Lohengrin) geht von der Bühne und schickt Gottfried als Schwan nach Hause. Da Lohengrin eindeutig bisexuell war, hegte er für die Beziehung von Gottfried und Waldemar größte Sympathien. Solange es irgend ging, deckte er die beiden, schenkte ihnen sogar den Gral, damit sie im dunklen Wald Licht hatten. Ob Lohengrin als angeheirateter Onkel mit Gottfried und Waldemar auch Sex hatte, wissen wir nicht. Fest steht nur, dass Elsas dauerndes Genörgel alle in den Wahnsinn trieb und Lohengrin sich völlig genervt — und ein klein wenig in Gottfried verliebt — zur Flucht entschloss. Die Brabanter Gesellschaft war einfach nicht modern genug, um hier eine Lösung anzubieten. Wagner auch nicht. Alles klar also? Schauen wir noch kurz auf den Schluss der Oper: Der Kahn, in dem Lohengrin *unendlich traurig* (Regieanweisung) scheidet, entfernt sich. Ortrud sinkt bei Gottfrieds Anblick mit einem Schrei zu Boden. Elsa sinkt entseelt ebenfalls zu Boden (in Gottfrieds Armen) und das Volk (Chor) tut sein Entsetzen mit *Weh! Ach!* kund, bleibt aber erstmal stehen. Wie Gottfried und Waldemar sich bei alledem fühlen, interessiert niemanden. Typisch heteronormative Kacke halt.

Gottfried und Waldemar haben am 14. Juli ihren großen Auftritt, feiern also an diesem Datum ihren Gedenktag.

GOTTFRIED AND WALDEMAR

Connoisseurs of Wagner's opera *Lohengrin* will no doubt have always been very interested in Gottfried, who disappeared while taking a walk in the woods and was allegedly murdered by his sister Elsa. In actual fact, Gottfried simply ran away on an adventure with his friend Waldemar. According to the opera, back in Brabant, the tragedy takes its course. Ortrud schemes, Elsa stands accused, a knight appears, there's a fight, he wins, and then Elsa marries the knight. She can do anything but ask him his name. Let's take a look at the libretto: *You must never ask me or be at pains to discover from whence I journeyed here, nor what is my name and lineage!* Of course she does it anyway, the knight (Lohengrin) leaves the stage and sends Gottfried home as a swan. As Lohengrin was clearly bisexual, he had enormous sympathy for the relationship between Gottfried and Waldemar. He kept them safe for as long as possible, even giving them the Grail to light their way through the dark forest. Whether Lohengrin, as an uncle by marriage, had sex with Gottfried and Waldemar, remains unknown. One thing is certain: Elsa's constant nagging drove everyone insane and Lohengrin, thoroughly exasperated — and a little bit in love with Gottfried — decided to make his escape. Brabant society was simply not modern enough to offer a solution. Neither was Wagner. Any questions? Let's take a quick look at the opera's finale: the boat with the *infinitely sad* (according to the stage directions) Lohengrin on board leaves the shore. At the sight of Gottfried, Ortrud falls to the ground with a cry. Elsa also sinks lifeless to the ground (in Godfrey's arms), and the chorus expresses its horror with cries of *Woe! Alas!* and then continues to stand around pointlessly. No one cares about how Gottfried and Waldemar feel about any of this. Just your standard heteronormative crap.

Gottfried and Waldemar's grand finale is on July 14, so that's when they celebrate their feast day.

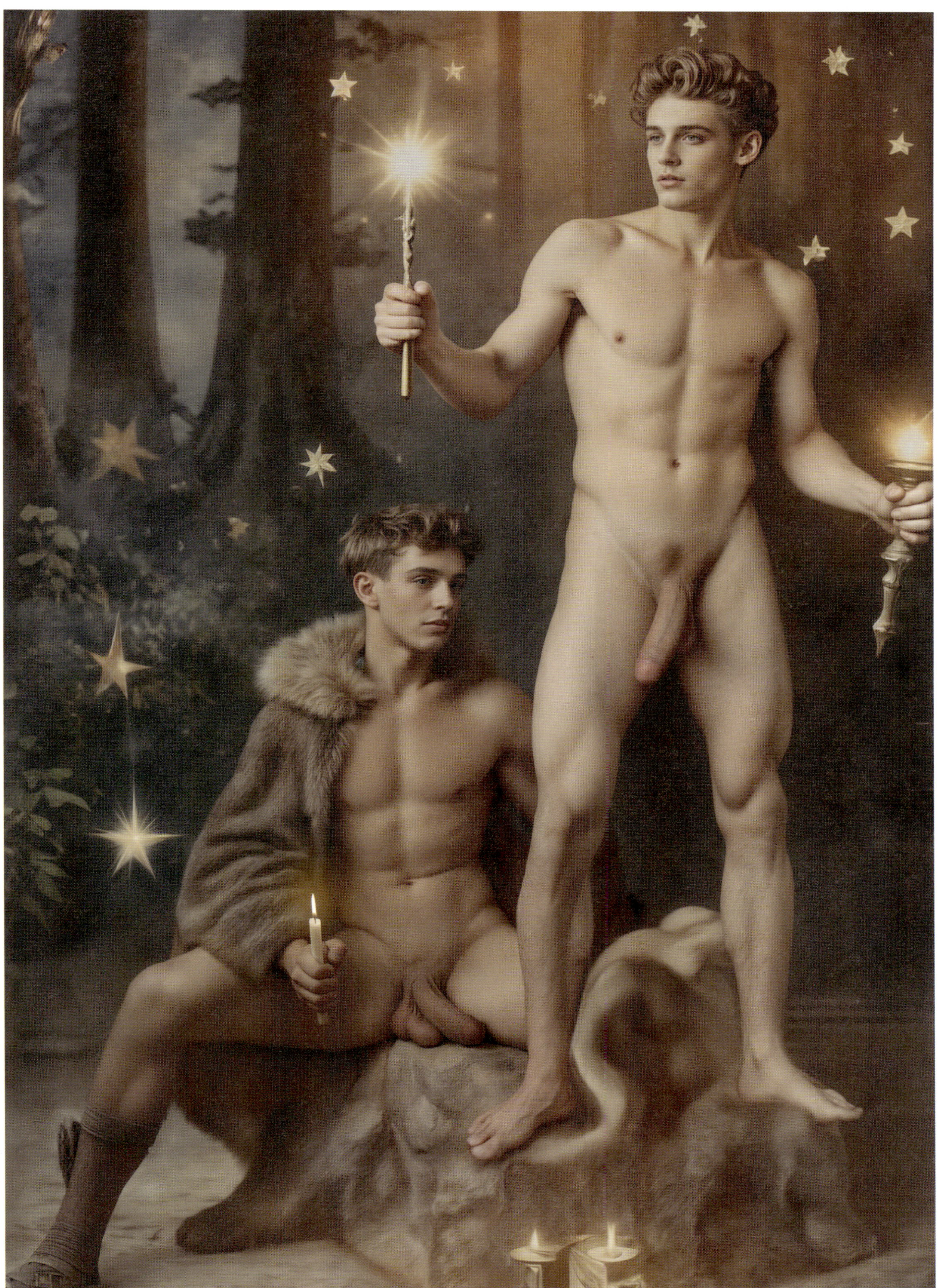

GOTTFRIED & WALDEMAR

HÄNSEL

Wie Geschichte von Hänsel wurde durch die Gebrüder Grimm im Geschmack der damaligen Zeit erzählt, und es lohnt sich ein genauerer Blick: Die Mutter von Hänsel entdeckte seine Homosexualität und schmiss ihn aus dem Haus. Leider kommt so etwas vor. Der Vater, ein sehr vermögender Holzgroßhändler, hatte mehr Verständnis für seinen Sohn, konnte sich aber nicht durchsetzen. Wie dann von Petula Clark sehr schön besungen, *When you're alone, and life is making you lonely / You can always go / Downtown*, ging auch Hänsel in die große Stadt und zog nach ein paar Tagen auf der Straße bei einem Freier ein. Dem ging es im Prinzip nur um Hänsels Penis, dessen Härte, Größe und Standfestigkeit. Eine echte *Size-Queen*, wie man heute sagen würde. Am liebsten hätte er den armen Hänsel eingesperrt und ganz allein für sich gehabt. Zum Glück schritt dann die schwule Selbsthilfe ein und verschaffte Hänsel ein Zimmer in einem schwulen Jugendwohnprojekt, das ganz idyllisch (siehe unsere Darstellung) auf dem Lande an einem kleinen Fluss gelegen war. Hier blieb Hänsel ein paar Jahre und machte eine Ausbildung. Er ging gerne im Wald spazieren und erlebte unter leuchtendem Sternenhimmel viele Abenteuer. Warum jetzt Hänsel und Gretel als Geschichte um versuchten Kindsmord, Kannibalismus und eine böse Mutter erzählt werden musste, ist uns schleierhaft, denn eigentlich ist die Geschichte schon traurig genug. Psychologisierende Interpretationen der Grimm'schen Version gehen sogar davon aus, dass die Hexe und die Mutter ein und dieselbe Person sein könnten und wir es möglicherweise sogar mit einem sexuellen Übergriff der Mutter auf den Sohn zu tun haben. Das Eingesperrtsein von Hänsel und *sein Stöckchen durchs Gitter schieben* lässt uns schaudern und in tiefe, tiefe Abgründe blicken.

Hänsels Geburtstag ist der 16. Oktober und mahnt uns, wachsam zu bleiben, um Not zu erkennen und Hilfe zu leisten.

HANSEL

The story of Hansel was told by the Brothers Grimm to suit contemporary tastes, and it is worth taking a closer look: Hansel's mother found out that he was gay and threw him out of the house. This kind of thing does happen, unfortunately. His father, a wealthy timber wholesaler, was more understanding but could never stand up for himself or his son. True to the song immortalized by Petula Clark *When you're alone, and life is making you lonely / you can always go / downtown*, Hansel headed for the big city and, after a couple of days of roaming the streets, moved in with a john, who was only interested in Hansel's penis: its firmness, size and stamina. Today we would call him a real *size queen*. Ideally, he would have liked to lock poor Hansel in a cage and keep him all to himself. Fortunately, a gay self-help organization stepped in and found Hansel a room in a gay youth housing project in an idyllic location (see our illustration) in the countryside by a small river. Hansel lived here for a couple of years and completed a vocational training course. He went on lots of walks in the forest and enjoyed plenty of adventures under a bright starry sky. Why the story of Hansel and Gretel had to be turned into a tale of attempted infanticide, cannibalism and an evil mother is beyond us — after all, the real story is sad enough as it is. Some psychoanalytic interpretations of Grimm's version even suggest that the witch and the mother are one and the same person and that the story might even be about a mother sexually assaulting her son. Then you have Hansel locked up in a cage and *pushing his twig through the bars*, and the story becomes just too chilling for words.

Hansel's birthday is October 16 and is a reminder to be on the lookout for people who need our help.

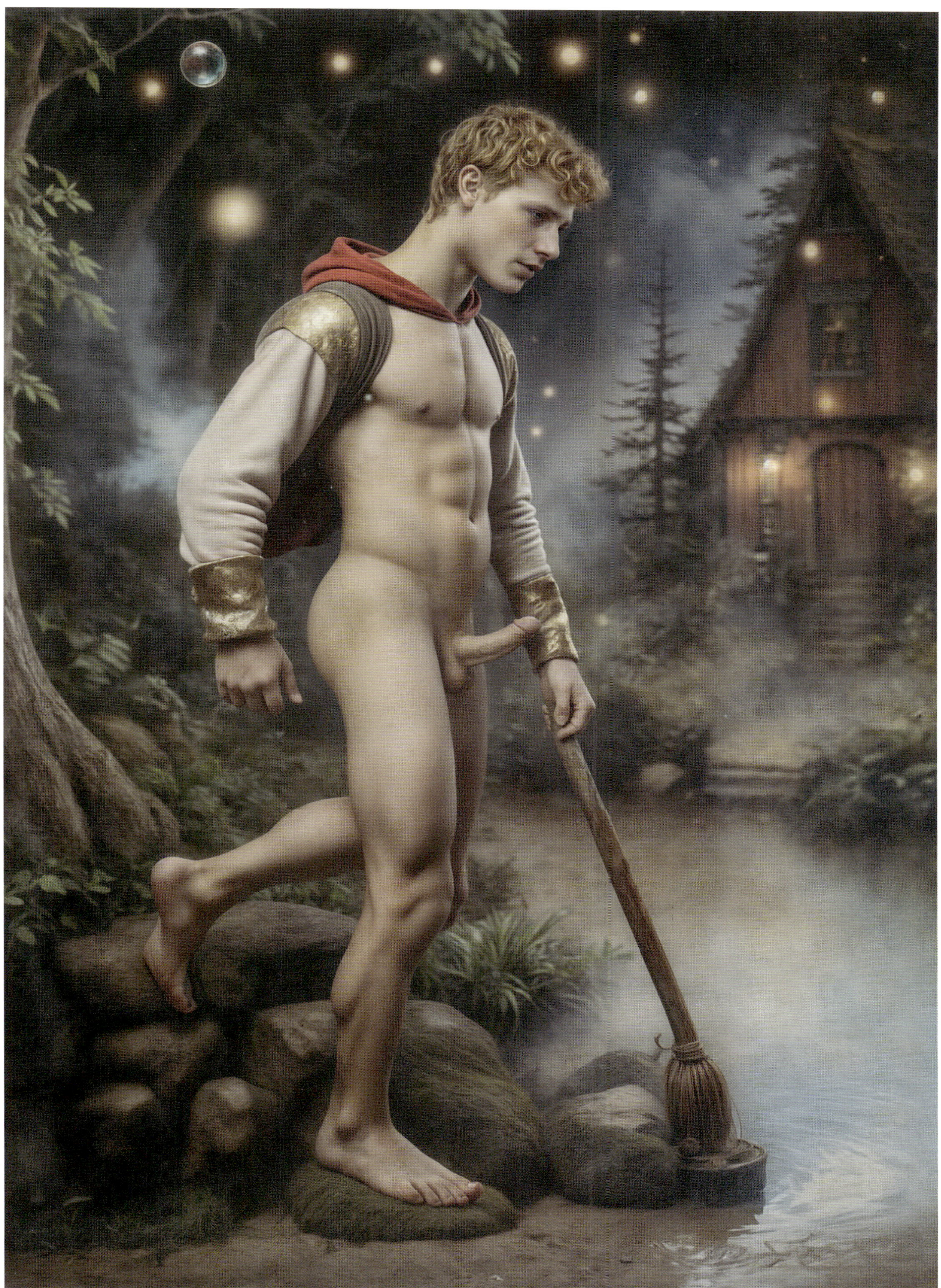

HÄNSEL · HANSEL

DER HEILIGE HANNO AUS KARTHAGO

Hanno wurde 372 in Karthago geboren, wo er auch 439 durch einen Vandalen starb. Der römische Kaiser Theodosius I. hatte 380 das Christentum zur Staatsreligion erklärt und 391 alle anderen Götterkulte verbieten lassen. Dies führte auch in Karthago zu Intoleranz und Gewalt, konkret zu Bücherverbrennungen, Enteignungen und Zerstörungen von Tempeln und sakralen Objekten. Auch der *Männer-lieben-Männer-Tempel* wurde verwüstet und sein Symbol (ein langer, spitzer Gegenstand, der in eine weiche Form eindringt; siehe Abbildung) sollte verboten werden. Hanno, selbst häufiger Besucher des *Männer-lieben-Männer-Tempels*, gelang es, immerhin das Symbol durch geschickte Umdeutung für die kommenden Jahrtausende zu bewahren. Seine von Johannes, Kapitel 13, Vers 34, abgeleitete Behauptung „Aus seiner (Jesus) geöffneten Seite strömen Blut und Wasser, aus seinem durchbohrten Herzen entspringen die Sakramente der Kirche. Das Herz des Erlösers steht offen für alle, damit sie freudig schöpfen aus den Quellen des Heiles" wurde zum festen Bestandteil der christlichen Liturgie. Damit war die Verehrung des Heiligsten Herzens Jesu geboren. Aber wir wissen, dass es in Wahrheit um etwas ganz anderes ging. Jesus sprach: „Ich bin nicht gekommen, Frieden zu bringen, sondern das Schwert" (Matthäus Kapitel 10, Vers 34) und Tätowierer, die leider die Oberarme und Schenkel heterosexueller Männer verunstalten, behaupten in völliger Unkenntnis der Herkunft des Symbols noch ganz andere Dinge. Hanno hatte in Karthago ein gutes Leben, gerade weil er durch das von ihm prominent getragene Symbol von anderen eingeweihten Männern erkannt wurde. Dennoch drohte Gefahr, denn aus Gebieten, die heute in Polen liegen, zogen ab 400 die Vandalen über Frankreich und Spanien nach Nordafrika, wo sie 439 Karthago erreichten. Sie haben Karthago übrigens nicht zerstört, sondern dort einfach nur ein neues Königreich gegründet. Hanno hatte allerdings das Pech, einem großgewachsenen Jungvandalen in einem öffentlichen Bad — plätschernd im warmen Wasser — zuzulächeln. Dieser erwiderte seine Annäherung so stürmisch, dass es für Hannos Herz zu viel war und er durch einen Herzinfarkt starb. Der Name des Jungvandalen war Geiserich und wir kennen ihn als den → HEILIGEN GEISERICH (siehe Seite 60).

In welchem Lebensabschnitt der heilige Hanno nun angerufen werden sollte, ist unklar, aber das ist ja bei vielen religiösen Dingen so. Gefeiert wird der heilige Hanno jedenfalls am 3. September.

SAINT HANNO OF CARTHAGE

Hanno was born in Carthage in 372, where he also died at the hands of a Vandal in 439. In 380, the Roman emperor Theodosius I decreed that Christianity was to be the state religion and banned all other religions in 391. This led to intolerance and violence in Carthage as well, specifically to book burnings, seizures of property and the destruction of temples and objects of worship. *The Temple of Men Who Love Men* was also destroyed and its symbol (a long, pointed object penetrating a soft shape; see illustration) was to be banned. Hanno, a frequent visitor to the *Temple of Men Who Love Men*, managed to preserve the symbol for the coming millennia by cleverly reinterpreting it. His declaration, derived from John, chapter 13, verse 34, "From His (Jesus') wounded side flowed blood and water, the fountain of sacramental life in the Church. To His open heart the Saviour invites all to draw water in joy from the springs of salvation" became an integral part of the Christian liturgy. This is how the veneration of the Most Sacred Heart of Jesus began. But we know that it was really about something entirely different. Jesus said: "I did not come to bring peace, but a sword." (Matthew chapter 10, verse 34) and tattoo artists, who sadly disfigure the upper arms and thighs of so many heterosexual men and are completely unaware of the symbol's origin, claim something else altogether. Hanno had a great life in Carthage precisely because the symbol he displayed prominently allowed him to be recognized by other like-minded men. Danger nevertheless loomed, as in 400 the Vandals began to migrate from present-day Poland to North Africa via France and Spain, reaching Carthage in 439. They did not destroy Carthage, by the way, but rather founded a new kingdom there. Hanno, however, had the misfortune of smiling at a tall young Vandal splashing alluringly in the warm water of a public bath. Said young Vandal returned his advances so enthusiastically that it was too much for Hanno's heart and he died of a heart attack. The young man's name was Gaiseric and we know him as → SAINT GAISERIC (see page 60).

It is unclear at what stage of life St. Hanno is meant to be invoked, but that is often the case in religious matters. In any case, the feast of St. Hanno is celebrated on September 3.

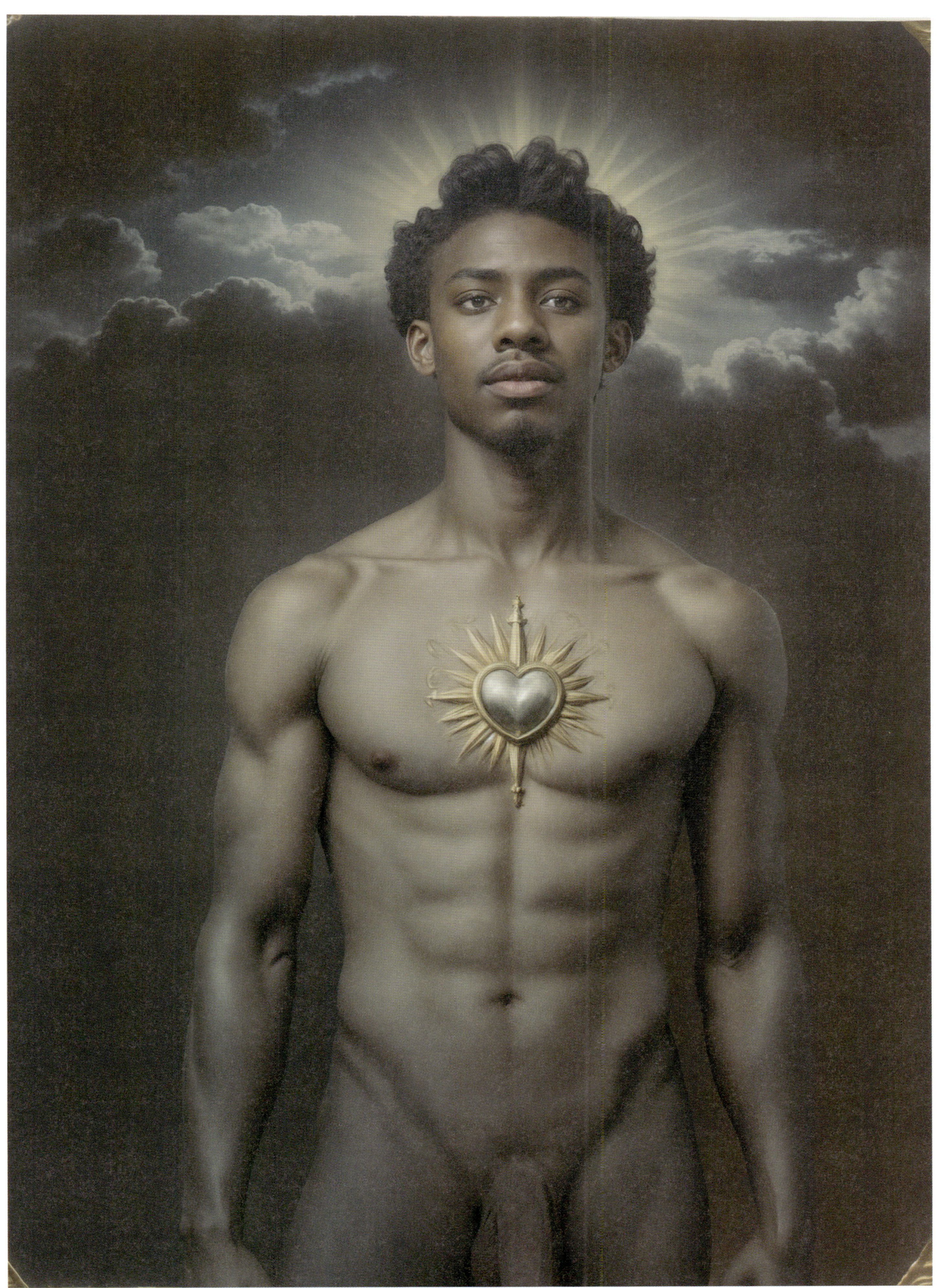

DER HEILIGE HANNO AUS KARTHAGO · SAINT HANNO OF CARTHAGE

DER HEILIGE HARALD AUS FUCKING

Harald verstarb 1122 in Rom und wurde 1070 im damals noch bayerischen Fucking geboren. Seit 1779 gehört das bei Braunau gelegene Dorf zu Österreich, 2020 wurde es in Fugging umbenannt. Schon früh waren die besonderen Talente des Bauernsohns Harald erkennbar. Er begeisterte durch einen komplexen Charakter, denn er war gleichzeitig *aktiv und passiv, hart und weich, gebend und nehmend, ruhig und bewegt, fordernd und beschwichtigend* ... ab hier ergänzen Sie bitte selber weiter. In der chinesischen Philosophie wurde das *Harald-Prinzip* im 11. Jahrhundert aufgegriffen, *Yin und Yang* (Chinesisch 陰陽 / 阴阳) genannt und auch auf heterosexuelle Menschen übertragen, aber alles in allem war der Methode wenig Erfolg beschieden: Kriege wurden geführt, Länder erobert, Reiche gegründet, Kulturen zerstört, aber Frieden fanden die geschätzten 250 bis 350 Millionen Menschen, die damals die Welt bevölkerten, selten. Eine kleine Gruppe sogenannter *Haraldisten* lernte dennoch mit dem eigenen Körper und den eigenen Aggressionen konstruktiv umzugehen, wobei der heilige Harald sie zu Lebzeiten *aktiv* und *passiv* unterstützte. Bekanntere und nicht gecancelte Heilige wie Dominikus, Franziskus von Assisi oder Ignatius von Loyola werden in der Regel mit einer Weltkugel dargestellt, auf der dann häufig noch Maria steht. Es gibt auch Freimaurerlogen mit drei Weltkugeln. Der heilige Harald jedoch wird grundsätzlich mit zwei Weltkugeln abgebildet.

Die zwei Kugeln des heiligen Haralds werden am 19. Februar gefeiert — übrigens zeitgleich mit → CONNOR UND CARSON (Seite 26).

SAINT HARALD OF FUCKING

Harald died in Rome in 1122 and was born in Fucking, which was still part of Bavaria at the time, in 1070. Located near Braunau, this village has been part of Austria since 1779 and was renamed Fugging in 2020. The unique talents of Harald, the son of a peasant, were evident from an early age. Everyone was thrilled by the complexity of his character, for he was simultaneously *active and passive, hard and soft, giving and taking, calm and animated, demanding and appeasing*... add your own suggestions here. The *Harald principle* was adopted by Chinese philosophers in the 11th century, called *Yin and Yang* (Chinese 陰陽 / 阴阳) and also applied to heterosexuals, but on the whole the method was not very successful: wars were waged, countries conquered, empires founded, cultures destroyed, but the estimated 250 to 350 million people who populated the world at the time rarely found peace. A small group of so-called *Haraldists* nevertheless learned more constructive ways of relating to their own bodies and feelings of aggression, with the *active* and *passive* support of St. Harald. Better-known and uncancelled saints such as Dominic, Francis of Assisi or Ignatius of Loyola are usually depicted with a globe with Mary on top. Some Freemason lodges also have three globes. St. Harald, however, is always depicted with two.

The twin globes of St. Harald are celebrated on February 19 — incidentally on the same day as → CONNOR AND CARSON (page 26).

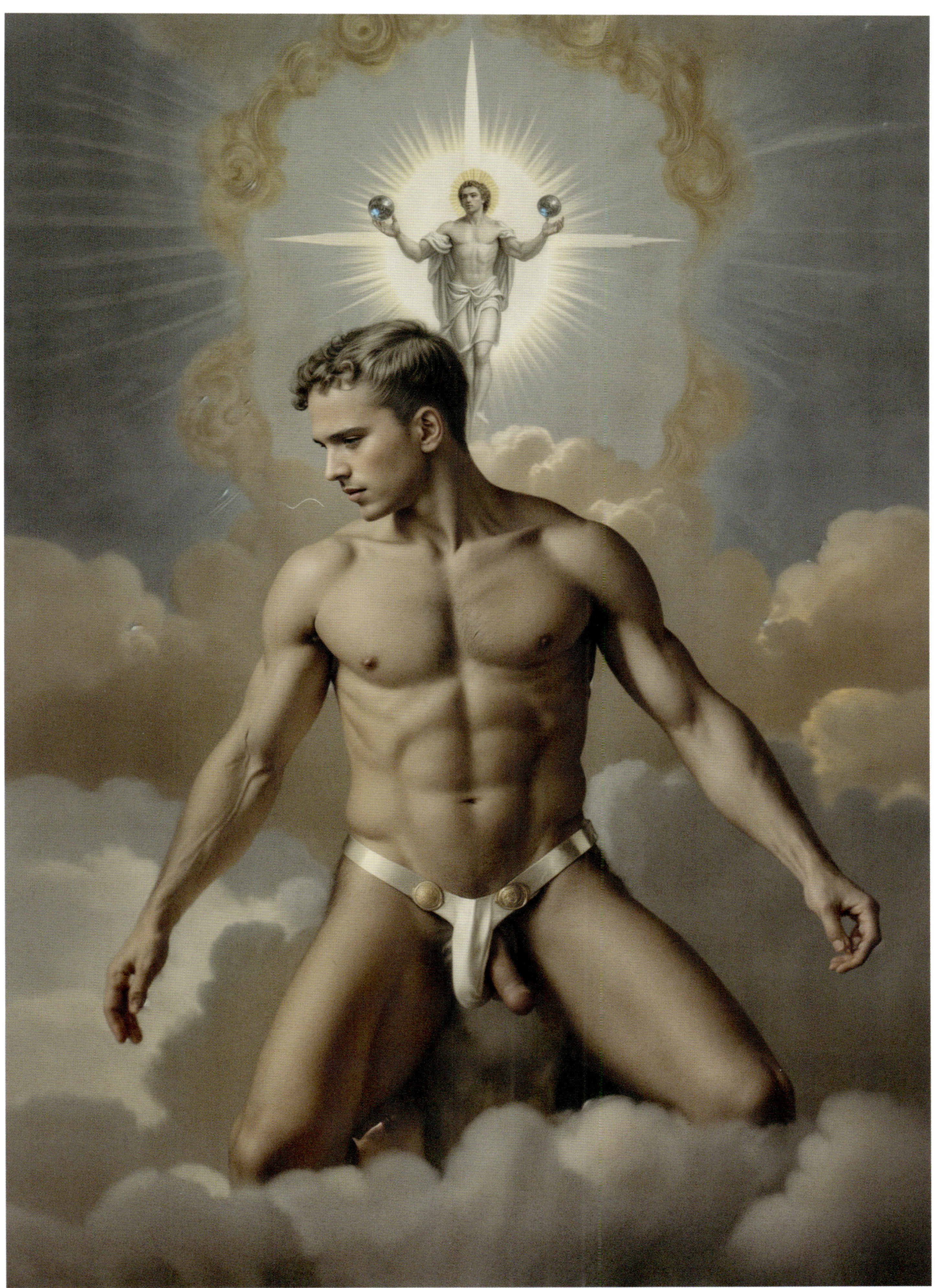

DER HEILIGE HARALD AUS FUCKING · SAINT HARALD OF FUCKING

DER HEILIGE HARRY UND DER HEILIGE SAM AUS NEW ORLEANS

Harry (*1832; †1896) stammte aus der Familie des Stadtgründers von New Orleans. Der trug den Nachnamen *Le Moyne de Bienville*, aber Harry nannte sich stolz *Legrand*, denn er war das Ergebnis einer Liebesbeziehung seines Vaters mit einem französischen Au-pair-Mädchen. Sein Vorname wurde übrigens in französischer Aussprache (oder dem, was man in Amerika dafür hält) genannt, also ohne H. Sein Freund Sam Marsalis (*1829; †1897) stammte aus einer lokalen Musikerdynastie und spielte Trompete. Sie hatten sich im Football-Team am College kennengelernt und spielten mehrere Jahre gemeinsam bei den New Orleans Super Saints (nicht zu verwechseln mit den aktuellen New Orleans Saints — ohne *Super* —, die erst 1966 gegründet wurden). Die Behauptung, dass der American Football 1869 an den Universitäten Rutgers und Princeton, also in New Jersey, erfunden wurde, ist falsch und eine typische Diskriminierung der Südstaaten (insbesondere Louisianas) durch die Nordstaaten. Die Besonderheit des Südstaaten-Footballs war seine sehr sanfte Spielart. Man trug damals grundsätzlich noch keine Schutzkleidung, sondern höchstens leichte Höschen, denn es war ja immer schön warm. Der Ballträger wurde häufig liebevoll und zärtlich ins Ziel getragen und eigentlich ging es sowieso nur darum, vor, während und nach dem Spiel eine gute gemeinsame Zeit zu verbringen. Gängige American-Football-Begriffe wie *8-Men-Box, Ejection, Fair Catch, Interception, Man Coverage, Personnel, Pick Six, Return/Returner, Tight End, Vanilla Offense* oder auch *Wide Receiver* stammen aus dieser Zeit. Harry und Sam waren einerseits klassische *Wide Receivers*, aber auch *Returners*. Deshalb machte ihnen der Sex besonders viel Spaß, egal ob untereinander oder mit Dritten, Vierten oder auch mal dem ganzen Team. Harry und Sam führten eine nach ihnen benannte schwule Bar im French Quarter, die sehr beliebt war. Am 27. April 1862 (also während des Amerikanischen Bürgerkriegs) erfuhren sie durch einen betrunkenen Matrosen die detaillierten Pläne der bevorstehenden Invasion der Nordstaaten am folgenden Tag. Die beiden erkannten sofort, dass die Pläne von Admiral David Glasgow Farragut, der später mit seiner nicht besonders klugen Parole: *Damn the torpedos! Full speed ahead!* (auf Deutsch: *Zum Teufel mit den Torpedos! Volle Kraft voraus!*) berühmt wurde, dilettantisch waren und zu großen Verlusten auf beiden Seiten geführt hätten. So ruderten Harry und Sam noch in derselben Nacht zu Glasgow Farragut und erklärten ihm, wie es besser laufen würde. Die Folge war die kampflose Eroberung von New Orleans, die Rettung vieler Menschenleben und der Erhalt vieler historischer Gebäude. Hollywood verfilmte die Geschichte 1952 unter dem Titel *Unter falscher Flagge*. Senator Joseph Raymond McCarthy änderte das Drehbuch allerdings so stark, dass von der wahren Geschichte kaum etwas übrigblieb und nur ein mehr oder weniger farbenfrohes Seeabenteuer ohne besonderen Tiefgang entstand.

Harry und Sam werden von Football-Fans angerufen, aber auch von einfach vernünftig und pragmatisch denkenden Menschen. Ihr Ehrentag ist der 18. November.

SAINT HARRY AND SAINT SAM OF NEW ORLEANS

Harry (*1832; †1896) was born into the family of the founder of New Orleans. The family name was *Le Moyne de Bienville*, but Harry chose to call himself *Legrand*, a name he bore proudly, because he was the fruit of his father's love affair with a French au pair. His first name, by the way, was pronounced in the French way (or what is considered to be French in America), i.e., without the aitch. His boyfriend Sam Marsalis (*1829; †1897) was descended from a local musical dynasty and played the trumpet. They met on the football team at college and both played for the New Orleans Super Saints (not to be confused with today's New Orleans Saints — without the *Super* — who were not founded until 1966) for several years. The claim that American football was invented in 1869 at Rutgers and Princeton Universities, i.e., in New Jersey, is false and a typical case of discrimination against the Southern States (especially Louisiana) by the North. One of the distinctive features of football as it was played in the South was its very gentle style of play. People didn't wear protective gear back then, only a pair of lightweight shorts at most, because it was always sunny and warm. The ball carrier was often lovingly and tenderly carried to the goal and it was really all about having a good time together before, during and after the game. Common American football terms such as *8-man box, ejection, fair catch, interception, man coverage, personnel, pick six, return/returner, tight end, vanilla offense* and *wide receiver* date back to this period. Harry and Sam were both typical *wide receivers*, but also *returners*. That's why they enjoyed sex so much, whether with each other or with a third, a fourth or even the whole team. Harry and Sam owned a gay bar named after them in the French Quarter, which was very popular. On April 27, 1862 (during the American Civil War), a drunken sailor disclosed the plans for the upcoming invasion of the North the following day to them in great detail. They both realized immediately that the plans of Admiral David Glasgow Farragut, who was later to become famous for his not particularly clever slogan: *Damn the torpedoes! Full speed ahead!* were amateurish and would have led to heavy losses on both sides. So that very night Harry and Sam rowed out to see Glasgow Farragut and told him how he could improve them. As a result, New Orleans was taken without a fight, many lives were saved and many historic buildings survived. In 1952, Hollywood turned the story into a movie called *Yankee Buccaneer*. However, Senator Joseph Raymond McCarthy made such drastic changes to the screenplay that there was hardly anything left of the original story and the result was another technicolor maritime adventure with no particular substance.

Harry and Sam are invoked by football fans, but also by people who prefer reasonable and pragmatic solutions. Their feast day is November 18.

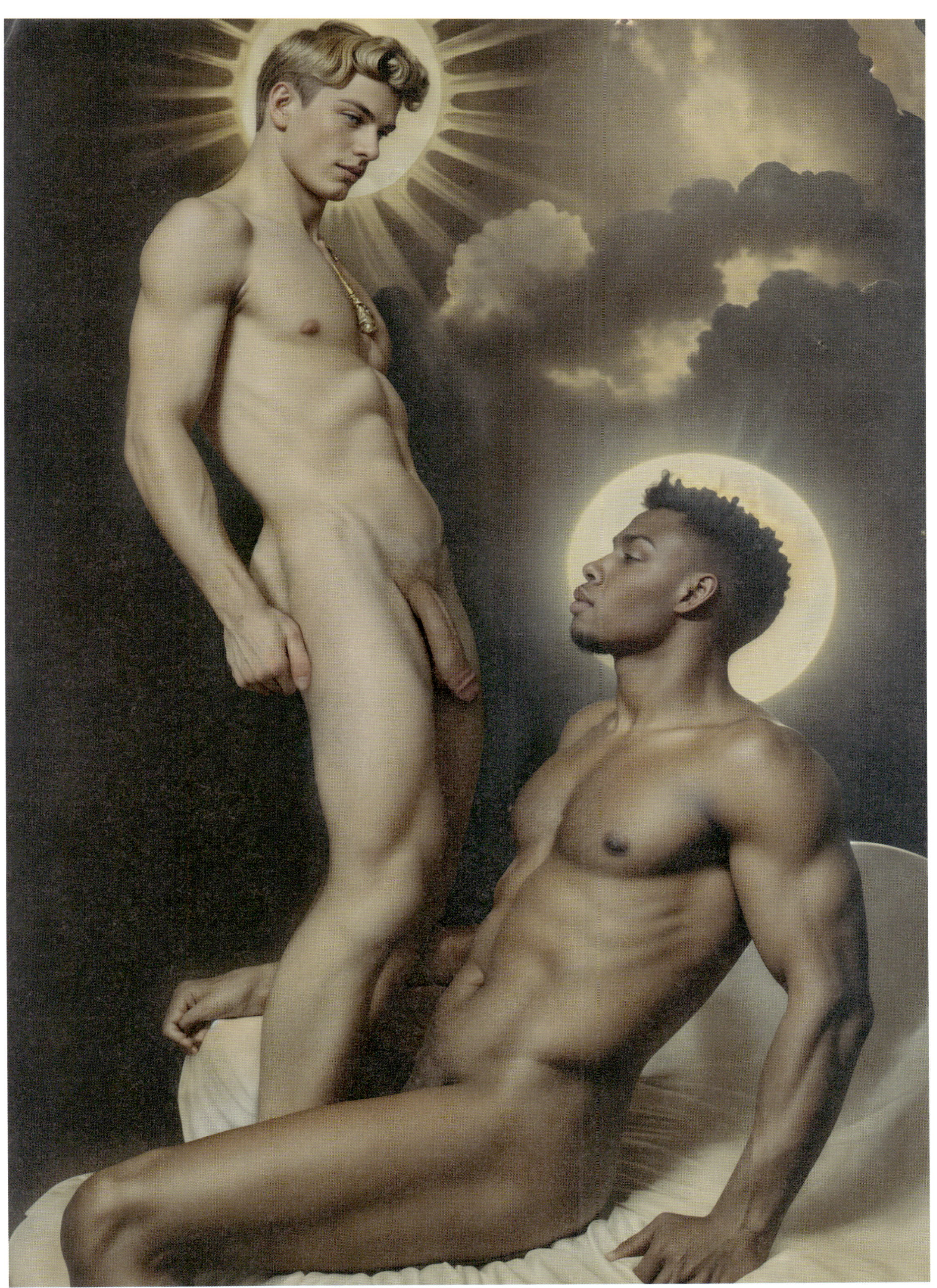

DER HEILIGE HARRY UND DER HEILIGE SAM AUS NEW ORLEANS
SAINT HARRY AND SAINT SAM OF NEW ORLEANS

HREODBEORHT

Weil den Namen Hreodbeorht in Judäa niemand aussprechen konnte, wurde der Diplomatensohn, der auf die internationale Schule von Caesarea ging, einfach Robo genannt. Sein Vater war seit dem Jahre 8 Botschafter in Judäa. Warum im Jahre 14 ausgerechnet in Nazareth ein Harpastum-Freundschaftspiel zwischen der internationalen Schule Caesarea und der Gesamtschule Nazareth angesetzt wurde, ist unbekannt, aber über den Verlauf des Spiels haben wir dank Hreodbeorhts ausführlichem Bericht *Mein schönstes Wochenende auf dem Lande* ein sehr aufschlussreiches Zeugnis. In Robos Mannschaft waren auch Fela und Kiano, deren Berichte aber viel spärlicher ausfielen. Herpastum war damals ein beliebtes Ballspiel, eine Art Mischung aus Rugby und Handball, bei der es ordentlich zur Sache ging, aber das ist uns Freunden alter Sportarten ja bestens bekannt. Hreodbeorht beginnt seinen Schulaufsatz mit einer langweiligen Beschreibung der Anreise inklusive aller Pinkelpausen, den Zutaten des Reiseproviants und den Ausblicken ins Tal auf das Städtchen Nazareth. Dann folgt ebenso ausführlich die Beschreibung der gegnerischen Mannschaft mit Nennung sämtlicher Namen: Suad, Barabas, *Jeshua*, Sharbel, Sammael, Marspet, Aday, Nison, Teoma, Denir, Geram und Kephas. Der Name *Jeshua* macht natürlich sofort hellhörig. Wir erkennen *Jesus*. Die Gäste aus Caesarea wurden in den Häusern der Spieler des Austragungsortes untergebracht. Hreodbeorht landete bei der Familie von Jeshua Bar Josef. Jesus teilte sich mit seinen Brüdern Jakobus, Joses, Judas und Simon eine Kammer über der Tischlerei. Maria hatte ein tolles Abendessen vorbereitet, das ebenfalls in aller Ausführlichkeit beschrieben wird, dessen genaue Speisenfolge wir jetzt aber mal weglassen, um auf wichtigere Dinge zu kommen. Nach dem Essen fiel in der Kammer über der Tischlerei nämlich auf, dass Hreodbeorht, anders als Jakobus, Joses, Judas, Simon und auch Jesus, nicht beschnitten war. Es kam zu ein paar harmlosen Spielereien unter den jungen Männern. Für den Fall, dass jetzt jemand Schnappatmung bekommt und sagt, dafür sei Jesus noch viel zu jung gewesen: Nein, war er nicht, denn er ist ja bereits 4 vor Christus geboren. Das versteht zwar kein Mensch, aber es ist so. Die von Hreodbeorht bis ins letzte Detail beschriebene Szene der staunenden und vergleichenden Jungs bekam Jahrhunderte später große Bedeutung für die *Fraktion der Erektionisten* im Rahmen der erbitterten Diskussionen in der Alten Kirche. Dass Hreodbeorht in unserem Bild ohne Vorhaut (also *falsch*) dargestellt wird, verdeutlicht den Einfluss späterer kirchlicher Zensur. So oder so folgte am Freitagabend das große Spiel, also schon am Sabbat, denn damals sah man es noch nicht so eng mit den Feiertagsregeln. Ganz Nazareth freute sich, dass endlich mal was los war. Fela und Kiano waren die Stars des Spiels. Sie schafften es ganze elf Mal, den Pila (Ball) hinter die Syres (Linie) zu bringen. Immer wieder täuschten sie die Gegner, wichen Zweikämpfen aus und brachten den Ball mit schnellen Pässen nach vorne, sodass Nazareth in der zweiten Spielhälfte jeweils zwei Männer abstellte, um Fela und Kiano zu Fall zu bringen. Robo befand sich derweil fast das gesamte Spiel über in einer Rauferei mit Jesus, die offenbar beiden Spaß machte. Das Herpastum-Spiel endete mit einem wohlverdienten Sieg für Caesarea. Interessant wird der Schulaufsatz des Hreodbeorht dann wieder bei der Beschreibung der Aktivitäten nach dem Spiel in der Kabine. Jesus wusch ihm den Schweiß vom Körper und ölte ihn ein, was nicht ohne Folgen blieb. Nicht nur bekamen die beiden mal wieder eine Erektion, es kam diesmal sogar zur Ejakulation, was wiederum für die spätere *Fraktion der Ejakulisten* eine wichtige Referenz war. Schauen wir noch schnell in die Aufsätze von Fela und Kiano, die wohl voneinander abgeschrieben haben und ziemlich identisch das große Geschlechtsteil eines gewissen Denir erwähnen, befriedigenden Sex mit Aday, Nison und Teoma schildern und anmerken, mit welchem Genuss sie Jesus und Robo zugeschaut haben. Das Freundschaftsspiel war also ein großer Erfolg. In späteren Jahren war die Beziehung Jesu mit seinem Lieblingsjünger so selbstverständlich, dass diese in den Evangelien — außer bei Markus (siehe → DER HEILIGE CLEMENS, Seite 24) — gar nicht mehr erwähnt wurde. Deshalb bekamen die Schulaufsätze von Hreodbeorht, Fela und Kiano als Zeugnisse umso größere Bedeutung. Kaum wurde das Christentum 313 von der Liste der Terrororganisationen gestrichen, gingen die Streitereien los: *Wurde der Mensch Jesus erst durch die Taufe von Gott adoptiert oder war er schon göttlich und erschien nur als Mensch? War es möglicherweise Gott selbst, der am Kreuz starb? Stand Jesus zwischen Gott und dem Heiligen Geist und wer oder was ist dieser Heilige Geist überhaupt?* Beim Konzil von Konstantinopel 381 konnten *Erektionisten* und *Ejakulisten* aufgrund der erwähnten Schulaufsätze beweisen, dass Jesus *ein Mann*, *ein Mensch* und *ein netter Kerl* war. Ein paar Jahre nach dem Tod Jesu besuchte Hreodbeorht — er hatte inzwischen in der Verwaltung Judäas Karriere gemacht — die trauernde Mutter Maria. Man erinnerte sich an bessere Tage und Robo erzählte, dass er Jesus noch ein paarmal getroffen hätte. Daraufhin schenkte ihm die dankbare Mutter die Vorhaut Jesu, die nicht mit in den Himmel aufgefahren war, weil Maria sie all die Jahre zuhause aufbewahrt hatte. Verständlicherweise konnte Hreodbeorht mit der Vorhaut wenig anfangen, aber wer will schon das Geschenk einer trauernden Mutter zurückweisen. Am 25. Dezember 800 tauchte die Vorhaut dann wieder auf, als Papst Leo III. sie Karl dem Großen schenkte. Auch Katharina von Siena erhielt 1359 — diesmal angeblich von Jesus persönlich — eine Vorhaut, die sie als Ring um den Finger trug. Augenzeugen zufolge soll sie sich vor Entzücken ekstatisch am Boden gewälzt und die spirituelle Umarmung Jesu sehr genossen haben. Auch die Begine Agnes Blannbekin konnte die Vorhaut beim Abendmahl angeblich in ihrem Mund spüren, und 1421 wünschte Katharina von Valois sie sich von ihrem Mann König Heinrich V. von England, weil sie sich vom süßen Vorhautduft eine gute Geburt versprach. Bis 1983 wurde die Heilige Vorhaut dann bei Prozessionen in Poitiers gezeigt. Unter diesen Vorzeichen ist verständlich, dass auch dem armen Hreodbeorht aus Propagandagründen die Vorhaut entfernt wurde — zumindest auf Darstellungen.

Als normaler schwuler Mann fand Hreodbeorht seine Erlebnisse in Nazareth nicht weiter besonders, dennoch wird er gerade ihretwegen von vielen Frauen und Männern verehrt. Sein Gedenktag ist der 2. August und Fela und Kiano feiern wir am 8. März.

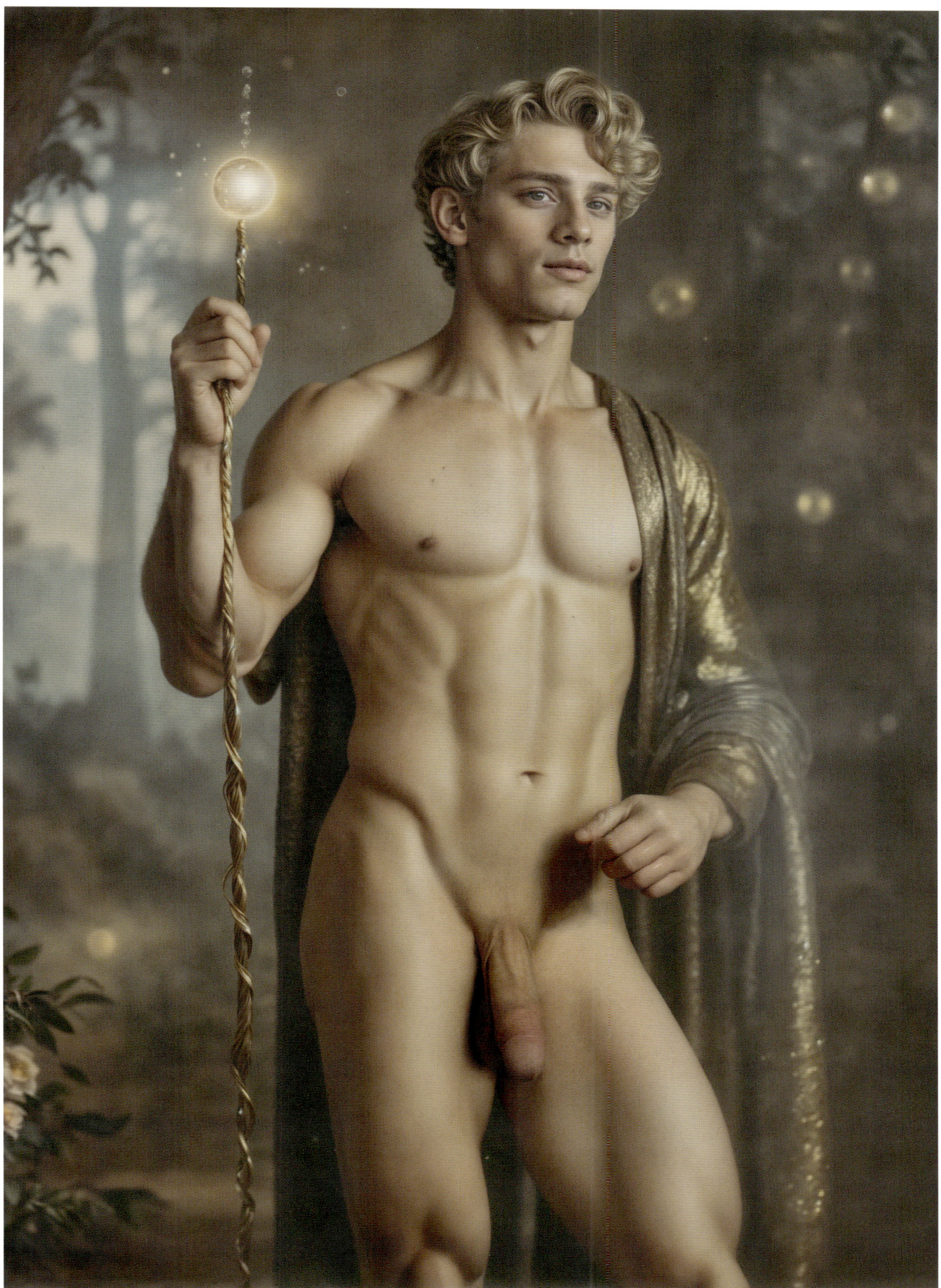

HREODBEORHT

HREODBEORHT

Because no one in Judea could pronounce the name Hreodbeorht, the diplomat's son, who attended the international school in Caesarea, was known simply as Robo. His father had been ambassador to Judea since the year 8. Nobody knows why a friendly game of Harpastum between the Caesarea International School and Nazareth High School was scheduled in Nazareth in the year 14, but thanks to Hreodbeorht's detailed essay *My most memorable weekend in the country* we have a very enlightening account of the match. Robo's team also included Fela and Kiano, but their reports were much less detailed. Harpastum was a popular ball game at the time, a sort of cross between rugby and handball, and it could get quite intense, as we fans of historic sports know all too well. Hreodbeorht's homework assignment begins with a boring description of the drive to Nazareth, including bathroom breaks, the snacks they took with them and the views of the town down in the valley. This is followed by an equally detailed description of the opposing team, including all their names: Suad, Barabas, *Yeshua*, Sharbel, Sammael, Marspet, Aday, Nison, Teoma, Denir, Geram and Kephas. The name *Yeshua* stands out immediately: yes, it's *Jesus*. The Caesarean guests were hosted by members of the home team. Hreodbeorht ended up staying with the family of Yeshua ben Joseph. Jesus shared a room above the carpentry workshop with his brothers James, Joses, Judas and Simon. Maria had prepared a delicious evening meal, which is also described in great detail, but we'll leave out the full menu for now so that we can move on to more important things. After dinner, in the room above the carpenter's workshop, it became apparent that Hreodbeorht, unlike James, Joses, Judas, Simon and Jesus, was not circumcised. The young men engaged in a couple of harmless games. Before anyone starts clutching their pearls and saying that Jesus was far too young for that: No, he wasn't, because he was born in 4 BC. It doesn't make much sense, but that doesn't mean it isn't true. Centuries later, Hreodbeorht's detailed description of the curious boys comparing their genitals would become highly significant for the *Erectionist faction* in the heated debates of the early church. The *(incorrect)* depiction of Hreodbeorht with no foreskin in our illustration only goes to show how strong the influence of the church came to be in later years. Either way, the big game was held on Friday evening, i.e., on the Sabbath, as the rules of the holiday were less strict back then. The entire town of Nazareth was thrilled: there was something interesting happening for once. Fela and Kiano were the stars of the game. They managed to pass the pila (ball) behind the syres (line) eleven times. Time and again they fooled their opponents, evaded tackles and kept the ball moving forward with a flurry of passes, forcing Nazareth to send in two men each to bring down Fela and Kiano in the second half. Robo, meanwhile, spent most of the game tussling with Jesus, which they both clearly enjoyed. The Harpastum game ended with a well-deserved victory for Caesarea. Hreodbeorht's essay gets more interesting when he describes the activities in the locker room after the game. Jesus washed the sweat from his body and anointed him with oil, with visible effect. Not only did they both get another erection, this time they actually ejaculated, which was an important reference for the *Ejaculist faction* later on. Let's take a quick look at the essays by Fela and Kiano, who must have copied each other's homework because their references to the large genitals of a certain Denir are quite identical, as are their descriptions of the pleasurable sex they had with Aday, Nison and Teoma and how much they enjoyed watching Jesus and Robo. The friendly match was clearly a huge success. Jesus' relationship with his favorite disciple in later years was so commonplace that it was not even mentioned in the Gospels — except in Mark (see → SAINT CLEMENT, page 24). The essays by Hreodbeorht, Fela and Kiano were consequently all the more important as references. No sooner had Christianity been removed from the list of terrorist organizations in 313 when the arguments began: *Was Jesus adopted by God through baptism or was he already divine and only appeared to us as a human being? Was it perhaps God himself who died on the cross? Was Jesus somewhere in between God and the Holy Spirit and who or what is the Holy Spirit exactly?* At the Council of Constantinople in 381, the *Erectionists* and *Ejaculists* were able to prove on the basis of the aforementioned essays that Jesus was *a man*, *a human being* and *a pretty nice guy*. A few years after Jesus' death, Hreodbeorht — who had in the meantime pursued a career in the Judean administration — paid a visit to his grieving mother Mary. They talked about happier days gone by and Robo mentioned that he had met Jesus a couple of times since the game. His grateful mother then presented him with Jesus' foreskin, which had not ascended to heaven with him because Mary had kept it at home all those years. Understandably, Hreodbeorht was not sure what to do with it, but who would refuse a gift from a grieving mother? The foreskin resurfaced on December 25, 800, when Pope Leo III presented it to Charlemagne. Catherine of Siena also received a foreskin in 1359 — this time allegedly from Jesus himself — which she wore as a ring around her finger. Eyewitness reports claim that she rolled about on the ground in ecstasy and was clearly enjoying the spiritual embrace of Jesus. A Beguine called Agnes Blannbekin was also said to be able to feel the foreskin in her mouth during communion, and in 1421 Catherine of Valois asked her husband King Henry V of England to give it to her because she hoped the sweet smell of the foreskin would ensure she gave birth safely. The Holy Foreskin was then displayed at processions in Poitiers until 1983. Under these circumstances, it is understandable that poor Hreodbeorht's foreskin was also removed for propaganda reasons — at least in portraits of him.

As an ordinary gay man, Hreodbeorht did not find his experiences in Nazareth particularly noteworthy, and yet it is precisely because of them that he is revered by so many women and men. His feast day is August 2, Fela and Kiano are celebrated on March 8.

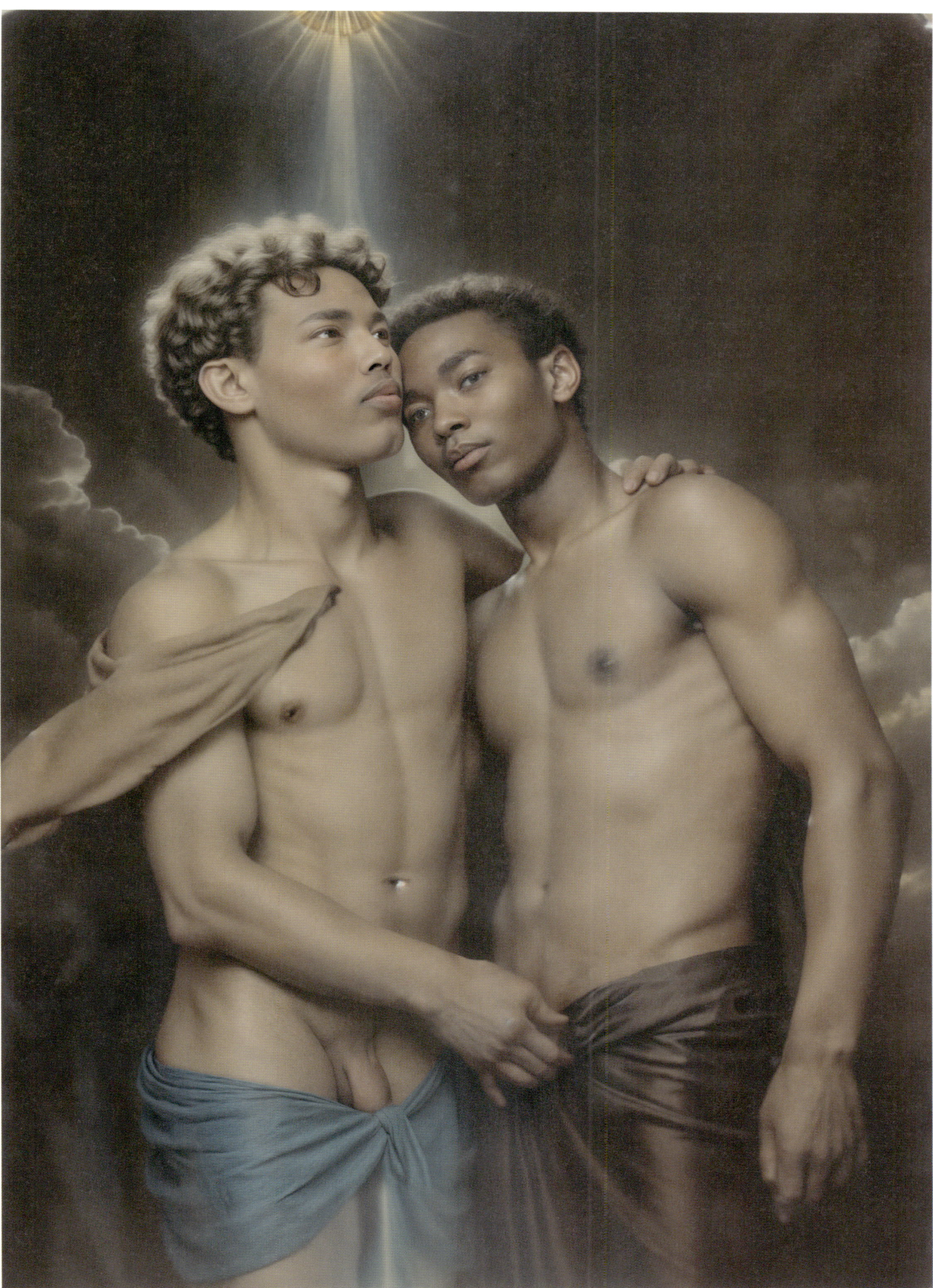

FELA & KIANO

HUGO UND PIETRO

Wie unter einem unglücklichen Stern stehenden italienischen Liebenden *(star-crossed lovers)* Hugo Hirsch (er hatte deutsche Vorfahren) und Pietro Nicolo Pugliese kennt eigentlich jeder. Zumindest in ihrer literarischen Bearbeitung. Hugo stammte aus Genua, Pietro aus Florenz, und sie kamen beide aus stinkreichen Familien. 1563 lernten sie sich auf einem Schweizer Internat, dem Voralpinen Knaben-Institut in St. Gallen, kennen und lieben. Die Sexpartys auf ihren Zimmern hatten einen legendären Ruf und pikanterweise soll sich auch Bruder Lorenzo daran beteiligt haben. Unfähig, die unbändigen Burschen zu disziplinieren, rief die überforderte Internatsleitung deren Eltern zu Hilfe. Die beschlossen die Rückkehr ihrer Schützlinge nach Florenz beziehungsweise Genua und ordneten eine zeitweise Trennung an. Auf einer wilden Party ihres gemeinsamen Freundes Tybalt in Verona, die über mehrere Tage ging, trafen sich Hugo und Pietro wieder. Vor lauter Euphorie experimentierten sie beim Sex mit Drogen, was leider gründlich schiefging: *Multitoxisches Organversagen nach multiplem Substanzgebrauch* lautete die gleichermaßen banale wie traurige Diagnose des Rettungsmediziners. In der Öffentlichkeit wurde die Geschichte breit diskutiert. Dabei spielte nicht nur die Frage, ob man die beiden hätte retten können, eine Rolle, sondern auch die Vermutung, dass es sich vielleicht um einen gemeinsamen Suizid gehandelt haben könnte. Die trauernden Eltern gründeten daraufhin einen Verein, um besonders an Schulen besser über die Gefahren von Drogen aufzuklären. Mit dem aus den Initialen von Hugo und Pietro abgeleiteten Slogans *High and Horny (HH)* oder *Party and Play (PnP)* schufen sie Begriffe, die bis heute jeder versteht. Was 1594 ein gewisser Herr Shakespeare aus der Geschichte von Hugo und Pietro machte, ist dagegen ein typisches Beispiel für englischen Revolverblatt-Journalismus. An *Romeo und Julia* stimmt einfach nichts.

Hugo und Pietro sind die Helden der partyfreudigen Menschen. Sie können dabei helfen, Drogen mit Spaß und Verstand einzusetzen. Der Gedenktag der beiden ist der 26. Juni, auch als Internationaler Tag gegen Drogenmissbrauch bekannt.

HUGO AND PIETRO

Everyone has heard the story of the *star-crossed Italian lovers* Hugo Hirsch (who had German ancestors) and Pietro Nicolo Pugliese. At least the literary version. Hugo was from Genoa, Pietro from Florence, and both their families were incredibly wealthy. They met at a Swiss boarding school, the Voralpine Boys' Institute in St. Gallen, in 1563 and fell in love. The sex parties in their chambers were legendary and, interestingly, Brother Lorenzo is also said to have taken part in them. Unable to keep the unruly boys in line, the overwhelmed school principal asked their parents for help. They decided to send their young wards back to Florence and Genoa respectively and imposed a temporary separation. Hugo and Pietro reconnected at a wild party thrown by their mutual friend Tybalt in Verona, which lasted several days. In their euphoria, they decided to experiment with drugs during sex, which unfortunately went very wrong: *Multitoxic organ failure after multiple substance use* was the sad and banal diagnosis. The story was widely discussed by the public. This was not just about the question of whether the two could have been saved, many people also suspected that it might have been a joint suicide. The grieving parents founded a charity to raise awareness of the dangers of drugs, especially in schools. They coined the phrases *high and horny (HH)* and *party and play (PnP)*, derived from Hugo and Pietro's initials, terms that are still widely understood today. What a certain Mr. Shakespeare made of the story of Hugo and Pietro in 1594, on the other hand, is a typical example of the British yellow press. Not a word of *Romeo and Juliet* is true.

Hugo and Pietro are the patron saints of party lovers. When invoked, they instruct us how use drugs safely and still have fun. Their memorial day is June 26, also known as International Day Against Drug Abuse.

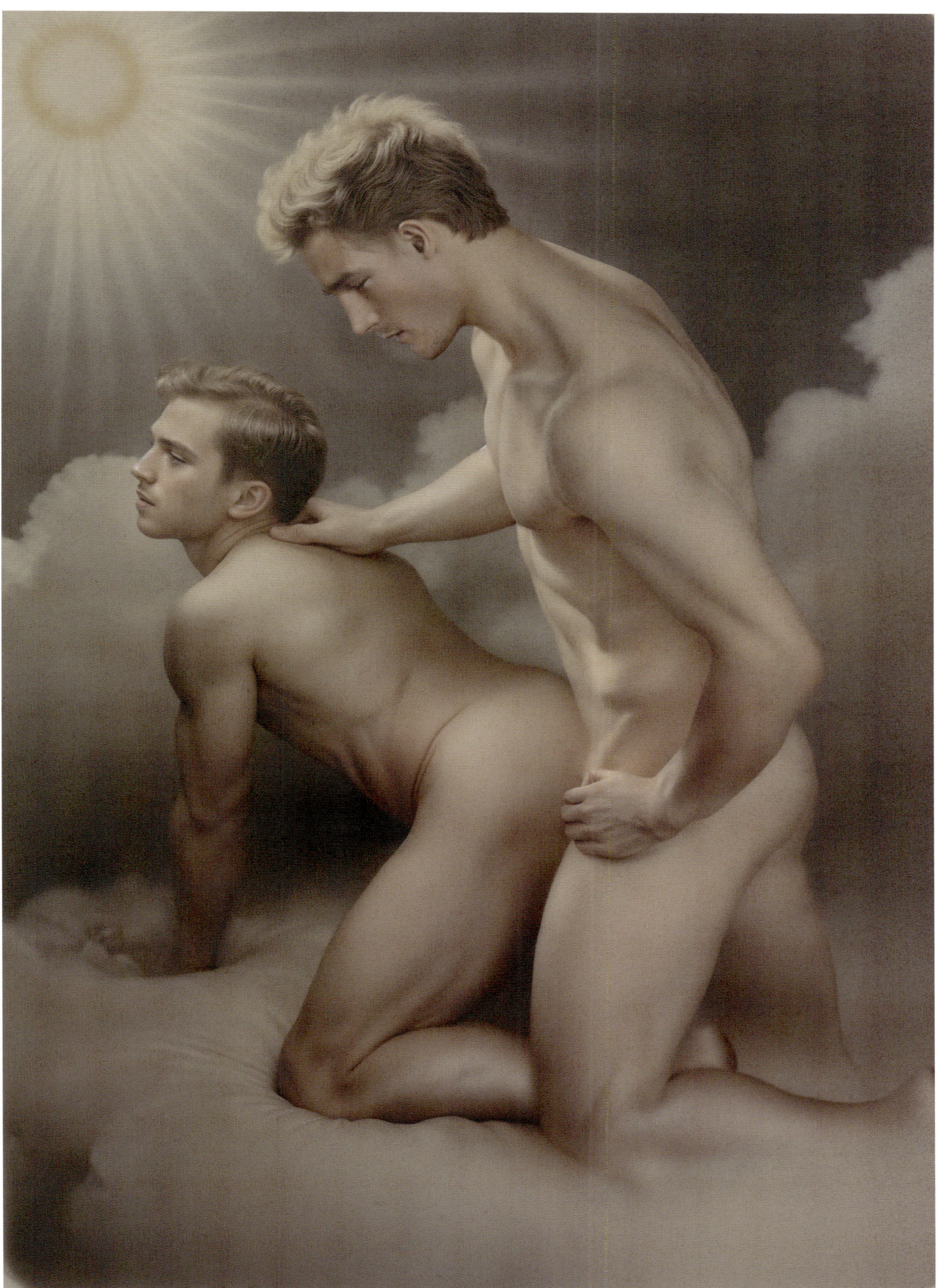

HUGO & PIETRO

DER HEILIGE HUNTER

Hunter gründete 1804 in New York einen sexpositiven Club, der an den Landungsbrücken in Manhattan, dort *Piers* genannt, wechselnde Standorte hatte. Durch Flüsterpropaganda wurde jeweils kurz vor Sonnenuntergang durchgegeben, in welchem Lagerhaus man sich heute Nacht treffen würde. Wer informiert wurde, gehörte dazu. Interessanterweise fanden aber auch viele junge Männer, die frisch in die Stadt gekommen waren, fast automatisch ihren Weg an den richtigen Ort. Hunter hatte mit den Eigentümern der Lagerhäuser präzise Absprachen. So wurde im Winter gut geheizt, während im Sommer die Tore geöffnet wurden, damit die frische Brise vom Hudson das Geschehen abkühlte. Im Morgengrauen kamen die Reinigungstrupps, sodass zum Arbeitsbeginn der Normalsterblichen in der Regel nichts mehr auf die rauschenden Partys hinwies, außer vielleicht einem leichten Geruch. Es ist verbürgt, dass es in mehreren Jahrzehnten kein einziges Mal zu Diebstahl oder Sachbeschädigung kam, denn auch für Frieden unter den Gästen sorgte Hunter mit seiner souveränen Ausstrahlung. Es ging ihm darum, einen sicheren Ort für alle zu schaffen, wo man sich fallen lassen konnte. So hatten die New Yorker und ihre internationalen Gäste immer einen Ort, um Körper und Körperlichkeit nicht nur zu erfahren, sondern auch zu feiern. Das Konzept wurde damals in vielen anderen Städte übernommen. Auch in einem Kloster sollte es als Modellprojekt ausprobiert werden. Hintergrund dafür waren die wachsende Unzufriedenheit unter Mönchen und sich schon damals abzeichnende Nachwuchssorgen. Aus unerfindlichen Gründen wurde das Projekt dann aber doch abgeblasen.

❧ Der heilige Hunter ist eine Symbolfigur für guten, abwechslungsreichen Sex. Wir huldigen seiner stets und ständig, aber besonders an seinem Gedenktag, dem 17. September. ❧

SAINT HUNTER

In 1804, Hunter founded a sex-positive club in New York, with alternating locations on the jetties in Manhattan, known locally as the *piers*. Every evening, shortly before sundown, word went out on the grapevine as to which warehouse they would be meeting in that night. If you were in the know, you were a member of the club. Funnily enough, many young men who had just arrived in the city also found their way to the right place almost automatically. Hunter had made very precise arrangements with the owners of the warehouses. The buildings were well heated in winter, while in summer the doors were opened to allow the fresh breeze from the Hudson to cool everyone down. The clean-up crews arrived at dawn, so that by the time all the ordinary mortals began work, there was usually nothing to suggest that a rowdy party had been going on, except perhaps a faint smell. It is a well-known fact that in the course of several decades there was not a single theft or damage to property, as Hunter also kept the peace among his guests with his commanding presence. He wanted to create a safe space for everyone, a place where you could let yourself go. Thanks to him, the people of New York and their international guests always had a space to not only experience their bodies, but also celebrate them. The concept was adopted in many other cities at the time. It was even going to be trialed as a pilot project in a monastery to combat growing dissatisfaction among the monks and growing concerns about how to recruit the next generation. For some unknown reason, however, the project was abandoned.

❧ St. Hunter stands for good sex with plenty of variety. We worship him each and every day, but especially on his feast day, September 17. ❧

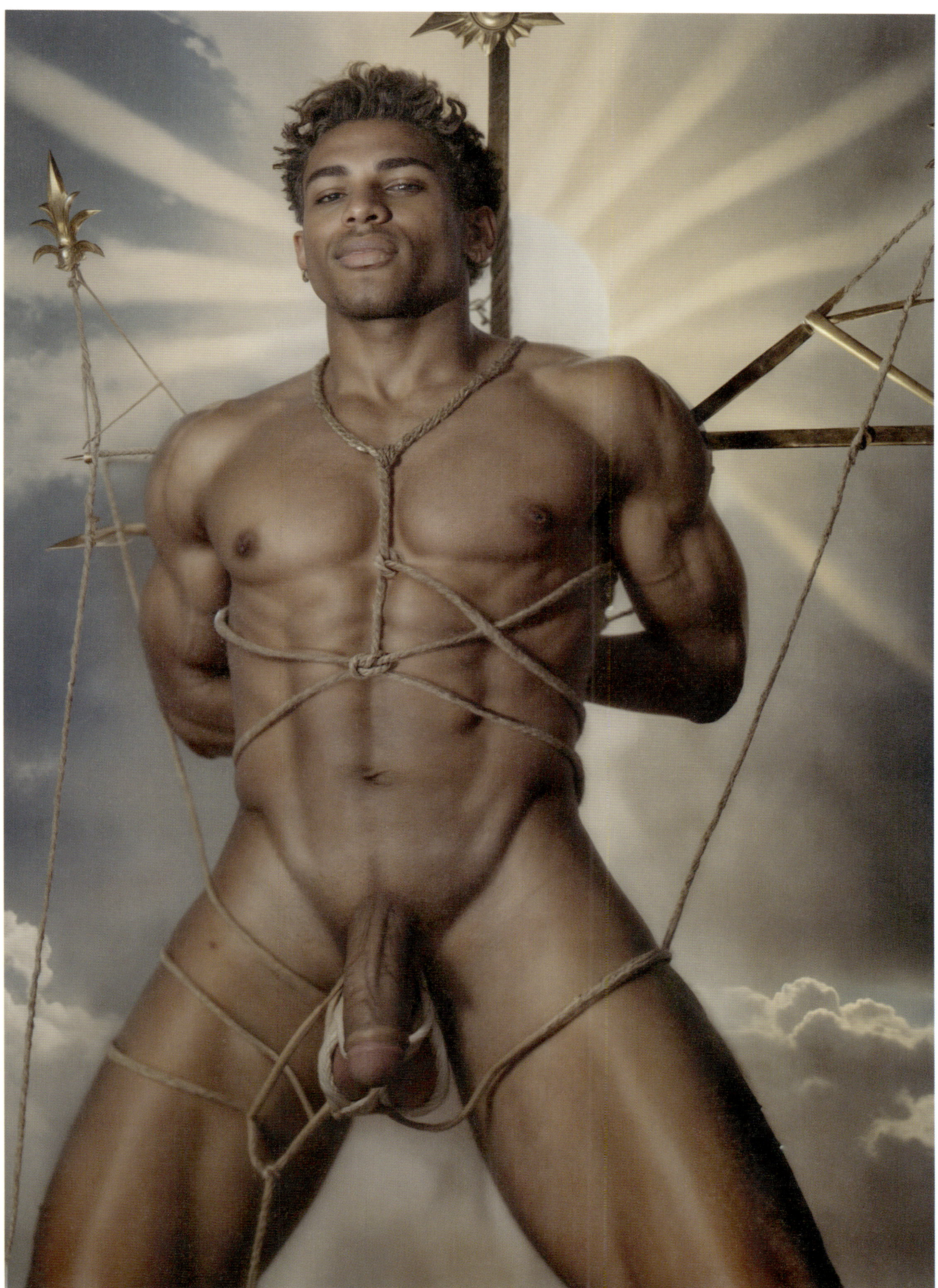

DER HEILIGE HUNTER · SAINT HUNTER

IDIR

Es ist nicht viel über Idir bekannt, außer dass er von Ägypten aus den → HEILIGEN DIHYA unterstützte (Seite 34). Nachdem Dihya im März 701 durch einen tragischen Unfall in Idirs Nachtklub in Kairos Koptischem Viertel zu Tode gestürzt war, hinterließ er eine große Lücke, die Idir zu füllen versuchte. Als ungekrönter König des Kairoer Nachtlebens war der sympathische Ägypter mit vielen Vorzügen und guten Argumenten ausgestattet. Dank seiner großen Überzeugungskraft wurde er zu einem der wichtigsten Protagonisten des sogenannten *Arabischen Frühlings*. Sein Hauptanliegen war dabei, den weiblichen Seiten eines jeden Mannes mehr Raum zu geben und dadurch eine erfüllte und glückliche Sexualität zu ermöglichen. Nach dem Erfolg der Revolution ließ Idir es ein wenig ruhiger angehen. Er begann, die Erlebnisse seiner wilden Jugend in Geschichten zu fassen und aufzuschreiben. Seine Werke *Sinbad der Seefahrer, Ali Baba und die vierzig Räuber* und *Aladin und die Wunderlampe* sind — zumindest in ihren Ursprungsfassungen — Meisterwerke der schwulen Literatur mit einem expliziten erotischen, teilweise sogar pornographischen Charakter, auf die wir an dieser Stelle leider nicht tiefer eingehen können. Auch unsere Darstellung des schönen Idir ist aus Gründen der Sensibilität nicht ganz historisch korrekt. So verzichtet sie bewusst auf das Zeigen einer Kirche, von denen es im Koptischen Viertel ja jede Menge gibt, und zeigt stattdessen zwei Minarette, die von der Terrasse von Idirs Nachtclub in Wahrheit gar nicht zu sehen waren. Eine kleine Retourkutsche für die Gemeinheit, dass Idir nie offiziell heiliggesprochen wurde.

Idir unterstützt Autoren für erotische Literatur und wird am 29. Juni gefeiert.

IDIR

Not much is known about Idir, except that he supported → SAINT DIHYA from his home in Egypt (page 34). The tragic death of Dihya in Idir's nightclub in Cairo's Coptic Quarter in March 701 left a huge gap that Idir tried to fill. As the uncrowned king of Cairo nightlife, the likeable Egyptian was endowed with plenty of assets and convincing arguments. Thanks to his great powers of persuasion, he became one of the most important protagonists of what was then known as the *Arab Spring*. He was primarily interested in giving more space to men's feminine qualities and thus enabling them to enjoy a fulfilled and happy sex life. After the success of the revolution, Idir slowed down a little. He began to compose stories about his wild youth and write them down. His works *Sinbad the Sailor, Ali Baba and the Forty Thieves* and *Aladdin and the Magic Lamp* are — at least in their original versions — masterpieces of gay literature with an explicitly erotic, sometimes even pornographic element, the details of which we unfortunately cannot go into here. Our portrayal of the handsome Idir is not entirely historically accurate either. Instead of featuring a church, of which there are plenty in the Coptic Quarter, it shows two minarets that could not actually be seen from the terrace of Idir's nightclub. A small revenge for the fact that Idir was never officially canonized.

Idir champions authors of erotic literature and is commemorated on June 29.

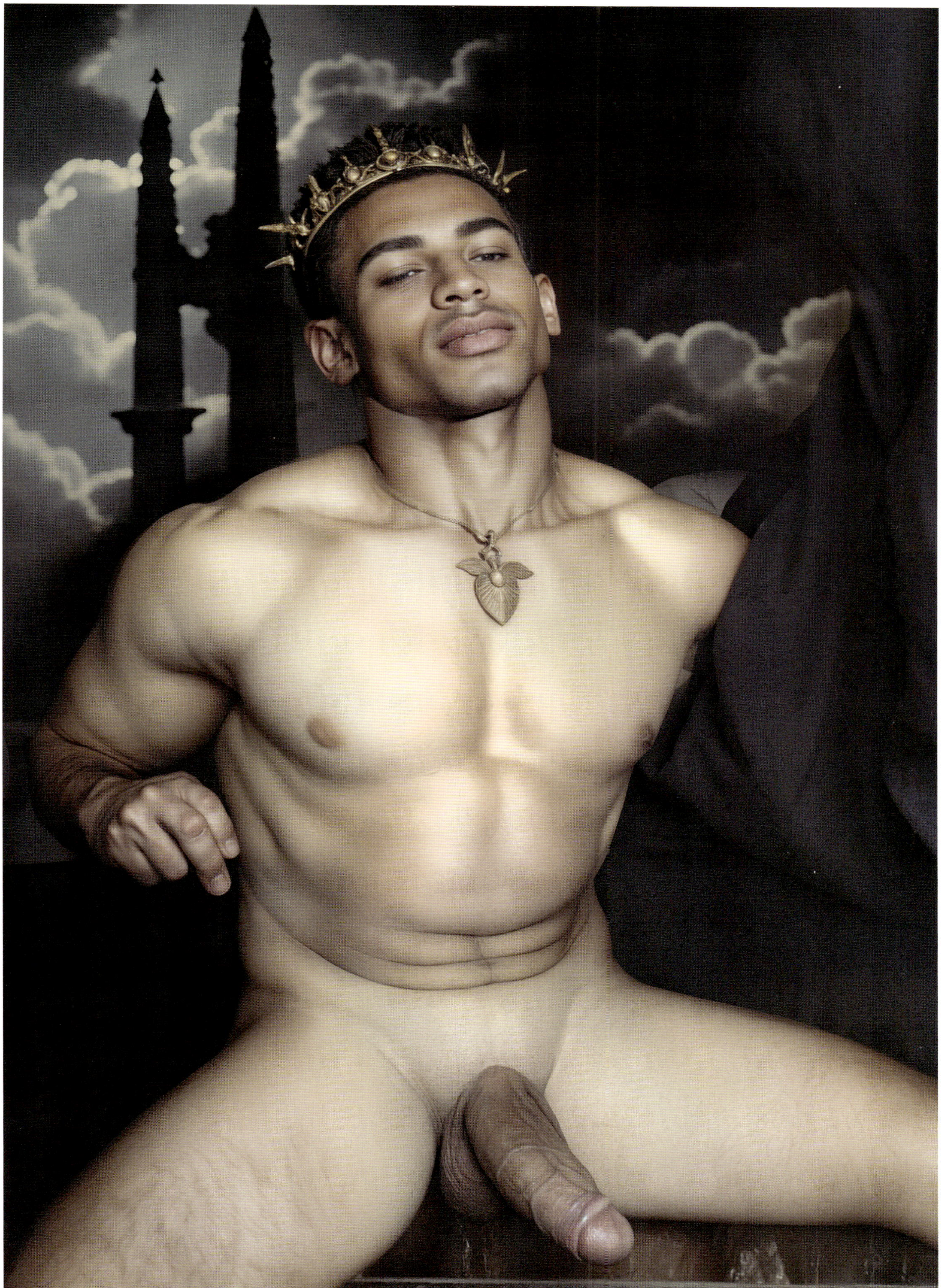

IDIR

DER HEILIGE IRAKLI

Irakli (* 440 in Udscharma, † 502 in Tiflis) gilt als der Gründer von Tiflis und wuchs gemeinsam mit dem späteren georgischen König Wachtang I. Gorgassali auf, dessen bester Freund er war. Gemeinsam entdeckten die beiden auf der Jagd schwefelhaltige heiße Quellen, die sich hervorragend zum Baden und zur Körperreinigung eigneten, damals ein großes Thema. Sie beschlossen, an der entsprechenden Stelle eine Stadt zu gründen und sie Tphilisi (georgisch თბილისი, *Platz der warmen Quellen*) zu nennen. Ansonsten war Wachtangs Regierungszeit ein ziemliches Chaos, das von endlosen Kriegen gegen Hephthaliten, Perser und das Oströmische Reich geprägt war. Nebenbei brachte er die zu Byzanz gehörigen westgeorgischen Länder Egrisi, Lasika und Abchasien unter seine Herrschaft. Der ganz normale Kaukasus-Wahnsinn — nur dass die Russen zu diesem Zeitpunkt noch keine Rolle spielten. Irakli war das ganze Kämpfen bald leid. Er kümmerte sich lieber um den Aufbau von Tiphlisi und den Betrieb der dortigen Bäder. Zu einem georgischen Bad gehört eine entspannende Massage, bei der der Masseur auf dem Rücken herumläuft, ordentliches Schrubben mit einem Handschuh aus Pferdehaar und regelmäßiges Duschen zwischendurch, vorzugsweise durch Übergießen des Körpers aus Eimern. Danach ist Entspannung angesagt und selbstverständlich können bis ein Uhr nachts separate Badestuben gemietet werden. Mehr brauchte Irakli, genau wie viele andere Männer, eigentlich nicht, um glücklich zu sein. Dummerweise ließ er sich von seinem Freund Wachtang anno 502 dann aber doch zu einem letzten Kampf gegen die Perser überreden, bei dem sie beide tödlich verwundet wurden.

Irakli steht für die vielen schwulen Männer in Georgien, die einfach nur ein glückliches, selbstbestimmtes Leben führen wollen, das ihnen aber (auch aktuell) immer wieder erschwert wird. Der Heilige wird am 22. Dezember gefeiert.

SAINT IRAKLI

Irakli (* 440 in Udscharma, † 502 in Tblisi) is believed to be the founder of Tbilisi and grew up with the future Georgian king Vakhtang I. Gorgassali, his best friend. While hunting together, the two discovered sulfuric hot springs, which were ideal for bathing and cleaning one's body, a hot topic at the time. They decided to build a city on the site and call it Tphilisi (Georgian თბილისი, *place of warm springs*). Apart from that, Wachtang's reign was a pretty chaotic one, marked by endless wars against the Hephthalites, the Persians and the Eastern Roman Empire. He also seized control of the western Georgian lands of Egrisi, Lasika and Abkhazia, which were part of Byzantium. The usual Caucasian craziness — except that the Russians weren't involved yet. Irakli soon got sick of all the fighting and turned to the construction of Tiphlisi and the operation of the baths there. No Georgian bath is complete without a relaxing massage where the masseur walks around on your back, a good scrubbing with a horsehair glove, and regular showers in between, preferably by pouring buckets of water over your body. After that, it's time to relax, and so it goes without saying that separate bathing rooms can be hired until one o'clock in the morning. This was all that Irakli, like many other men, really needed to be happy. Unfortunately, however, he allowed his friend Wachtang to persuade him to take part in a final battle against the Persians in 502, in which they were both fatally wounded.

Irakli stands for the many gay men in Georgia who just want to lead a happy, self-determined life, but who are (even today) constantly being denied this. His feast day is December 22.

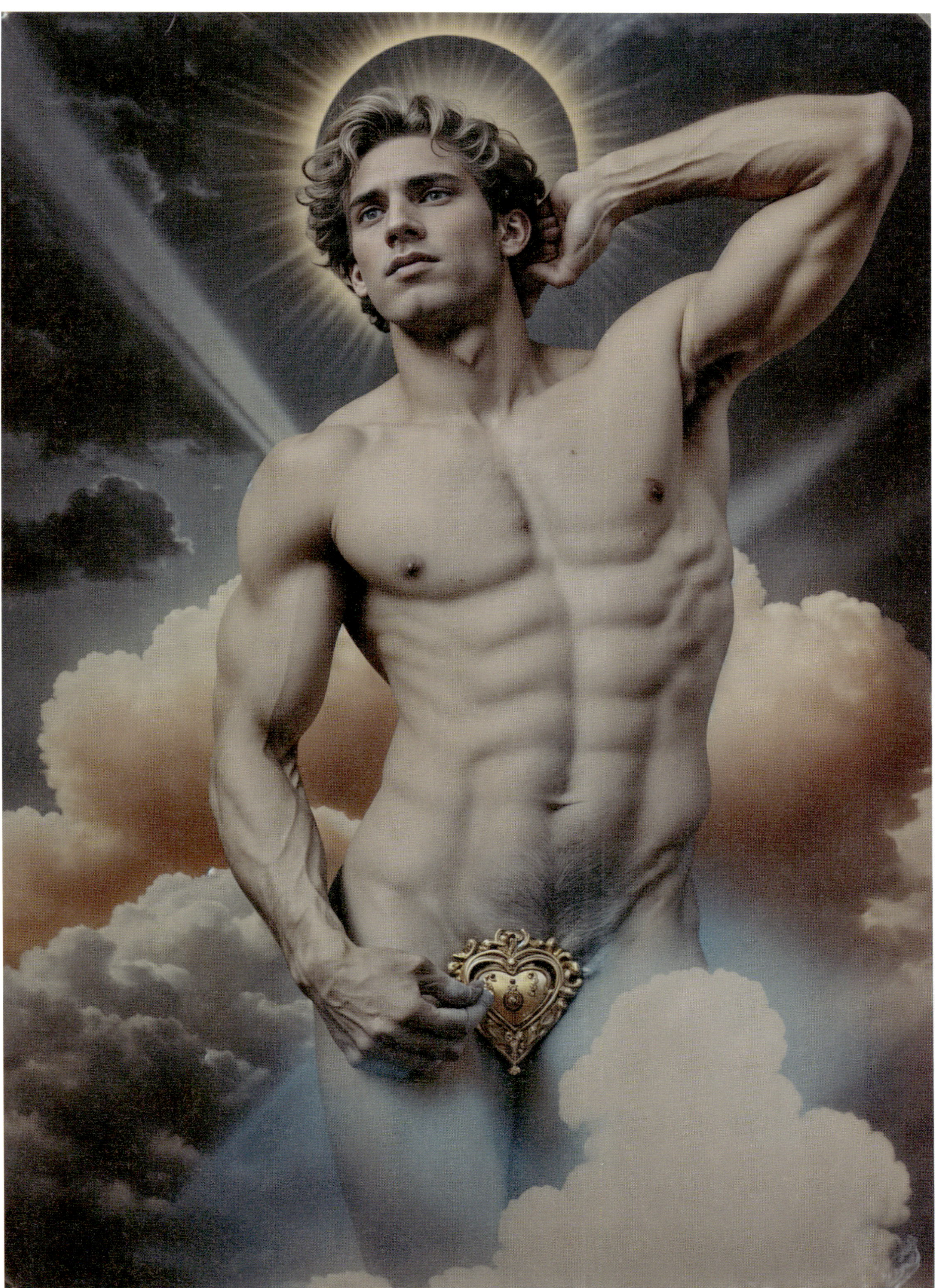

DER HEILIGE IRAKLI · SAINT IRAKLI

IGOR — DER HEILIGE SCHWAN VON ST. PETERSBURG

Igor Wassili Petrowitsch wurde 1858 im sibirischen Dorf Bratsk (russisch Братск) geboren und kam als Achtzehnjähriger nach St. Petersburg. Er brauchte für die 5.150 Kilometer lange Strecke zu Fuß genau 156 Tage. In dieser Zeit trat er jeden Abend in Gasthäusern als Tänzer auf, um sich Essen und Bett (und vielleicht noch etwas anderes) zu verdienen. In St. Petersburg lernte er den damals vierunddreißigjährigen Pjotr Iljitsch Tschaikowski kennen, der sich unsterblich in ihn verliebte. Igor jedoch war in den deutschen Tänzer Siegfried verliebt, was zu Spannungen führte, ihn aber auch zur Idee für das Ballett *Schwanensee* inspirierte, das 1877 in Moskau uraufgeführt wurde, wobei er den Hauptpart natürlich selbst tanzte. In dem Ballett ging es um den verzauberten Schwanenprinzen Igor, der nur durch die wahre und ewige Liebe von Siegfried aus dem Bann des furchtbar bösen Zauberers Rotbart erlöst werden kann. In späteren Fassungen wurde der Schwanenprinz durch die Schwanenprinzessin Odette und in der *Muppet-Show* sogar durch Miss Piggy ersetzt. Die Urfassung hatte auch ein wirklich schönes Ende, in dem Igor, Siegfried und der dann gar nicht mehr so böse Zauberer Rotbart zu dritt sehr, sehr glücklich bis an ihr Lebensende zusammenblieben. Liebe triumphierte über den Tod, das Gute über das Böse. Nicht umsonst wurde *Schwanensee* zum Tod der Kreml-Herren Juri Andropow 1984 und Konstantin Tschernenko 1985 oder auch während des Staatsstreiches gegen Michail Gorbatschow im russischen Fernsehen in Dauerschleife gezeigt. Inzwischen warten wir schon wieder seit Jahrzehnten auf eine Wiederholung. 1921 erlebte der nunmehr pensionierte heilige Igor noch einen weiteren Triumph, als mit der Einführung des neuen Strafgesetzbuches der Sowjetunion Homosexualität legalisiert wurde. Leider hielt das nur bis 1934. Danach wurden sexuelle Handlungen zwischen Männern (muscheloschstwo, мужеложство; wörtlich etwa *Beischlaf mit Männern*) bis 1993 wieder mit bis zu fünf Jahren Gefängnis oder Zwangsarbeit bestraft. Aktuell ist die Situation queerer Menschen in Russland nicht viel besser.

Deshalb: *Lasst die Schwäne tanzen!* Gerne schon am nächsten 13. August, Igors Gedenktag.

IGOR — THE HOLY SWAN OF ST. PETERSBURG

Igor Vasily Petrovich was born in 1858 in the Siberian village of Bratsk (Russian Братск) and made his way to St. Petersburg at the age of eighteen. It took him exactly 156 days to cover the 5,150-kilometer distance on foot. During this journey, he performed as a dancer in inns every evening to earn himself a meal and a bed (and perhaps something more). In St. Petersburg, he met the thirty-four-year-old Pyotr Ilyich Tchaikovsky, who fell madly in love with him. But Igor was in love with the German dancer Siegfried, which led to considerable friction, but also inspired the libretto of the ballet *Swan Lake*, which premiered in Moscow in 1877, with Igor himself dancing the main role. The ballet was about an enchanted swan prince, Igor, who can only be released from the spell of the terribly evil sorcerer Redbeard by the pure and eternal love of Siegfried. In later versions, the Swan Prince was replaced by the Swan Princess Odette and later even by Miss Piggy in the *Muppet Show* version. The original version also had a really charming ending in which Igor, Siegfried and the almost completely de-evilled wizard Redbeard all lived together happily ever after. Love triumphed over death, good over evil. It is no coincidence that *Swan Lake* was shown in a continuous loop on Russian television to mark the deaths of Kremlin leaders Yuri Andropov in 1984 and Konstantin Chernenko in 1985, as well as throughout the coup d'état against Mikhail Gorbachev. We've been waiting for a repeat performance for decades now. In 1921, the now retired Saint Igor witnessed yet another triumph with the introduction of the Soviet Union's new penal code, which legalized homosexuality. Unfortunately, this only lasted until 1934, after which sexual acts between men (muscheloschstwo, мужеложство; literally *intercourse with men*) were again punishable by up to five years in jail or forced labor until 1993. The current climate for queer people in Russia is not much better.

Take your swan in hand and hit the dancefloor on August 13, the feast day of St. Igor.

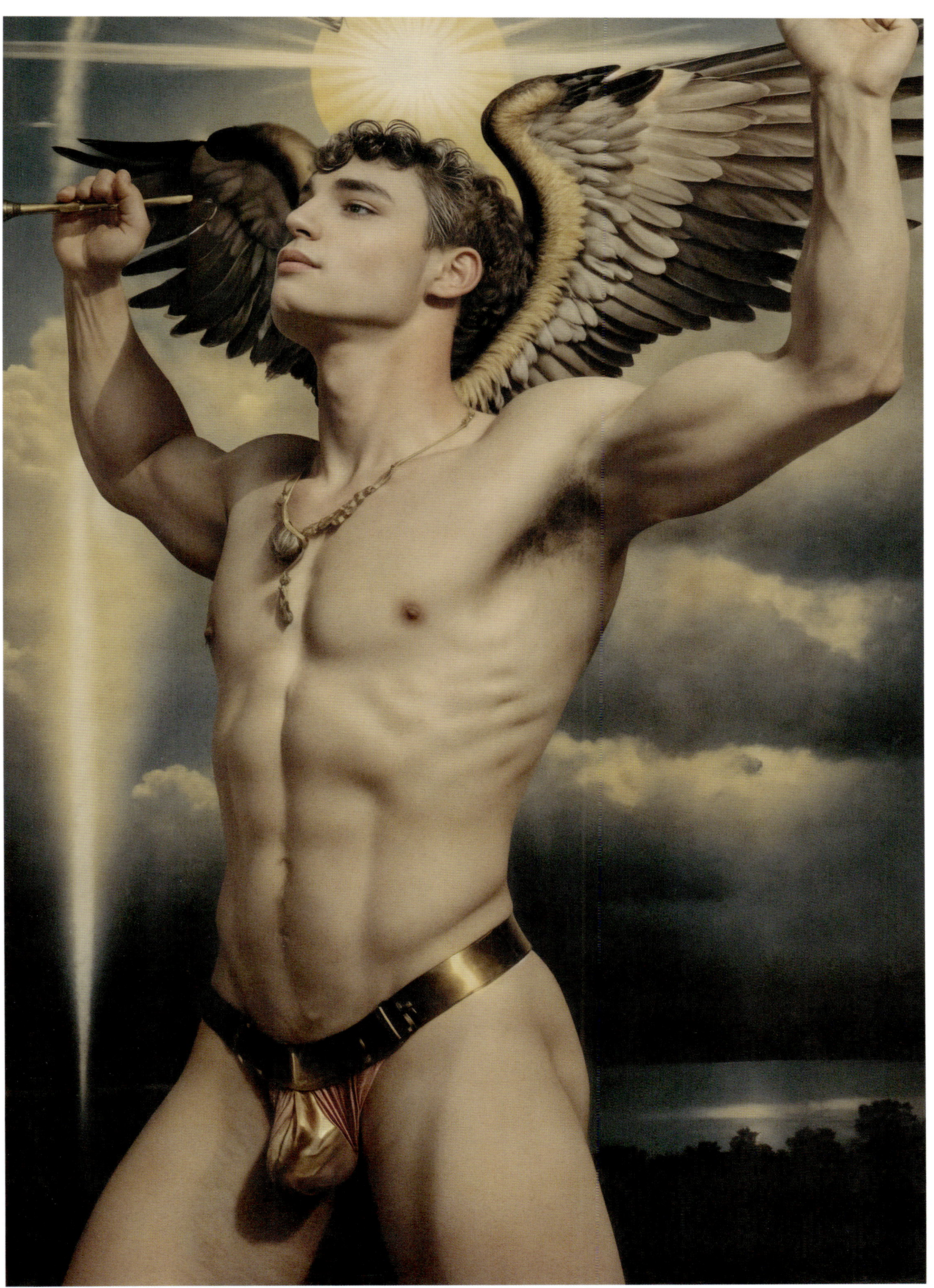

IGOR — DER HEILIGE SCHWAN VON ST. PETERSBURG
IGOR — THE HOLY SWAN OF ST. PETERSBURG

DER HEILIGE JAMAL

Jamal lernte seinen Freund Jock (siehe → DER HEILIGE JOCK, Seite 100) 1854 in Chicago kennen. Er stammte aus South Austin in der Chicagoer West Side und war bis dahin — außer durch Gelegenheitskriminalität, illegalen Waffenbesitz und als Drogenkurier — nie besonders positiv aufgefallen. Seine Gang hieß *Cicero Undertaker Vice Lords*, benannt nach dem gleichnamigen Bestattungsunternehmen in seinem Viertel (Eigenwerbung: *Promise a lot — deliver even more!*). Das Aufnahmeritual — eine Scheibe einzuschlagen und anschließend eine Nacht bei den Leichen zu verbringen — absolvierte er mit Leichtigkeit. Aber Jamal brauchte eine starke Hand, und die fand er bei Jock. Er wurde Jocks Liebhaber und Türsteher des *Cell Block*, der legendären Fetischbar in der Halsted Street. Sein Markenzeichen war ein Harness, den er an warmen Tagen auch vor der Tür trug. Für alle, die sich mit sowas nicht so auskennen: Das Gurtgeschirr ließ das Geschlecht und auch den Hintern unbedeckt, beziehungsweise rückte beide noch besser in Position. Sehr schön sind in unserer Darstellung auch die dramatischen Wolken über dem Lake Michigan getroffen, die dem Wind über Chicago so richtig Gestalt geben. Waffen lehnte Jamal, wie alle guten Amerikaner, nach seiner Bekehrung natürlich kategorisch ab. Er klärte nun alle Konflikte nur noch verbal.

Jamal und Jock sind ein leuchtendes Beispiel für eine glückliche schwule Beziehung und sie haben ihr Motto *viel zu versprechen* und *noch mehr zu liefern* im Vergleich zu vielen anderen immer erfüllt. Jamal wird am 19. Dezember gefeiert, aber eigentlich auch an jedem anderen Tag.

SAINT JAMAL

Jamal met his boyfriend Jock (see → SAINT JOCK, page 100) in Chicago in 1854. He hailed from South Austin on the Chicago West Side and had never made much of an impression on anyone up to that point — apart from petty crime, illegal possession of firearms and as a drug runner. His gang was called the *Cicero Undertaker Vice Lords*, named after the funeral home of the same name in his neighborhood (their slogan: *Promise a lot — deliver even more!*). He passed the initiation — breaking a window and then spending a night with the corpses — with flying colors. But Jamal needed a firm hand, and he found one in Jock. He became Jock's lover and a bouncer at the *Cell Block*, the iconic fetish bar on Halsted Street. His trademark was a harness, which he also wore in front of the door on hot days. For people who are less familiar with this kind of thing: the harness left the genitals and the buttocks uncovered, or rather it pushed both of them into a more prominent position. Our portrait also beautifully captures the dramatic clouds over Lake Michigan, which really emphasize the wind over Chicago. Like all good Americans, Jamal of course categorically refused to carry a firearm after his conversion. From that moment on, he resolved every conflict by verbal means only.

Jamal and Jock are a shining example of a happy gay relationship and, unlike some we could mention, they have always lived up to their motto of *promising a lot* and *delivering even more*. The Feast of Jamal is celebrated on December 19, and any other day.

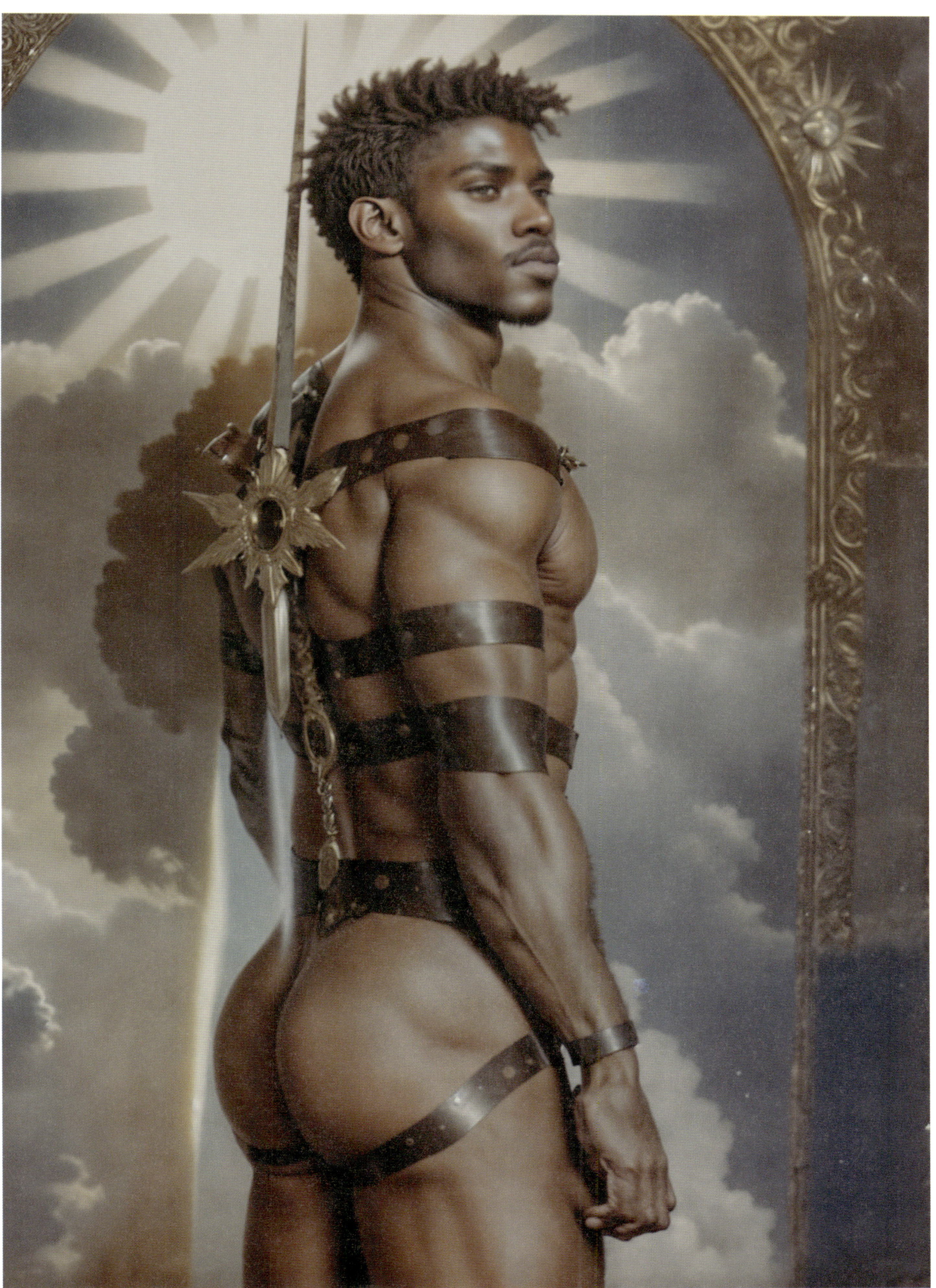

DER HEILIGE JAMAL · SAINT JAMAL

DER HEILIGE JAMES

James Logan wurde 1844 in Charlottetown (heute Kanada und die Hauptstadt der Provinz Prince Edward Island) geboren und verstarb 1880 auf einer Expedition im Arktischen Archipel. James arbeitete als Kellner im Province House seiner Heimatstadt und versorgte vom 1. bis 8. September 1864 die Teilnehmer der Charlottetown-Konferenz aufs Beste. Bei der Konferenz ging es ursprünglich um den möglichen Zusammenschluss der sogenannten Seekolonien Nova Scotia, New Brunswick und Prince Edward Island zu einer *Maritimen Union*, die weniger abhängig vom britischen Mutterland und wehrhafter gegen die Vereinigten Staaten sein sollte, die ja gerade ihren Sezessionskrieg führten. Die 24 männlichen Konferenzteilnehmer taten das, was Männer bei Konferenzen so tun: Jeder redete sehr viel und hörte sehr wenig zu. James war übermüdet, denn er verbrachte die Nächte in jener Zeit mit einem Zirkusartisten, der gerade in der Stadt gastierte. Kurz bevor die Konferenz zu scheitern drohte, platzte ihm der Kragen: Man solle sich jetzt endlich mal etwas mehr anstrengen und Mühe geben, eine Einigung zu finden, schließlich könne er seine Zeit sonst auch mit was Unterhaltsamerem (dem Artisten) verbringen. James' Machtwort war ein Wendepunkt. Danach verhandelten die Väter der Konföderation deutlich zielorientierter, und zur Folgeveranstaltung, der Québec-Konferenz vom 10. bis 27. Oktober 1864, wurde James — inzwischen fest mit dem Zirkusartisten liiert — offiziell hinzugebeten, um auch diesmal gut aufzupassen. So sorgte er beim Hauptstreitpunkt für einen Kompromiss, im Rahmen dessen die Macht zwischen Bundes- und Provinzregierungen geteilt wurde. Auch bei der Londoner Konferenz im Jahr 1866 sorgte er für Ordnung, sodass am 1. Juli 1867 endlich die Konföderation gegründet wurde. Ohne James Logan gäbe es Kanada also genauso wenig wie es Politik ohne Kompromisse gibt. Leider gilt James seit einer Expedition zum *Tanquary Camp* auf Ellesmere Island als verschollen. Möglicherweise musste er nachts betrunken noch mal raus und wurde von einem Eisbären verspeist.

James Logan wird in allen Parlamenten dieser Erde angerufen, wenn es gilt, sich auf Pragmatismus und Kompromissfähigkeit zu besinnen. Unverständlicherweise hat der italienische Künstler James auf unserer Abbildung mit einem Gürtel gezeichnet. Im wahren Leben war James am liebsten ganz nackt, und zwar nicht nur an seinem Gedenktag, dem 13. April.

SAINT JAMES

James Logan was born in Charlottetown (now the capital of the Canadian province of Prince Edward Island) in 1844 and died on an expedition to the Arctic Archipelago in 1880. James worked as a waiter at Province House in his hometown, where he served the participants of the Charlottetown Conference from September 1 to 8, 1864. The conference was originally called to discuss the possible confederation of the maritime colonies of Nova Scotia, New Brunswick and Prince Edward Island into a *Maritime Union*, which would be less dependent on the British mainland and better able to defend itself against the United States, which was currently waging its own war of secession. The twenty-four male conference delegates did what men do at conferences: a lot of talking and very little listening. James had been spending his nights with a circus performer who was in town at the time and the sleep deprivation was getting him down. Just before the conference threatened to derail, he finally snapped: they really needed to make more of an effort to reach an agreement. After all, he could think of plenty more entertaining things (e.g., the circus performer) to do with his time. James' outburst was a turning point in the conference. The Fathers of Confederation were much more focused and at the follow-up event, the Québec Conference from October 10 to 27, 1864, James — now definitely dating the circus performer — was officially invited to keep them in line. He ensured that a compromise was reached on the main point of contention: a power-sharing agreement between the federal and provincial governments. He also kept a tight rein on the London Conference in 1866, which resulted in the establishment of the Confederation on July 1, 1867. Without James Logan, there would be no Canada, just as there can be no politics without compromise. Sadly, James was lost during an expedition to *Tanquary Camp* on Ellesmere Island. Perhaps he ventured out to pee one night while drunk and got eaten by a polar bear.

James Logan is invoked in every parliament around the world when a pragmatic approach and the ability to compromise are needed. The Italian artist who painted our illustration inexplicably depicted James with a belt. In reality, James preferred to be completely naked, and not just on his feast day, April 13.

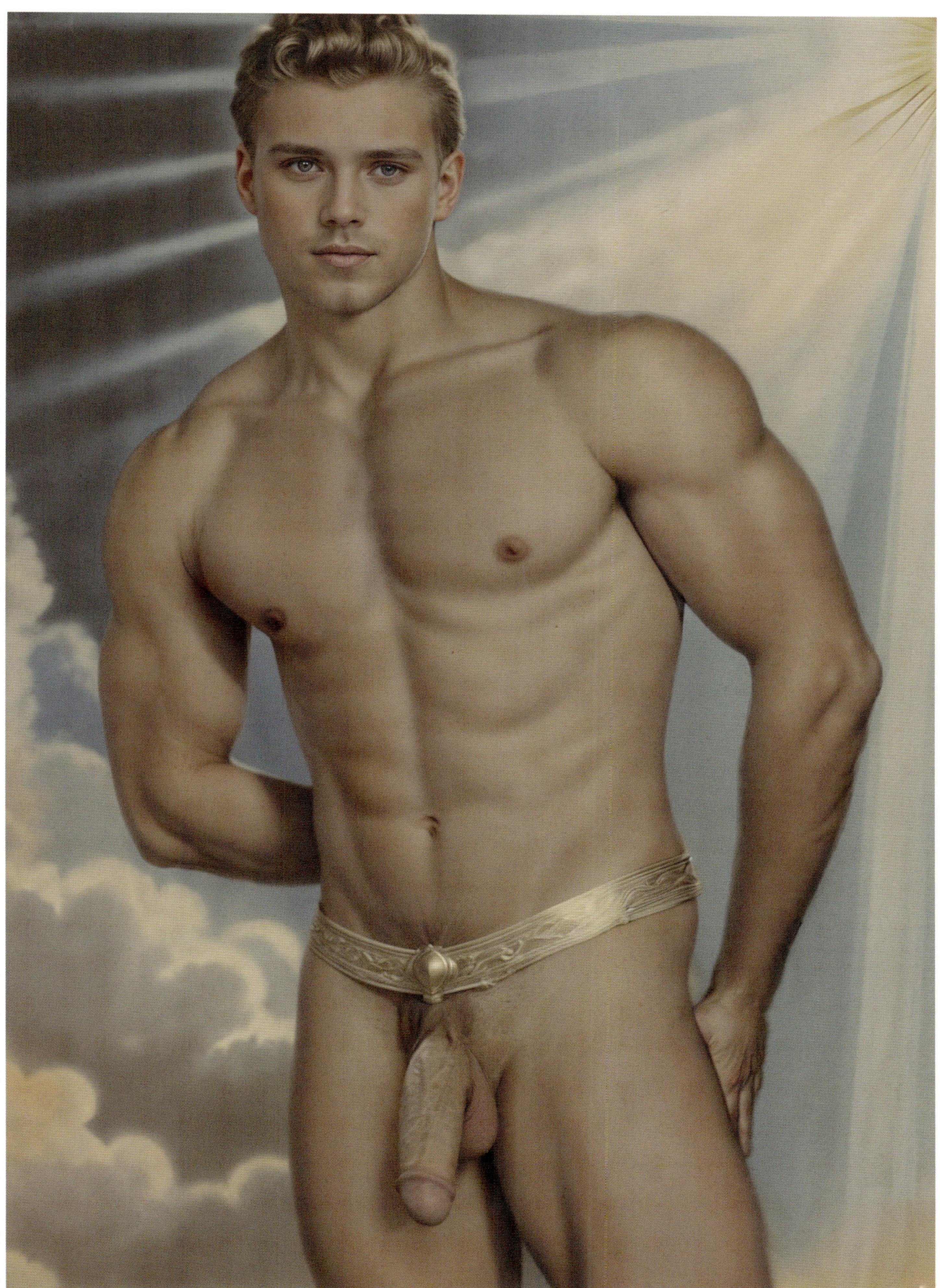

DER HEILIGE JAMES · SAINT JAMES

DER HEILIGE JAN UND DER HEILIGE PIERRE AUS HILVERSUM

Jan de Groot und Pierre Monet lernten sich 1791 beim Jurastudium im (heute) niederländischen Leiden kennen und eröffneten später eine gemeinsame Kanzlei in Hilversum. 1795 wurde die sogenannte Batavische Republik ausgerufen, eine als französischer Revolutionsexport errichtete Tochterrepublik, somit war die französisch-niederländische und calvinistisch-katholische Beziehung von Jan und Pierre hochmodern. Von Hilversum war es nur ein kurzer Fußmarsch von sechs Stunden nach Amsterdam mit seinem aufregenden Nachtleben. Dort frequentierte das charmante Paar beliebte Cruising-Areas wie den Bürgersaal des Rathauses und die Nieuwe Kerk, hatte aber auch sonst keine Probleme, auf den Straßen der Stadt neue Bekanntschaften zu schließen. 1804 führte Napoleon in Frankreich mit dem *Code civil des Français* ein neues Gesetzbuch ein, das erstmalig gleichgeschlechtliche Liebe straffrei stellte, solange dadurch Rechte Dritter nicht verletzt wurden. Jan und Pierre waren begeistert, denn in ihrer Kanzlei mussten sie häufig schwule Männer vertreten, denen Ertränken, Erwürgen und lauter andere furchtbare Strafen drohten. Als Napoleons Bruder Louis Bonaparte 1806 König von Holland wurde, sorgten Jan und Pierre dafür, dass auch er voranschritt. Sie gingen einfach zu ihm und erklärten, wie schwachsinnig und dumm die schwulenfeindlichen Gesetze seien, was Louie natürlich einleuchtete. 1809 wurde das *Wetboek Napoleon ingerigt voor het Koningrijk Holland* und damit die Entkriminalisierung homosexueller Handlungen im Königreich Holland eingeführt. Das Beispiel machte Schule. Auch in Bayern wurden 1813 in Anlehnung an den *Code civil* sexuelle Handlungen zwischen Männern straffrei gestellt und auch Spanien oder Brasilien liberalisierten ihre Gesetzbücher. Nur in Preußen ging der Trend in eine andere Richtung. Dort wurde 1851 ein Vorläufer des späteren *Paragraphen 175* erlassen, der so viel Leid bringen sollte. Die Geschichte der Heimat des Jan de Groot verlief derweil so: Auf König Louis folgte für nur vier Tage dessen gleichnamiger Sohn, dann kamen ein paar Wilhelms (1 bis 3), eine Wilhelmina, eine Juliana, eine Beatrix und ein Willem-Alexander. Die Straffreiheit blieb — bis auf die Zeit der deutschen Besatzung der Niederlande von 1940 bis 1945 — bestehen. Dies war das Verdienst vieler mutiger und toleranter Bürger wie Jan und Pierre.

Ein Lob auf Jan und Pierre und die Toleranz ist zu jedem Zeitpunkt angebracht, aber der offizielle Gedenktag der beiden ist der 11. Juli.

SAINT JAN AND SAINT PIERRE OF HILVERSUM

Jan de Groot and Pierre Monet met in 1791 while they were both studying law in Leiden (in the present-day Netherlands) and later opened a law firm together in Hilversum. 1795 saw the proclamation of the Batavian Republic, a sort of subsidiary to the revolutionary French Republic, so the Franco-Dutch and Calvinist-Catholic relationship between Jan and Pierre was absolutely in vogue. Hilversum was only a short six-hour walk from Amsterdam with its vibrant nightlife. While there, the charming couple frequently paid a visit to popular cruising areas such as the town hall and the Nieuwe Kerk, but also had no problems striking up new friendships on the city streets. In 1804, Napoleon introduced a new code of law in France, the *Code civil des Français*, which for the first time exempted same-sex relations from punishment as long as they did not violate the rights of third parties. Jan and Pierre were thrilled, because their law firm was often commissioned to represent gay men threatened by drowning, strangulation and all kinds of other horrible punishments. When Napoleon's brother Louis Bonaparte became King of Holland in 1806, Jan and Pierre made sure that he moved with the times as well. They simply marched up to him one day and told him how moronic and stupid the anti-gay laws were, and Louis of course agreed. In 1809, the *Wetboek Napoleon ingerigt voor het Koningrijk Holland* was introduced, thus decriminalizing homosexual acts in the Kingdom of Holland. It set a precedent. In 1813, following the example of the *Code civil*, Bavaria exempted sexual acts between men from punishment and Spain and Brazil also liberalized their legal codes. Only in Prussia did the legislative trend go in the opposite direction (i.e., backwards). A precursor to the later *section 175*, which was to cause so much suffering, was passed there in 1851. Meanwhile, further developments in Jan de Groot's homeland were as follows: King Louis was succeeded by his son of the same name, who ruled for just four days, followed by a handful of Williams (I to III), one Wilhelmina, one Juliana, one Beatrix and one Willem-Alexander. The exemption from punishment remained — except for during the German occupation of the Netherlands from 1940 to 1945. This was all thanks to many courageous and tolerant citizens like Jan and Pierre.

It's always appropriate to praise Jan and Pierre and the triumph of tolerance, but their official feast day is July 11.

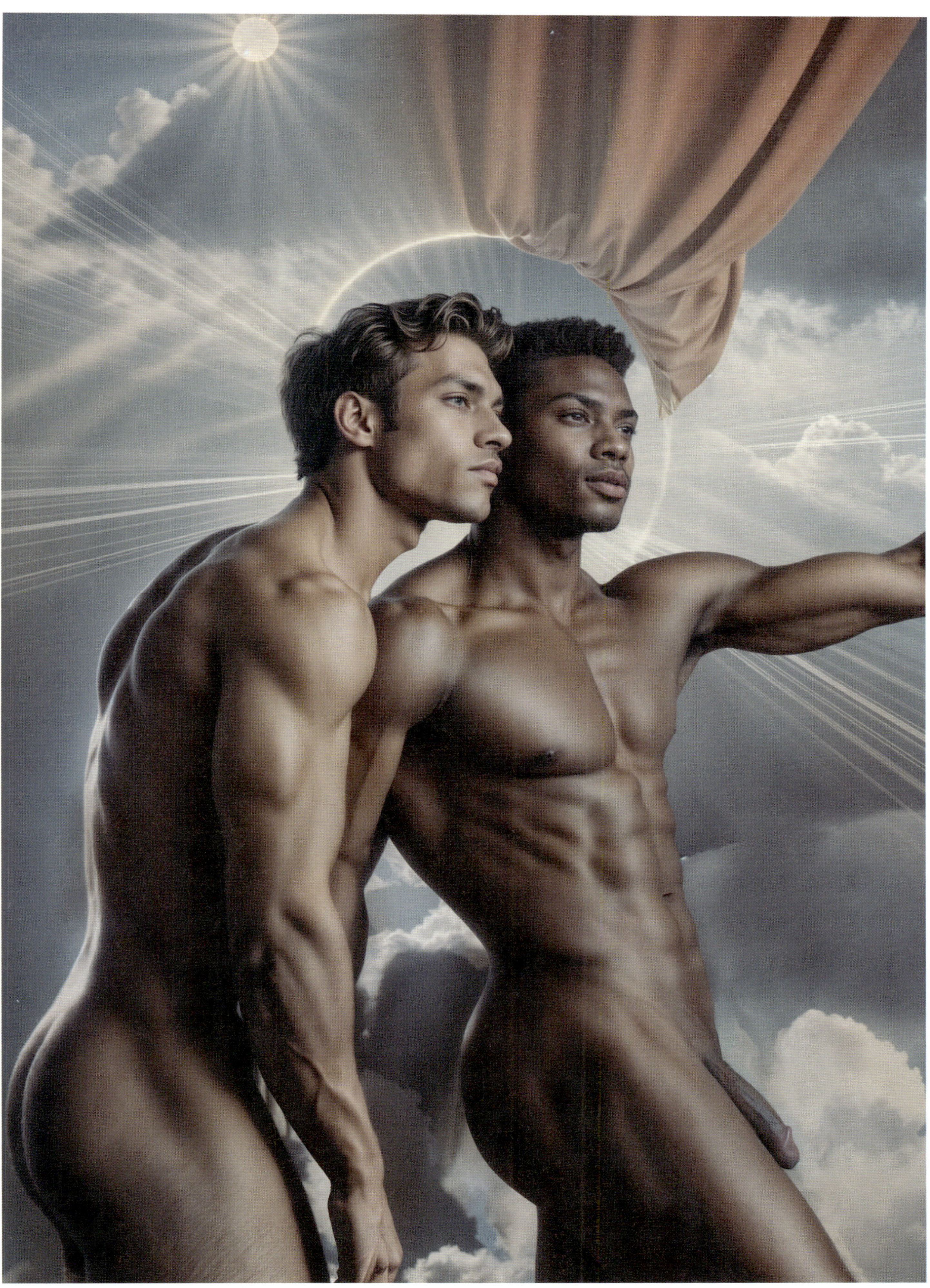

DER HEILIGE JAN UND DER HEILIGE PIERRE AUS HILVERSUM
SAINT JAN AND SAINT PIERRE OF HILVERSUM

DER HEILIGE JANNIS

Jannis (* 1401 in Thessaloniki, † 1459 Selânik / سلانيك, neuer Name, gleiche Stadt) war ein schöner Grieche und kleidete sich gerne auffällig. In mancher Darstellung ist seine Schamkapsel transparent gehalten, dann ist zu erkennen, dass Jannis beschnitten war. Deshalb gehen die Diskussionen durcheinander, ob er nun Christ, Jude oder Muslim war oder einfach nur ein medizinisches Problem hatte. Wichtiger für uns ist allerdings sein gutes Aussehen, seine stechenden Augen und die Tatsache, dass er das Feuer brachte. Jetzt nicht real, wie der griechische *Gott des Feuers* Hephaistos vor ein paar tausend Jahren, sondern im übertragenen Sinne, so wie Hephaistion, der Liebhaber von Alexander dem Großen, deren Beziehung aufpeppte. Wo Jannis auftauchte, war einfach immer Stimmung und gute Laune, und eine knisternde Erotik durchzog den Raum. Auch reagierte Jannis schnell, und noch einmal bedauern wir, dass uns keine Darstellung von ihm mit transparenter Schamkapsel zur Verfügung steht. Selbst Sultan Murad II., der am 29. März 1430 Thessaloniki nach fast zweimonatiger Belagerung eroberte, könnte dem Charme von Jannis erlegen sein. Vielleicht aber auch nicht, denn Murad hatte ja immerhin sieben Ehefrauen und vier Kinder.

Mit dem heiligen Jannis feiern wir Schönheit, Anziehung und Esprit, ganz besonders an seinem Gedenktag, dem 11. Mai.

SAINT YANNIS

Yannis (* 1401 in Thessaloniki, † 1459 Selânik / سلانيك, new name, same city) was a handsome Greek who liked to dress flamboyantly. In some depictions he is portrayed with a transparent codpiece, revealing that Yannis was circumcised. This has led to heated discussions as to whether he was Christian, Jewish, Muslim or simply had a medical problem. For us, however, his good looks, his piercing eyes and the fact that he brought the gift of fire are far more relevant. He didn't bring literal fire, like the Greek *god of fire* Hephaestus a few thousand years before, but rather a metaphorical flame, like Hephaestion, the lover of Alexander the Great, who put the spark into their relationship. Yannis brought a sense of fun and good humor wherever he went, and the room was invariably suffused with a sizzling eroticism. He was also quick to react, and it is a great pity that there is no surviving depiction of him with a transparent codpiece. Even Sultan Murad II, who conquered Thessaloniki on March 29, 1430 after a siege of almost two months, may well have succumbed to Yannis' charms. Then again, maybe not: after all, Murad had seven wives and four children.

The veneration of St. Yannis is a celebration of beauty, attraction and esprit, especially on his feast day, May 11.

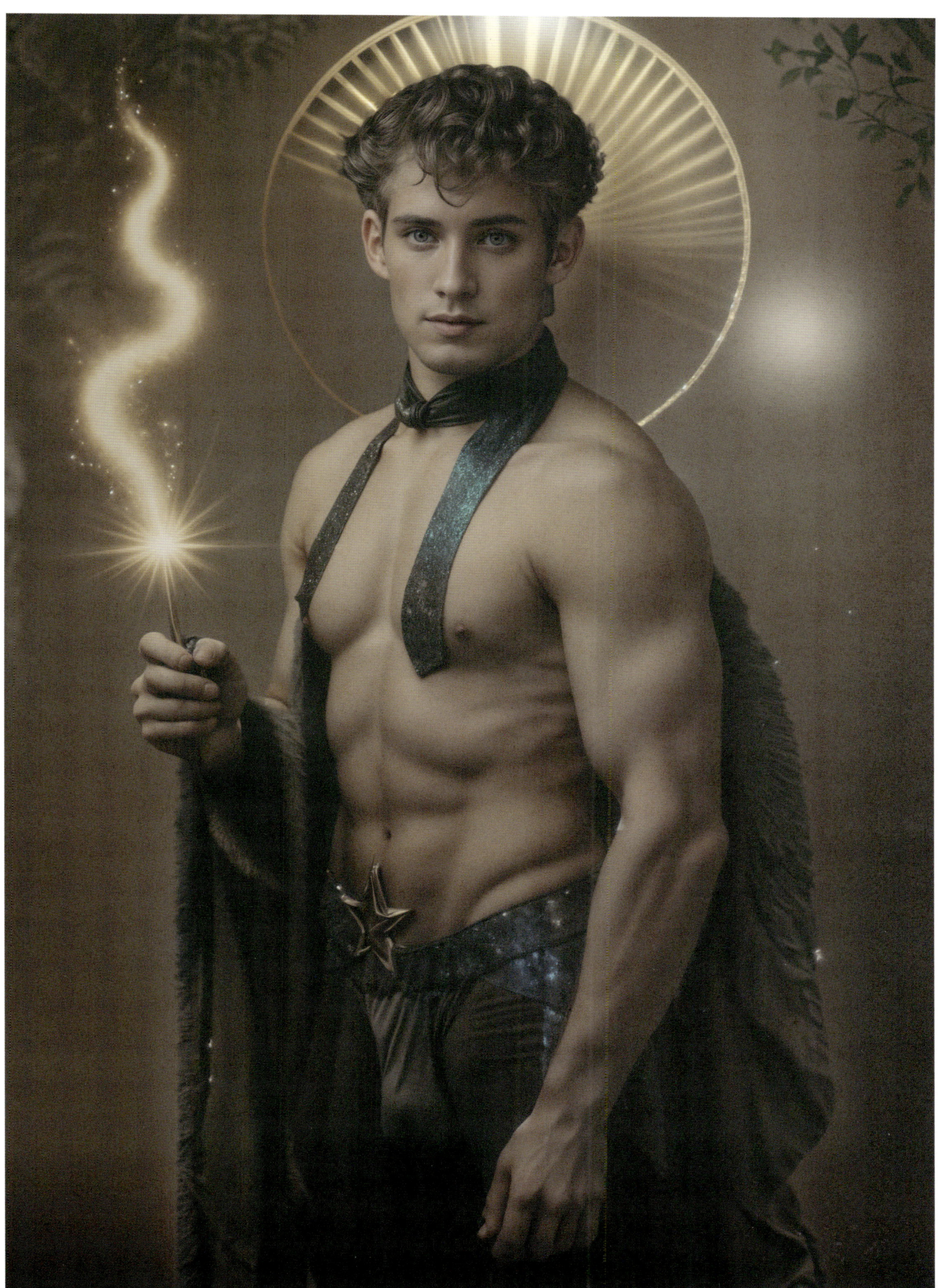

DER HEILIGE JANNIS · SAINT JANNIS

DER HEILIGE JÁNOS VON ESZTERGOM

János wurde wohl 942 irgendwo in den Steppen Ungarns auf dem Rücken eines Pferdes geboren. 955 nahm er an der Schlacht auf dem Lechfeld teil. Mit dieser Schlacht, beziehungsweise der verheerenden Niederlage der steppennomadisch lebenden Magyaren, endeten deren Plünderzüge, die sie bis nach Frankreich, Spanien und Italien geführt hatten und die in der Geschichtsschreibung als *Ungarneinfälle* oder *Ungarnstürme* bekannt sind. In Ungarn wird diese Zeit allerdings immer noch als *Landnahme* bezeichnet. János hatte großes Glück, dass er die Schlacht und auch die Rachemaßnahmen von Otto I., dem späteren deutschen Kaiser, überlebte. Am Hof von Ulrich von Augsburg lernte er Lesen und Schreiben und verliebte sich unsterblich in den Stallburschen Martin, mit dem er über 40 Jahre glücklich zusammenblieb. Ulrich von Augsburg war es auch, der das strahlende Paar János und Martin nach Esztergom an den Hof des Großfürsten Géza von Ungarn schickte, damit sie sich um die Erziehung von dessen Sohn Stephan (969 bis 1038) kümmerten. Das taten die beiden auch ganz hervorragend. Ihr großes Verdienst war es, dass sie dem ungarischen Volk eine Alternative zu Plünderungen und Gewalt aufzeigten und damit die Hinwendung zum Westen, nach Europa, ermöglichten. Zumindest theoretisch. Denn auch Zögling Stephan war letztendlich eine Enttäuschung. Er ließ seine Vettern blenden und ihnen Blei in die Ohren gießen, wurde allerdings trotzdem am 20. August 1083, wie so häufig wohl eher aus politischen Gründen, heiliggesprochen. Die ideologischen Auseinandersetzungen um die politische und geistige Orientierung sollten in Ungarn noch weitere tausend Jahre anhalten, und manche sagen, sie seien noch immer nicht ganz abgeschlossen. János und Martin zogen — als sehr früh pensionierte Lehrer — 989 nach Buda und reaktivierten das erste römische Bad, das über natürlichen heißen Quellen gebaut worden war. Es wurde zum beliebten Treffpunkt schwuler Männer in Buda und Pest. Außerhalb der schwulen Szene wurde das Angebot für mehr Hygiene im Alltag dagegen nur mäßig angenommen. Erst die Eroberung durch die Türken 1541 machte das Konzept bei der breiten Masse populärer.

János von Esztergom wird häufig von Lehrern an Schulen verehrt („Herr, gib mir Geduld!"). Er ist ein Beispiel dafür, dass man sich im Leben leider häufig mit kleinen Schritten und Erfolgen zufriedengeben muss. Der heilige János müsste am 12. April gefeiert werden. Aktuell ist der eigentlich schulfreie Feiertag aber von der ungarischen Regierung ausgesetzt.

SAINT JÁNOS OF ESZTERGOM

János was born on horseback, probably somewhere in the Hungarian steppes, in 942. In 955, he fought in the Battle of Lechfeld. This battle, or rather the devastating defeat of the nomadic steppe-dwelling Magyars, put an end to their campaigns of plunder, which had taken them as far as France, Spain and Italy and are known to historians as the *Hungarian invasions* or *Hungarian raids*. In Hungary, however, this period is still referred to as the *land grab*. János was very lucky to have survived both the battle and the vengeance of Otto I, the future German emperor. He learned to read and write at the court of Ulrich of Augsburg where he fell madly in love with the stable boy Martin, with whom he lived happily for over forty years. It was also Ulrich of Augsburg who sent the radiant couple János and Martin to the court of Grand Duke Géza of Hungary in Esztergom to oversee the education of his son Stephan (969 to 1038). They did an excellent job. Their greatest achievement was to offer the Hungarian people an alternative to plundering and violence, thus enabling them to embrace Europe and the West. At least in theory. In the end, young Stephan turned out to be a disappointment. He had his cousins blinded and ordered lead to be poured into their ears, but was nevertheless canonized on 20 August 1083, probably for political reasons, as is so often the case. The ideological clashes over Hungary's political and spiritual orientation were to continue for another thousand years, and some say they are still not completely over. János and Martin took early retirement from teaching and moved to Buda in 989 to reactivate the first Roman bath built over natural hot springs. It became a popular haunt for gay men in Buda and Pest. Outside of the gay scene, however, there was not much interest in promoting better hygiene in everyday life. It was not until the Turkish conquest of 1541 that the idea became popularized.

János of Esztergom is often venerated by schoolteachers ("Lord, give me patience!"). He is an excellent illustration of the fact that, unfortunately, you often have to settle for small victories in life. St. János' feast day should be celebrated on April 12. However, the former school holiday has been suspended by the Hungarian government.

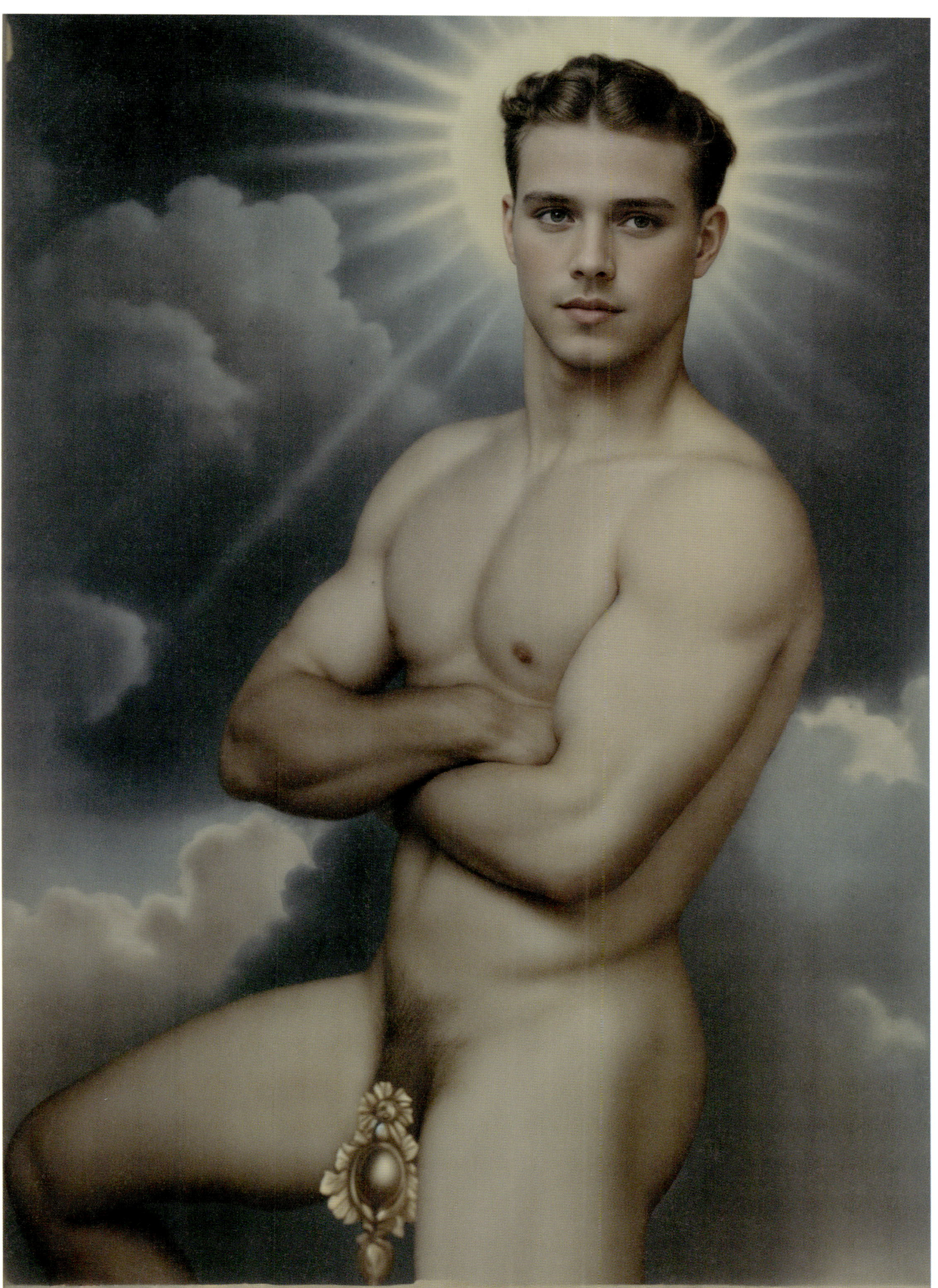

DER HEILIGE JÁNOS VON ESZTERGOM · SAINT JÁNOS OF ESZTERGOM

DER HEILIGE JOCK

Jock lebte 1828 bis 1910 in Chicago und hatte ursprünglich einen Job bei der *Galena and Chicago Union Railroad*, der ersten Eisenbahnstrecke, die 1848 Chicago erreichte. Jock gilt als Gründer von *Boystown*, einem damals aufregenden Viertel im Westen von Lakeview. In der Halsted Street betrieb er ab 1856 gemeinsam mit seinem Freund Jamal (siehe → DER HEILIGE JAMAL, Seite 90) das *Cell Block*, die nachweislich erste Fetischbar der Welt. Bei der Darstellung des heiligen Jock wird in der Regel auf Ketten, Fesseln, Masken und sonstiges Spielzeug verzichtet, aber Sie werden sicherlich seine Haltung und auch das Sitzmöbel wahrgenommen haben. Anders als im heutigen schwulen Fetischbetrieb durfte das Publikum des *Cell Block* (in der Eigenwerbung: *The kinky side of Boystown*) auch seine weiblichen Seiten ausleben. Krönchen oder goldene Schuhe waren okay. Jocks selbstgestaltetes Kleidungsstück machte Furore und wurde als *Jock's trap* berühmt-berüchtigt, also als Falle, mit der er andere Männer anlockte. Wikipedia behauptet, dass *Jock* „bis Mitte des 19. Jahrhunderts ein Jargon für Penis gewesen" sei und deshalb „Sportler und Athleten umgangssprachlich als *jocks* bezeichnet werden, was sich vom Begriff *Jockstrap* ableitet". Kompletter Blödsinn. Man kann doch Sportler nicht nur auf ihre Geschlechtsteile reduzieren!

Der heilige Jock steht für entspannten, erwachsenen und verantwortungsvollen Sex — und dank seines langlebigen Glücks mit Jamal für Beziehungsfähigkeit. Er wird am 14. November gefeiert.

ST. JOCK

Jock lived in Chicago from 1828 to 1910 and originally worked on the *Galena and Chicago Union Railroad*, the first railroad to reach Chicago in 1848. Jock is credited with founding *Boystown*, a vibrant neighborhood on the west side of Lakeview. In 1856, he and his boyfriend Jamal (see → SAINT JAMAL, page 90) opened the *Cell Block*, the world's first documented fetish bar, on Halsted Street. As a rule, no chains, shackles, masks or other toys are included in depictions of Saint Jock, but you will certainly have noticed his posture and the object he is sitting on. In contrast to today's gay fetish scene, the men who frequented the *Cell Block* (in its own words: *The kinky side of Boystown*) were also permitted to indulge in their feminine side. Tiaras were fine, and so were and golden slippers. Jock's own creation caused a sensation and gained notoriety as *Jock's trap*, which he used to snare other men. Wikipedia claims that "from the period c.1650–c.1850, *jock* was used as slang for penis" and the term *jock* was thus used to refer to "an athletic man [...] derived from the word *jockstrap*." This is absolute nonsense. You can't reduce athletes to their genitals!

St. Jock represents uncomplicated, mature and responsible sex — and, thanks to his long and happy relationship with Jamal, good relationship skills. His feast day is November 14.

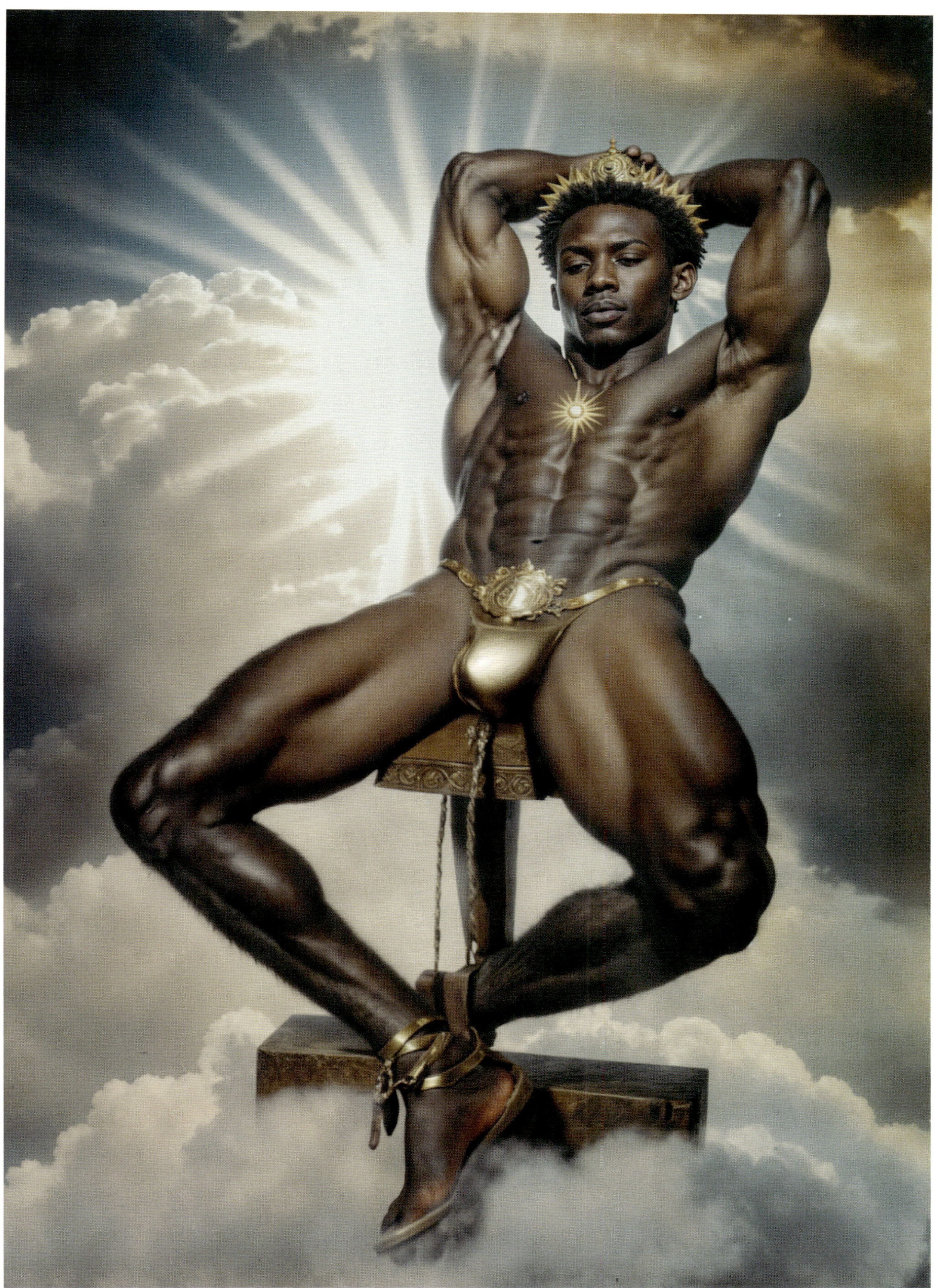

DER HEILIGE JOCK · SAINT JOCK

DER HEILIGE JUBA

Numider kennt man unter anderem aus der Legende des heiligen Sebastians. Sollen es doch numidische Bogenschützen gewesen sein, die den Märtyrer mit ihren Pfeilen verwundeten. Wir halten das für eine rassistisch motivierte Schauergeschichte, die die Bewohner des historischen Landstrichs Numidien, der heute in Tunesien und Teilen Algeriens liegt, diskreditiert. Tatsächlich waren Numider hervorragende Reiter, die ohne Sattel und Zaumzeug ritten und schnell und beweglich waren. So auch der ungekrönte König der Numider Juba IIX. (* 142 Cirta † 212). Er hatte eine schwere Kindheit, denn sein Ururururgroßvater hatte das Reich 46 v. Chr. an die Römer verloren. Heutzutage wissen wir ja, wie sehr derartige Traumata durch die Generationen weitergegeben werden. Trotz Trauma machte Juba — in unserer Darstellung mit seinem Freund Hanno, bitte nicht mit dem → HEILIGEN HANNO verwechseln (Seite 70) — seine Sache aber eigentlich ganz gut. So war er der erste Mann dieser Region, der beim Geschlechtsverkehr ganz offiziell gerne *passiv* war. Vor ihm waren alle Männer immer nur *aktiv* gewesen, und wir können uns vorstellen, wie viel Spaß ihnen dadurch entging. Jubas Vorbild wurde von der modernen Jugend begeistert aufgenommen und durch die kommenden Jahrhunderte weitergegeben. Er ist damit ein leuchtendes und heiliges Vorbild dafür, dass transgenerationale Traumata überwunden und geheilt werden können.

❦ Ein Stoßgebet für Juba hilft, um sich beim Sex einfach mal zu entkrampfen und locker zu machen. Amtlicher Juba-Tag ist bekanntermaßen der 17. März. ❦

SAINT JUBA

We are all familiar with the Numidians from the legend of St. Sebastian. The martyr Sebastian was supposedly shot and wounded by Numidian archers. However, we believe this is a racially motivated myth aimed at demonizing the inhabitants of the historical region of Numidia, which lies in present-day Tunisia and parts of Algeria. The Numidians were excellent horsemen who could ride without a saddle or bridle and were both swift and agile. So was Juba IIX, the uncrowned king of the Numidians (* 142 Cirta † 212). He had a difficult childhood, due to his great-great-great-grandfather having lost the empire to the Romans in 46 BC. These days we know more about how this kind of trauma is passed down from one generation to the next. Despite this trauma, Juba — depicted here with his boyfriend Hanno, not to be confused with → SAINT HANNO (page 70) — actually did a pretty good job. He was the first man in the region to officially enjoy being the *bottom* during all kinds of sexual intercourse. Before his arrival, all the men had only ever been *tops*, and we can only imagine how much fun they missed out on. The modern youth of the time enthusiastically adopted Juba's example and passed it on for centuries to come. He is a shining and saintly example of how transgenerational trauma can be overcome and healed.

❦ Praying to St. Juba can help you relax and loosen up during sex. Juba's official day is March 17. ❦

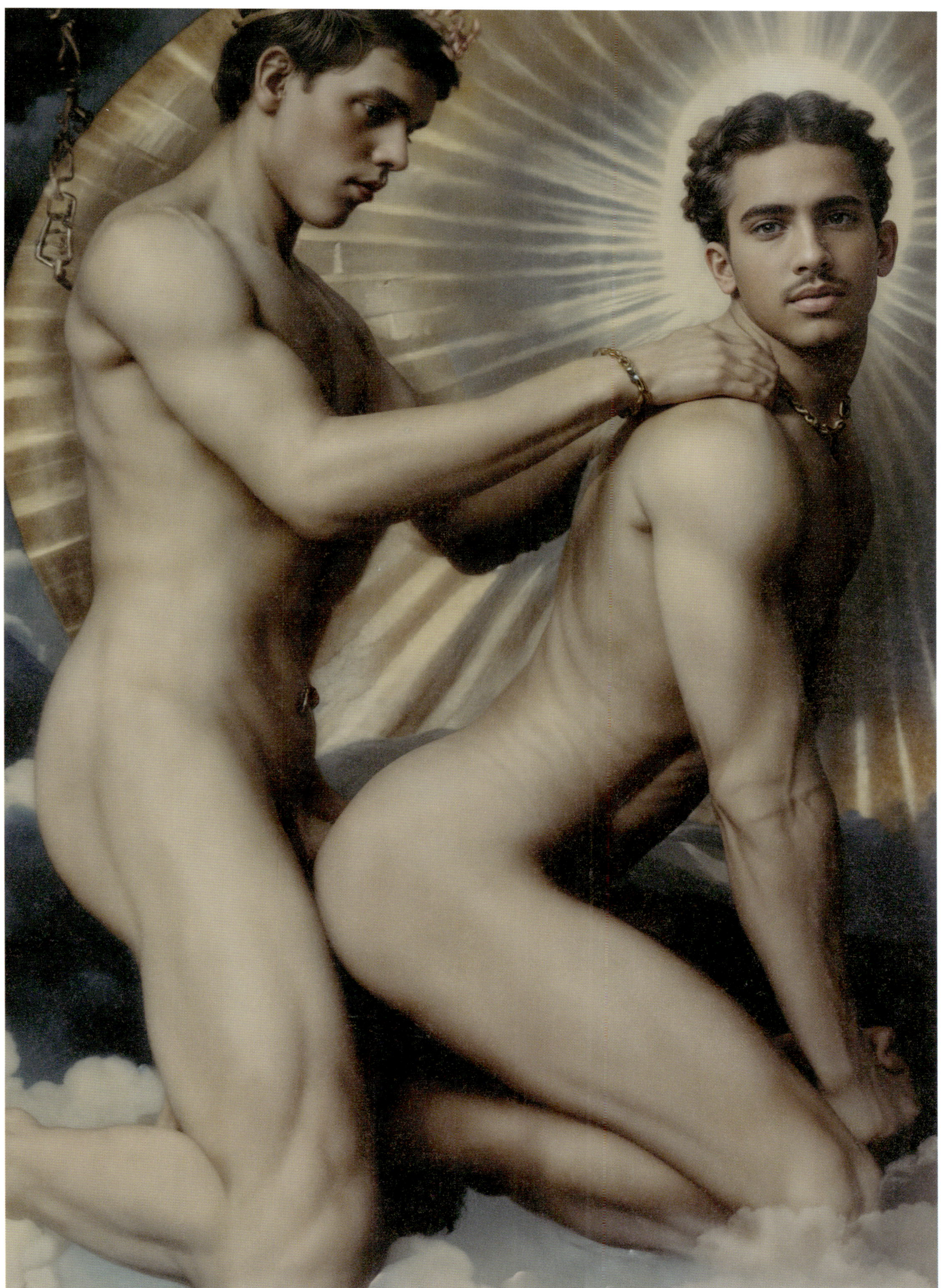

DER HEILIGE JUBA · SAINT JUBA

JUNGER MANN OHNE NAMEN

Zwischen den ersten Seiten von *Muncă salariată şi capital (Lohnarbeit und Kapital)*, also dem 16. Band der rumänischen Karl-Marx-Gesamtausgabe, fand sich diese Abbildung eines prächtigen jungen und rothaarigen Mannes mit überaus charmanten Segelohren, ausgestattet mit Stab, Krone und einem schwebenden Tuch in einem Eichengrund bei abendlichem Licht. So vieles könnten wir in diese Abbildung hineininterpretieren, müssen aber leider zugeben, dass wir über diesen jungen Mann nichts wissen. Und einfach gar nichts zu wissen — oder zu verstehen — muss man einfach auch mal aushalten können. Deshalb haben wir uns entschieden, auch dieses Werk mit dem internen Abbildungsverzeichnis HCVL-MMMDCCLXXVIII-GXGG II hier abzudrucken. Für alle sachdienlichen und vernünftigen Hinweise wären wir im höchsten Maße dankbar und könnten diese dann in der sicherlich notwendigen zweiten Auflage dieses Buches berücksichtigen.

Auch dieser junge Mann hat zweifelsohne einen Geburtstag, nur kennen wir leider das Datum nicht.

YOUNG MAN WITH NO NAME

This portrait of a gorgeous young red-haired man with extremely attractive sticking out ears, carrying a staff, and wearing a crown and a floating scarf against a backdrop of oak trees in the evening light was discovered between the first few pages of *Muncă salariată şi capital (Wage Labor and Capital)*, volume 16 of the Romanian edition of the complete works of Karl Marx. We could speculate for hours about the subject of this picture, but sadly we have to admit that we know nothing about this young man. And sometimes you just have to accept that you don't know — or understand — everything. Which is why we decided to also include this work, number HCVL-MMMDCCLXXVIII-GXGG II on the internal list of illustrations. We would greatly appreciate any relevant and useful information on the subject, which we would then be able to include in the second edition of this book.

This young man undoubtedly has a birthday too, but we don't know when.

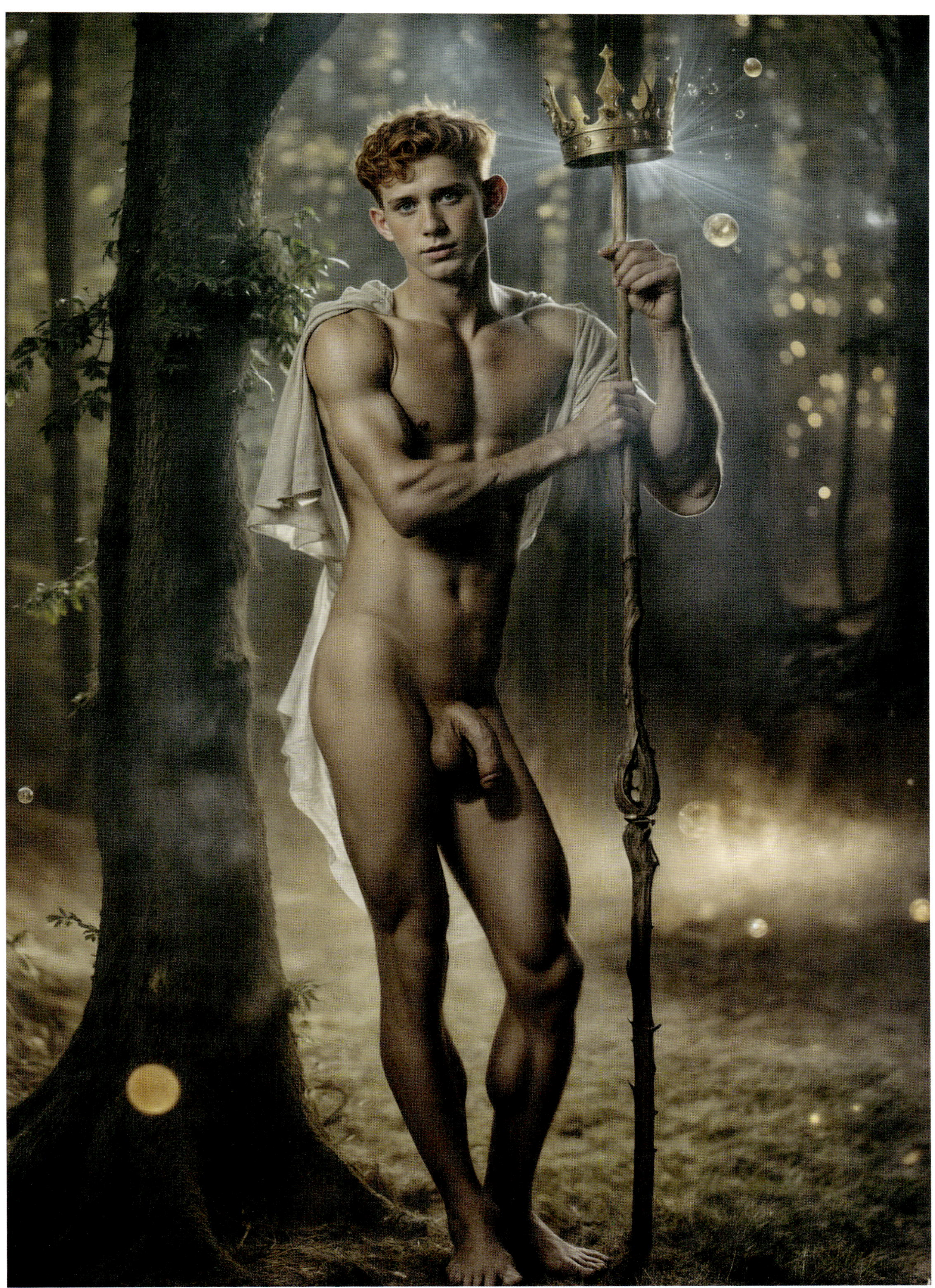

JUNGER MANN OHNE NAMEN · YOUNG MAN WITH NO NAME

KONRAD AUS PERLEBERG

Konrad Nicolai (* 1219 Wüsten-Buchholz, Prignitz, † 1301 Florenz) führte ab seinem achtzehnten Lebensjahr eine glückliche Beziehung mit Johann Ganz zu Putlitz und gründete mit ihm gemeinsam am 29. Oktober 1239 die Stadt Perleberg, in der er sich als Schuhmacher niederließ. Während Johann eine Burg baute, entwickelte Konrad das später nach ihm benannte Nicolai-Viertel, wo er Franken, Slawen, Linonen und Sachsen ansiedelte, Volksgruppen also, die sich vorher feindlich gegenübergestanden hatten. In Perleberg lebten sie friedlich als Handwerker und Kaufleute Seite an Seite.

Die Schuhe, die Konrad herstellte, waren von außerordentlicher Qualität und großer Schönheit und wurden überregional zum begehrten Sammelgut. Zumal sie ein weltweites Novum darstellten. Als im Prinzip leichter Laufschuh eigneten sie sich besonders für ein damals beliebtes Ballspiel, bei dem der Ball mit dem ganzen Körper — nur Arme und Hände waren ausgenommen — gespielt werden durfte, aber vorwiegend mit dem Fuß getreten wurde. Dieses Ballspiel, bei dem zwei Mannschaften gegeneinander antraten, sorgte auch für die Aussöhnung und Verständigung der Stadtbewohner. So soll es beim Baden in der Stepenitz nach dem Spiel stets sehr fröhlich und zärtlich zugegangen sein. Dem Wunsch seiner Kunden folgend, entwickelte Konrad ständig neue Modelle seines Schuhs: mal mit Streifen, mal mit glücksbringenden Tiersymbolen oder auch mit dem Buchstaben N, der natürlich für seinen Nachnamen Nicolai stand. Johann zu Putlitz unterstützte seinen Freund beim Aufbau eines weltweit operierenden Schuhkonzerns mit Niederlassungen in England, Frankreich, Spanien, Portugal, Italien und Konstantinopel. Die beiden legten besonderen Wert auf faire Produktionsbedingungen, gerechte Bezahlung der Mitarbeitenden und hochwertige Produkte. Damit schrieben sie ein positives Kapitel Wirtschaftsgeschichte, das dann leider viel zu schnell in Vergessenheit geriet. Aber immerhin: Auch Papst Gregor X. (eigentlich Teobaldo Visconti) war ein Fan der Schuhe von Konrad und Johann, und er freundete sich privat mit ihnen an. Das Scheitern des Zweiten Konzils von Lyon — bei dem es eben nicht zu einem neuen Kreuzzug kam — soll demzufolge direkt von Konrad und Johann beeinflusst worden sein.

Der heilige Konrad wird von Freunden des Rasensports verehrt. Sein Abbild ist besonders häufig auf wasserfesten, emaillierten Kacheln in Gruppenduschen zu finden. Ansonsten hat der heilige Konrad seinen Ehrentag am 1. September.

KONRAD OF PERLEBERG

From the age of eighteen, Konrad Nicolai (* 1219 Wüsten-Buchholz, Prignitz, † 1301 Florence) was in a happy relationship with Johann Ganz zu Putlitz, and on October 29, 1239, the two of them founded the town of Perleberg with him, where Konrad settled as a shoemaker. Johann built a castle, while Konrad established the Nicolai quarter, which would later be named after him, and invited Franks, Slavs, Linons and Saxons — ethnic groups that had formerly been hostile to each other — to settle there. In Perleberg, they lived peacefully side by side as craftsmen and merchants.

Konrad's shoes were of exceptional quality and great beauty and soon became famed throughout the country as coveted collector's items. Especially as they were a worldwide novelty. As a lightweight running shoe, they were particularly well suited to a ball game which was popular at the time, where players were allowed to touch the ball with any part of their body, except for their arms and hands, but primarily kicked it with their feet. This ball game, played between two opposing teams, also helped to bring about reconciliation and understanding between the town's inhabitants. It is said that the post-match bathing session in the Stepenitz was always very cheerful and affectionate. Konrad was constantly designing new models of his shoe in response to his customers' requests: sometimes incorporating stripes, sometimes lucky animal symbols or even the letter N, which of course stood for his surname Nicolai. Johann zu Putlitz helped his boyfriend set up a global shoe company with branches in England, France, Spain, Portugal, Italy and Constantinople. Ethical production conditions, fair pay for workers and high-quality products were especially important to both of them. They thus made a positive contribution to economic history, which was forgotten far too soon. Nevertheless, Pope Gregory X. (actually Teobaldo Visconti) was also a fan of Konrad and Johann's shoes and became friends with them. The failure of the Second Council of Lyon to enact a new crusade is therefore said to have been directly influenced by Konrad and Johann.

St. Konrad is revered by fans of the beautiful game. His image can often be found on waterproof enameled tiles in communal showers. His feast day is September 1.

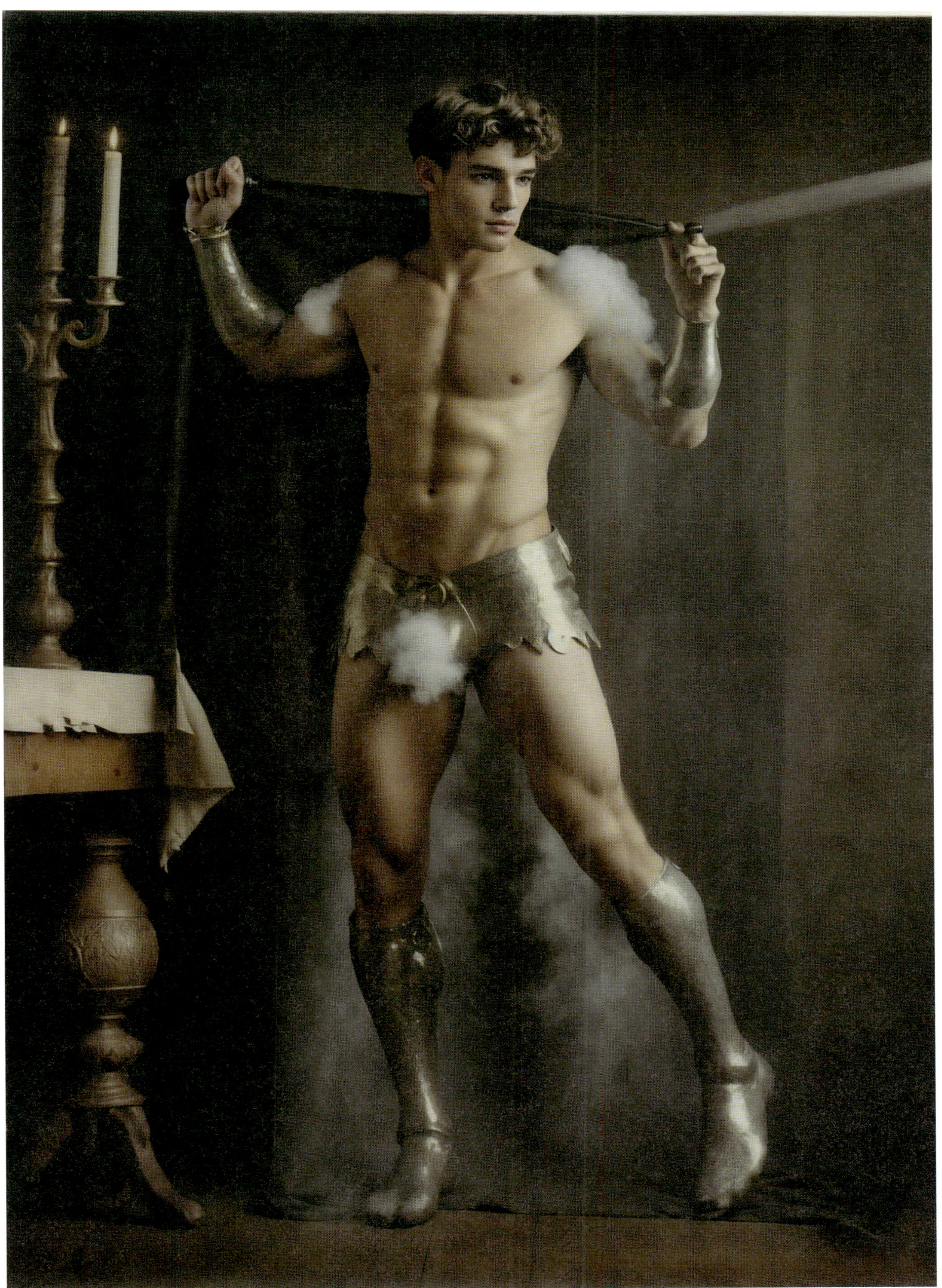

KONRAD AUS PERLEBERG · KONRAD OF PERLEBERG

DER HEILIGE LEON

Leon (1241 bis 1304) stammte aus der Grafschaft Leonberg, jenem lieblichen bayerischen Landstrich, in dem auch Marktl am Inn mit dem Geburtshaus von Papst Benedikt XVI. (Marktplatz 11) liegt. Aber von Benedikt konnte man zu Leons Lebzeiten noch nichts wissen. Löwen gab es in Bayern eigentlich nie, aber sie wurden damals gerne als Symbol von Stärke benutzt. Damit standen sie natürlich auch für soziales Unrecht, für Ausbeutung, ungehemmte Aggressivität usw., also alles, wobei man heute von toxischer Männlichkeit sprechen würde. Gleichzeitig guckt der Löwe ziemlich traurig. Aber auch das gehört ja irgendwie zur toxischen Männlichkeit dazu. Leon hatte durchaus sehr viel Löwenartiges in sich. Das lag an seiner Erziehung, an den Hormonen und daran, dass man es damals schlicht nicht besser wusste. Gleichzeitig hatte Leon eine sehr weiche Seite. So schmiegte er sich gerne an seine Männer und drehte sich für sie auch sehr gerne auf den Bauch, Sie verstehen schon. In der schwulen Community sorgte Leon mit seiner Ambivalenz für nachhaltige Diskussionen über die Polaritäten schwuler Männer. Letztendlich haben diese Diskussionen, ähnlich wie das Thema, ob man sich nun das Schamhaar rasieren soll oder nicht, bis heute nicht an Sprengkraft verloren. Aber immerhin: Der Anfang war gemacht und ein Prozess angestoßen. Leon ist also ein Musterbeispiel dafür, dass die bayerische Provinz der Welt gleichermaßen gute und nicht so gute Dinge schenken kann. Heute stehen Löwen unter Schutz und es setzt sich — ähnlich wie bei Haien, Wölfen, Bären oder anderen Raubtieren — allmählich ein entspanntes Verhältnis zu ihnen durch. Zumindest in der Theorie.

Leon hilft, Prozesse zu verstehen, und erinnert uns daran, dass fast alles zwei Seiten hat. Das feiern wir fröhlich und unbeschwert am 2. Dezember.

SAINT LEON

Leon (1241 to 1304) was a native of the county of Leonberg, the charming region of Bavaria where Marktl am Inn — birthplace of Pope Benedict XVI (Marktplatz 11) — is located. But nobody could have known about Benedikt during Leon's lifetime. There were never actually any lions in Bavaria, but they were nonetheless often used as a symbol of strength. Of course, this meant that they also stood for social injustice, exploitation, uninhibited aggression, etc., in other words, everything that we today would call toxic masculinity. The lion looks a bit sad. But that's also a part of toxic masculinity. Leon certainly had a lot of lion-like qualities. This was due to his upbringing, his hormones and the fact that people simply didn't know any better back then. At the same time, he also had a gentler side. He liked to snuggle up to his men and also liked to roll over onto his belly for them, if you know what I mean. Leon's ambivalence sparked a lingering debate in the gay community about the polarities of gay men. The debates, like the issue of whether or not to shave your pubic hair, rages on to this day. But at least the first step had been taken and a process set in motion. Leon is therefore a prime example of how Bavaria is the source of many wonderful things — and many not so wonderful things. Today, lions are protected by law and, like sharks, wolves, bears and other predators, humanity's relationship with them is gradually becoming less hostile. Theoretically at least.

Leon helps us to understand processes and reminds us that there are two sides to almost everything. We celebrate this on December 2.

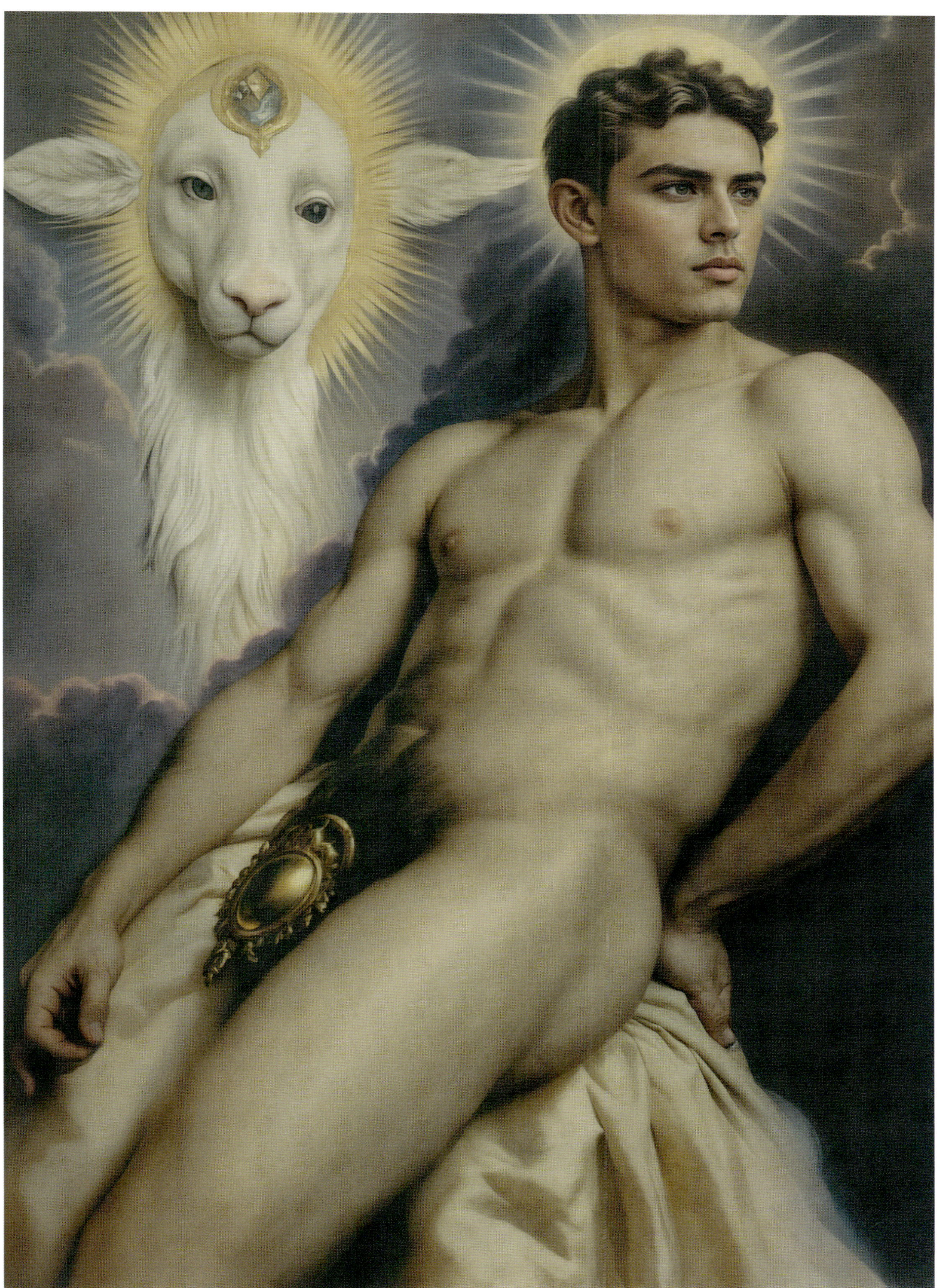

DER HEILIGE LEON · SAINT LEON

DER HEILIGE LSD

Lucius Spurius Dellius war ein Enkel von Quintus Dellius, den wir als *Wechselreiter der Bürgerkriege (desultor bellorum civilium)* kennen, weil er 43 v. Chr. zunächst von Publius Cornelius Dolabella zu Gaius Cassius Longinus überlief, um dann 42 v. Chr. zu Marcus Antonius zu wechseln, den er 31 v. Chr. wiederum zugunsten von Octavian verließ. Lucius Spurius Dellius (von guten Freunden *LSD* genannt) wurde im Jahre Null am 23. Dezember in Rom geboren und von Sarmentus, Octavians ehemaligem Geliebten, erzogen. Quintus Dellius soll sich in früheren Jahren mal bei Cleopatra über Sarmentus beschwert haben, aber dabei ging es nur um Rotweinversorgung, nie um schwule Liebe. Was das betraf, war Quintus, wie bei seinen politischen Entscheidungen, offenbar Pragmatiker. Sein Enkel *LSD* wuchs also zu einem fröhlichen jungen Mann heran und experimentierte schon früh mit halluzinogenen Substanzen für medizinische, religiöse und sonstige Zwecke. Sein Spezialgebiet waren psilocybinhaltige Pilze, die er teilweise sogar aus Sibirien importieren ließ. Zum Gebrauch von Stechapfel, Bilsenkraut, Cannabis und Mohn schrieb er Standardwerke, die das Wissen von Homer aufgriffen und später bei Herodot und Diodor zitiert wurden. Gleichzeitig warnte *LSD* vor dem maßlosen Genuss von Alkohol, denn Wein war ja damals ein weitverbreitetes Grundnahrungsmittel. So verdanken wir *LSD*, dass es damals üblich wurde, weißen, roten und gelben Wein, ganz egal ob süß oder gewürzt, kalt oder heiß mit Wasser zu verdünnen. Das erhöhte nicht nur die Schlagkraft der römischen Legionen gegen die dauerbetrunkenen Germanen, sondern war auch der allgemeinen Volksgesundheit zuträglich.

Kenner der Materie wissen, dass Lucius Spurius Dellius immer mit dezenten bunten Farben in seinem Heiligenschein dargestellt wird. Wir feiern ihn offiziell am 11. April. Er steht aber auch sonst jederzeit gerne zur Verfügung.

SAINT LSD

Lucius Spurius Dellius was the grandson of Quintus Dellius, whom we know as the *desultor bellorum civilium*, because he first defected from Publius Cornelius Dolabella to Gaius Cassius Longinus in 43 BC and then joined Marcus Antonius in 42 BC, whom he left for Octavian in 31 BC. Lucius Spurius Dellius (known to his close friends as *LSD*) was born in the year zero on December 23 in Rome and was brought up by Sarmentus, Octavian's former lover. Quintus Dellius is said to have complained to Cleopatra about Sarmentus in earlier years, but it was only about red wine supplies, never about gay love. As far as this was concerned, as with his political decisions, Quintus was clearly a pragmatist. His grandson *LSD* thus grew up to be a cheerful young man and began experimenting early on with hallucinogenic substances for medical, religious and other purposes. He was particularly interested in psilocybin mushrooms, which he had imported from as far away as Siberia. He wrote the definitive works on the use of datura, henbane, cannabis and poppy, which drew on the wisdom of Homer and were later quoted by Herodotus and Diodorus. At the same time, *LSD* warned against the excessive consumption of alcohol, as wine was a widespread staple food at the time. Thanks to *LSD*, it became common practice to dilute white, red and yellow wine, whether sweet or spiced, cold or hot, with water. Not only did this increase the effectiveness of the Roman legions against the perpetually drunk Germanic tribes, it also had a positive impact on public health.

Historians know that Lucius Spurius Dellius is always depicted with a subtle array of colors in his halo. His official feast day is 11 April. But he is also available at any other time.

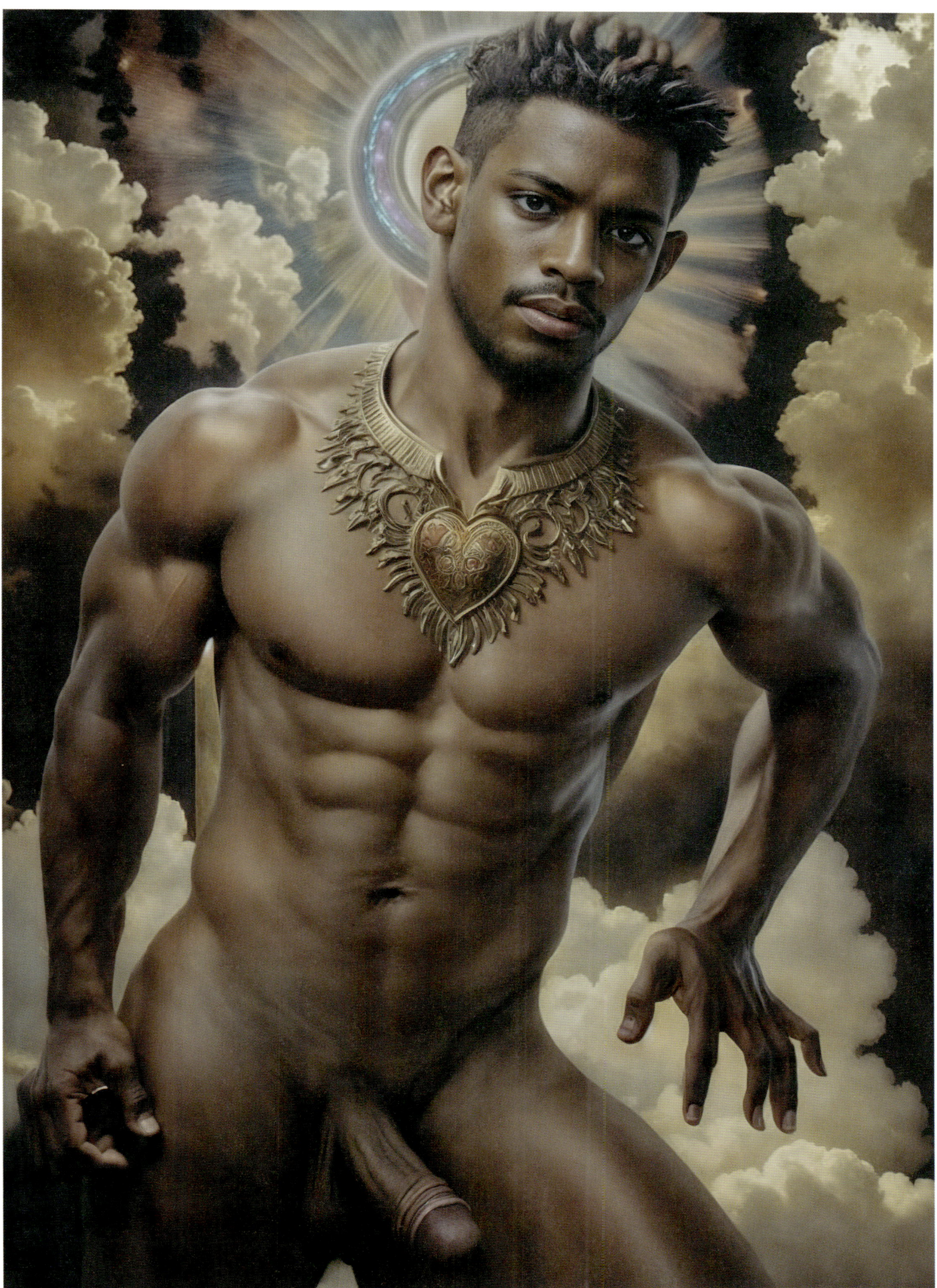

DER HEILIGE LSD · SAINT LSD

DER HEILIGE MANIUS POSTUMUS

Manius Postumus (* 503 in Gerasa; † 551 Berytus) wurde von seinen wohlhabenden Eltern zum Jurastudium nach Berytus (heute Beirut) geschickt. Was anfänglich nur eine Verlegenheitslösung war — man ging davon aus, dass Manius wie der Vater Makler werden würde –, entwickelte sich bei dem jungen Mann zu einer Leidenschaft. Er hatte an der *Rechtsschule von Berytus* (übrigens neben Konstantinopel und Rom die einzige offiziell anerkannte juristische Lehranstalt im Römischen Reich) sein Coming-out, organisierte die dortige Schwulengruppe und zog nach dem Studium mit viel Enthusiasmus in die Kämpfe für eine bessere Welt. Dazu gehörte auch, dass Manius schon als junger Mann für Kaiser Justinian die sogenannten *Pandekten* erstellte, eine Sammlung von Schriften der römischen Rechtswissenschaft, deren Lehren teilweise noch heute die Grundlage vieler Rechtssysteme in Europa und Lateinamerika bilden. Die *Pandekten* unterschieden zwischen Schuld-, Sach-, Familien- und Erbrecht. Manius entwickelte dieses Ordnungssystem auf Basis von Erfahrungen, die er im privaten Bereich machte: Jahrelang hatte er Buch geführt, mit welchem Mann er wann und wo das erste oder weitere Mal welche Art von Sex gehabt hatte. Die Fülle an Informationen bedurfte einer sensiblen Analyse und einer speziellen Sortierung, zumal sie aufgrund von Manius' Vorbildfunktion in der Schwulengruppe von anderen Männern in Berytus adaptiert wurde. Alle fingen an zu zählen und zu sortieren, und man traf sich regelmäßig, um die Ergebnisse abzugleichen, was später weltweit Schule machte. Der ganze Spaß endete 551 mit einem Erdbeben, infolgedessen Berytus durch eine Flutwelle zerstört wurde, in der auch Manius zu Tode kam. Das römische Recht wäre ohne Manius Postumus, beziehungsweise seine *Pandekten*, zweifelsohne verlorengegangen, und sicher nicht so hübsch sortiert worden. Dafür sind ihm noch heute viele Menschen dankbar, zumindest in Ländern, in denen kein religiöses Recht gilt.

Der heilige Manius Postumus ist der Schutzheilige der Juristen und wird am 15. Mai gefeiert.

SAINT MANIUS POSTUMUS

Manius Postumus (* 503 in Gerasa; † 551 Berytus) was sent by his wealthy parents to study law in Berytus (present-day Beirut). Initially, this was just a stop-gap measure — the family assumed that Manius would become a broker like his father — but the young man developed a passion for the subject. He first came out at the *Berytus School of Law* (the only officially recognized law school in the Roman Empire apart from Constantinople and Rome), organized the local gay men's group there and, after graduating, enthusiastically enlisted in the fight for a better world. As a young man, Manius compiled the *Pandects* — a compendium of writings on Roman law, some of which still form the basis of many legal systems in Europe and Latin America — for Emperor Justinian. The *Pandects* are divided into categories: law of obligations, property law, family law and inheritance law. Manius developed this classification system on the basis of his own personal experiences: for years he kept a record of the men he had sex with, as well as when, where, what kind of sex, and whether or not he had had it for the first time. All this information necessitated careful analysis and sorting, especially as it was adapted by other men in Berytus due to Manius' pioneering role in the local gay men's group. Everyone began counting and sorting, and regular meetings were held to compare the results, which later became a worldwide trend. In 551, an earthquake put an end to all the fun, causing Berytus to be destroyed by a tidal wave, in which Manius also perished. Without Manius Postumus, or rather his *Pandects*, Roman law would undoubtedly have been lost and certainly would not have been so neatly categorized. Many people are still grateful to him to this day, at least in countries where religious law does not apply.

St. Manius Postumus is the patron saint of lawyers and is celebrated on May 15.

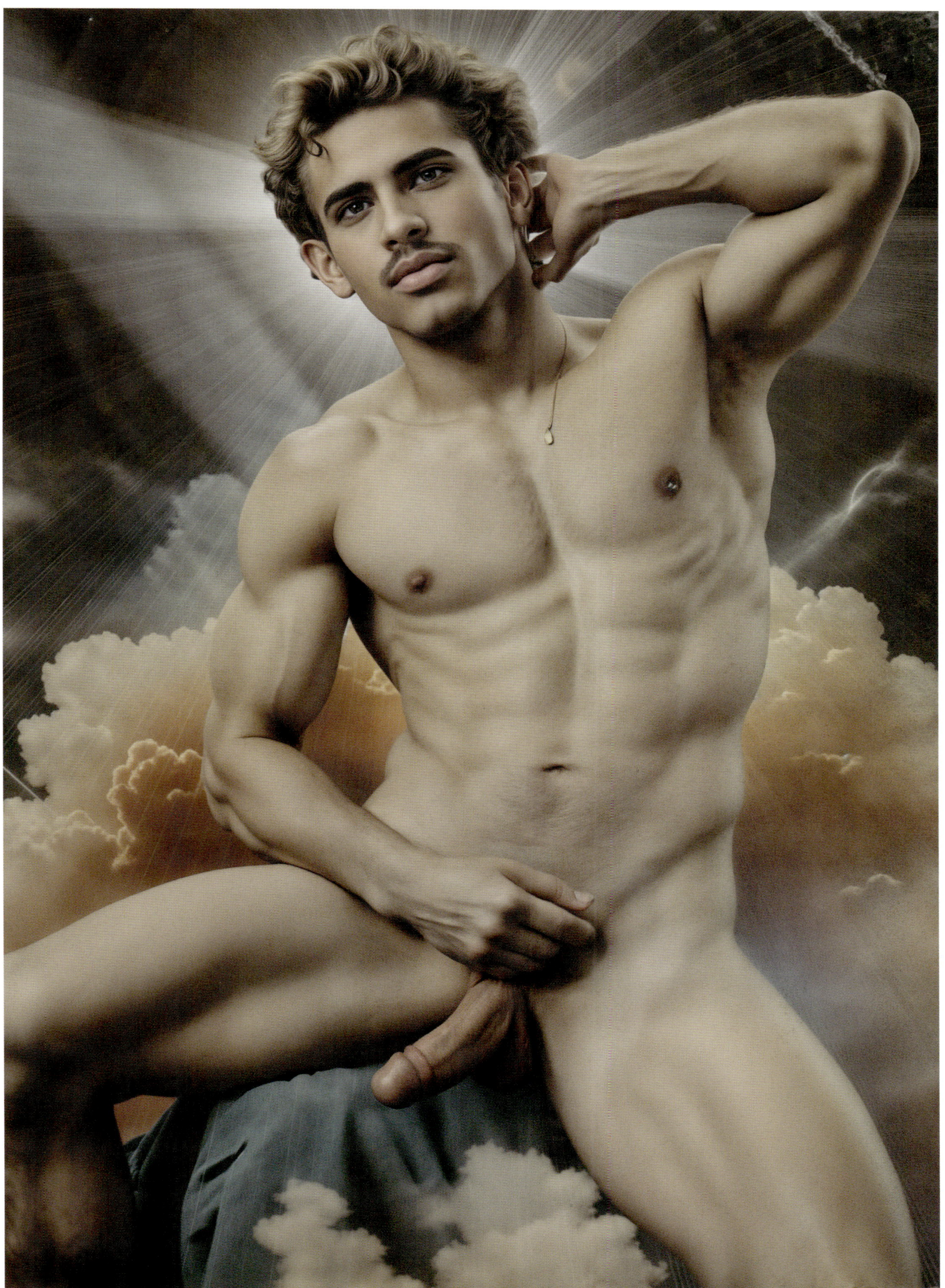

DER HEILIGE MANIUS POSTUMUS · SAINT MANIUS POSTUMUS

SECHS MÄNNER IM EIS: FINNIAN, KEVYN, LORCAN, LUGH, RONAN UND SIODA

Im Sommer 1890 brach unter großem Jubel der schwulen Gemeinschaft eine Gruppe von sechs unerschrockenen Männern in die Antarktis auf. Das Ziel war der Südpol, der am 14. Dezember 1891 auch erreicht wurde. Es ist ja bekannt, dass fast alle großen naturwissenschaftlichen Expeditionen von abenteuerlustigen schwulen Männern durchgeführt wurden und — von Reinfällen wie der Reise der *Bounty* mal abgesehen — auch meist ein gutes Ende nahmen. Solche Expeditionen wurden früher gerne mit Spenden aus der Community finanziert, denn die Entdeckung neuer Länder, Lebensformen und Männer ist nun mal im Interesse aller Schwulen. Dass sich am Südpol nicht besonders viele Männer rumtreiben, ahnten die charmanten Polarforscher natürlich, aber sie wollten sich selbst davon überzeugen. Die sechs stammten aus dem kleinen irischen Dorf Cloonbigeen bei Galway und hatten sich auf einem Rave kennengelernt. Ihre Namen (inklusive sinngemäßer Übersetzung): Finnian *(Der Helle, der Blonde)*, Kevyn *(Der Hübsche, der Anmutige)*, Lorcan *(Der kleine Wilde)*, Lugh *(Der Leuchtende)*, Ronan *(Kleine Robbe)* und Sioda *(Der Sanfte)*. Dass Ronan in unserer Darstellung mit einem Dinosaurier statt mit einer Robbe abgebildet wurde, liegt vermutlich daran, dass der italienische Zeichner einem Übersetzungsfehler aufgesessen ist. Wir bitten, das zu entschuldigen, und weisen darauf hin, dass er immerhin die irischen Wälder sehr schön getroffen hat. Ansonsten wird es wohl die wenigsten wundern, dass die sechs ein unschlagbares Team bildeten. Ihre Reise zum Südpol verlief dementsprechend reibungslos: Man packte die Hunde aus, setzte sich auf die Schlitten und schlüpfte des Nachts jeweils zu zweit in einen Schlafsack zwecks gegenseitiger Erwärmung. So erreichte man am 14. Dezember den Pol, feierte dort Siodas Geburtstag mit einem kleinen Rave und trat anschließend fröhlich den Rückzug an. Die verdiente Anerkennung blieb leider aus, denn am 15. Mai 1891 erließ Leo XIII. ja seine schwulenfeindliche Enzyklika und tilgte alle schwulen Heiligen aus der Geschichte. Zu allem Überfluss stiftete der Papst 1911 dann auch noch Roald Amundsen und Robert Falcon Scott zu einem völlig unnötigen Wettrennen zum Südpol an, das auf Seiten von Scott zu einem katastrophalen Ausgang mit fünf Toten führte. Hätte er sich an die *Zwei-Mann-in-einem-Schlafsack-Regel* unserer sechs Heiligen gehalten, wäre das sicher nicht passiert. Unser Sextett machte auf dem Rückweg von der Dezember-Expedition jedenfalls noch länger Ferien in Brasilien und kehrte dann nach Hause zurück, um die irische Gesellschaft mit Abenteuergeschichten und Körperwärme zu versorgen.

Unsere sechs Männer im Eis befeuern jugendlichen Abenteuergeist. Man feiert sie am 4. Oktober (Finnian), 9. Juni (Kevyn), 4. August (Lorcan), 25. November (Lugh), 11. Juni (Ronan) und — natürlich — 14. Dezember (Sioda). Also eigentlich das ganze Jahr und das macht natürlich auch Sinn.

THE SIX ICE SAINTS: FINNIAN, KEVYN, LORCAN, LUGH, RONAN AND SIODA

In the summer of 1890, amid much applause from the gay community, a group of six intrepid men set off for Antarctica. They were headed for the South Pole, which they reached on December 14, 1891. As we all know, almost all great scientific expeditions were carried out by adventurous gay men and — with the exception of the voyage of the *Bounty* — usually ended well. In the past, such expeditions were often financed by donations from the community, because gay men have always had a vested interest in the discovery of new countries, ways of life and men. Of course, the charming polar explorers suspected that there weren't many men wandering around the South Pole, but they wanted to make sure. The six men all came from the small Irish village of Cloonbigeen near Galway and had met at a rave. Their names (and approximate translations): Finnian *(Bright or Blonde One)*, Kevyn *(Handsome or Graceful One)*, Lorcan *(Little Wild One)*, Lugh *(Shining One)*, Ronan *(Little Seal)* and Sioda *(Gentle One)*. The fact that Ronan is depicted with a dinosaur instead of a seal is probably due to a translation error on the part of the Italian artist. We apologize and would like to draw your attention instead to the Irish forests, which he has captured beautifully. That said, few people will be surprised to learn that the six men made an unbeatable team. Their journey to the South Pole went off without a hitch: they unpacked the dogs, climbed onto the sleds and snuggled up at night, two men per sleeping bag, to keep each other warm. They reached the South Pole on December 14, celebrated Sioda's birthday there with a small rave and then happily set off back home. Sadly, they were robbed of their well-deserved recognition by Leo XIII, who issued his homophobic encyclical on May 15, 1891 and erased all gay saints from church history. To make matters worse, in 1911 the Pope also incited Roald Amundsen and Robert Falcon Scott to compete in a completely unnecessary race to the South Pole, which led to the death of five men in a catastrophic outcome for Scott. This would almost certainly not have happened if he had only stuck to the *two men, one sleeping bag rule* taught by our six saints. Our sextet stopped off in Brazil for an extended vacation on the way back from the December expedition and then returned home to regale Irish society with tales of adventure and body heat.

The Six Ice Saints inspire a youthful spirit of adventure. They are celebrated on October 4 (Finnian), June 9 (Kevyn), August 4 (Lorcan), November 25 (Lugh), June 11 (Ronan) and — of course — December 14 (Sioda). In other words, all year round, which of course makes sense.

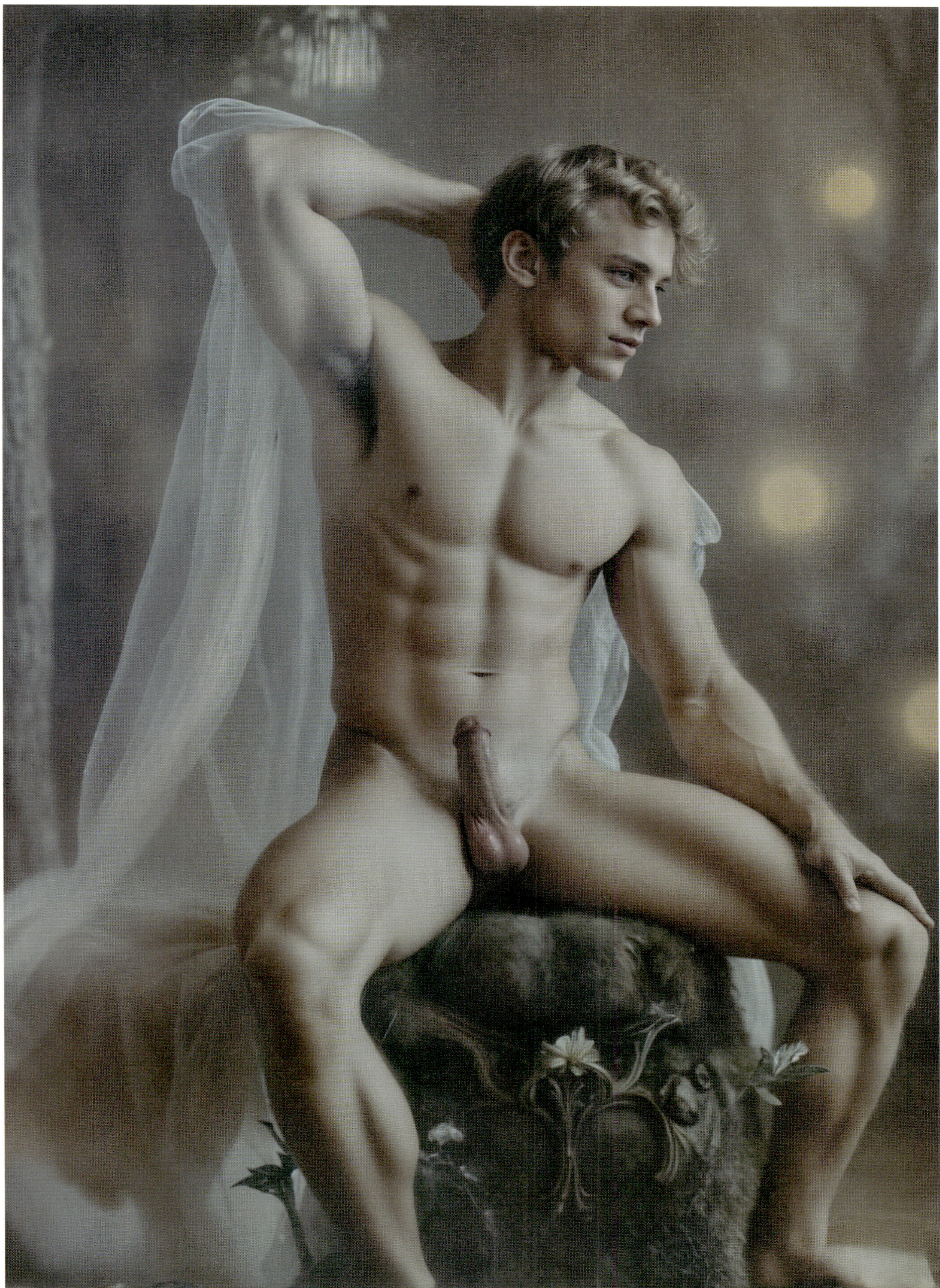

FINNIAN

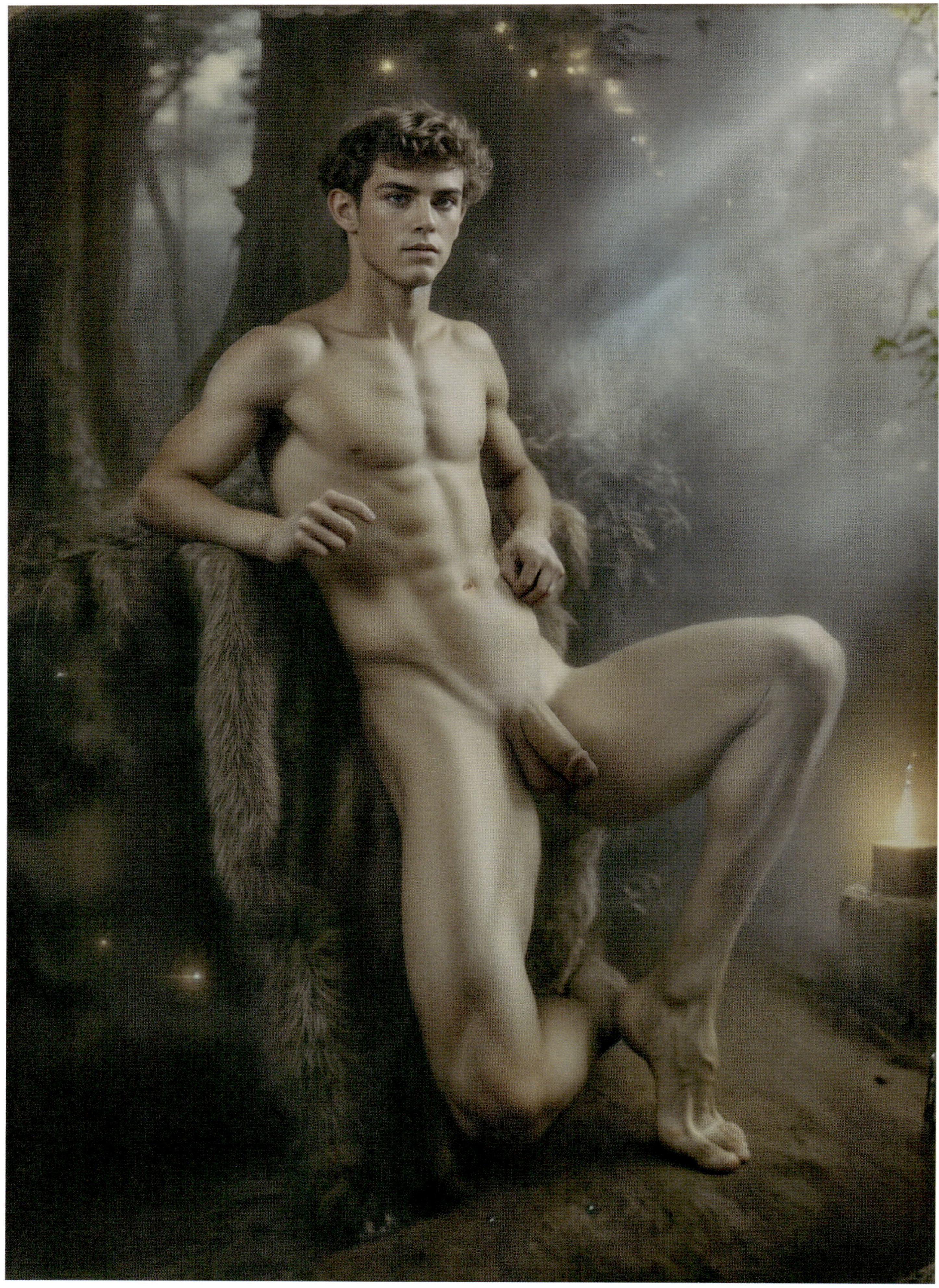

KEVYN

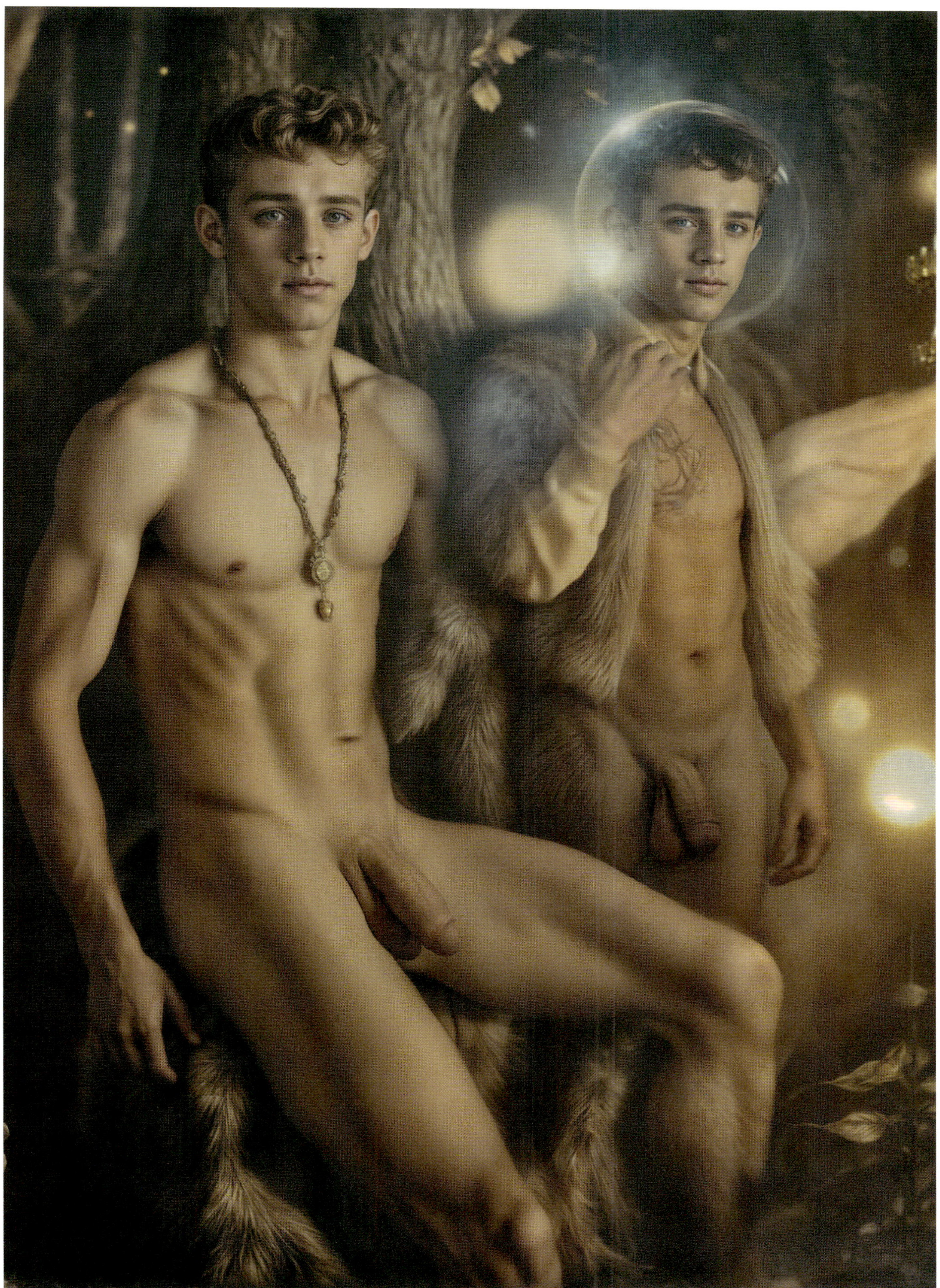

LORCAN UND LUGH

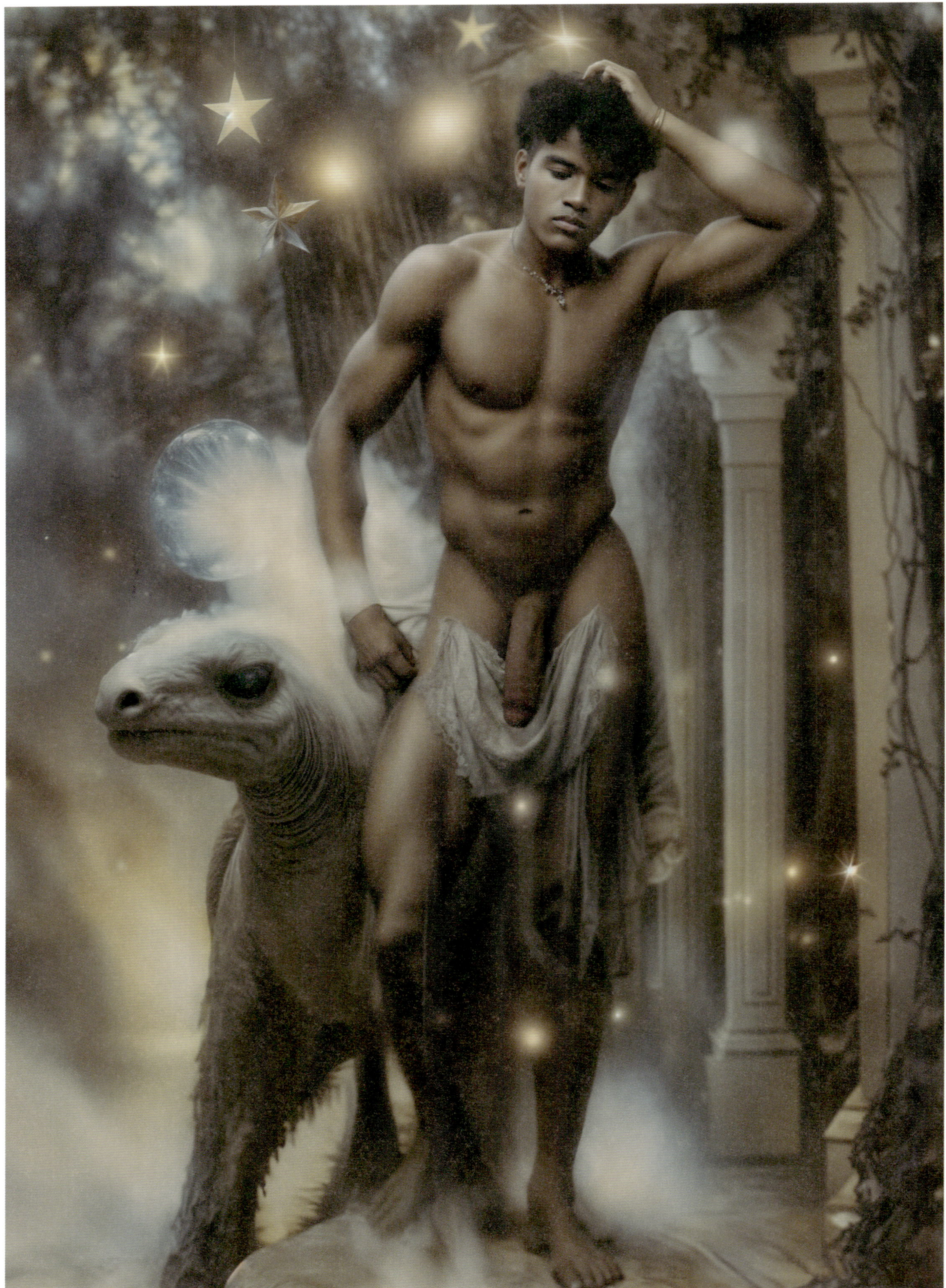

RONAN

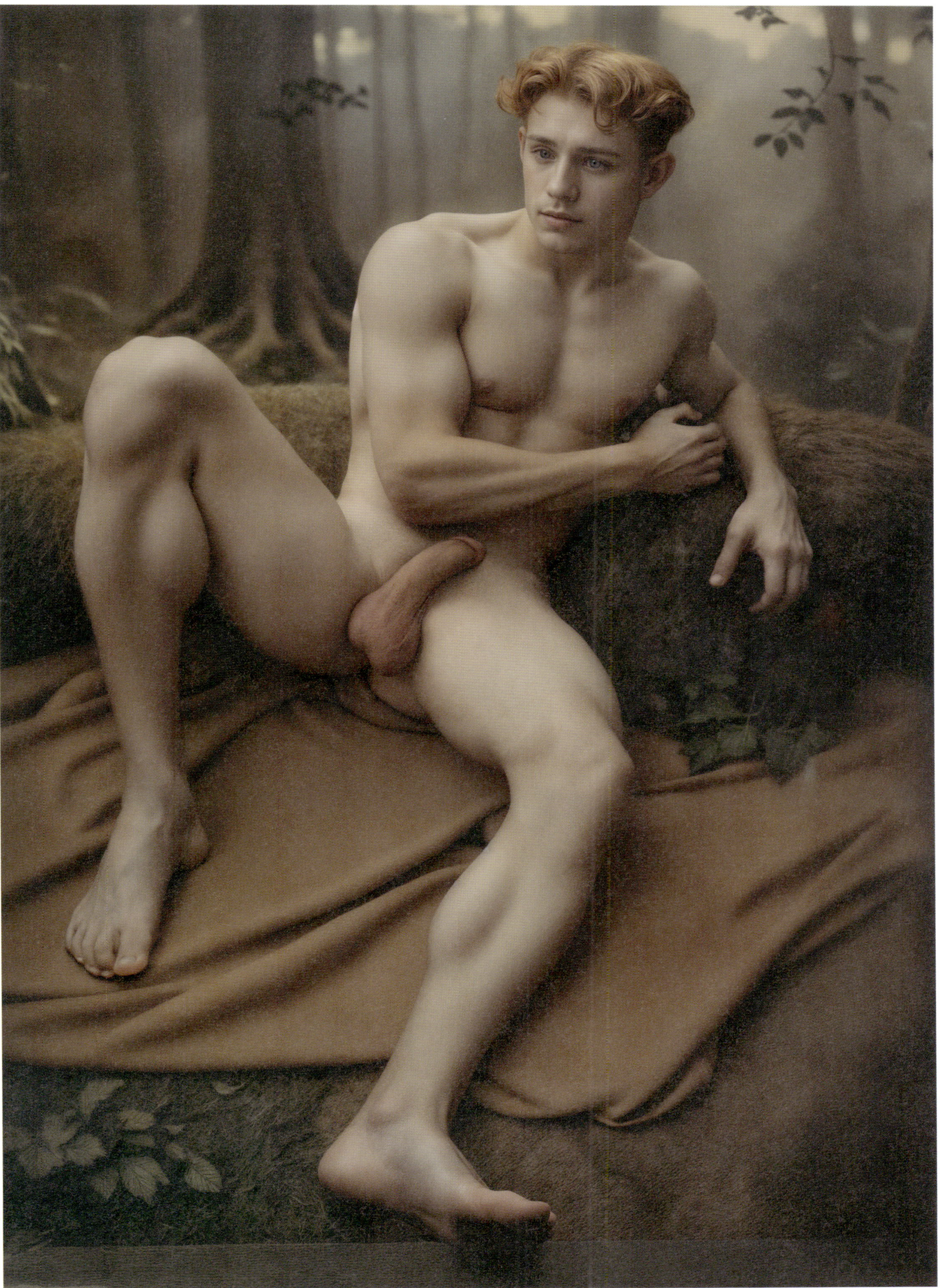

DER HEILIGE MAKSYM VON POLTAWA

Maksym von Poltawa lebte 1620 bis (vermutlich) 1657. Er war Wassermüller am Fluss Worskla in der Stadt Poltawa, die damals zu Polen-Litauen (auch *Rzeczpospolita* oder *Königliche Republik der Polnischen Krone* oder — lateinisch — *Respublica Poloniae*) gehörte und heute in der Ukraine liegt. Polen-Litauen war ein Vielvölkerstaat, in dem neben Polen und Litauern auch Deutsche, Letten, Esten, Ukrainer, Belarussen, Russen und Tartaren lebten. Die konfessionelle Vielfalt war dementsprechend groß und reichte von orthodoxen, katholischen und protestantischen Christen über Juden und Muslimen bis hin zu Anhängern der litauischen Mythologie. Maksym von Poltawa war getaufter (aber vernünftigerweise nicht besonders ambitionierter) Katholik und lebte mit seinen beiden Liebhabern Doron, einem aus Vilnius stammenden Juden, und Kritikija, einem orthodoxen Kosaken aus dem Gebiet der Dnepr-Stromschnellen, zusammen in einer Mühle. Zeitzeugen zufolge huldigten die drei dort auch Potrimpos, einem *ährengekrönten Jüngling*, der aus der (heidnischen) Prußischen Religion als *Gott des Wassers* bekannt ist. Ansonsten wurde Maksym von Poltawa wegen seines besonders fein gemahlenen Mehls hochgeschätzt, das er durch mehrfaches Sieben herstellte. Weil demzufolge keine Steinchen im Mehl waren, verbesserte sich die Zahngesundheit bei den Einwohnern der Region Poltawa gewaltig. Das sprach sich herum. Bald lieferten Maksym, Doron und Kritikija ihr Mehl im ganzen Land aus. Das taten sie stets persönlich und sie waren überall geschätzte Gäste. Viele Gasthäuser stellten ihnen dabei ein besonders breites Bett (das sogenannte *Maksym-Bett*; später *Maxi-Bett*) zur Verfügung. Beim Chmelnyzkyj-Aufstand der orthodoxen Kosaken wurde die Mühle am Worskla zerstört und ausgerechnet Kritikija erschlagen. Maksym hätte seinen Status durch Konversion erhalten können, entschied sich aber dafür, bei Doron zu bleiben, der als Sklave nach Konstantinopel verkauft wurde. Dort verlieren sich die Spuren der beiden. Über Ferdinand von Fürstenberg erfuhr Papst Alexander VII. vom Schicksal des Maksym von Poltawa und dachte wohl kurzzeitig über einen Freikauf nach. Schließlich stand er mit Sultan Mehmed IV. aufgrund des Krieges um Kreta in engem Kontakt. Über den Bau der Kolonnaden am Petersplatz und andere prestigeträchtige Bauprojekte vergaß der Papst das Ganze aber offenbar. In Polen-Litauen wurde Maksym von Poltawa dagegen weiterhin vom einfachen Volk für sein vorbildhaftes friedliches Leben in Ehren gehalten. Es bürgerte sich sogar der Brauch ein, die Köpfe männlicher Neugeborener mit etwas Mehl zu bestäuben, in der Hoffnung, dass der Junge schwul werden und sich ähnlich tugendhaft wie Maksym von Poltawa entwickeln würde. In den Nordkarpaten hat sich dieser Brauch bis heute gehalten.

Maksym von Poltawa wird häufig bei Zahnschmerzen angerufen, denen ansonsten das tägliche Anlächeln seines Heiligenbildes — verbunden mit regelmäßiger Mundhygiene — vorbeugen soll. Wir gedenken Maksym, Doron und Kritikija am 11. Juli.

SAINT MAKSYM OF POLTAVA

Maksym of Poltava was born in 1620 and lived until (presumably) 1657. He was a water miller on the Worskla River in the city of Poltava, which at the time belonged to Poland-Lithuania (also known as the *Rzeczpospolita* or *Royal Republic of the Polish Crown* or — in Latin — *Respublica Poloniae*) and is now part of Ukraine. Poland-Lithuania was a multi-ethnic state where Germans, Latvians, Estonians, Ukrainians, Belarusians, Russians and Tartars lived alongside Poles and Lithuanians. It was home to a correspondingly wide variety of faiths, ranging from Orthodox, Catholic and Protestant Christians to Jews, Muslims and devotees of Lithuanian mythology. Maksym of Poltava was baptized as a (not particularly ambitious) Catholic and lived in a mill with his two lovers: Doron, a Jew from Vilnius, and Kritikija, an Orthodox Cossack from the Dnepr Rapids region. According to contemporary witnesses, the three also worshipped Potrimpos, a *corn-crowned youth* who is known in the Old (pagan) Prussian religion as the *God of Water*. Maksym of Poltava was held in high esteem for his particularly finely ground flour, which he produced by sifting it several times over. There were no stones in Maksym's flour, which greatly improved the dental health of the inhabitants of the Poltava region. Word got around. Soon Maksym, Doron and Kritikija were distributing their flour all over the country. They always did this in person and were highly respected guests everywhere they went. Many inns took to offering them a particularly wide bed (known as a *Maksym bed*; later a *maxi bed*). The mill on the Vorskla was destroyed during the Khmelnytsky uprising of the Orthodox Cossacks and Kritikiya was killed. Maksym could have kept his status by converting, but decided to stay with Doron, who was enslaved and trafficked to Constantinople. This was the last anyone heard of them. Ferdinand von Fürstenberg told Pope Alexander VII about the fate of Maksym of Poltava and the Pope briefly considered buying his freedom. After all, he was in close contact with Sultan Mehmed IV because of the war over Crete. But the Pope was distracted by the construction of the colonnades in St. Peter's Square and other prestigious building projects, and forgot all about it. In Poland-Lithuania, however, Maksym of Poltava continued to be honored by the common people for his exemplarily peaceful life. It even became customary to dust the heads of newborn boys with a little flour in the hope that the boy would turn out gay and become as virtuous as Maksym of Poltava. In the Northern Carpathians, this custom has survived to this day.

Maksym of Poltava is often invoked for toothache, which you can also prevent by smiling at his portrait every day — and brushing your teeth regularly. We honor the memory of Maksym, Doron and Kritikija on July 11.

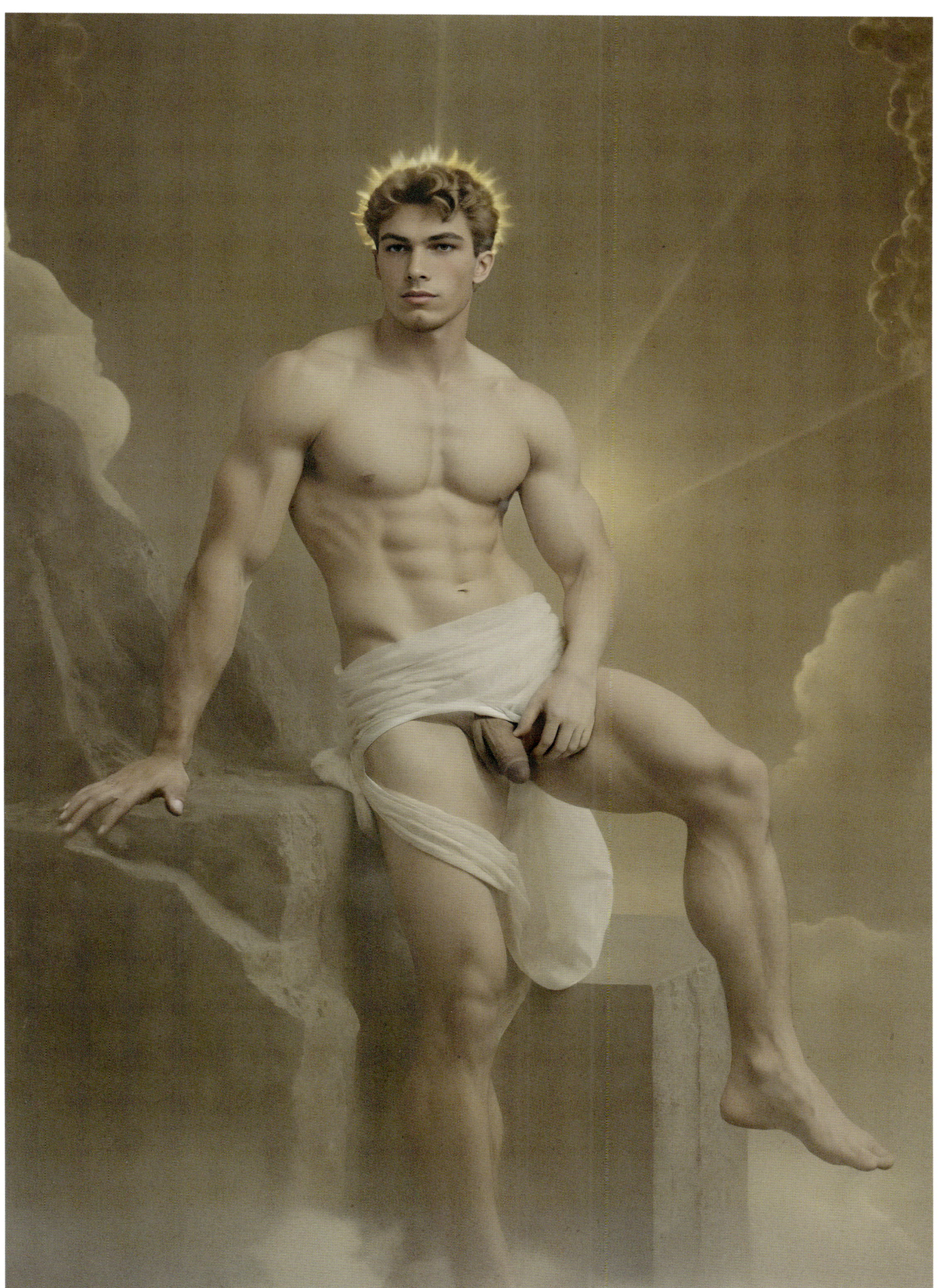

DER HEILIGE MAKSYM VON POLTAWA · SAINT MAKSYM OF POLTAVA

DER HEILIGE MANUEL

Manuel wurde 1530 im Lissaboner Stadtteil Bairro Alto geboren. Dort besuchte er mangels Alternativen eine Jesuitenschule. Mit sechzehn Jahren wurde er von seiner Ordensgemeinschaft (*Gesellschaft Jesu* oder *Societas Jesu*) nach Goa geschickt, wo er Francisco de Xavier (spanisch *Francisco de Gassu y Javier* oder *Francisco de Jassu y Azpilcueta*) bei der Missionierung in Ostasien unterstützen sollte. Am 15. August 1549 erreichten die beiden Japan, konkret den Hafen von Kagoshima auf der Insel Kyūshū. Dort missionierten sie knapp zwei Jahre vor sich hin. Als sie sich dann 1551 als einfache Pilger nach Kyōto begaben, war Manuels Verhältnis zu Francisco bereits getrübt. Er hatte nämlich herausgefunden, dass der Gefährte den Jesuitenkollegen in der Heimat geschrieben hatte, die Japaner hätten einen großen *Fehler*: „Niemand findet die widernatürliche Sünde abnormal oder abscheulich." Manuel fand diesen *Fehler* wunderbar, denn er war bis über beide Ohren in Takeda und Kasuga verliebt — Sie wissen schon, Takeda Shingen, der japanische Kriegsherr, der anno 1542 im Alter von 22 Jahren seinem eifersüchtigen 16-jährigen Geliebten Kasuga Gensuke schriftlich bescheinigte, dass er niemals mit einem gewissen Yashichiro Sex hatte oder jemals haben werde. Sex zu dritt mit Takeda und Manuel fand Kasuga aber ganz großartig und Manuel ging es genauso. Mit Francisco de Xavier und seinen Missionsbemühungen ging es nach der Pilgerei nach Kyōto bergab. Zum japanischen Kaiser Go-Nara wurde er gar nicht erst vorgelassen, weil Manuel ein Treffen der beiden durch eine List verhinderte. Kurz darauf musste Francisco Japan verlassen. Er wollte daraufhin sein Glück in China versuchen, aber die Chinesen waren vorgewarnt und ließen ihn nicht ins Land. Manuel blieb derweil in Japan mit Takeda und Kasuga zusammen. Als Takeda im Jahr 1573 starb, hatte der Portugiese das Jesuitentum und den Missionierungseifer längst hinter sich gelassen und sinnvollere Aufgaben für sich entdeckt. So stieß er in Japan wichtige Reformen an, verantwortete ein neues Steuersystem, ordnete den Bau von Bewässerungs- und Abwasserkanälen an und schuf ein Straßenbausystem, das der Kultur der Verantwortung und des Gemeinwohls diente — sprich Schäden wurden schnell gemeldet und repariert, was bis heute weltweit einzigartig ist. Manuel starb 1630 als Hundertjähriger in Kyōto eines natürlichen Todes. Er wird häufig auf dem Gipfel des Fujiyama stehend in einem von Kasuga, der als Modedesigner arbeitete, entworfenen Kleidungsstück aus japanischem Kunstpelz abgebildet. In unserem Bild ist im Hintergrund außerdem die Kyokujitsuki (japanisch: 旭日旗, deutsch: *Flagge der aufgehenden Sonne*) zu sehen, allerdings in ihrer früheren, friedlichen Version, die im Zeichen eines langen und erfüllten Sexuallebens stand und erst später von japanischen Nationalisten umgedeutet wurde.

Der heilige Manuel kümmert sich gerne um so ziemlich alle, die gute Organisation zu schätzen wissen. Er wird am 13. September gefeiert.

SAINT MANUEL

Manuel was born in the Bairro Alto district of Lisbon in 1530. In the absence of alternative options, he attended a Jesuit school there. At the age of sixteen, the Society of Jesus (*Societas Jesu*) sent him to Goa, where he was to assist Francisco de Xavier (Spanish: *Francisco de Gassu y Javier* or *Francisco de Jassu y Azpilcueta*) in his missionary work in East Asia. The two arrived in Japan, specifically the port of Kagoshima on the island of Kyūshū, on August 15, 1549. There they spent the next two years doing missionary stuff. By the time they made their way to Kyōto as pilgrims in 1551, Manuel's relationship with Francisco had already soured. He had discovered that his companion had written to his Jesuit colleagues back home that the Japanese had a major *flaw*: "No one finds unnatural sin abnormal or abhorrent." Manuel thought this *flaw* was wonderful because he was head over heels in love with Takeda and Kasuga — that's right, Takeda Shingen, the Japanese warlord who in 1542, at the age of twenty-two, wrote to his jealous sixteen-year-old lover Kasuga Gensuke that he had never had or ever would have sex with a certain Yashichiro. Three-way sex with Takeda and Manuel, on the other hand, was absolutely fine by Kasuga, and Manuel felt the same way. Everything went downhill for Francisco de Xavier and his missionary efforts after the pilgrimage to Kyōto. He was not even permitted to see the Japanese Emperor Go-Nara because Manuel used a ruse to prevent the two from meeting. Francisco was forced to leave Japan shortly afterwards. He hoped to try his luck in China, but the Chinese were forewarned and refused to let him into the country. Manuel remained in Japan with Takeda and Kasuga. By the time Takeda died in 1573, his Portuguese lover had abandoned Jesuitism and missionary work altogether and moved on to more meaningful tasks. He launched a number of vital reforms in Japan, introduced a new tax system, ordered the construction of irrigation channels and sewer systems and created a road construction system that fostered a culture of responsibility and the common good — any defects were quickly reported and repaired — a system that is still the only one of its kind in the world today. Manuel died of natural causes at the age of one hundred in Kyōto in 1630. He is frequently depicted standing on the summit of Mount Fujiyama in a garment made of Japanese faux fur designed by Kasuga, who worked as a fashion designer. In our illustration, the Kyokujitsuki (Japanese: 旭日旗, English: *Flag of the Rising Sun*) can also be seen in the background, albeit in its earlier, peaceful version, which stood for a long and fulfilling sex life before it was later redefined by Japanese nationalists.

St. Manuel is happy to help just about anyone who appreciates good organization. His feast day is September 13.

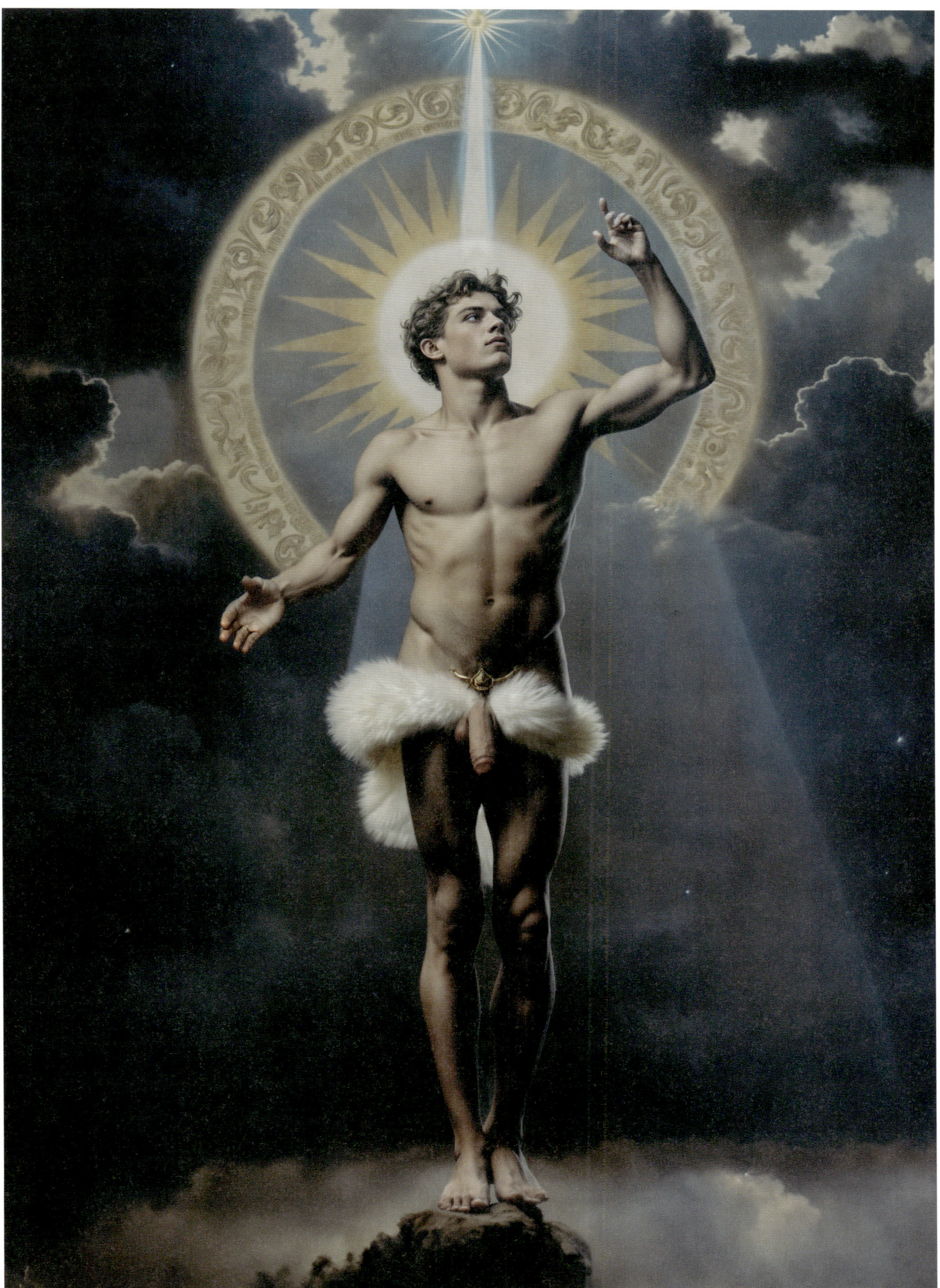

DER HEILIGE MANUEL · SAINT MANUEL

DER HEILIGE MAREADES

Schon bei der Schreibweise Mareades (auch *Mereades, Mariades, Mariadnes* oder *Cyriades*) gibt es Streit. Außerdem wird ihm von Veruntreuung öffentlicher Gelder, die eigentlich zum Bau eines Hippodroms gedacht waren, über Perserfreundlichkeit bis hin zum Vatermord so ziemlich alles in die Schuhe geschoben, was bei den Römern verpönt war. Schauen wir genauer hin und gehen ins Antiochia des Jahres 244. Zu jener Zeit zählte die Hauptstadt der Provinz Syria 500.000 Einwohner und war neben Rom, Alexandria und Karthago eine der wichtigsten Städte des Römischen Reiches. Mareades war durch den Import von Waren aus Indien und China sehr vermögend geworden und engagierte sich stark für die schwule Community von Antiochia. Damit das nächtliche Cruisen mehr Spaß machte, führte er Straßenbeleuchtung ein, und für alle, die nicht nur Sex haben, sondern auch tanzen wollten, errichtete er oberhalb der Stadt eine Großraumdiskothek, in der man eine schöne Aussicht hatte und ungestört die ganze Nacht feiern konnte. Mareades taufte den Club *Charonion*, frei nach *Charon*, dem Kosenamen seines Liebhabers. Der Name spricht Bände. Alle, denen *Charon* (altgriechisch Χάρων) als Fährmann zur Unterwelt ein Begriff ist, können erahnen, was Mareades mit seinem *Charon* so trieb und wie es in ihrem Club zugegangen sein muss. Das *Charonion* wurde von einem fünf Meter hohen Steinrelief des Mareades (eine Tiara tragend) überragt, das bis heute besichtigt werden kann. So viel hedonistischer Pomp rief natürlich Neider auf den Plan. So wurden unzählige ehrenrührige Gerüchte und Diffamierungen über Mareades verbreitet, gerade auch in den sozialen Medien. Genervt verließ er die Stadt, behaupten die einen. Er wehrte sich und feierte noch viele Jahre weiter, behaupten die anderen.

Mareades kümmert sich um die Clubkultur und ist damit gut ausgelastet. Wir feiern ihn am 3. Januar, aber eigentlich jeden Freitag oder Samstag und auch gerne mal mitten in der Woche.

SAINT MAREADES

Even the spelling of Mareades (also known as *Mereades, Mariades, Mariadnes* or *Cyriades*) is a source of controversy. He was also accused of just about everything that the Romans disapproved of, from embezzling public funds intended for the construction of a hippodrome to being too friendly towards the Persians. And patricide. But let's take a closer look at Antioch in the year 244. At that time, the capital of the province of Syria had 500,000 inhabitants and was one of the most important cities in the Roman Empire, alongside Rome, Alexandria and Carthage. Mareades had amassed a great deal of wealth by importing goods from India and China and was very active on behalf of Antioch's gay community. He introduced street lighting to make cruising at night more enjoyable, and for everyone who wanted to dance as well as have sex, he built a large discotheque above the city, which offered beautiful views and undisturbed all-night partying. Mareades named the club *Charonion* after *Charon*, the nickname he gave his lover. Aptly named, as it turns out. If you are familiar with *Charon* (ancient Greek Χάρων) as the ferryman to the underworld, you can probably guess what Mareades got up to with *Charon* and the kind of goings-on that took place at their club. Towering above the *Charonion* was a five-meter-high stone carving of Mareades (wearing a tiara), which can still be seen today. Of course, this hedonistic opulence attracted its share of envy. Countless slanderous rumors and allegations about Mareades were circulated, especially on social media. Some say he left the city in annoyance. Others maintain that he fought back and kept on partying for many years.

Mareades is the patron saint of club culture which keeps him very busy. We celebrate his feast day on January 3, but you can also come by every Friday or Saturday and sometimes in the middle of the week as well.

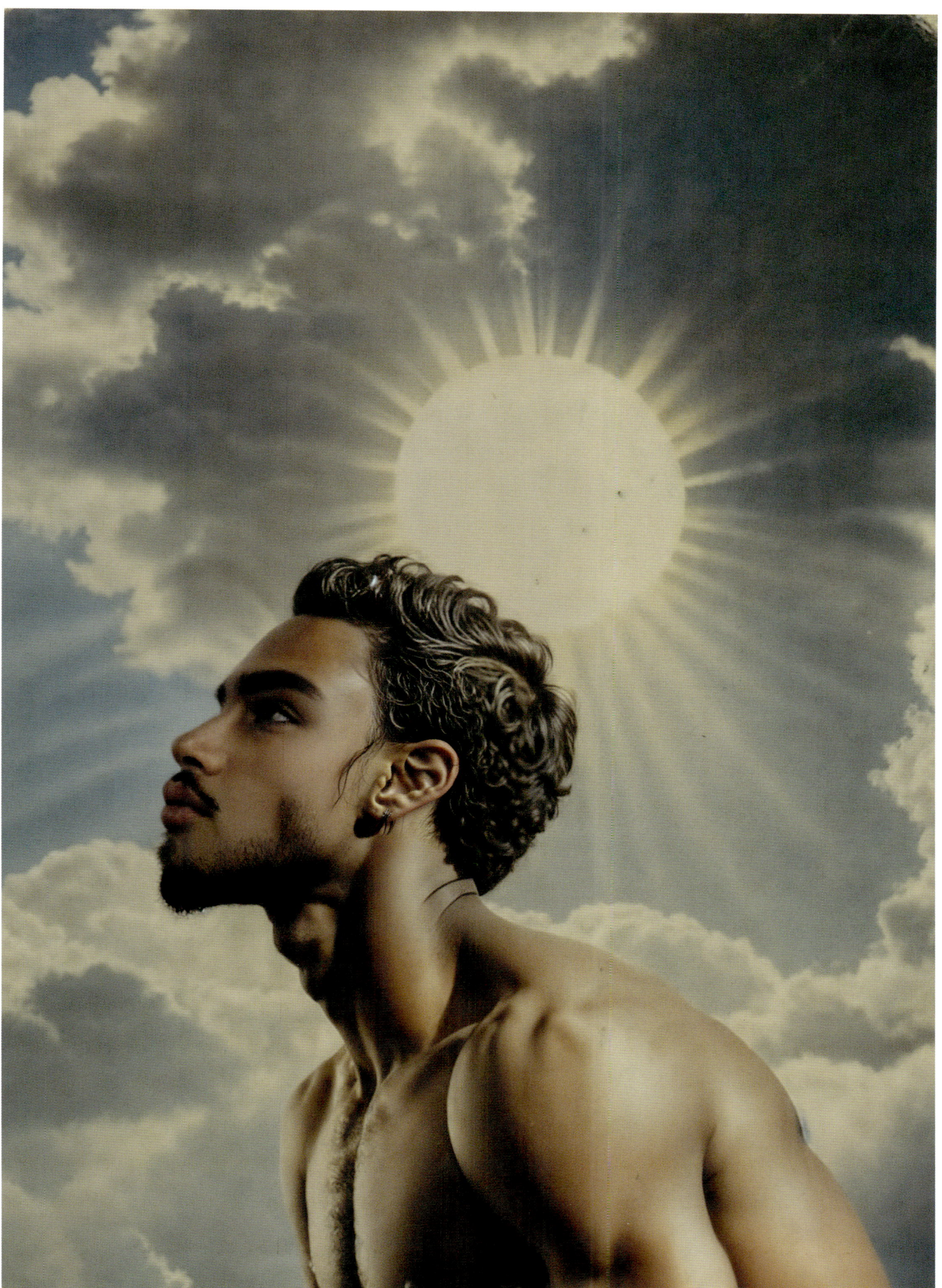

DER HEILIGE MAREADES · SAINT MAREADES

DER HEILIGE MATEO

Die Unabhängigkeit des wunderschönen Kolumbiens ist untrennbar mit der *Llorente-Vase* verbunden, einem mysteriösen Symbol, dessen Geschichte bis dato falsch erzählt wurde. Die Vase wird von der kolumbianischen Bevölkerung immer dann heranzitiert, wenn ein unzufriedener Geist Grund für Streit, Debatten oder sonstigen Aufruhr sucht. Das geht auf das Jahr 1810 und irgendeine wirre Geschichte um das Ausleihen eines Gegenstands für eine Party zurück, die der Leihgeber dem Leihenden nicht geben wollte, was dann zu einer Revolte und Simón Bolívars erster Unabhängigkeitserklärung und nicht zuletzt zu langen Kämpfen gegen die Spanier führte. In Wahrheit ist das aber die Geschichte von Mateo (*1780 in Cartagena de Indias), einem erfolgreichen Innenausstatter aus Bogotá, der ab 1801 auch der Liebhaber von Alexander von Humboldt war, mit dem er eine glückliche Fernbeziehung führte, aber das nur am Rande. Mateo bevorzugte einen eher opulenten Stil mit Säulen, vielen Vorhängen und gerne auch mal mit Krönchen. Am 20. Juli 1810 erschien in seinem Laden eine zickige spanische Kundin, also eine Angehörige der herrschenden Kolonisten-Klasse, die Mateo schwer rassistisch und homophob beleidigte. Die Worte sind zwar überliefert, aber eine Niederschrift des genauen Zitats verbietet sich. Nur so viel: Die Bitch verglich ein Körperteil Mateos mit einer im Laden stehenden großen Vase mit breiter Öffnung. Das war dann selbst dem geduldigen Mateo zu viel. Er trug seinen Zorn auf die Straße und gewann im Handumdrehen die Sympathien seiner Mitmenschen. Die Folge waren die erwähnte Revolution, einige Jahre Krieg und 1821 die Wahl von Simón Bolívar zum Präsidenten. Simón hatte Mateo übrigens ursprünglich die Abschaffung der Sklaverei versprochen, ein Versprechen, das er (typisch Politiker, typisch Wahlkampfgetöse) am Ende nicht einlöste. Erst in den 1850er Jahren, als klar war, dass schlechte Arbeitslöhne sich noch besser rechnen als Sklaverei, ließen sich die Großgrundbesitzer auf ein entsprechendes Gesetz ein.

Der heilige Mateo hilft allen Menschen, denen zu Recht mal der Kragen platzt, und ist natürlich auch für die Zunft der Innenausstatter zuständig. Sein offizieller Gedenktag ist der 26. September.

SAINT MATEO

The independence of enchanting Colombia is inextricably linked to the *Vase of Llorente*, a mysterious symbol whose story has never been told properly until now. The vase is invoked by the Colombian people whenever a discontented spirit is looking for a reason to start an argument, a dispute or any other kind of disturbance. This tradition dates back to 1810 and a rather confusing story about an object being borrowed for a party, which the lender refused to give to the borrower, leading to a revolt, the first declaration of independence by Simón Bolívar and protracted battles against the Spanish. In reality, however, this is the story of Mateo (*1780 in Cartagena de Indias), a successful interior decorator from Bogotá, who in 1801 also became the lover of Alexander von Humboldt, with whom he enjoyed a happy long-distance relationship. But that's another story. Mateo favored a rather opulent style, featuring columns, lots of drapery and sometimes even coronets. On July 20, 1810, a Spanish customer, i.e., a member of the ruling colonial class, showed up in his store and subjected Mateo to racist and homophobic abuse. Decency prevents us from quoting the exact words but suffice it to say that this horrible bitch compared a part of Mateo's anatomy to a large vase with a wide mouth that was on display in his store. That was too much even for the patient Mateo. He took his rage to the streets and quickly won the support of his fellow citizens. This led to the aforementioned revolution, several years of war and the election of Simón Bolívar as president in 1821. Simón had originally promised Mateo that he would abolish slavery, a promise that he (like politicians and their campaign promises all over the world) ultimately failed to keep. It was not until the 1850s, when it became apparent that paying low wages was even more profitable than enslaving people, that the big landowners agreed to outlaw slavery.

St. Mateo helps everyone who is justifiably upset and is of course also the patron saint of interior decorators. His official feast day is September 26.

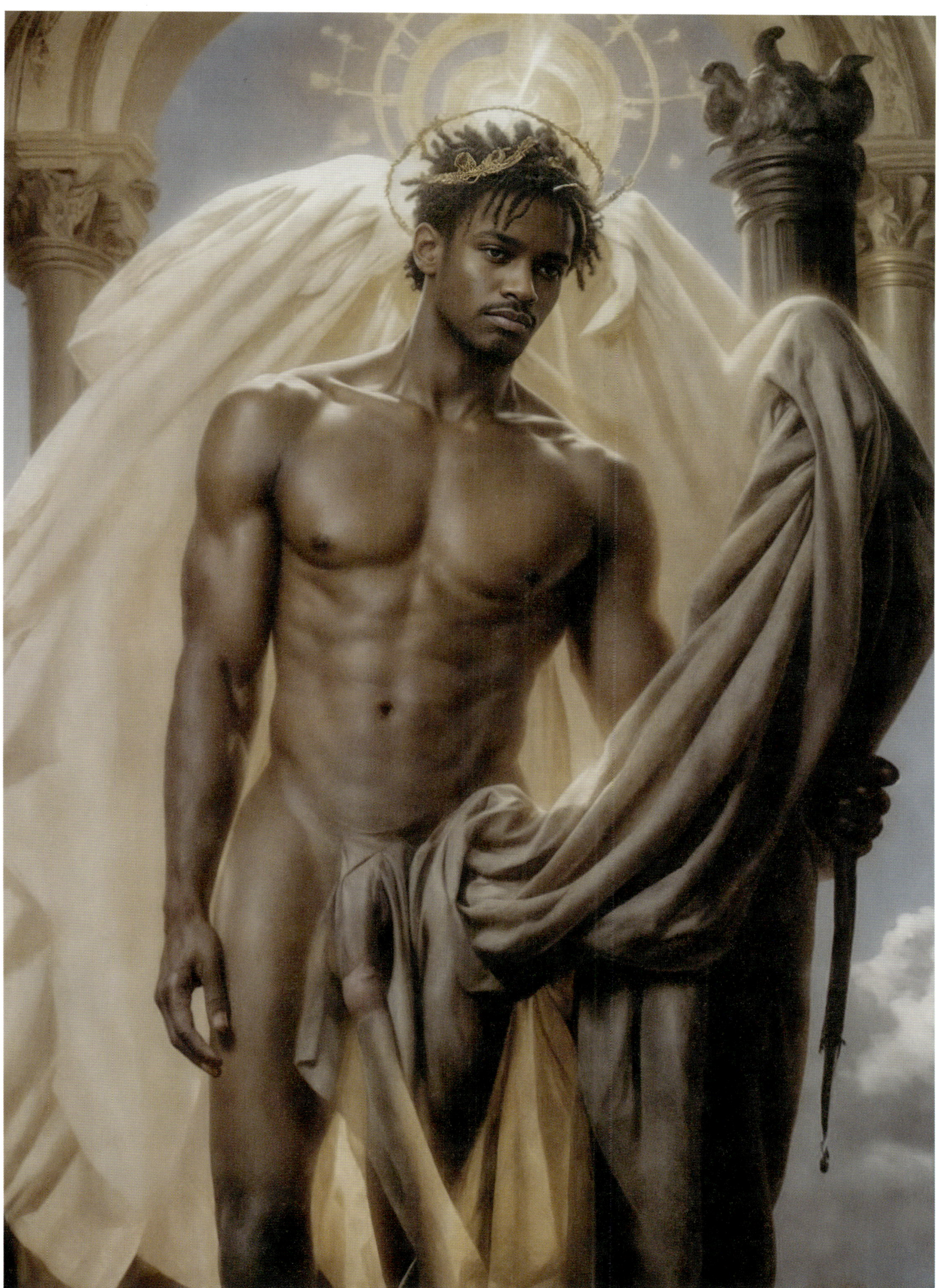

DER HEILIGE MATEO · SAINT MATTEO

DER HEILIGE MICHAŁ

Michał wurde etwa 1420 in Puck (deutsch *Putzig*; kaschubisch *Pùck*) geboren und gehörte dem westslawischen Volk der Kaschuben (auch Kassuben, polnisch Kaszubi, kaschubisch Kaszëbi) an. Er war von kleiner Statur, hatte ein sehr fröhliches und einnehmendes Wesen und arbeitete in der Logistik des Fischmeisteramts seiner Heimatstadt. Dort lernte er seinen Lebensgefährten Heinrich Reffle von Richtenberg (* etwa 1415 in Schwaben; † 1477 in Königsberg) kennen, der ab 1470 *Hochmeister des Deutschen Ordens* war. Dann kam der *Dreizehnjährige Krieg* (1454 bis 1466, auch als *Preußischer Städtekrieg* oder polnisch *Wojna trzynastoletnia* bekannt), ein Gerangel zwischen *Deutschem Orden* und einer Interessenvertretung preußischer Städte und Landadliger gemeinsam mit dem Königreich Polen, bei dem es im Prinzip um Macht- und Zukunftsfragen ging: Auf der einen Seite stand der religiös geprägte *Ordensstaat*, auf der anderen das sich emanzipierende Bürgertum. Michał konnte über seinen Freund Heinrich immer wieder ausgleichend in den Konflikt eingreifen. Am Ende ging der Krieg für den *Deutschen Orden* verloren, aber die Beziehung zwischen Michał und Heinrich hielt. 1470 geriet Heinrich dann selbst in schwere Konflikte mit Rom, weil er sich gegen den Ablasshandel des neuen Bischofs von Samland, Dietrich von Cuba, stellte. Überdies machte Heinrich der *Preußische Pfaffenkrieg* (1467 bis 1479), der genauso unverständlich und unnötig war wie der *Dreizehnjährige Krieg*, zu schaffen. Zum Glück hatte er Michał, der auch in der Beziehung ausgleichende Kräfte entwickelte, sodass die beiden trotz der ganzen dummen Auseinandersetzungen um sie herum eine glückliche und harmonische Partnerschaft führten. Gemäß seiner Herkunft spielte Michał nämlich gerne den Puck (später auch *Puk*), also einen fröhlichen, erotischen und wohlgelaunten Hausgeist. Was genau er da so trieb, schrieb er in sehr intimen Tagebüchern nieder. Nach Heinrichs Tod im Jahr 1477 zog Michał Puck nach Mallorca und betrieb dort bis zu seinem eigenen Ableben 1492 eine Finca für spirituelle und sexuelle Einkehr und Erholung. Über hundert Jahre nach seinem Tod, konkret im Jahr 1595, fielen Michałs Tagebücher durch einen Zufall William Shakespeare in die Hände. Was der Dichter dort las, inspirierte ihn derart, dass er es erst im *Sommernachtstraum* (1595/96) und später in seinen *Sonetten* (1609) verarbeitete.

Michał Puck wurde über Jahrhunderte besonders von Frauen verehrt, die etwas dümmliche Männer abbekommen hatten, die sie aber trotzdem liebten. Da ein Puk meist eine Tarnkappe trägt, huldigen ihm aber auch Mützen- und Hutmacher. Der Gedenktag des heiligen Michał ist der 16. August.

SAINT MICHAŁ

Michał was born circa 1420 in Puck (German *Putzig*; Kashubian *Pùck*) and belonged to the West Slavic Kashubian people (or Cassubian, Polish Kaszubi, Kashubian Kaszëbi). He was small, with a very cheerful and engaging personality and worked in the logistics department of the fish master's office in his hometown. It was there that he met his life partner Heinrich Reffle von Richtenberg (* circa 1415 in Swabia; † 1477 in Königsberg), who later became *Grand Master of the Teutonic Order* in 1470. Then the *Thirteen Years' War* broke out (1454 to 1466, also known as the *War of the Cities* or *Wojna trzynastoletnia* in Polish), a dispute between the *Teutonic Order* and a group representing the interests of Prussian cities and landed gentry together with the Kingdom of Poland, which was essentially about questions of power and the future, with the religious state of the *Teutonic Order* on one side and the emancipated bourgeoisie on the other. Michał repeatedly stepped in to help mediate the conflict through his boyfriend Heinrich. In the end, the *Teutonic Order* lost the war, but the relationship between Michał and Heinrich survived. In 1470, Heinrich himself came into serious conflict with Rome because he opposed the sale of indulgences by the new Bishop of Samland, Dietrich von Cuba. Heinrich was also struggling with the Prussian *War of the Priests* (1467 to 1479), which was just as silly and pointless as the *Thirteen Years' War*. Fortunately, he still had Michał, who also applied his mediation skills to their relationship, so that the two of them enjoyed a happy and harmonious union despite all the idiotic conflicts going on around them. In keeping with his roots, Michał occasionally liked to take on the role of Puck, a cheerful, erotic and happy-go-lucky household spirit. He recorded Puck's shenanigans in a series of very intimate diaries. After Heinrich's death in 1477, Michał Puck moved to Mallorca where he ran a finca for men seeking spiritual and sexual recreation until his own death in 1492. In 1595, over a hundred years after his death, Michał's diaries happened to fall into the hands of William Shakespeare. The bard was so inspired by these writings that he incorporated them into *A Midsummer Night's Dream* (1595/96) and later into his *Sonnets* (1609).

For centuries, Michał Puck was worshipped by women who had somehow ended up with rather dim-witted men but loved them anyway. As Puck usually wears a cap of invisibility, he is also worshipped by cap and hat makers. The feast day of St. Michał is August 16.

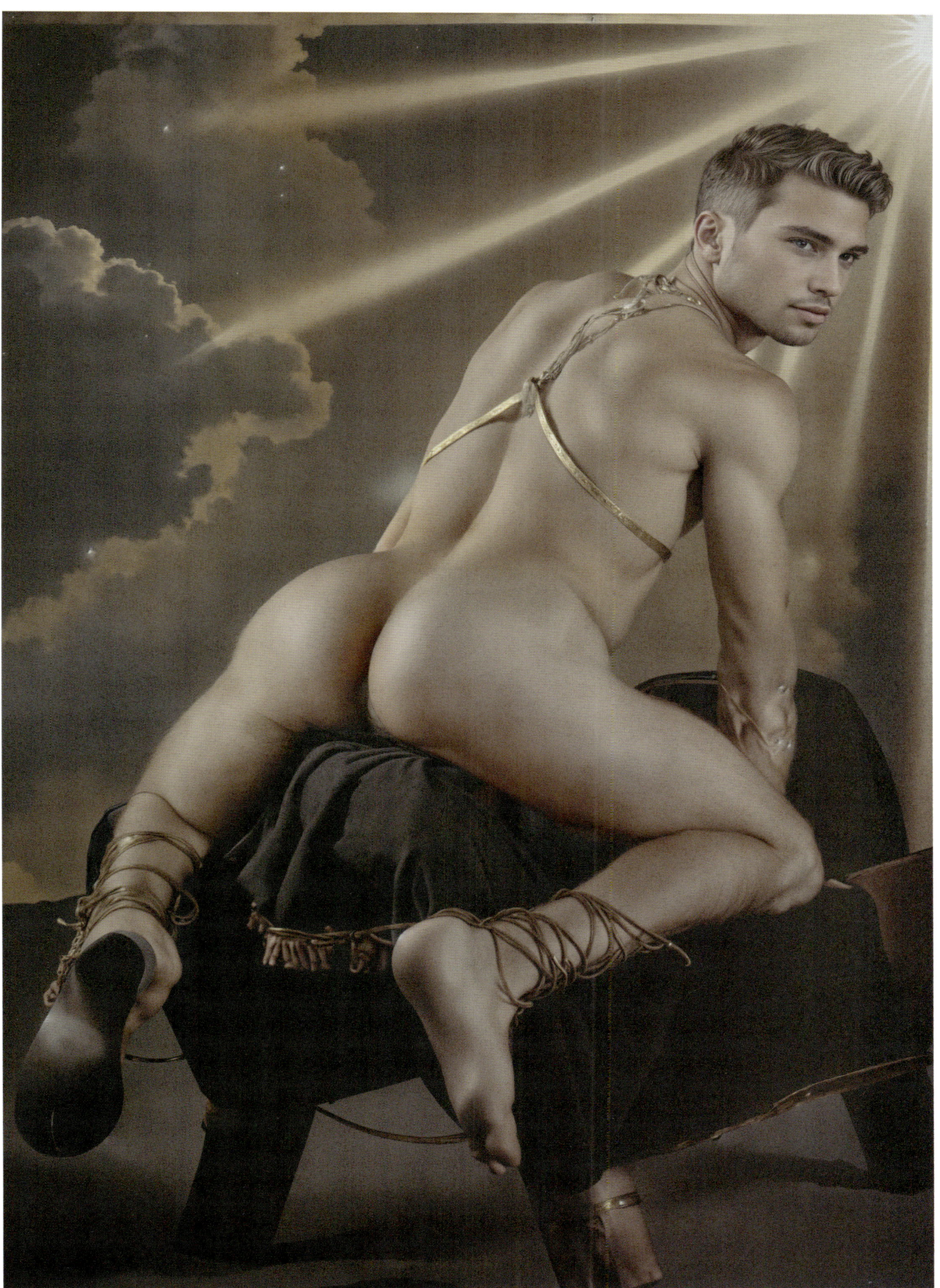

DER HEILIGE MICHAŁ · SAINT MICHAŁ

DER HEILIGE NADIM

Nadim ist etwas ganz Besonderes, denn er ist Engel und Heiliger zugleich. Diese Doppelfunktion entspricht seiner wichtigen Aufgabe als Gleichstellungsbeauftragter an der Himmelspforte. Dort wird selbstverständlich überkonfessionell operiert und selbst die schlimmsten Agnostiker sind willkommen. Detailbeschreibungen über das turbulente Treiben dort kennen wir ja irgendwie alle. Aber Nadim hat uns bestätigt, dass es in Wirklichkeit noch viel turbulenter zugeht — und viel schöner.

Warum der heilige Nadim ausgerechnet am 28. Dezember gefeiert wird, lässt sich historisch nicht mehr genau nachvollziehen. Sehen wir es als Wink des Himmels und nehmen es einfach mal ganz ohne Turbulenzen hin.

SAINT NADIM

Nadim is a very special individual because he is both an angel and a saint. This dual function reflects his important role as Equal Opportunities Officer at the Gates of Heaven. Needless to say, he takes a non-denominational approach, and even the toughest agnostics are welcome. We are all more or less familiar with detailed descriptions of the turbulent goings-on there. But according to Nadim, it's even more turbulent up there in reality — and much nicer.

Why St. Nadim is celebrated on December 28 of all days cannot be precisely reconstructed. Let's treat it as a sign from the heavens and just accept it without too much turbulence.

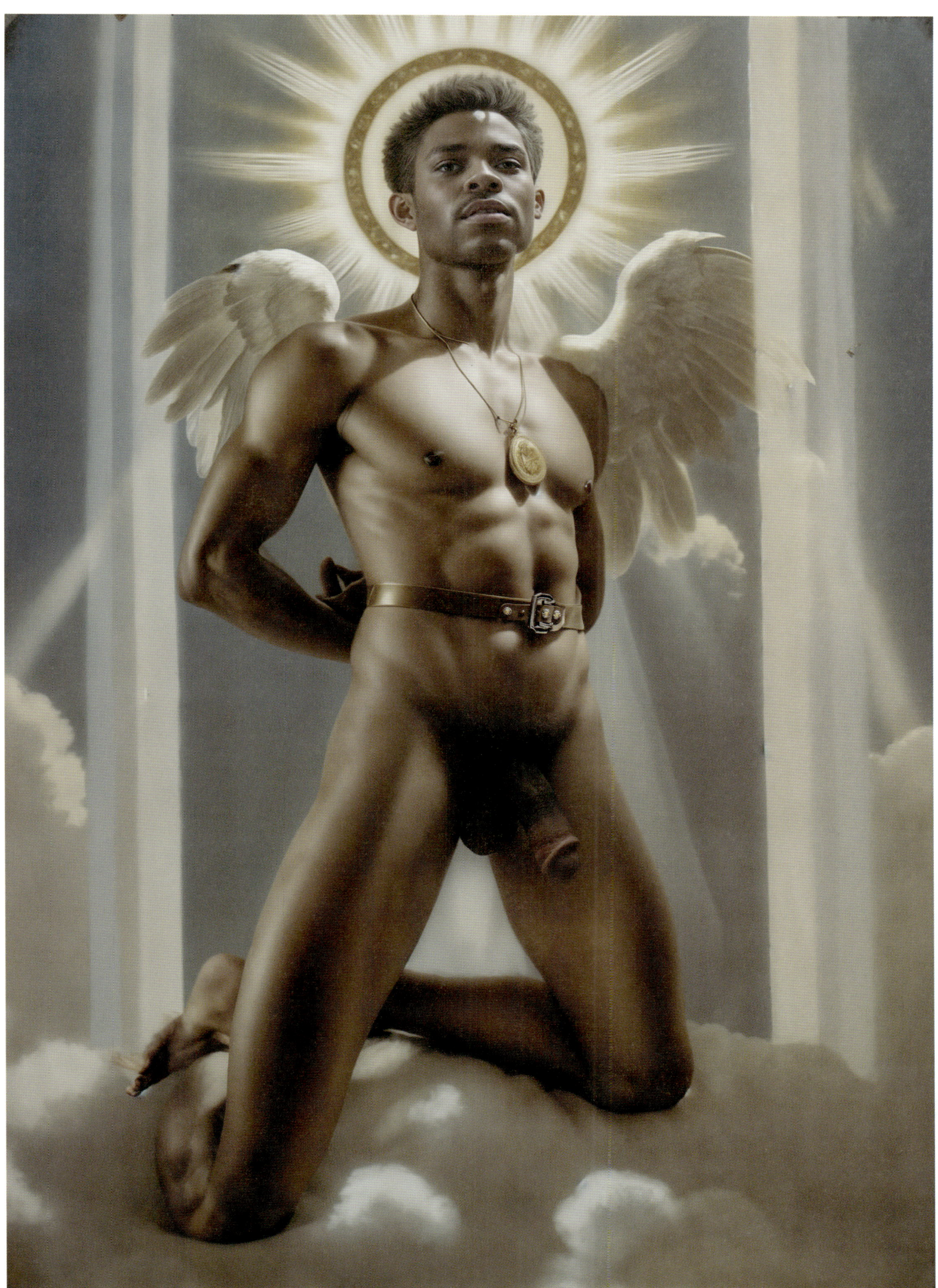

DER HEILIGE NADIM · SAINT NADIM

DER HEILIGE NATHAN UND DER HEILIGE YANNICK

Als nordafrikanische Invasoren im Jahr 904 die Insel Malta eroberten, waren Nathan und Yannick schon seit Jahren ein Paar. Außerdem waren sie erfolgreich im Gewürzhandel tätig. Sie vertrieben Kümmel. Angebaut wurde dieser auf der zu Malta gehörenden Insel *Comino* (maltesisch: *Kemmuna*, deutsch: *Kümmel*). Nach der Invasion wurden die Einwohner Maltas gezwungen, zum Islam überzutreten oder als Menschen zweiter Klasse weiterzuleben und Tribute sowie eine Sondersteuer (Dschizya) zu zahlen. Viele Christen, die die Dschizya nicht aufbringen konnten, wurden versklavt. So wurde Malta zum Hauptumschlagplatz des arabischen Sklavenhandels. Nathan und Yannick halfen zahlreichen jungen Männern, der Sklaverei zu entgehen, indem sie deren Dschizya bezahlten. Das konnte natürlich nicht lange gutgehen. Bald waren Nathan und Yannick pleite, gerieten selbst in Sklaverei und wurden nach Mauretanien verkauft (wo übrigens am 8. August 2007 erstmals ein Gesetz verabschiedet wurde, das Sklaverei unter Strafe stellte). Was danach mit unseren beiden Heiligen passierte, ist nicht bekannt. Auf Malta überlebte das Andenken an sie noch eine Weile. Nachdem die Insel im Jahr 1090 von den Normannen erobert worden war, die die muslimischen Herrscher vertrieben, baute man zwischen Marsaxlokk und Birżebbuġa ein *Nathan-und-Yannick-Sanktuarium*. Doch dann kamen Papst Leo XIII. und seine Enzyklika *Rerum Novarum* mit dem geheimen Zusatzprotokoll. Im Zuge des Verbots der schwulen Heiligenverehrung wurde das Sanktuarium im Juni 1891 bis auf die Grundmauer geschleift.

Der heilige Nathan und der heilige Yannick werden seit jeher von Betroffenen und Gegnern altertümlicher und moderner Sklaverei um Beistand angerufen. Sie haben ihren Gedenktag am 8. Oktober.

SAINT NATHAN AND SAINT YANNICK

Nathan and Yannick had already been in a serious relationship for years when the island of Malta was captured by North African invaders in 904. They were also successful spice traders who traded exclusively in caraway seeds, which were cultivated on the Maltese island of *Comino* (Maltese: *Kemmuna*). After the invasion, the inhabitants of Malta were forced to either convert to Islam or become second-class citizens and pay tribute and a special tax (jizya). Many Christians who could not afford to pay the jizya were enslaved. Malta thus became the main hub of the Arab slave trade. Nathan and Yannick helped many young men escape enslavement by paying their jizya. Of course, this couldn't go on forever. Before long, Nathan and Yannick had run out of money, became enslaved themselves, and were sold to Mauritania (where, incidentally, the first law criminalizing slavery was passed as late as August 8, 2007). Nobody knows what happened to our two saints afterwards. Their memory survived for a while in Malta. In 1090, the island was conquered by the Normans, who drove out the Muslim rulers and built a sanctuary dedicated to Nathan and Yannick between Marsaxlokk and Birżebbuġa. But then Pope Leo XIII came along with his encyclical *Rerum Novarum* and the secret additional protocol. The sanctuary was razed to the ground in June 1891 in the wake of the ban on the veneration of gay saints.

St. Nathan and St. Yannick are invoked by victims and opponents of slavery, both ancient and modern. Their feast day is October 8.

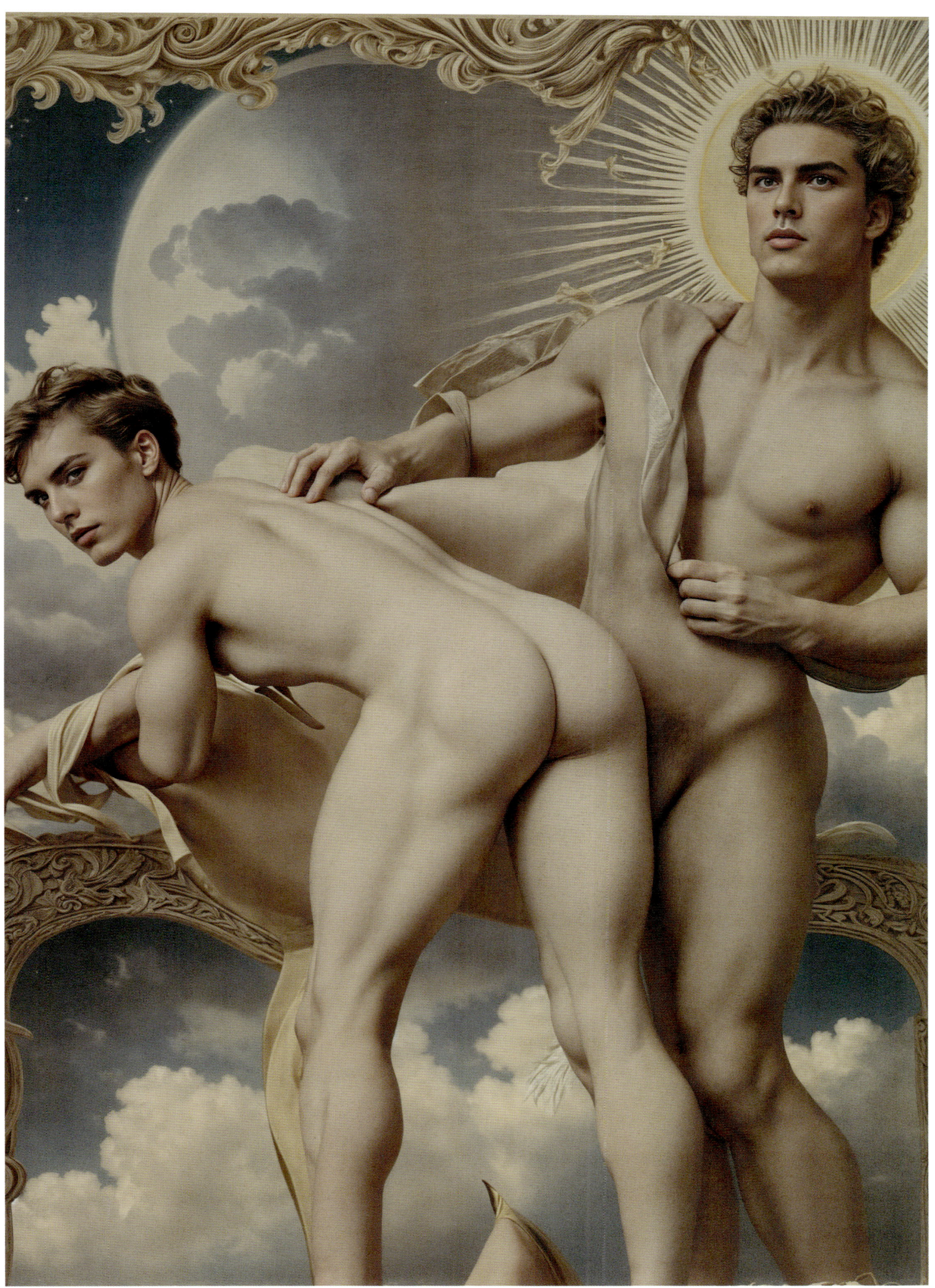

DER HEILIGE NATHAN UND DER HEILIGE YANNICK
SAINT NATHAN AND SAINT YANNICK

DER HEILIGE NIKOLAOS VON BYZANZ

Nikolaos war Masseur am Hof des byzantinischen Kaisers Alexander (Alexandros Porphyrogennētos), der uns wegen seiner anrüchigen Beziehung zu Basilitzes ja bestens bekannt ist. Angeblich wollte Alexander sogar den rechtmäßigen Thronfolger (seinen Neffen Konstantin Porphyrogennetos) entmannen lassen, um dem *slawischen Burschen* („Σκλαβηνόν μειράκιον"), wie Arethas von Caesarea den hübschen Baselitzes betitelte, die Herrschaft der Römer übergeben zu können. Aber darum geht es hier nicht. Schließlich wurde nicht Alexander heiliggesprochen, sondern Nikolaos. Der hatte seinen großen Auftritt, als der *Schnelle Oleg* (andere sprechen auch vom *Großen Oleg*, siehe → DER HEILIGE OLEG, Seite 138) 907 mit einer Streitmacht aus Warägern, Ilmensee-Slowenen, Tschuden, Slowenen, Kriwitschen, Merern, Drewlanen, Ramimitschen, Poljanen, Sewerjanen, Wjatitschen, Chorwwaten, Duleben und Tiwerzen vor den Toren Konstantinopels auftauchte, um die Stadt zu plündern. Unerschrocken trat Nikolaos vor die Stadtmauer, ging auf Oleg zu, machte diesem ein paar Komplimente und bot ihm eine Massage an. Oleg nahm gerne an. Chronisten berichteten, dass die Massage mehrere Tage und Nächte gedauert haben soll und währenddessen mehrere schwere Gewitter über die Stadt zogen. Oleg zeigte sich beeindruckt von Nikolaos' Qualitäten und erklärte nach der Massage, dass er Konstantinopel nun nicht mehr plündern wolle, dafür aber einen Handelsvertrag mit dem Kaiser abschließen werde. Gesagt, getan. Nikolaos zog dann mit Oleg nach Kiew, wo er das *Badehaus Byzanz* eröffnete, das die ortsansässige Bevölkerung eifrig frequentierte. Weil allerdings kaum jemand den Namen aussprechen konnte, bürgerte sich unter den Besuchern die liebevolle Abkürzung *Banja* ein. Zu den Besonderheiten des Badehauses gehörte der Brauch, dass die Gäste sich gegenseitig mit eingeweichten Birkenzweigen auspeitschten — der Legende nach eins der erotischen Spiele, mit denen sich Oleg und Nikolaos in den Gewitternächten vor den Toren Konstantinopels in Stimmung gebracht hatten. Nikolaos teilte mit Oleg übrigens wohl auch dessen Liebe zu Gold, das er allerdings nicht an den Füßen, sondern modebewusst in der Körpermitte trug. Andere sprachen auch davon, er habe *Goldene Hände* gehabt. Aber das muss man nicht wortwörtlich verstehen.

Dass der heilige Nikolaos von Byzanz vor dem Besuch einer Banja angerufen wird, versteht sich von selbst. Sein Bild fehlt in keiner russischen Badeanstalt. Leider lässt sich das heutzutage von nur von einem sehr kleinen Teil der Weltbevölkerung überprüfen. Dass sich das bald ändern möge, erbitten wir am 27. Juli, dem Feiertag des heiligen Nikolaos — sicherlich ein guter Tag, um ein Badehaus zu besuchen.

SAINT NIKOLAOS OF BYZANTIUM

Nikolaos was a masseur at the court of the Byzantine Emperor Alexander (Alexandros Porphyrogennētos), best known for his disreputable relationship with Basilitzes. Alexander is even reputed to have wanted to have the rightful heir to the throne (his nephew Constantine Porphyrogennetos) emasculated in order to hand over Roman rule to the *Slavic lad* (Σκλαβηνόν μειράκιον), as Arethas of Caesarea dubbed the handsome Baselitzes. But that's enough about Alexander. After all, Nikolaos is the one who was canonized. His big moment was in 907, when *Oleg the Swift* (aka *Oleg the Great*, see → SAINT OLEG, page 138) showed up at the gates of Constantinople with an army of Varangians, Ilmensee Slovenes, Chudes, Slovenes, Krivichs, Merers, Drevlanes, Ramimichs, Polyans, Severyans, Vyatichs, Khorvats, Duvets and Tivets intent on raiding the city. Nikolaos fearlessly stepped outside the city wall, approached Oleg, paid him a few compliments and offered him a massage. Oleg was happy to accept. Chroniclers reported that the massage lasted several days and nights, during which powerful thunderstorms swept over the city. Oleg was impressed by Nikolaos' qualities and after the massage was finally over, he declared that he no longer wished to sack Constantinople but would instead conclude a trade agreement with the emperor. No sooner said than done. Nikolaos then accompanied Oleg back to Kyiv, where he opened the *Byzantium Bathhouse*, which was very popular with the local residents. Hardly anyone could pronounce the name, however, so patrons soon adopted the affectionate abbreviation *banya*. One of the bathhouse's more distinctive features was the practice of guests whipping each other with birch branches soaked in water — according to legend, this was one of the erotic games that Oleg and Nikolaos used to get themselves in the mood on stormy nights at the gates of Constantinople. Incidentally, Nikolaos probably also shared Oleg's love of gold, although he didn't wear it on his feet, but rather more stylishly around his waist. Some people also said that he had *golden hands*. But probably not literally.

It goes without saying that St. Nicholas of Byzantium is invoked before visiting a banya. No Russian bathhouse is complete without a portrait of him. Unfortunately, only a very small proportion of the world's population can verify this today. Let's pray that this changes soon, maybe on July 27, the feast day of St. Nikolaos — a good day to visit a bathhouse.

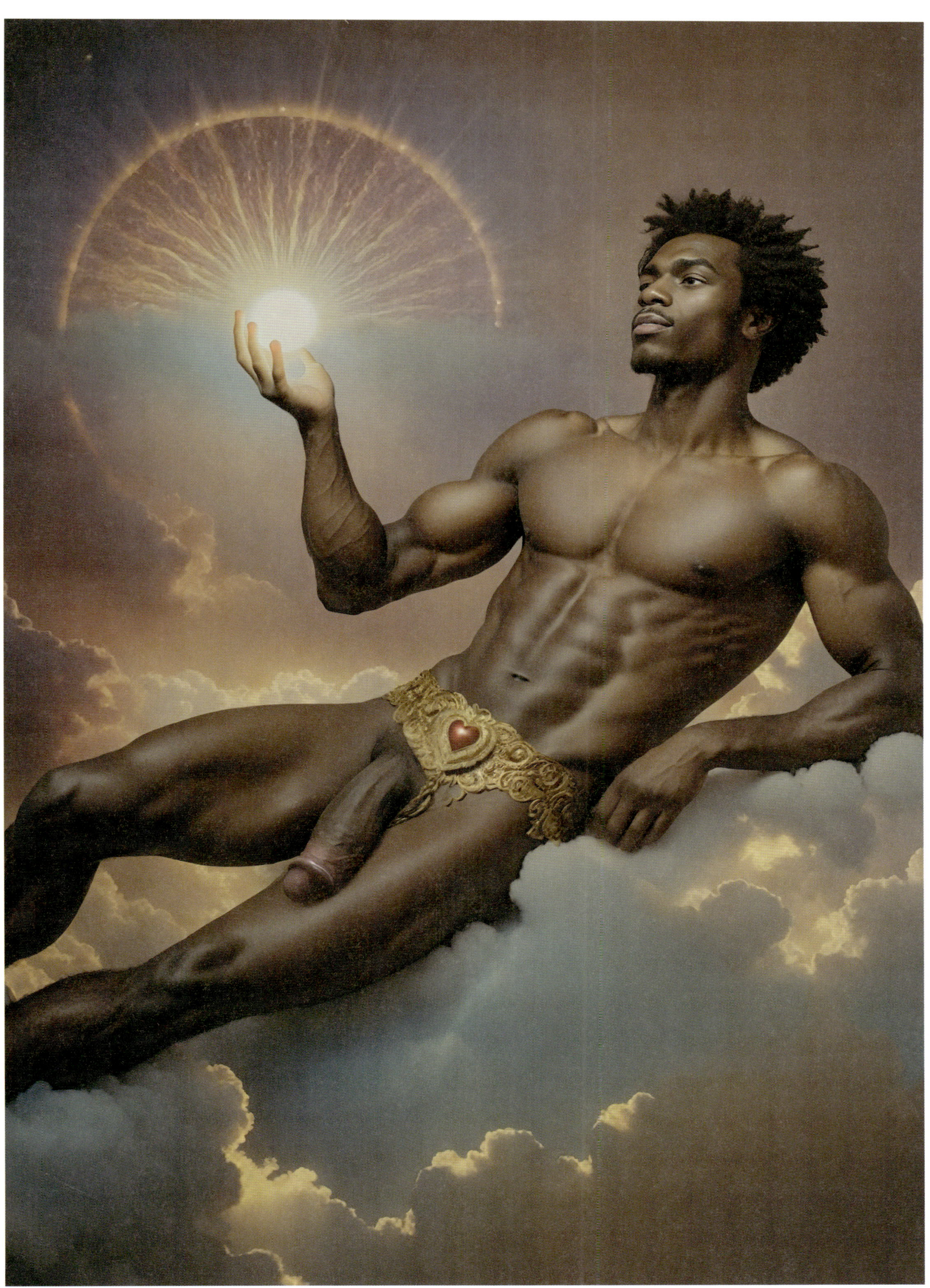

DER HEILIGE NIKOLAOS VON BYZANZ
SAINT NIKOLAOS OF BYZANTIUM

DER HEILIGE OLE UND DER HEILIGE STIG

Ole Hansen Egede wurde am 4. Januar 1823 in Kabelvåg auf den nordnorwegischen Lofoten (nordsamisch Lufuohta oder Váhki) geboren und verstarb am 29. November 1905 in Kristiania (heute Oslo). Sein Freund Stig Johannsen erblickte etwas später, am 15. Juni 1824, im benachbarten Sørvågen das Licht der Welt, verstarb dafür aber einen Tag früher, am 28. November 1905, ebenfalls in Kristiania. Oles Vater war Fischer, kam aber an einem trüben Tag im Jahr 1837 nicht mehr von seiner Arbeit auf dem Meer zurück, sodass der junge Ole schon im zarten Alter von 14 Jahren die Schule verlassen musste, um für den Familienunterhalt zu sorgen. Mit 18 Jahren besorgte er sich ein eigenes kleines Fischerboot und enterte zusammen mit Stig Johannsen die See. Wenn von Mitte Januar bis Mitte April hunderte von Booten ausschwärmten, um Kabeljau zu fangen, waren die beiden Freunde immer ganz vorne mit dabei. Der Kabeljau wurde dann durch Trocknung an der kühlen, salzigen Luft zu Klippfisch oder Stockfisch *(Tørrfisk)* verarbeitet, wie er in katholischen Ländern gerne verzehrt wird. Ole und Stig waren nicht religiös, hatten dafür aber ein besonders gutes Gespür dafür, die Kabeljau-Schwärme ausfindig zu machen, was ihnen unter den anderen Fischern viel Bewunderung einbrachte. Ein katholischer Missionar, der sich auf die Lofoten verirrte und ziemlich erfolglos blieb, versuchte den Spürsinn von Ole und Stig als Wunder („*Fischer, die über das Wasser gehen!*") zu deuten, was die Menschen in Kabelvåg mit Wohlwollen zur Kenntnis nahmen. Als der Missionar 1846 allerdings damit anfing, die beiden von ihrer Homosexualität *heilen* zu wollen, kam es zur Revolte, im Rahmen derer die Bewohner Kabelvågs den Missionar zurück nach Schweden jagten. Ole und Stig konnten aber nicht nur fischen, sie waren auch gut bei Stimme. So sangen sie im berühmten Männerchor der Lofoteninseln, der 1905 im Parlament von Kristiania ein Ständchen beitrug, als der frischgekrönte König Haakon VII. (ursprünglich hatte er Carl geheißen) als erster Monarch eines unabhängigen Norwegens seit 518 Jahren seinen Eid auf die Verfassung leistete. Dem König wurde warm ums Herz und er war zu Tränen gerührt, als er die beiden hochbetagten Männer händchenhaltend singen sah. Leider reichte seine Herzenswärme an diesem Tag offenbar nur für ihn selbst. Ole und Stig hingegen verkühlten sich bei der anschließenden Feier und verstarben danach kurz hintereinander am 28. und 29. November. Ihren fast zeitgleichen Tod deuteten manche Menschen dann auch gleich wieder als Wunder. Bis heute erfahren Ole und Stig auf den Lofoten und in ganz Norwegen große Wertschätzung.

Fischer, die auf eine reiche Beute hoffen, stellen sich einfach Ole und Stig bei ihrer Lieblingsbeschäftigung vor (und damit ist jetzt nicht das Singen gemeint), und dann klappt das schon! Offiziell werden der heilige Ole und der heilige Stig am 4. Januar gefeiert.

SAINT OLE AND SAINT STIG

Ole Hansen Egede was born on January 4, 1823 in Kabelvåg in the northern Norwegian Lofoten Islands (Lufuohta or Váhki in North Sami) and died on November 29, 1905 in Kristiania (present-day Oslo). His boyfriend Stig Johannsen was born a little later, on June 15, 1824, in neighboring Sørvågen, but died the day before him, on November 28, 1905, also in Kristiania. Ole's father was a fisherman, but one dreary day in 1837 he went out to sea and never came back, so young Ole had to leave school at the tender age of fourteen to help support the family. At the age of eighteen, he bought his own small fishing boat and set out to sea with Stig Johannsen. Every year from mid-January to mid-April, hundreds of boats set out to catch cod, and the two friends were always right at the forefront. The cod was then dried in the cool, salty air and turned into stockfish *(tørrfisk)*, a popular dish in Catholic countries. Ole and Stig were not religious but had a special knack for spotting shoals of cod, a skill that earned them much admiration from the other fishermen. A Catholic missionary who had wandered onto the Lofoten Islands and had not had much success there witnessed Ole and Stig's talent and decided it must be a miracle *("fishermen who walk on water!")*. And the people of Kabelvåg were happy to go along with it. However, when the missionary began trying to *cure* them of their homosexuality in 1846, a riot broke out and the inhabitants of Kabelvåg chased the missionary back to Sweden. But Ole and Stig weren't just good at fishing, they were also excellent singers. They joined the famous Lofoten Islands Male Choir, with whom they sang in the Kristiania Parliament in 1905 when the newly crowned King Haakon VII (originally called Carl), the first monarch of an independent Norway in 518 years, took the oath of allegiance to the constitution. When he laid eyes on the heartwarming sight of two elderly men holding hands and singing, the King was moved to tears. Unfortunately, it seems that his heart was only warm enough for himself that day. Ole and Stig caught a chill during the ensuing celebration and died shortly afterwards on November 28 and 29. Some people interpreted their almost simultaneous deaths as yet another miracle. Ole and Stig are still held in high esteem in Lofoten and throughout Norway to this day.

Fishermen hoping for a rich haul simply picture Ole and Stig doing their favorite thing (not singing) and voilà! St. Ole and St. Stig are officially commemorated on January 4.

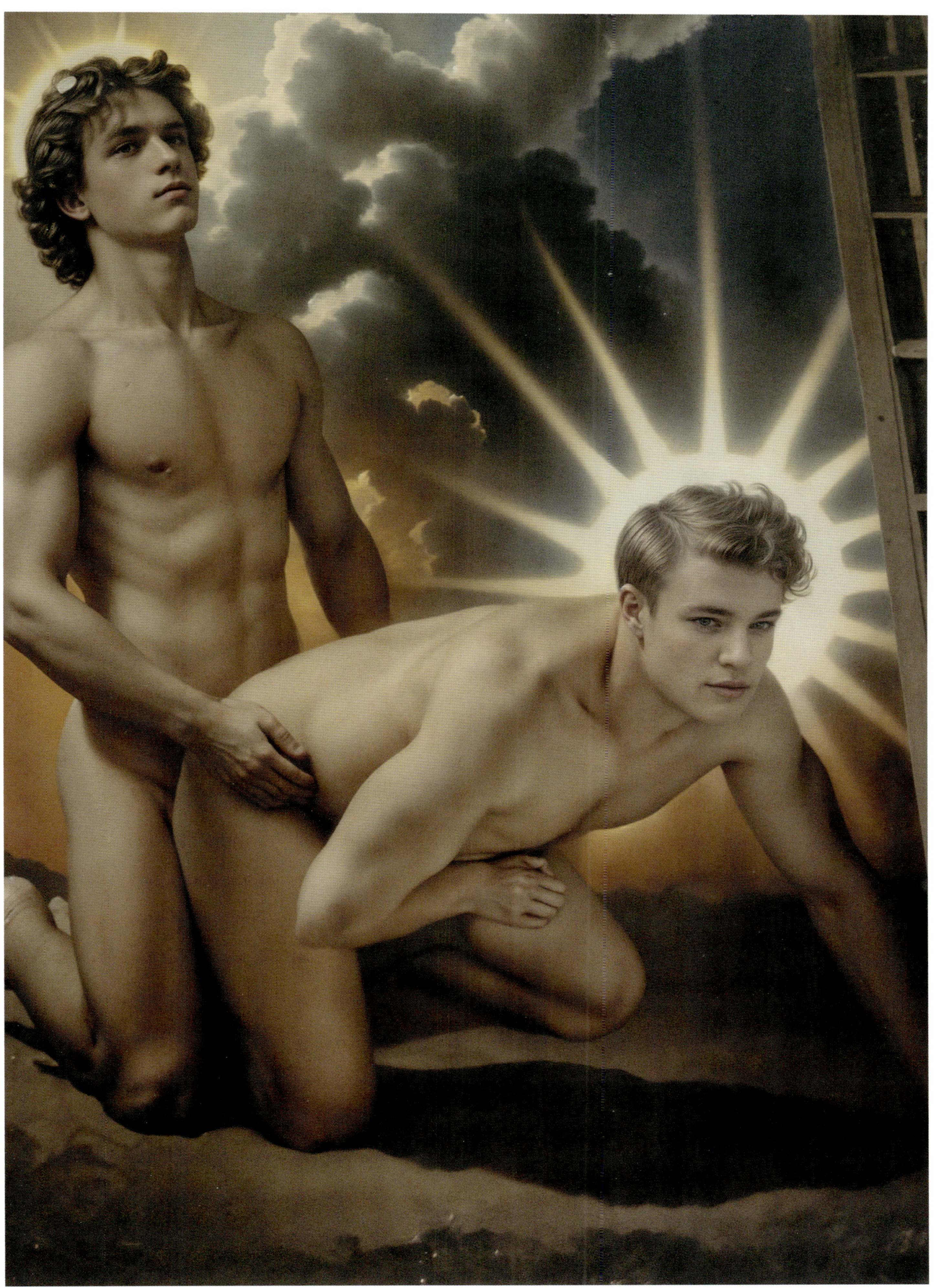

DER HEILIGE OLE UND DER HEILIGE STIG
SAINT OLE AND SAINT STIG

DER HEILIGE OLEG

Oleg (kyrillisch Олег; altostslawisch Ольгъ/Ѡлегъ; kirchenslawisch Ольгъ Вѣщии und altnordisch *Helgi*) war ein Herrscher der Rus. Er wurde 860 in Alt-Uppsala *(Gamla Uppsala)* geboren und verstarb 922 in Kiew. Er wurde auch *Oleg der Schnelle* genannt. Diesen Beinamen hatte er nicht, weil er beim Sex besonders schnell zum Orgasmus kam (bedeutende Forscher konnten das Gegenteil beweisen), sondern weil er in der Kontaktanbahnung wahnsinnig schnell war. Mit seinem offenen und freundlichen — eben slawischen — Wesen bezauberte er jeden Mann im Handumdrehen. Andere bedeutende Forscher wiederum behaupten, die korrekte Übersetzung müsse *Oleg der Große* lauten, was sich wohl auch ohne einen Blick auf unsere Darstellung von selbst erklärt. Ansonsten verlegte er das Machtzentrum seines Reiches 882 von Nowgorod nach Kiew und gilt deshalb als Gründer des Großreiches Kiewer Rus. Dort wurde Vielfalt großgeschrieben. Oleg selbst war Waräger, aber zu seinen Sexualpartnern gehörten Waräger, Ilmensee-Slowenen, Tschuden, Slowenen, Kriwitschen, Merer, Drewlanen, Ramimitschen, Poljanen, Sewerjanen, Wjatitschen, Chorwwaten, Duleben und natürlich auch Tiwerzen. Also so ziemlich alle Volksgruppen, die damals zwischen Ostsee und Schwarzem Meer lebten. Mit einer entsprechend buntgemischten Schar zog er 907 dann auch in kriegerischer Absicht nach Konstantinopel, wo ihm der → HEILIGE NIKOLAOS (Seite 134) erschien, beziehungsweise begegnete, und ihm die kriegerischen Absichten austrieb. Oleg sah ein, dass Sex und Handel besser sind als Gewalt. Anstatt die Stadt zu zerstören (das passierte dann erst 1453), schloss er einen Handelsvertrag mit dem byzantinischen Kaiser, der dazu führte, dass Oleg ziemlich viel Geld verdiente. Die Folge war ein aufwendiger Lebensstil. Man beachte seinen höchst modischen Beinschmuck aus massivem Gold (hier leider leicht außerhalb des Bildes). Dass später in Kiew ein goldenes Tor gebaut wurde, kommt auch nicht von ungefähr. Olegs enge Verbindung zum Byzantinischen Reich führte später übrigens auch dazu, dass die dortige Orthodoxie auch im Kiewer Rus ihre Spuren hinterließ, was die heutigen orthodoxen Prägungen in der Ukraine und Russland erklärt. Oleg selbst soll gesagt haben, dass ihm das mit der Religion *eher egal* war. Ihm soll es immer *nur um die wirklich wichtigen Dinge* gegangen sein.

Der heilige Oleg wird entweder bei den Themen *Größe* und *Geschwindigkeit* angerufen oder aber bei allen Angelegenheiten, die Gold betreffen. Sein Gedenktag ist der 13. Mai, und noch in jedem Jahr ist an diesem Tag der Goldkurs gestiegen.

SAINT OLEG

Oleg (Cyrillic Олег; Old East Slavic Ольгъ/Ѡлегъ; Church Slavonic Ольгъ Вѣщии and Old Norse *Helgi*) was a prince of the Rus. He was born in Old Uppsala *(Gamla Uppsala)* in 860 and died in Kiev in 922. He was also known as *Oleg the Swift*. This sobriquet was not because he was able to orgasm especially quickly (prominent researchers have shown that the opposite is in fact true), but because he was incredibly quick to initiate contact. He could charm every man in an instant with his open and friendly — in other words Slavic — nature. Other prominent researchers, on the other hand, claim that the correct translation should be *Oleg the Great*, which is probably self-explanatory even if you haven't seen our illustration. In 882, he shifted the center of power of his empire from Novgorod to Kiev and is therefore considered the founder of the great empire of Kievan Rus. Diversity was very important there. Oleg was a Varangian, but his sexual partners included Varangians, Ilmensee Slovenes, Chudes, Slovenes, Krivichs, Merers, Drevlanes, Ramimichs, Polyans, Severyans, Vyatichs, Khorvvats, Duives and, of course, Tiverts. In other words, pretty much every ethnic group living between the Baltic Sea and the Black Sea at the time. In 907, with a correspondingly diverse army, he set off for Constantinople with the intention of conquering it but was instead met by → SAINT NIKOLAOS (page 134), who persuaded him to abandon his military plans. Oleg realized that sex and trade were better than violence. Instead of destroying the city (which did not happen until 1453), he concluded a highly lucrative trade agreement with the Byzantine emperor, and thus ended up with large amounts of money which he spent on a highly extravagant lifestyle. Readers will note his ultra-fashionable solid gold greaves (unfortunately not displayed in their entirety here). It is no coincidence that a golden gate was built in Kiev years later. Oleg's close ties to the Byzantine Empire later led to the Orthodox faith leaving its mark on Kievan Rus, which explains the present-day Orthodox influences in Ukraine and Russia. Oleg himself is said to have remarked that he *didn't really care* about religion. He was allegedly only interested in *really important things*.

St. Oleg is invoked in matters of *size* and *speed* and anything to do with gold. His feast day is May 13, and the price of gold always rises on this day.

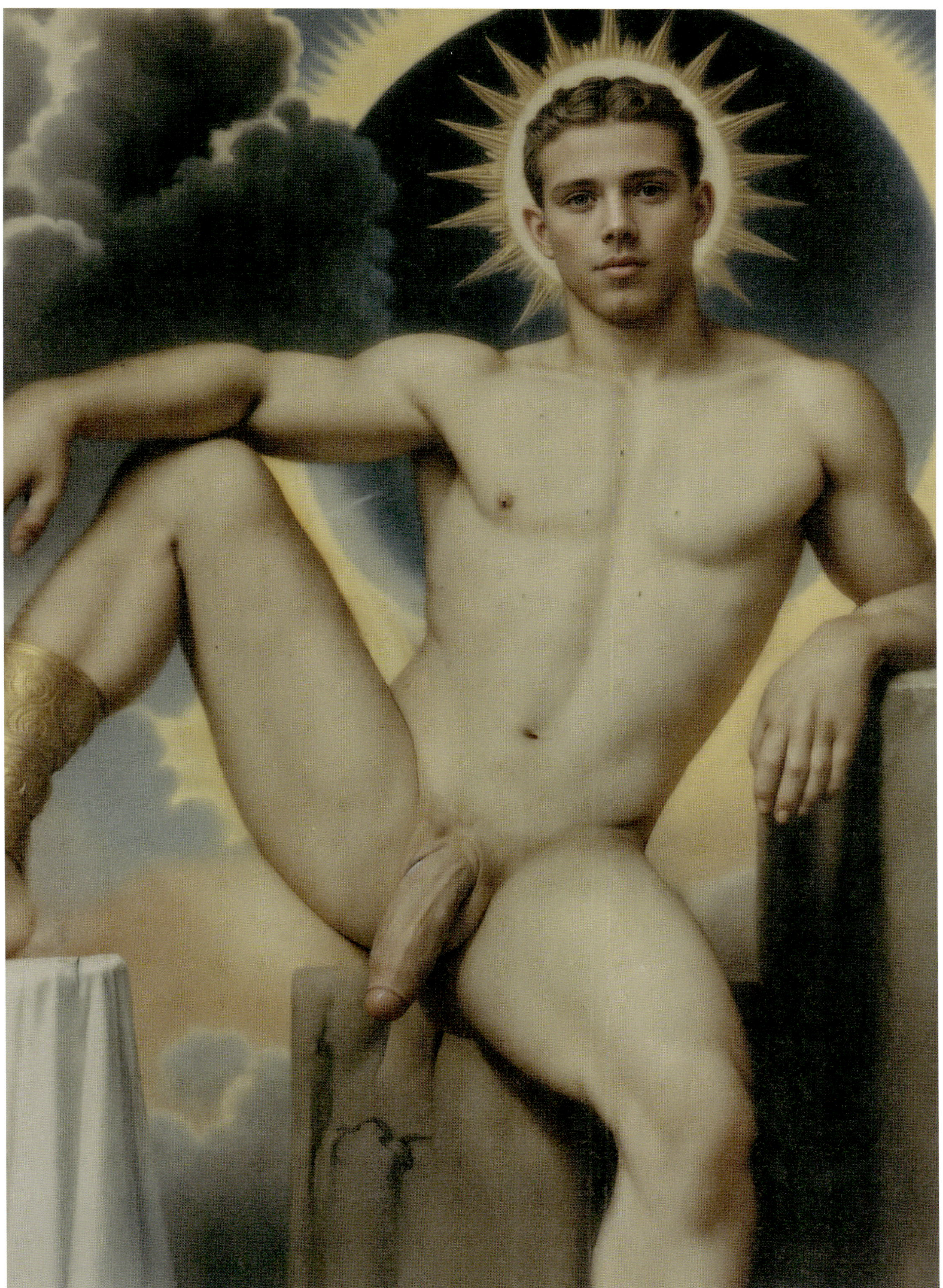

DER HEILIGE OLEG · SAINT OLEG

OSCAR UND FRANK

Oscar Schmidt und Frank Hollenberg wurden 1862 mit einem Abstand von nur wenigen Tagen auf einem Planwagen Richtung Westen, irgendwo in Illinois, Missouri oder Kansas, geboren. Franks Vater gründete 1872 in dem nach ihm benannten Städtchen Hollenberg am Little Blue River in Kansas einen Laden mit Postfiliale, den Sie immer noch an der Ecke Main und Fuller Street besuchen können. Oscar und Frank waren allerbeste Freunde und wuchsen ungezwungen und frei auf. Unsere Abbildung zeigt die beiden beim Spielen im Wald und die auffällige Dominanz der Farbe Rot. Für seine roten Schuhe hatte Oscar jahrelang gespart und so ziemlich jeden Job angenommen, um die Schuhe in einem Versandkatalog bestellen zu können und sie dann zu Fuß an der 21,2 Kilometer (13,2 Meilen) entfernten *Hollenberg Pony Express Station* abzuholen. Natürlich wurde er von Frank begleitet. Oscar und Frank waren glückliche Rednecks und folgten dem → HEILIGEN GLÖCKCHEN (siehe Seite 64), von dem ihnen schon ihre Eltern begeistert erzählt hatten. Die Behauptung, dass der Begriff *Redneck* von einem bei der Feldarbeit durch die Sonne verbrannten Nacken stammt, ist nicht richtig. Junge Männer in den USA trugen Halstücher, mit denen sie sich schützen und gleichzeitig ihre sexuellen Wünsche artikulieren konnten. Die roten Schuhe standen für etwas anderes, aber für was genau, konnte nie genau erforscht werden und bleibt ein Geheimnis. Das gilt auch für die roten Schuhe der Päpste oder auch Dorothys Schuhe in *Der Zauberer von Oz*, einer ganz anderen Geschichte aus Kansas. Immerhin war *Friend of Dorothy* oder *a friend of Dorothy's (ein Freund von Dorothy)* früher ein Begriff für einen schwulen Mann und Judy Garland, die Darstellerin der Dorothy im Film *Der Zauberer von Oz*, zweifelsohne eine Ikone der Schwulenbewegung. Das kann man von irgendeinem Papst eher nicht behaupten. Oscars und Franks Eltern hatten den beiden Jungs in der East Street ein schönes Haus gebaut, das die beiden aber nur gelegentlich bewohnten. Sie zogen es vor, in Kansas City den *Side Kicks Saloon (For cowboy-loving cowboys …)* zu betreiben und ihren sexuellen Erfahrungshorizont um neue Spielarten zu erweitern.

Der genaue Geburtstag von Oscar und Frank wurde leider nicht erfasst, denn man war ja mit dem Planwagen unterwegs. Wir feiern ihre Experimentierfreude und die roten Schuhe — gemeinsam mit Schuhmachern in aller Welt — am 28. September.

OSCAR AND FRANK

Oscar Schmidt and Frank Hollenberg were born in 1862, just a few days apart, on a covered wagon heading west, somewhere in either Illinois, Missouri or Kansas. In 1872, Frank's father founded a store and post office in a small town named after him, Hollenberg, on the Little Blue River in Kansas, which you can still visit today — it's on the corner of Main Street and Fuller Street. Oscar and Frank were best friends and grew up without constraints or inhibitions. Our illustration shows the two of them playing in the forest; the color red is especially prominent. Oscar saved for years for those red shoes, taking just about any job he could get so he could order them from a mail-order catalog and then walk 13.2 miles to pick them up at the *Hollenberg Pony Express station*. Frank came with him of course. Oscar and Frank were happy-go-lucky rednecks and followers of → SAINT TINKER BELL (see page 64), whose story they had heard from their parents. Some people claim that the term *redneck* stems from farm workers getting a sunburnt neck from working in the fields. This is incorrect. Young men in the USA wore bandanas to protect their skin and signal their sexual preferences at the same time. The red shoes stood for something else, but it has never been possible to find out exactly what. It's a mystery. The same applies to the red shoes worn by the Popes and Dorothy's shoes in *The Wizard of Oz*, a completely different story from Kansas. After all, a *friend of Dorothy* used to mean a gay man, and Judy Garland, who played Dorothy in the film *The Wizard of Oz*, was undoubtedly an icon of the gay rights movement. You couldn't really say that about a Pope, no matter which one. Oscar and Frank's parents had built a nice house for the two boys in East Street, but the happy couple only lived there from time to time. They preferred to run the *Side Kicks Saloon (For cowboy-loving cowboys …)* in Kansas City and expand their sexual horizons.

There is no record of Oscar and Frank's exact birthdates, as they were both born in a covered wagon. We celebrate their passion for experimentation and red shoes — along with shoemakers all over the world — on September 28.

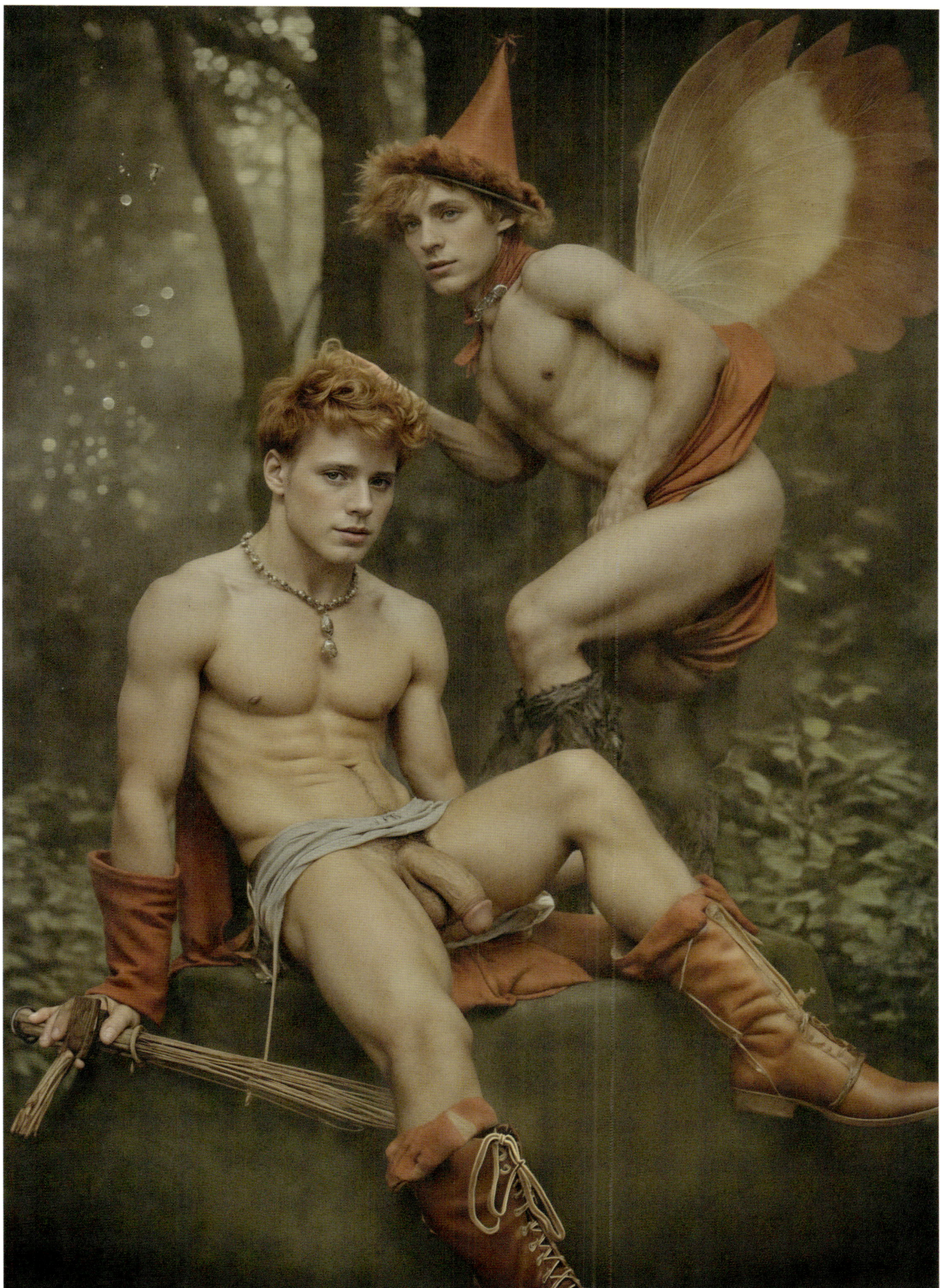

OSCAR & FRANK

DER HEILIGE PASQUALINO

Der heilige Pasqualino gehört zur Gruppe der *fliegenden Heiligen*. Sein Name geht auf das lateinische *Pascha (Osterfest)* mit all seinen Wundern zurück, wobei *Pascha* wiederum auf *Pessach* zurückgeht, das jüdische Fest, mit dem der Auszug aus Ägypten gefeiert wird, aber das wissen wir ja alle. Weniger bekannt ist dagegen, dass Pasqualino wie alle fliegenden Heiligen nach Lust und Laune quer durch die Jahrhunderte und Jahrtausende flattern kann und zur Muse vieler Künstler wurde. Ohne Pasqualino hätte es keinen Michelangelo, keinen Caravaggio, keinen Bernstein und nicht mal einen Tschaikowski gegeben. Ja, selbst ins frostige St. Petersburg hat sich dieser Heilige vorgewagt. Pasqualino hat wortwörtlich Steine, ja manchmal sogar Gebirge, zur Seite gerollt, um verkümmerte, tote Talente wieder zum Leben zu erwecken. Er war es natürlich auch, der die Menschen aus der Sklaverei ins gelobte Land führte. Alles hängt mit allem zusammen und Pasqualino ist immer mittendrin. Er verknüpft *Exodus* mit *Osterwundern*, zerrissene Vorhänge mit vor Farbenfreude berstenden Leinwänden, Regen mit Sonne, Hitze mit Schnee und sämtliche Widersprüche, die sonst noch auf dieser Welt bestehen können. Eigentlich kann und weiß er alles. Das einzige Problem ist, dass er oft zu faul ist, davon Gebrauch zu machen, und deshalb entweder zu selten oder zu spät erscheint. Wenn er allerdings mal da ist, geht es richtig zur Sache.

❧ *Pasqualino ist zurück!* Diesen Satz möchten wir doch alle in unserem Leben mindestens einmal ausrufen können. Darauf warten wir. Ganz besonders am 7. Dezember, dem offiziellen Pasqualino-Feiertag. ❧

SAINT PASQUALINO

St. Pasqualino is a member of the group of *flying saints*. His name derives from the Latin *Pascha (Easter)* with all its miracles, which in turn derives from *Pesach* or *Passover*, the Jewish festival celebrating the exodus from Egypt — but of course everyone knows that. What most people don't know is that Pasqualino, like all flying saints, can flit across the centuries and millennia at will and has served as a muse and source of inspiration for countless artists. Without Pasqualino, there would have been no Michelangelo, no Caravaggio, no Bernstein and no Tchaikovsky. Yes, this saint even made the journey to the freezing city of St. Petersburg. Pasqualino literally pushed boulders, sometimes even mountains, aside in order to bring withered and dead talents back to life. Of course, he was also the one who led people out of slavery and into the promised land. Everything is connected, and Pasqualino is always at the heart of it all. He is the link between *Exodus* and *Easter miracles*, torn veils and canvases exploding in color, rain and sun, heat and snow and all the other contradictions that can be found in this world. He knows everything and can do anything. The only problem is that he is frequently too lazy to make use of his abilities and therefore shows up either too little or too late. But when he does show up, the show really gets going.

❧ Don't we all wish we could cry *Pasqualino is back!* at least once in our lives? That's what we're all waiting for. Especially on December 7, Pasqualino's official holiday. ❧

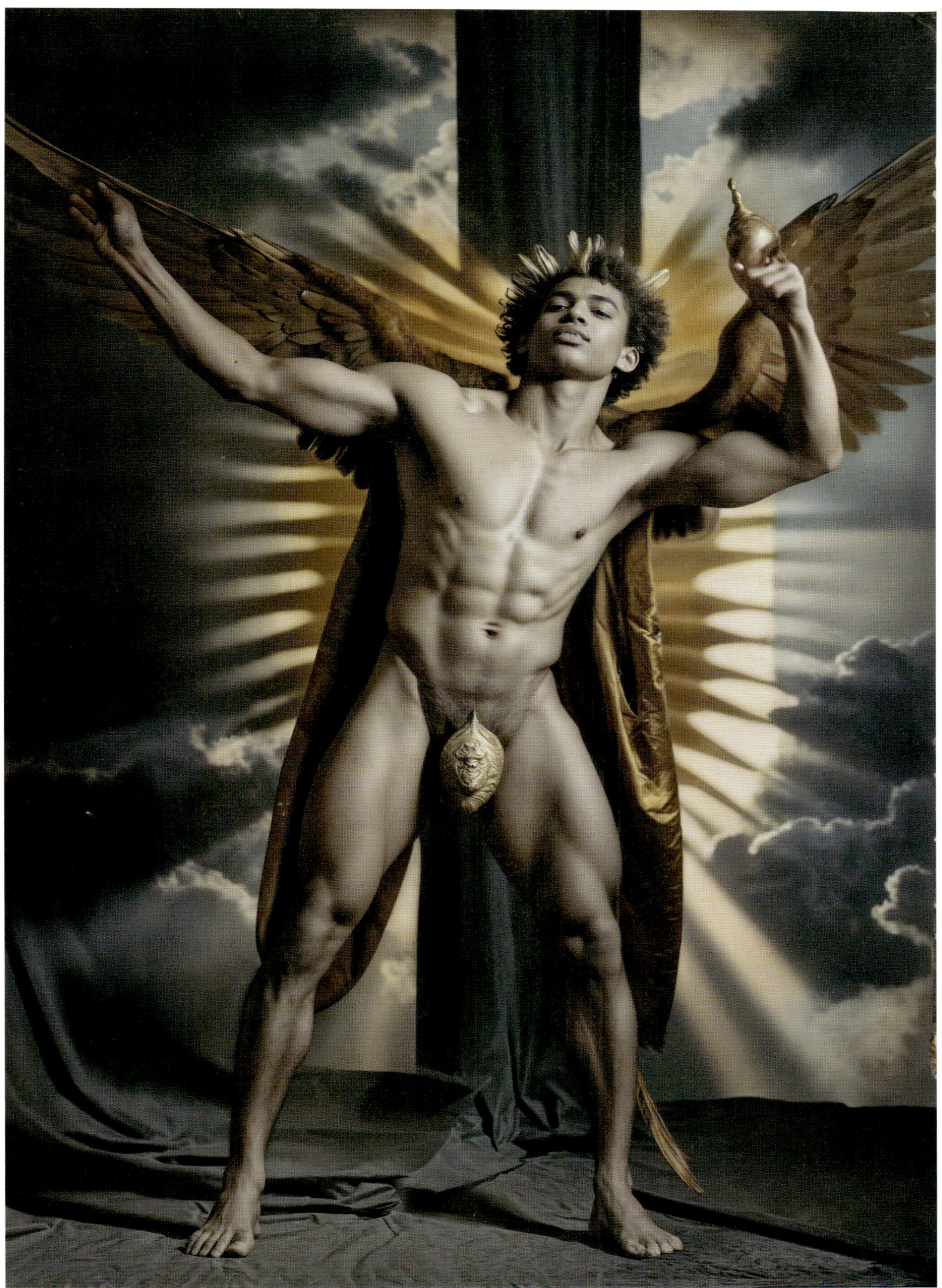

DER HEILIGE PASQUALINO · SAINT PASQUALINO

DER HEILIGE PETER UND DER HEILIGE EDMUND

Die Geschichte von Peter und Edmund wird häufig falsch erzählt. Es geht darin um Kleiderschränke, Märchenfiguren, eine Weiße Hexe, eine Biberfamilie, den Weihnachtsmann, Warzenweiber, einen Steintisch, einen Löwen und dessen freiwilligen Opfertod — eine komplett wirre Story also, auf die wir hier aus Platzgründen nicht in Gänze eingehen können. Fest steht, dass Peter und Edmund (beide *16. Oktober 1852) als schwules Zwillingspärchen in Dublin aufwuchsen und dort 1871 am *Trinity College* den genau zwei Jahre jüngeren Oscar Fingal O'Flahertie Wills Wilde kennenlernten. Peter und Edmund nahmen Oscar unter ihre Fittiche und brachten ihm so ziemlich alles bei. Darüber, ob es in diesem Zusammenhang auch zu einem *Zwillingsinzest* kam, wird viel spekuliert, aber es ist nicht überliefert. Es folgten Reisen nach Italien und schließlich der Wechsel nach Oxford ans *Magdalen College*. Peters und Edmunds dortiger Beitrag zur Gemeinschaft war ihre ästhetische Position: Sie waren der Meinung, dass die Kunst und auch der Sex sich selbst zu genügen hätten, also nicht äußeren Zwecken unterworfen werden sollten. Damit wendeten sich die Zwillinge gleichermaßen gegen konservative wie gegen progressive Positionen, was neue Spielräume für Experimente eröffnete. Betrachten Sie in diesem Zusammenhang bitte auch die überdimensionierte Schneeflocke in unserer Abbildung. Und die schimmernden Seifenblasen. Macht alles keinen Sinn, hat alles keinen Zweck, ist aber schön und ändert nichts daran, dass es am Ende eben doch nur um die Beule in Edmunds Hose geht.

Der heilige Peter und der heilige Edmund haben uns gelehrt, dass *Ästhetizismus als Lebensform* eine feine Sache ist. Dafür verehren wir sie — nicht nur, aber besonders an ihrem Gedenktag, dem 27. September.

SAINT PETER AND SAINT EDMUND

The story of Peter and Edmund is often told in garbled form, involving wardrobes, fairy tale characters, a white witch, a family of beavers, Santa Claus, a faun, a stone table, a lion and his sacrificial death — a thoroughly confusing tale that we don't have the space to go into here in full. We do know that Peter and Edmund (both born October 16, 1852) grew up as gay twins in Dublin, where they met Oscar Fingal O'Flahertie Wills Wilde, exactly two years their junior, at *Trinity College* in 1871. Peter and Edmund took Oscar under their wing and taught him pretty much everything. There is much speculation as to whether this also involved *incest between the twins*, but there is no record of it. They took several trips to Italy before finally transferring to *Magdalen College*, Oxford. Peter and Edmund's contribution to the Oxford community was their aesthetic position: they believed that art and sex should be self-sufficient and should not serve an external purpose. In doing so, the twins rejected both the conservative and progressive positions, which opened up new opportunities for experimentation. In this context, we would like to draw your attention to the giant snowflake in our illustration. And the iridescent soap bubbles. None of it makes sense, none of it serves any purpose, but it's pretty and doesn't change the fact that ultimately all that matters is the bulge in Edmund's pants.

St. Peter and St. Edmund teach us that *aestheticism as a way of life* can be an excellent choice. This is why we venerate them — not only, but especially on their feast day, September 27.

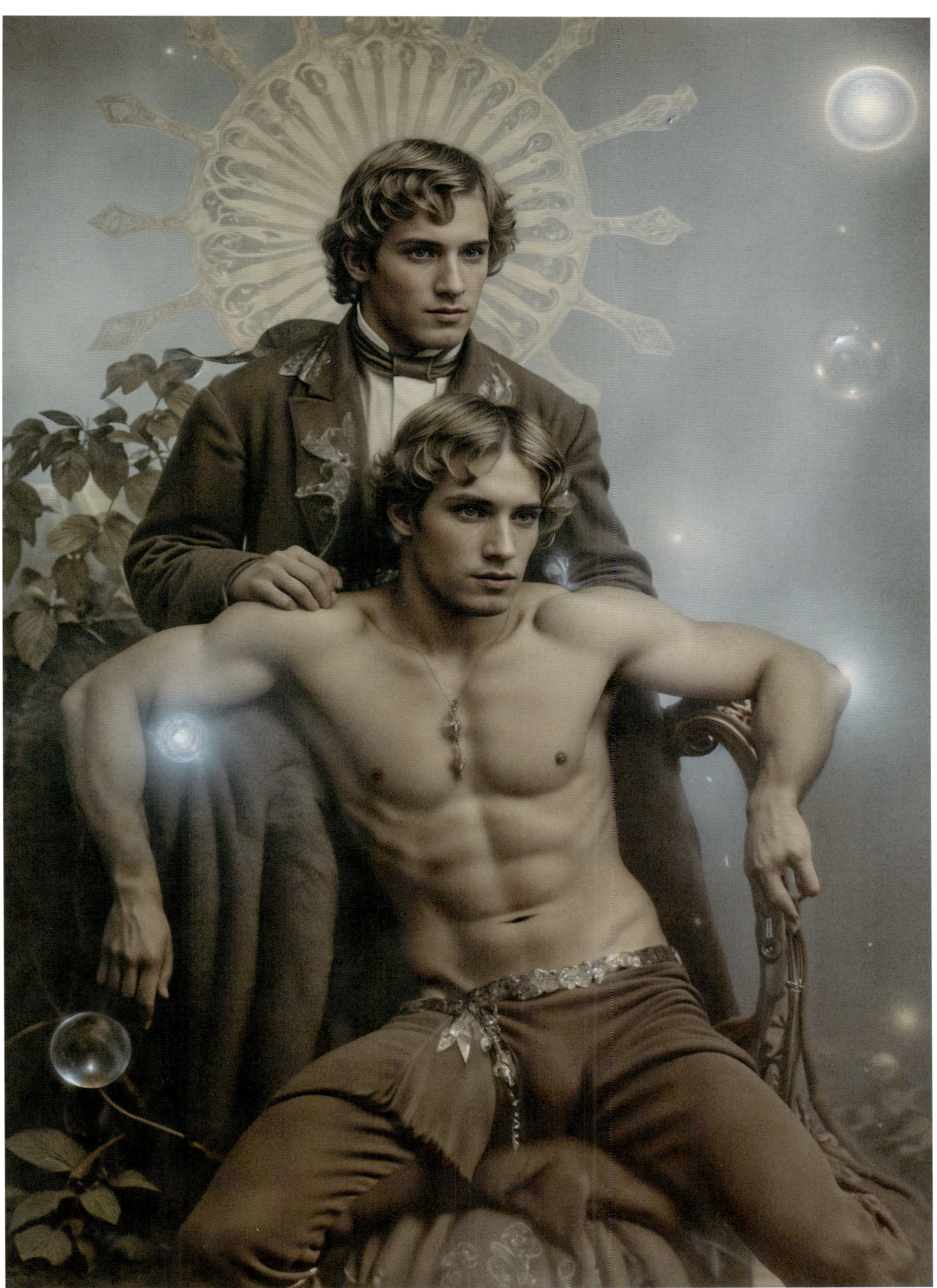

DER HEILIGE PETER UND DER HEILIGE EDMUND
SAINT PETER AND SAINT EDMUND

DER HEILIGE QUAO AUS NANNY TOWN

Es waren Granny Nanny und ihre Brüder Accompong, Cudjoe, Cuffy, Johnny sowie der Jüngste, Quao, die in Jamaika den als Maroon-Krieg (1730 bis 1739) bezeichneten Sklavenaufstand gegen die Briten organisierten. Als Maroons definierte man damals Menschen, die sich der Sklaverei durch Flucht oder aktiven Widerstand entzogen hatten. Die fünf Geschwister teilten sich auf, um ihren Kampf besser organisieren zu können. Nanny und Quao gründeten in den Blue Mountains im Nordosten der Insel mit dem Städtchen Nanny Town (heute *Moore Town*) einen Ort der Toleranz und sexuellen Vielfalt. Nanny wird in diesem Kontext stets als dominante und kluge Frau mit durchdringendem Blick beschrieben, die an der Befreiung von mehr als 800 Sklaven beteiligt gewesen sein soll. Noch heute ist das Porträt von *Nanny of the Maroons* auf dem 500-Jamaika-Dollar-Schein zu sehen (bei Redaktionsschluss knapp 3 Euro, Tendenz täglich sinkend). Der sanfte Quao mit den schönen Haaren wurde dagegen immer nur im Geheimen verehrt. Er kümmerte sich um die Musik in Nanny Town und entwickelte dabei eine charakteristische Offbeat-Phrasierung, bei der seine Gitarre — wie Wikipedia es ausdrückt — „auf die in den meisten anderen Musikrichtungen unbetonte zweite und vierte Taktzeit" spielte. Später nannte man sowas dann Reggae. Wie das schöne Jamaika trotz solcher Errungenschaften zu einem der homophobsten Orte der Welt werden konnte, kann kein Mensch erklären, geschweige denn verstehen. Körperliche Intimität unter Männern kann dort heutzutage mit bis zu zwei Jahren Haft bestraft werden, Analverkehr sogar mit bis zu zehn Jahren Gefängnis und schwerer Zwangsarbeit. Und die Musik, die ursprünglich mal für Freude und Entspannung sorgen sollte, kommt heute als Aggro-Dancehall mit Mordaufrufen (*Bun dem chichiman = Verbrennt die Schwulen*) daher. So hat sich Quao aus Nanny Town das bestimmt nicht vorgestellt, als er seinerzeit den Offbeat erfand. Möge er seinen schwulen Brüdern und Schwestern beistehen.

Quao lässt sein Licht auf all jene strahlen, die unserer Hilfe und unseres Zuspruchs bedürfen. Immer. Aber besonders hell an seinem Ehrentag, dem 29. Juni.

SAINT QUAO OF NANNY TOWN

It was Granny Nanny and her brothers Accompong, Cudjoe, Cuffy, Johnny and Quao, the youngest, who organized the slave rebellion against the British in Jamaica known as the Maroon War (1730 to 1739). The name "Maroon" was given to people who had escaped from slavery by running away or actively resisting. The five siblings split up in order to better organize their campaign. Nanny and Quao founded the small town of Nanny Town (present-day *Moore Town*) in the Blue Mountains in the north-east of the island as a place of tolerance and sexual diversity. Nanny is always described as an intelligent and commanding woman with piercing eyes, who is said to have helped liberate more than 800 slaves. The portrait of *Nanny of the Maroons* can still be seen today on the 500 Jamaican dollar bill (just under 3 Dollars at the time of writing, and falling daily). The gentle Quao with his beautiful hair, on the other hand, was only ever worshipped in secret. He handled the music in Nanny Town, developing a distinctive offbeat phrasing with his guitar: a rhythmic pattern that, as Wikipedia puts it, "accents the second and fourth beats in each bar." Later on, it came to be known as reggae. No one can explain, let alone understand, how despite such achievements, the beautiful island of Jamaica could become one of the most homophobic places in the world. Physical intimacy between males is punishable by up to two years in prison, and anal intercourse by up to ten years in prison and hard labor. And the music that was originally designed to bring joy and peace of mind has been transformed into aggressive dancehall anthems with incitements to murder (*Bun dem chichiman = Burn the gays*). This is certainly not what Quao from Nanny Town had in mind when he invented the offbeat. May he give aid and comfort to his gay brothers and sisters.

Quao shines his light on all those who need our help and support. Always. But it shines especially brightly on his feast day, June 29.

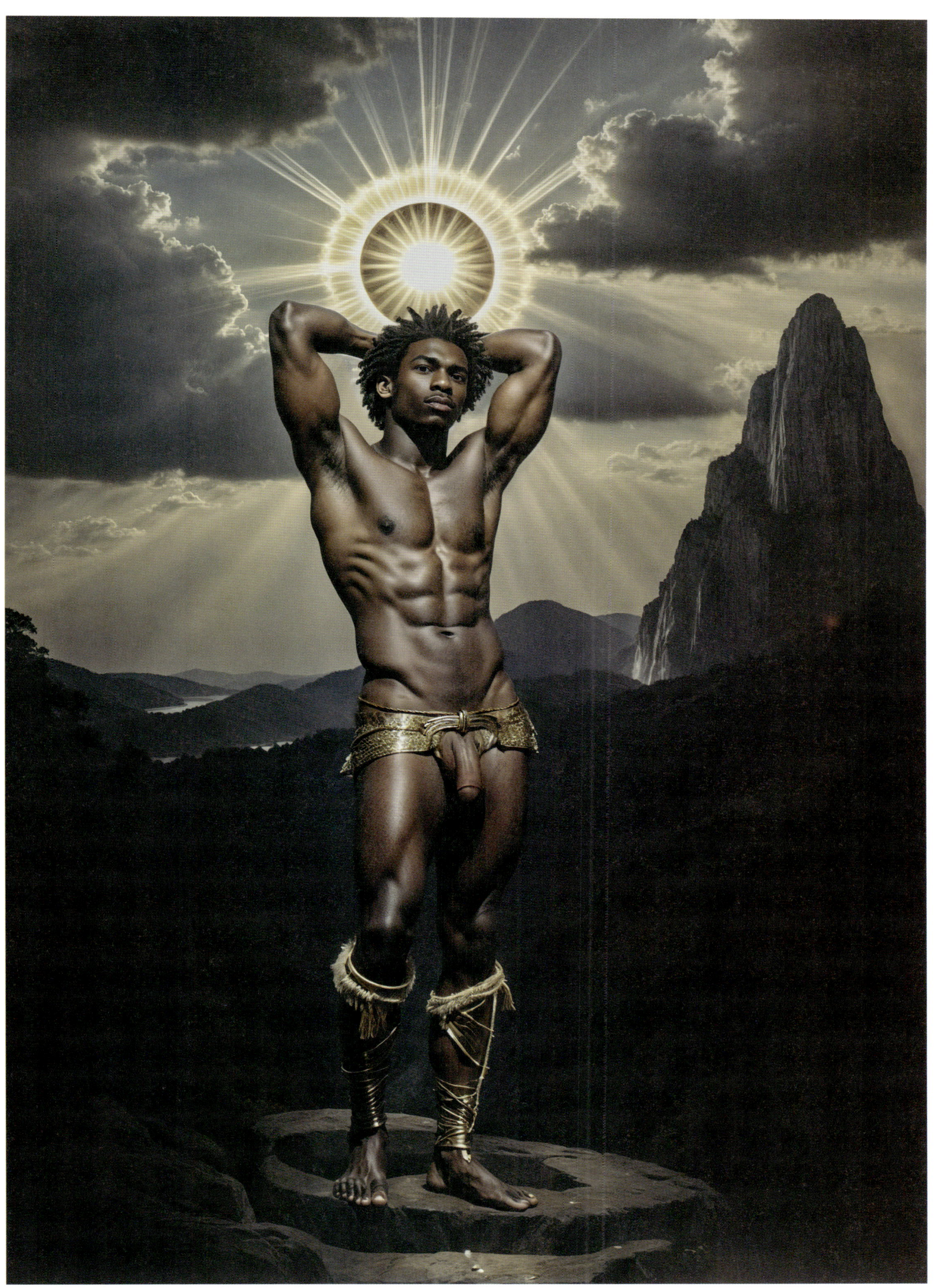

DER HEILIGE QUAO AUS NANNY TOWN
SAINT QUAO OF NANNY TOWN

DER HEILIGE QUENTIN UND SILVESTER

Quentin und Silvester arbeiteten in der Tempelprostitution als Hierodulen, also sogenannte heilige Diener. Sie lernten sich 160 in Smyrna (heute türkisch *İzmir*) kennen und verließen die Stadt 175 — also noch vor dem ersten großen Erdbeben — Richtung Mykonos. Interessanterweise wurde nur Quentin, der bei ihren sexuellen Rollenspielen häufig als schwarzer Engel auftrat, heiliggesprochen. Das störte aber ihre Beziehung nicht weiter. Als selbstbewusste Sexarbeiter ließen sie sich von Kunden gut bezahlen und boten gemeinsam in ihrem gut ausgestatteten Studio eine Reihe von Dienstleistungen an: Erotisches Tanzen, Massagen, SM-Shows und natürlich Geschlechtsverkehr. Ihre Kernkompetenz war allerdings das Zuhören. Demzufolge fühlten sich ihre Kunden nicht nur unterhalten, befriedigt und wahrgenommen, sondern auch verstanden — rundum glücklich also. An den Tempel mussten Quentin und Silvester nur fünf Prozent ihrer Einnahmen abgeben. Das Studio inklusive Heizung, fließend Wasser und Schutz stellte der Tempel sowieso. Und von der Einkommenssteuer waren Hierodulen auch befreit. So lief das damals. Quentin und Silvester wurden schnell ziemlich reich, oder jedenfalls vermögend genug, um sich auf Mykonos ein Haus mit Meerblick zu kaufen. Dort betrieben sie einen Souvenirladen und nahmen gelegentlich hungrige Touristen mit nach Hause.

Quentin und Silvester sorgen für faire und selbstbestimmte Arbeitskonditionen für Sexarbeiter. Ihr Gedenktag ist der 27. September.

SAINT QUENTIN AND SYLVESTER

Quentin and Sylvester were temple sex workers, known as hierodules or sacred servants. They met in Smyrna (present-day *İzmir* in Turkey) in 160 and left the city for Mykonos in 175 — before the first great earthquake. Interestingly, Quentin, who often posed as a black angel in their erotic role-playing games, was the only one to be canonized. That had no effect on their relationship, however. As self-assured sex workers, they charged high fees and offered their customers a range of services in their well-equipped studio: erotic dancing, massages, BDSM shows and, of course, sexual intercourse. Their main area of expertise, however, was listening. Not only were their clients entertained, satisfied and made to feel appreciated, but they also felt heard — in other words, completely happy. Quentin and Sylvester were only required to give five percent of their income to the temple, which also provided the studio including heating, running water and security. And hierodules were also not required to pay income tax. That's how things were back then. Quentin and Sylvester quickly became fairly wealthy, or at least wealthy enough to buy a house on Mykonos with a view of the sea. They opened a souvenir store there and occasionally took hungry tourists home with them.

Quentin and Sylvester support fair working conditions and self-determination for sex workers. Their official feast day is September 27.

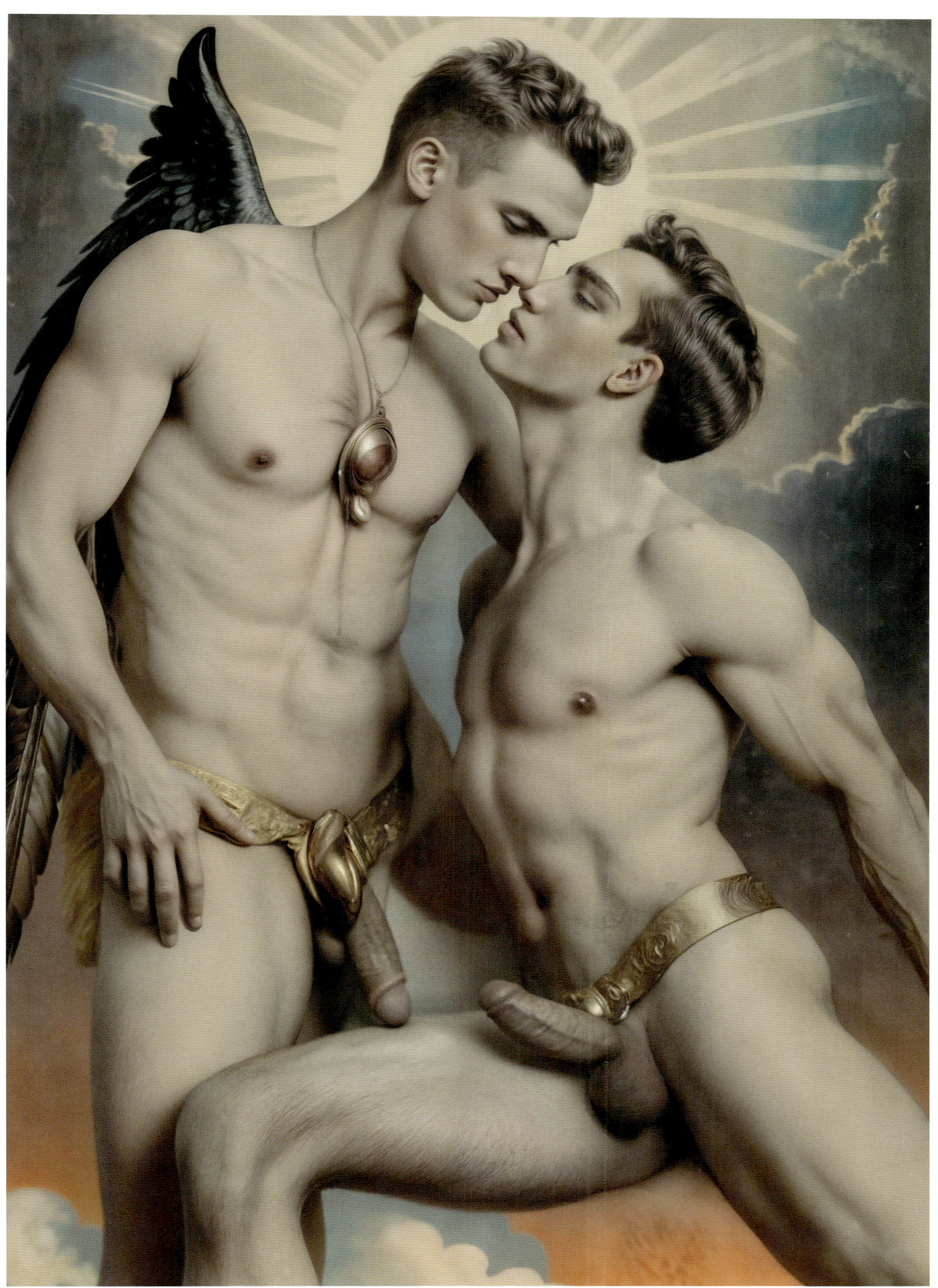

DER HEILIGE QUENTIN UND SILVESTER
SAINT QUENTIN AND SYLVESTER

RAHUL

Rahul stammte aus Dakha, Bengalen, und war ab 1852 zwei Jahre als Austauschstudent bei Dylan Parker und Moise Tellier in Montreal zu Gast (siehe → DER HEILIGE DYLAN, Seite 36). Anfangs bereitete er den beiden ein wenig Kummer, weil er fast jede Nacht unterwegs war und häufig einen, zwei oder auch mal mehr Männer mit nach Hause brachte. Dylans und Moises Schlafzimmer lag direkt unter der Mansarde, in der sie Rahul untergebracht hatten. Sie können sich den Krach mitten in der Nacht sicher vorstellen. Aber die drei fanden schnell einen Kompromiss. Rahul wurde kurzerhand in die Remise umquartiert. Dort hatte er einen eigenen Zugang, sodass weder er noch seine Gäste durch den Hausflur poltern mussten. 1854 ging Rahul (zu Deutsch *Bekämpfer der Missstände*) dann zurück nach Dhaka. Dort war er noch erfolgreicher als der heilige Dylan in Montreal. Rahul machte seine Heimatstadt innerhalb kürzester Zeit zur saubersten Stadt der Welt. Er sorgte für kristallklares Wasser im Buriganga-Fluss, ließ die Straßen mit Bäumen säumen, etablierte angenehme Wohnverhältnisse und ein pünktliches Nahverkehrssystem. Die etwa 80.000 Menschen, die damals in der Stadt lebten (heute sind es 20 Millionen oder mehr), waren zufrieden und glücklich. Unverschämterweise wurde Rahul trotzdem nie heiliggesprochen, weil Königin Victoria intervenierte. Als spätere Kaiserin von Indien schämte sie sich für den Dreck in London und wollte zu viel Aufmerksamkeit für die paradiesischen Verhältnisse in Dakha verhindern. In unserer monochromen Darstellung von Rahul sind deutlich Pfeile zu erkennen. Sie stehen für Krankheiten, können aber aufgrund konsequent umgesetzter Hygienemaßnahmen nicht mehr treffen.

Genau wie der heilige Dylan sorgt auch Rahul für Gesundheit. Wie das so ist bei schwulen Männern, arbeitet er dabei sehr harmonisch mit seinem Heiligenkollegen aus Montreal zusammen. Rahul wird am 30. Oktober gefeiert.

RAHUL

Rahul was originally from Dakha, Bengal, and came to Montreal in 1852 to spend two years with Dylan Parker and Moise Tellier (see → SAINT DYLAN, page 36) as an exchange student. In the beginning, the two of them lost hours of sleep on his account because he went out almost every night and often brought one, two or even more men home with him. Dylan and Moise's bedroom was directly below the attic where Rahul slept. You can imagine the ruckus they had to put up with in the middle of the night. But the three of them quickly found a compromise. Rahul simply moved to the coach house, where he had his own entrance, so neither he nor his guests had to tiptoe through the front hallway. In 1854, Rahul (English: *Conqueror of All Miseries*) went back to Dhaka, where he was even more successful than St. Dylan in Montreal. In no time at all, Rahul turned his hometown into the cleanest city in the world. He made the Buriganga River run crystal clear, lined the streets with trees, and established decent living conditions and a reliable public transportation system. The roughly 80,000 people who lived in the city at the time (there are 20 million or more today) were happy and content. Outrageously, Rahul was never canonized due to the interference of Queen Victoria. As the future Empress of India, she was ashamed of the squalid conditions in London and didn't want too much attention paid to the idyllic conditions in Dakha. Our monochrome depiction of Rahul clearly shows a number of arrows. They symbolize diseases but have been rendered harmless by the consistent implementation of sanitary measures.

Like St. Dylan, Rahul also looks after your health. Like all gay men, he works alongside his fellow saint from Montreal in perfect harmony. Rahul is celebrated on October 30.

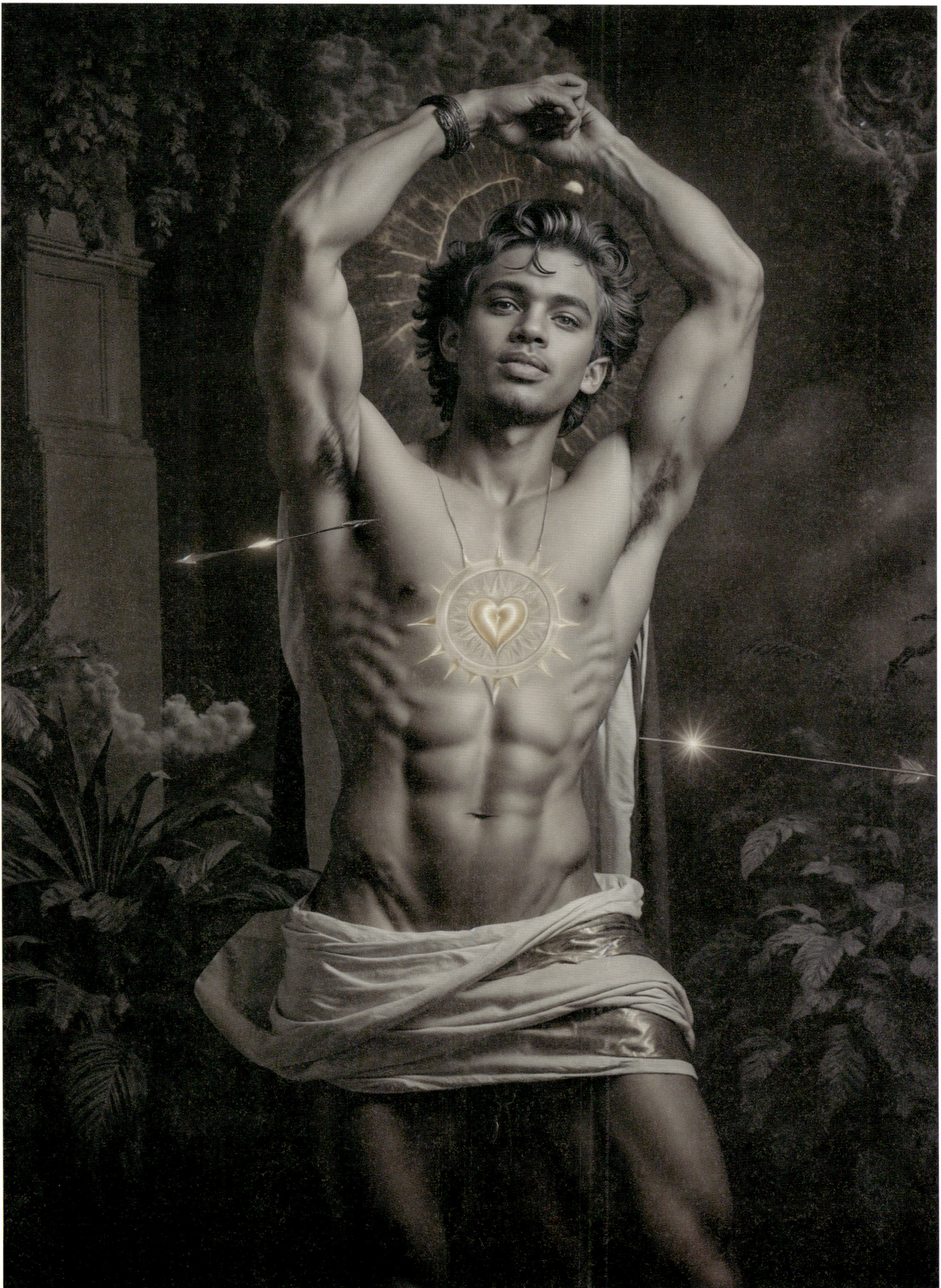

RAHUL

DER HEILIGE RIAAN ROARKE

Riaan Roarke (auch *der Erhabene, der Glanzvolle*) wurde 445 in Armagh (schottisch-gälisch *Airmagh*, irisch *Ard Mhacha Arm*) geboren. Der heilige Patrick war sein Taufpate. Gemeinsam mit seinem Ehemann Sean führte Riaan eine Apfelplantage am Loch Neagh. Dort kultivierten die beiden die besonders grünfarbige Apfelsorte Pelagia *(Malus Pelagia)*, die ihnen zu großem Wohlstand verhalf. Riaan war davon überzeugt, dass die menschliche Natur nicht durch die Erbsünde verdorben worden war, und vertrat den Standpunkt: „Alles, was von Gott geschaffen ist, muss gut sein!" Diese kluge und richtige Geisteshaltung, die er mit seinem Patenonkel in zahlreichen friedlichen Streitgesprächen diskutierte, benannte er nach seinen Äpfeln *Pelagianismus*. Kaum hatte er den heiligen Patrick fast vollständig von der Richtigkeit seiner Ansichten überzeugt, wurde aus Rom Germanus von Auxerre geschickt, um Patrick zur *rechten Lehre* zurückzuführen. Was dann geschah, ist nur lückenhaft überliefert. Riaan und Sean mussten Irland verlassen und sollen sich einer Expedition nach Grönland angeschlossen haben, wo sich ihre Spuren verlieren. Manche Quellen behaupten, sie wären in Amerika gelandet und hätten dort weiter für die Verbreitung des Apfelbaums gesorgt. Der heilige Patrick vermisste seinen Patensohn sehr. Er soll im Alter bitter bereut haben, die Vertreibung von Riaan und Sean mitverantwortet zu haben.

Riaan Roarke wird als Schutzheiliger der Apfelbäume verehrt. Er sorgt insbesondere dafür, dass frühe Blüten nicht durch Frost geschädigt werden. Zum *Saint Patrick's Day* (irisch *Lá Fhéile Pádraig*) am 17. März wird in Erinnerung an Riaan Roarke die grüne Farbe seiner Äpfel gefeiert, was der heilige Patrick noch persönlich veranlassen ließ. Der offizielle Gedenktag des heiligen Riaan Roarke ist allerdings der 21. Juli — weil es dann selbst in Irland schön warm ist und man besser feiern kann.

SAINT RIAAN ROARKE

Riaan Roarke (*The Exalted* or *The Magnificent*) was born in Armagh (Scottish Gaelic *Airmagh*, Irish *Ard Mhacha Arm*) in 445. His godfather was St. Patrick. Riaan and his husband Sean owned an apple orchard on Loch Neagh, where they cultivated the extra green apple variety Pelagia *(Malus Pelagia)*, which brought them great prosperity. Riaan was convinced that human nature had not been corrupted by original sin and believed that "everything that God created must be good." He called this school of thought, which was both wise and correct, *Pelagianism*, after his apples, and discussed it over and over again with his godfather. No sooner had he almost completely convinced St. Patrick that he was right than Germanus of Auxerre was sent from Rome to bring Patrick back to the *correct doctrine*. Only fragmentary records exist of what happened next. Riaan and Sean were forced to leave Ireland and are said to have joined an expedition to Greenland, after which all trace of them is lost. Some sources claim that they landed in America and continued to propagate their apple trees there. St. Patrick missed his godson very much. In later years, he is said to have bitterly regretted his part in the expulsion of Riaan and Sean.

Riaan Roarke is revered as the patron saint of apple trees. In particular, he prevents early blossoms from being damaged by frost. St. Patrick himself ordered the color green to be worn on *Saint Patrick's Day* (Irish: *Lá Fhéile Pádraig*) on March 17 in memory of Riaan Roarke and his apples. However, the official feast day of St. Riaan Roarke is July 21 — because it's nice and warm then, even in Ireland, and a better time of the year for celebrations.

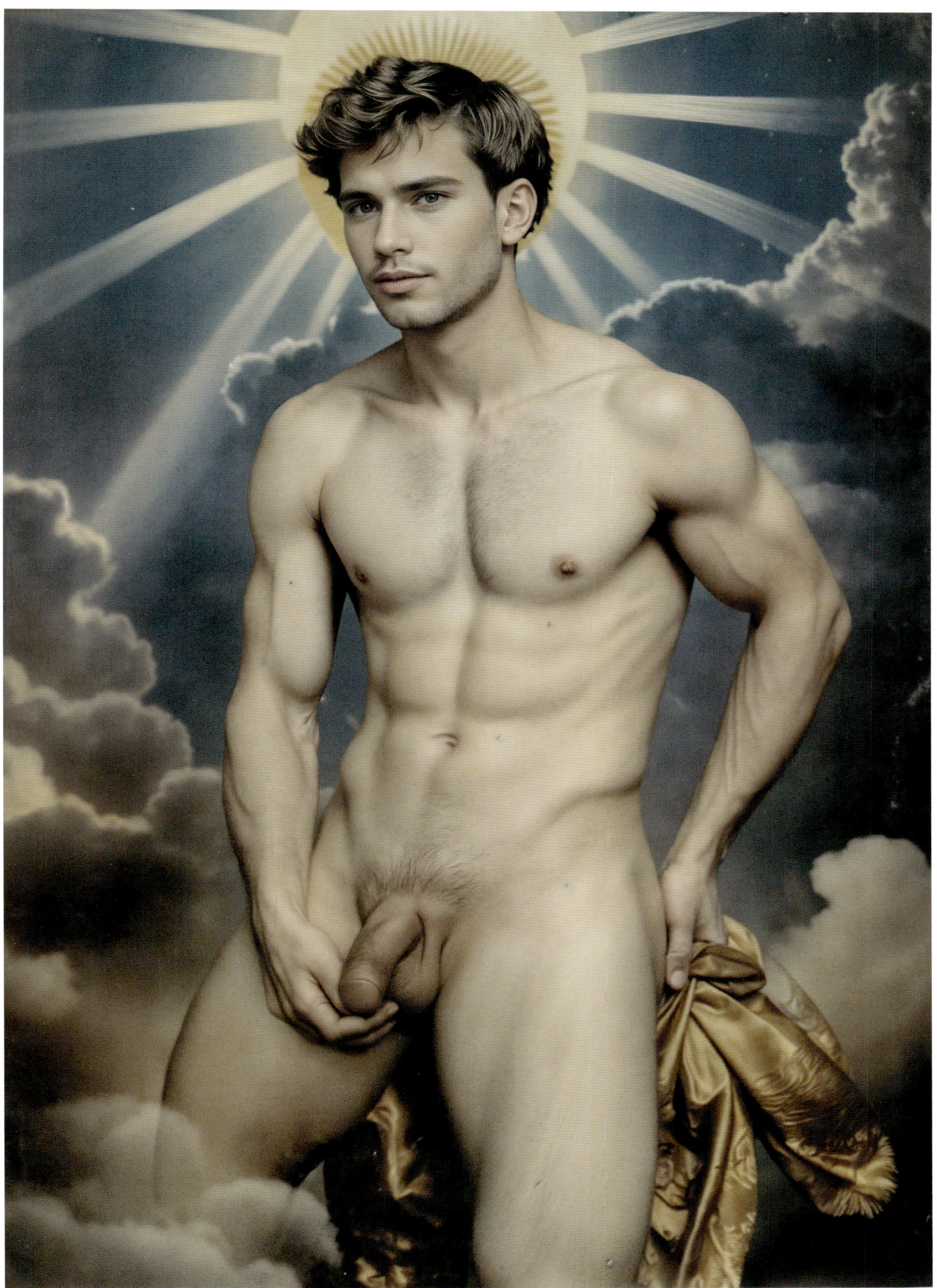

DER HEILIGE RIAAN ROARKE · SAINT RIAAN ROARKE

ROBYN

Wir erinnern uns: Die Charta Edwards III. (Englands König von 1327 bis 1377) besagte, dass an britischen Universitäten „ein jeder mit jedem verkehren dürfe, dieses aber diskret zu passieren habe" (siehe → DER HEILIGE CHARLES, Seite 22). Das klingt vergleichsweise fortschrittlich, war im Prinzip aber ein Rückschritt gegenüber dem von Robyn Hode *(Robin Hood)* unter Edward II. erwirkten Zustand. Hode war zusammen mit seinem Freund Littell John *(Little John)* und den Merry Men *(fröhlichen Gefährten)* Scarlok *(Will Scarlett)* und Much *(der Müllersohn)* im *Sherwood Forest* zuhause. Ihre Gemeinschaft dürfen wir uns ein bisschen wie ein Pfadfinderlager für Erwachsene oder einen Nudistenzeltplatz mit Lagerfeuer, Bärenfellen, gutem Essen und viel Animation vorstellen. In lustigen Rollenspielen durfte jeder mal Ritter, mal Sheriff spielen, wobei zuvor stets im fairen Losverfahren ermittelt wurde, wer diesmal bestimmen durfte, wo es lang ging. Besonders beliebte Spiele waren *Ball Scramble, Bandage a Buddy, Base Attack, Chain Gang Escape, Fist Ball, Grab Five, Hit the Bucket, I'm Taking, Tail Grab* und *Water Brigade*. Wie spaßig diese Spiele waren, sprach sich herum, sodass im Lauf der Jahre halb London in dem Männercamp vorbeikam, um mitzumachen. Auch Edward II. war 1323 trotz seines hohen Alters von schon 39 Jahren zusammen mit seinen Freunden Piers Gaveston und Hugh le Despenser im Sherwood Forest zu Gast. Welche Disziplinen der König gewann, beziehungsweise welche der schlaue Robyn ihn gewinnen ließ, ist leider nicht überliefert. Fest steht aber, dass Edward II. so begeistert war, dass er die Spiele in ganz England veranstalten ließ und dabei die Kirche zu Organisation und Finanzierung verdonnerte. Robyn und seine Freunde erhob Edward II. in den ehrwürdigen Stand der *Knights of the Bath*. Bei dieser Ritterwürde teilten die auserwählten Männer die *Badewanne* und die *Nächte* miteinander, und mit Robyn wollten natürlich viele baden. Bis 1327 hatten Englands Männer demzufolge sehr viel Spaß miteinander. Edwards Frau Isabelle de France und die Kirche fanden das Ganze dagegen weniger lustig. Genauer gesagt waren sie so sauer, dass sie Edward II. ermorden ließen. Wer genau den Auftrag erteilt hat, ist unklar, aber Gerüchten zufolge hat eine glühende Eisenstange eine Rolle gespielt. Robyn Hode wurde derweil von sozialistischen Bänkelsängern zum edlen Räuber, der den Reichen nimmt und den Armen gibt, umgedichtet, was ja irgendwie auch in Ordnung ist.

Robyns Heiligsprechung wurde im Zuge der ungelösten Schuldfrage bei der Ermordung Edwards II. zwar abgelehnt, trotzdem gilt er bis heute als kreativer und spielerischer Heilsbringer des mann-männlichen Sexuallebens. Wir feiern ihn am 9. November.

ROBYN

As we mentioned earlier, the charter of Edward III (King of England from 1327 to 1377) stated that "anyone may associate with anyone else at British universities, but must do so discreetly" (see → SAINT CHARLES, page 22). This sounds fairly progressive, but it was actually a step backwards compared to the situation established under Edward II thanks to the efforts of Robyn Hode *(Robin Hood)*. Hode lived in *Sherwood Forest* with his boyfriend Littell John *(Little John)* and the *two Merry Men* Scarlok *(Will Scarlett)* and Much *(the miller's son)*. Their community was a bit like a boy scout camp for adults or a nudist campsite with campfires, bearskins, good food and plenty of entertainment. They enjoyed playing role-playing games in which everyone got to be a knight or a sheriff, and where they drew straws to decide who would be in charge this time. Some of their favorite games were *ball scramble, bandage a buddy, base attack, chain gang escape, fist ball, grab five, hit the bucket, I'm taking, tail grab* and *water brigade*. Word got around about how much fun these games were, so that over the years half of London stopped by the men's camp to join in. Even Edward II paid a visit to Sherwood Forest in 1323, despite being the ripe old age of 39, along with his friends Piers Gaveston and Hugh le Despenser. History does not record which games the king won, or rather which ones the shrewd Robyn let him win. What we do know, however, is that Edward II was so delighted that he ordered the games to be held throughout England and forced the church to organize and finance them. Robyn and his friends were promoted to the honorable order of *Knights of the Bath*. The knights of this order shared both a *bathtub* and a *bed*, and of course many of them wanted to bathe with Robyn. As a result, the men of Olde England were very merry together until 1327. Edward's wife Isabelle de France and the church, on the other hand, found the whole thing less than amusing. They were so furious, in fact, that they had Edward II murdered. Nobody knows exactly who gave the order, but rumor has it that a red-hot iron poker played a role. Meanwhile, Robyn Hode has been recast by socialist balladeers as the noble robber who steals from the rich and gives to the poor, which is kind of cool.

Although Robyn's canonization was rejected due to his connection to Edward II and the unresolved question of who was to blame for the king's murder, he is still regarded as a creative and playful champion of man-on-man sexuality. We celebrate his memory on November 9.

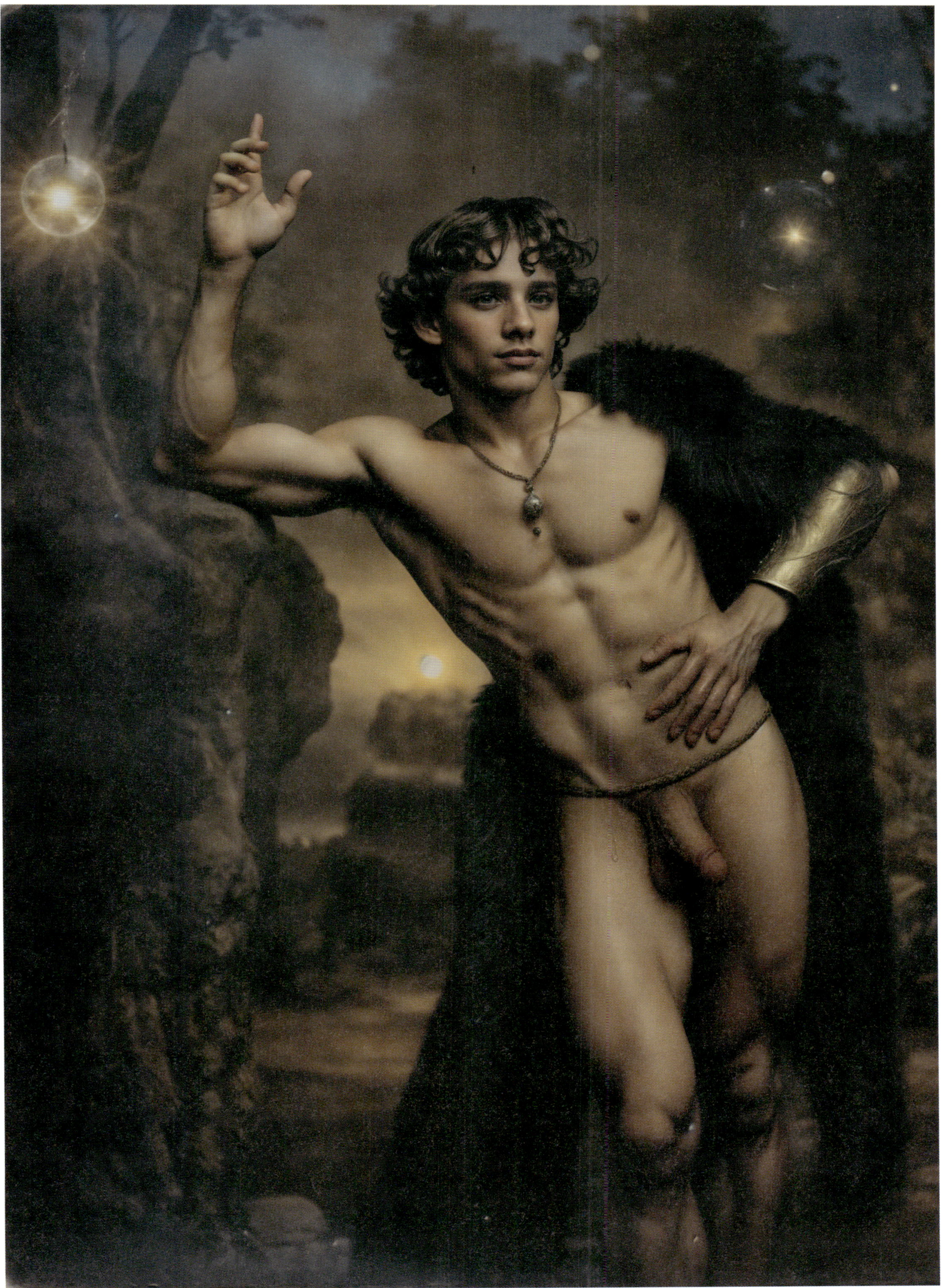

ROBYN

DER HEILIGE JOSEPH ALOIS LUDWIG SCHUMPETER

Joseph Alois *Ludwig* Schumpeter (* 20. April 1856 in Triesch; † 1. Januar 1888 auf Capri) war der Bruder des katholischen, deutschmährischen Tuchfabrikanten Joseph Alois *Karl* Schumpeter (* 15. März 1855 in Triesch; † 14. Januar 1887 ebenda) und damit der Onkel von Joseph Alois *Julius* Schumpeter (* 8. Februar 1883 in Triesch; † 8. Januar Taconic, Connecticut, USA). Nachdem Karl bei einem Jagdunfall ums Leben gekommen war, fiel die Erziehung des kleinen Julius unerwartet in den Zuständigkeitsbereich des lebensfrohen Ludwig. Der hatte sich sein Leben eigentlich anders vorgestellt. Als schwuler Mann fokussierte er seine Interessen auf guten Sex und ein gutes Leben und war überdies gut ausgelastet als Leiter des erfolgreichen Wiener Nachtclubs *Zur grellen Forelle* (den er aus Spaß gegründet hatte, denn Arbeiten hatte er als Spross einer reichen Familie eigentlich gar nicht nötig). Er ging pragmatisch mit der Situation um und gab dem kleinen Julius all die wertvollen Erkenntnisse mit auf den Weg, die er im Laufe seiner Karriere als Lebe- und Geschäftsmann gesammelt hatte. Zum Beispiel: Zur Wirtschaft gehört die Innovation! Reines gieriges Geldverdienen ist langweilig, denn der Spaß entsteht durch die Freude am Gestalten! Der Kapitalismus wird nicht überleben, weil er gestaltende Unternehmerpersönlichkeiten nicht fördert! Ein Kapitalist ist kein Unternehmer! Und so weiter. Der kleine Julius verinnerlichte all diese Ideen. Besonders blieb ihm folgender Grundsatz in Erinnerung: Eher legt sich ein Hund einen Wurstvorrat an als eine demokratische Regierung eine Budgetreserve. Wie es damals in Mode war, verbrachten Onkel und Neffe gerne ausgedehnte Urlaube auf Capri. Bei einem dieser Aufenthalte stürzte Ludwig 1888 in der Nähe der *Villa Lysis* von einer hohen Klippe. Er hatte seine Augen offenbar weniger auf den Weg als auf die Hinterbacken eines lokalen Führers gerichtet. Ein verhängnisvoller Fehler. Der Sturz endete tödlich. Julius trug die Lehren seines Ziehvaters weiter, studierte, wurde Professor und schließlich Finanzminister in Österreich. 1932 ging er nach Harvard. Dort traf er 1933 den frisch gewählten amerikanischen Präsidenten Franklin Delano Roosevelt und verklickerte ihm das mit *dem Hund* und *der Wurst* und seinem *schwulen Onkel*. Roosevelt war fasziniert. Im Nachgang sorgte er dafür, dass die USA keine neuen Schulden mehr aufnahmen, ein Beispiel, das dann weltweit Schule machte. Offiziellen Berechnungen zufolge hat diese Herangehensweise der Welt einen Schuldenstand von 226 Billionen Dollar erspart. Die entsprechenden Geldbeträge an gesparten Zinsen und was man mit ihnen alles anfangen könnte, kann sich jeder selbst ausrechnen.

Schumpeter *(der Onkel!)* wird von Lebe- und Geschäftsmännern und gleichermaßen hoch verehrt. Sein Feiertag ist der 20. April.

SAINT JOSEPH ALOIS LUDWIG SCHUMPETER

Joseph Alois *Ludwig* Schumpeter (* April 20, 1856 in Triesch; † January 1, 1888 in Capri) was the brother of the Catholic German-Moravian cloth manufacturer Joseph Alois *Karl* Schumpeter (* March 15, 1855 in Triesch; † January 14, 1887 in Capri) and thus the uncle of Joseph Alois *Julius* Schumpeter (* February 8, 1883 in Triesch; † January 8, Taconic, Connecticut, USA). After the death of Karl in a hunting accident, Ludwig unexpectedly became responsible for the upbringing of young Julius. This was not part of his life plans. As a gay man, his interests revolved around good sex and a comfortable life, and he was also very busy running the successful Viennese nightclub *Zur grellen Forelle* (which he had started as a hobby because, as the scion of a wealthy family, he didn't really need to work). He took a pragmatic approach to the situation and taught little Julius all the valuable lessons he had learned in the course of his career as a businessman and man about town. For example: Innovation is an essential part of business! Greed is boring. The joy of creativity is where the fun begins. Capitalism will not survive because it does not promote a creative entrepreneurial spirit! A capitalist is not an entrepreneur! And so on. Littel Julius internalized all these ideas. He particularly remembered the following principle: A dog is more likely to stock up on sausages than a democratic government is to build up a budget reserve. In keeping with the fashion of the time, Uncle Ludwig and his nephew liked to spend long vacations on Capri. It was on one of these trips that Ludwig fell off a high cliff near *Villa Lysis* in 1888. He had clearly spent too much time looking at the local guide's backside and not enough looking at the road. The error was fatal. So was the fall. Julius continued to follow the teachings of his foster father, went to university, became a professor, and was appointed the Austrian Minister of Finance. In 1932 he went to Harvard. In 1933, he met the newly elected American President Franklin Delano Roosevelt and told him about *the dog* and *the sausage* and his *gay uncle*. Roosevelt was intrigued. He subsequently stopped the USA from taking on any more debt, an example that set a global precedent. According to official calculations, this approach saved the world 226 trillion dollars in debt. You can work out the corresponding savings in interest yourself — and what you would do with it.

Schumpeter *(Uncle Ludwig!)* is held in high esteem by businessmen and bon vivants alike. His feast day is April 20.

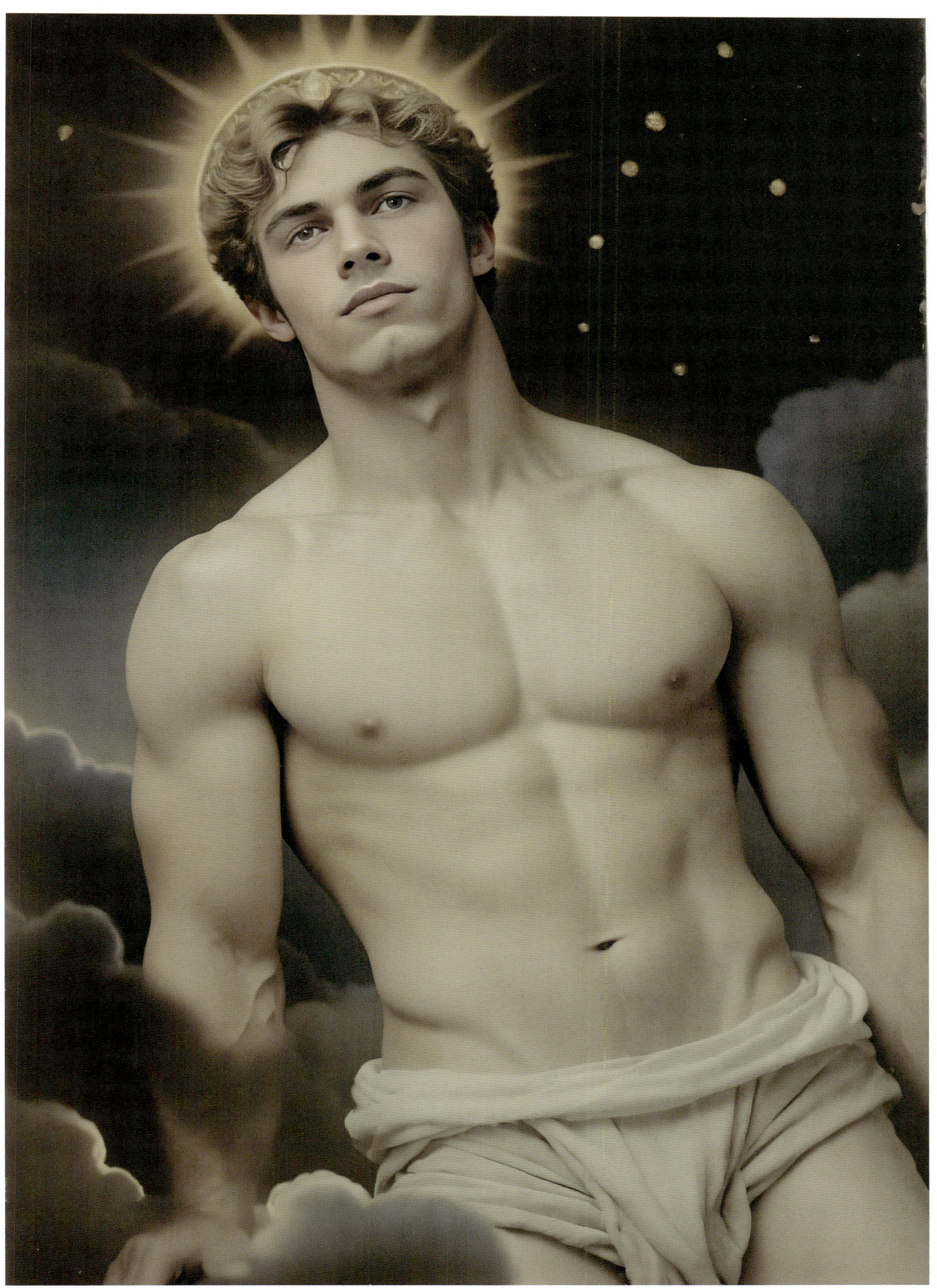

DER HEILIGE JOSEPH ALOIS LUDWIG SCHUMPETER
SAINT JOSEPH ALOIS LUDWIG SCHUMPETER

DIE GLORREICHEN UND HEILIGEN SIEBEN AUS SÃO PAULO

Jamiro, Elano, Matheus, Feliz, Neymar, Amarildo und Caique kennen in Brasilien alle! Nicht nur gründeten sie 1891 in São Paulo das Kaffeeimperium mit der Marke *Sete Glorioso,* sie bauten auch direkt neben dem Anwesen der Familie von Bülow eines der ersten Häuser auf der *Avenida Paulista.* Die rosa gestrichene Villa im orientalischen Stil hatte fünf Stockwerke und einen Keller, der zusätzlich zwei unterirdische Etagen umfasste, die eine Sauna namens *Veado* (portugiesisch *Schwuchtel*) beherbergten, die mit Schwimmbad, Bar, Massage- und Ruheräumen keine Wünsche offenließ. Dort fanden legendäre Partys statt. Im Erdgeschoss war das beliebte Kaffee und Restaurant *Puto* (ebenfalls ein Wort für *schwul*) untergebracht, das berühmt war für seine Feijoada, Moqueca und sein Quindim. Auch die ersten Caipirinhas wurden hier serviert, aber das ist eine andere Geschichte. Vom Erdgeschoss führte eine breite Treppe in den ersten Stock, wo die Buchhandlung *O Príncipe Feliz (Der Glückliche Prinz)* mit ihrem weltweit einzigartigen Angebot an schwuler Belletristik, Lyrik sowie Bildbänden zu Kultur und Kunst residierte. Die Buchhandlung hatte auch Räume, die für Gruppentreffen und Ausstellungen genutzt werden konnten. Im zweiten und dritten Stock befand sich die schwule Jugendhilfe mit Schlafräumen für Notfälle, einem umfangreichen Beratungsangebot und dem Boxclub *Boxear Cara* was auf Deutsch in etwa *Box-Kerle* bedeutet. Wenn Lesungen und Boxkämpfe gleichzeitig stattfanden, kam es gelegentlich zu Konflikten, die aber immer einvernehmlich gelöst wurden. Im vierten Stock folgte dann die Vermögensverwaltung der glorreichen Sieben. Die war nötig, denn sie besaßen im Rio-Paraíba-Tal und im Hochland von São Paulo Kaffeeplantagen und investierten in die Eisenbahnlinie zum Exporthafen Santos. Letzteres führte dazu, dass *Sete Glorioso* weltweit getrunken wurde und selbst der Papst in Rom dem hervorragenden Kaffee den Vorzug gab. Auf ihren Kaffeeplantagen gaben die glorreichen Sieben übrigens insbesondere Einwanderern aus Deutschland, Italien, Japan und dem Libanon eine faire Chance, in der neuen Heimat einen guten Start zu haben. Bleibt nur noch der fünfte Stock: das Wohn- und Schlafzimmer von Jamiro, Elano, Matheus, Feliz, Neymar, Amarildo und Caique mit einer riesigen umlaufenden Dachterrasse. So war die Villa an der *Avenida Paulista* jahrelang eine reine Männerwirtschaft. Dann kamen die Lesben. Erst forderten sie mehr Mitspracherecht, dann eine männerfreie Etage und letztendlich jagten sie die *Schwanzträger, Machos, Chauvinistenschweine* und so weiter zum Teufel und übernahmen das Haus komplett. Der rosa Anstrich wurde in grau geändert, der Saunaclub aus hygienischen Gründen geschlossen, das Restaurant auf vegetarisch-vegan und alkoholfrei umgestellt, die Buchhandlung mit lesbischen Fantasyromanen vollgestellt und die schwule Jugendhilfe in eine Favela umgesiedelt. *Sete Glorioso* verkauften sie an John Stith Pemberton, der nach dem Erfolg von Coca-Cola in weitere Produkte investieren wollte. Der Erlös diente angeblich zur Finanzierung mehrerer (erfolgloser) Revolutionen in Lateinamerika. Desillusioniert zogen sich Jamiro, Elano, Matheus, Feliz, Neymar, Amarildo und Caique zurück. Sie siedelten nach Praia de Forte um, wo sie Jahrzehnte später total verarmt, aber glücklich das Zeitliche segneten. Die Lesben verloren mit der Zeit das Interesse an dem grauen Haus an der *Avenida Paulista.* Es verfiel. 1952 wurde es abgerissen und durch ein 40-stöckiges Bürogebäude ersetzt, vor dem nun jährlich am Sonntag nach Fronleichnam bei der *Parada do Orgulho LGBTQ de São Paulo* (die mit fünf Millionen Teilnehmenden größte Parade dieser Art) ein Gedenkstopp eingelegt wird, zumindest von einigen schwulen Männern. Gerald Baldwin, Gordon Bowker und Zev Siegl spielten 1971 wohl sogar mal mit dem Gedanken, ihr erstes Kaffeegeschäft in Seattle nach den glorreichen Sieben zu benennen. Am Ende entschieden sie sich aber doch für eine Figur aus dem schwulen Romanklassiker *Moby Dick* — nicht etwa Ishmael oder Queequeg, sondern für den eher langweiligen Seemann Starbuck.

Barista rufen Jamiro, Elano, Matheus, Feliz, Neymar, Amarildo und Caique mit einem kurzen Stoßgebet an, wenn es um das Aufschlagen von Milch und deren Vermählung mit Kaffee zu goldbraunem Schaum, mit anderen Worten um die perfekte Crema auf einem frisch gezogenen Espresso, geht. In der Regel helfen unsere Sieben gerne. Ihre Gedenktage verteilen sich quer übers Jahr: 17. Februar (Elano), 18. Februar (Feliz), 8. Juni (Jamiro), 6. Oktober (Matheus) und 27. Dezember (Neymar). Für Amarildo und Caique, die am gleichen Tag Geburtstag hatten, ist der 12. August reserviert.

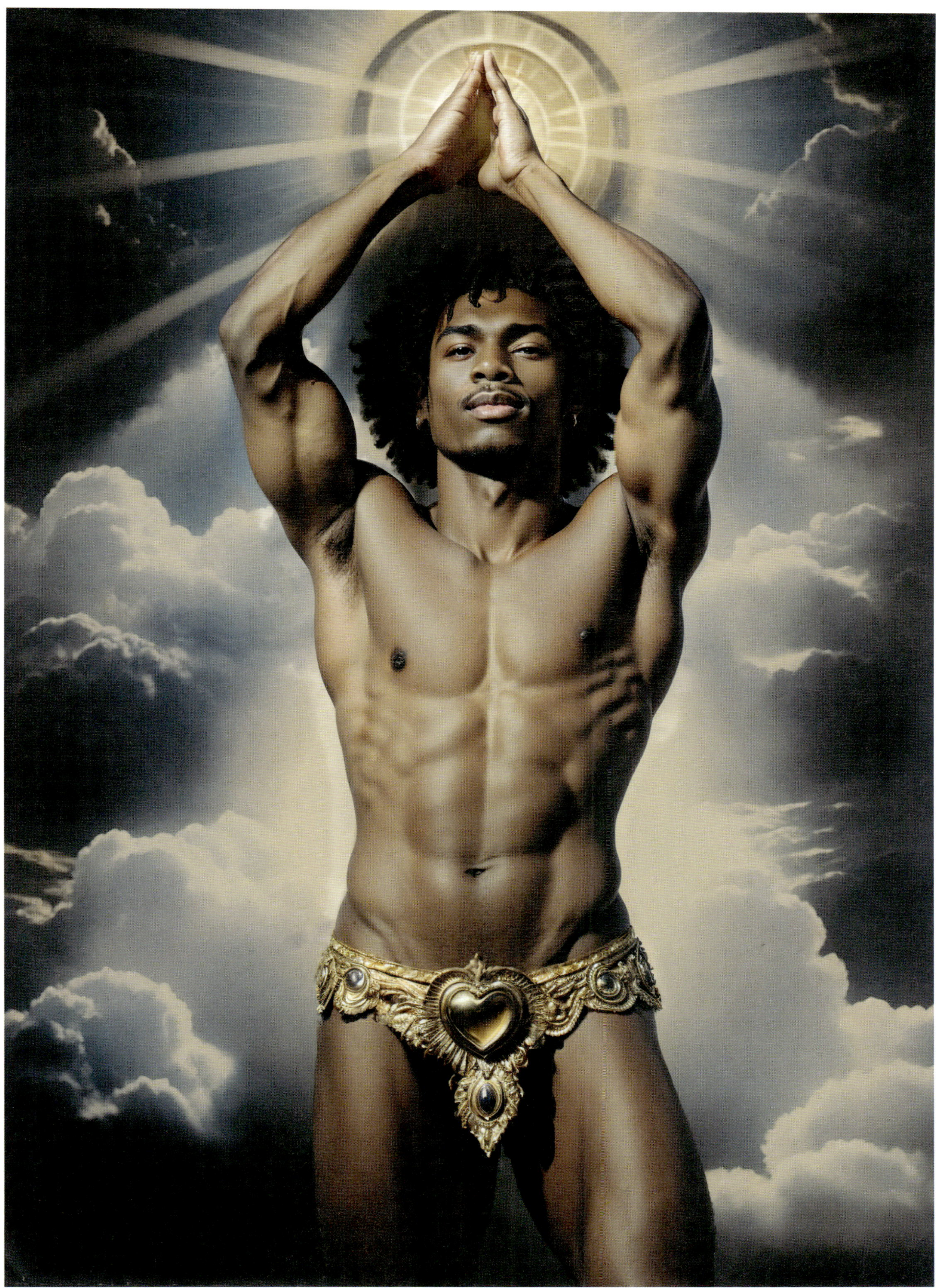

JAMIRO

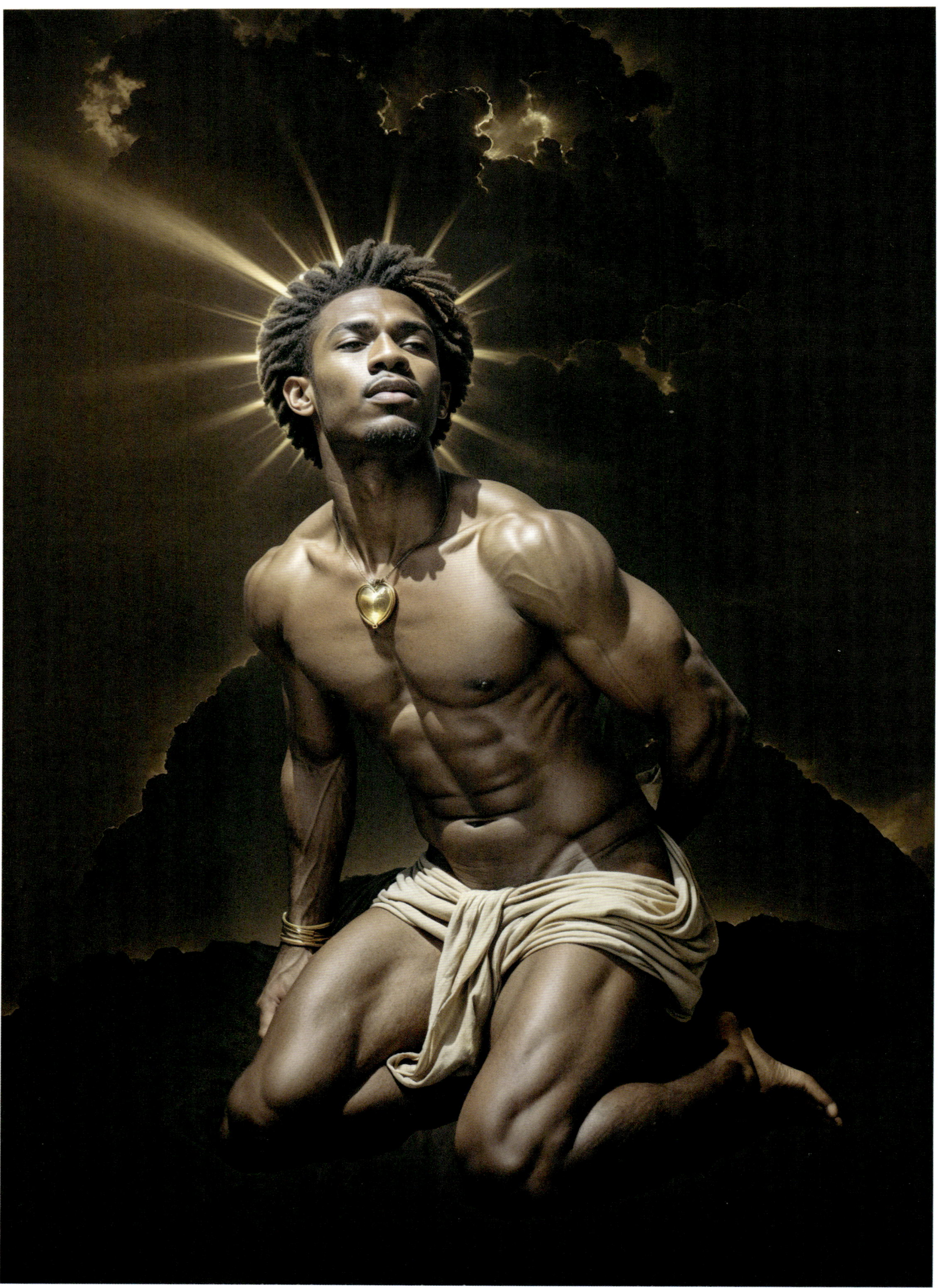

ELANO

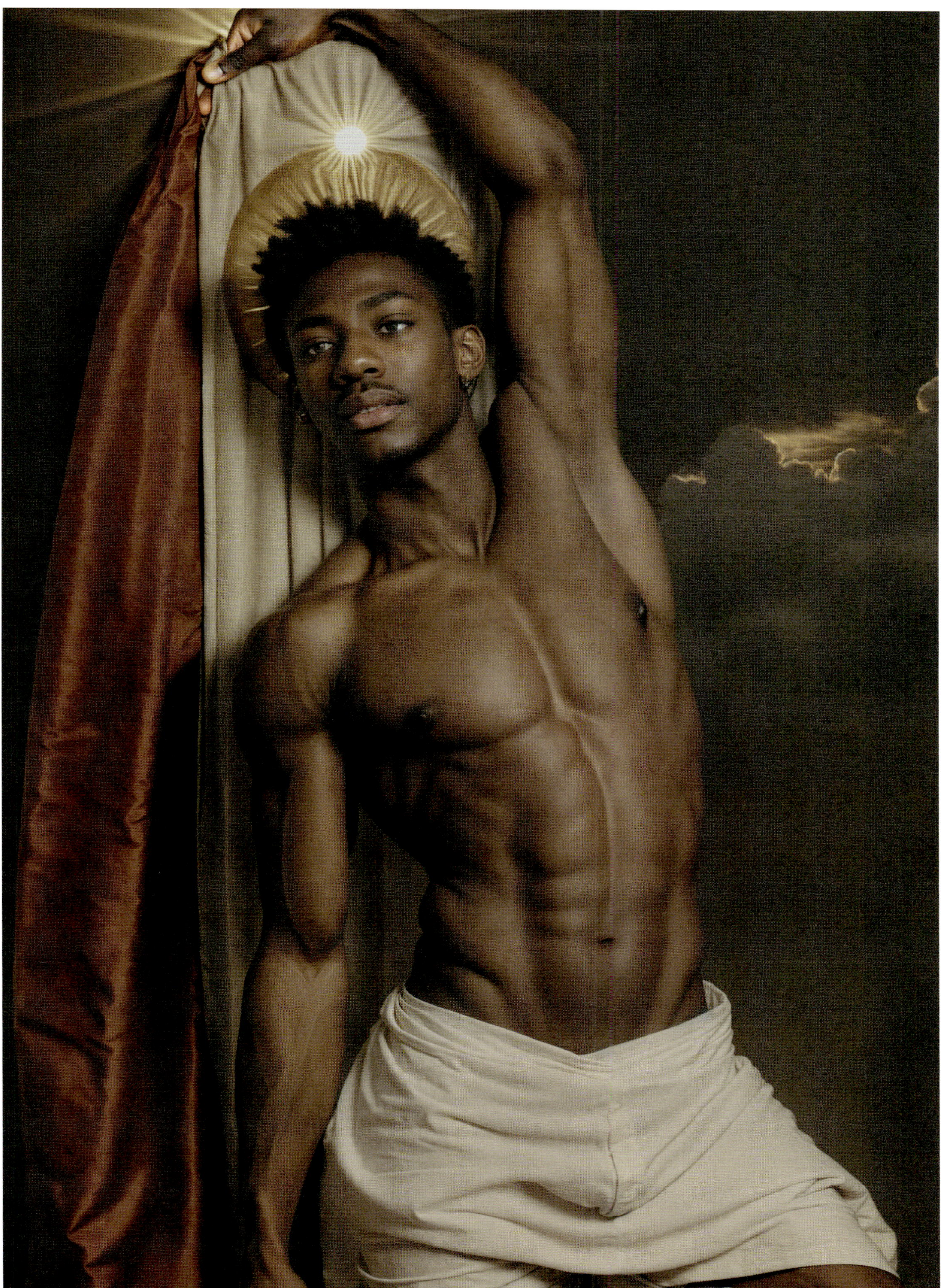

MATHEUS

THE MAGNIFICENT AND SAINTLY SEVEN OF SÃO PAULO

Every man and woman in Brazil knows Jamiro, Elano, Matheus, Feliz, Neymar, Amarildo and Caique! Not only did they launch the *Sete Glorioso* coffee emporium in São Paulo in 1891, they also built one of the first buildings on *Avenida Paulista* right next to the von Bülow family estate. The pink oriental-style villa had five floors and a basement with two additional levels that housed a sauna called *Veado* (*faggot* in Portuguese), a swimming pool, a bar, and massage rooms. The parties they hosted here were legendary. The first floor was home to the popular coffee shop and restaurant *Puto* (another word for *gay*), which was famous for its feijoada, moqueca and quindim. This is also where the first caipirinhas were served, but that's another story. A wide staircase led from the first floor up to the second floor, where you would find the bookshop *O Príncipe Feliz (The Happy Prince)* with its unique range of gay fiction, poetry and illustrated books on art and culture. The bookshop also had extra rooms that could be used for meetings and exhibitions. On the next two floors there was a gay youth support center with emergency accommodation, extensive counseling services and the *Boxear Cara* boxing club (loosely translated: *boxing guys*). Occasionally a conflict would arise when a book reading was scheduled at the same time as a boxing match, but these were always resolved amicably. The Magnificent Seven's asset management department was on the fourth floor. This was a very important department because the Seven owned coffee plantations in the Rio-Paraíba valley and the highlands of São Paulo and had invested in the railroad line to the port of Santos. This investment allowed them to export *Sete Glorioso* all over the world — even the Pope in Rome declared that this was his favorite brand of coffee. The Magnificent Seven gave immigrants from Germany, Italy, Japan and Lebanon in particular the opportunity to get off to a good start in their new homeland by giving them jobs on their coffee plantations. Then there was the top floor: Jamiro, Elano, Matheus, Feliz, Neymar, Amarildo and Caique's living room and bedroom with a huge panoramic roof terrace. For years, the villa on *Avenida Paulista* was an all-male business. Then along came the lesbians. First they demanded more of a say, then a woman-only floor and finally they chased off all the *dicks, machos, chauvinist pigs* and so on and took over the entire building. The pink walls were painted gray, the sauna club was closed for hygienic reasons, the restaurant switched to a vegetarian, vegan and alcohol-free menu, the bookshop was filled with lesbian fantasy novels and the gay youth support center was relocated to a favela. They sold *Sete Glorioso* to John Stith Pemberton, who was keen to invest in other products following the success of Coca-Cola. The proceeds were allegedly used to finance several (unsuccessful) revolutions in Latin America. Frustrated and disillusioned, Jamiro, Elano, Matheus, Feliz, Neymar, Amarildo and Caique retired. They moved to Praia de Forte, where they died decades later, destitute but happy. Over time, the lesbians lost interest in the gray building on Avenida Paulista and it fell into disrepair. In 1952, it was torn down and replaced by a 40-storey office building. Every year on the Sunday after Corpus Christi, the *Parada do Orgulho LGBTQ de São Paulo* (the largest parade of its kind, involving five million participants) briefly stops in front of the building in memory of the Magnificent Seven. At least, some of the gay men do. Gerald Baldwin, Gordon Bowker and Zev Siegl even considered naming their first coffee shop — founded in Seattle in 1971 — after them. In the end, however, they opted for a character from the classic gay novel *Moby Dick* — not Ishmael or Queequeg, but the rather boring seaman Starbuck.

Baristas say a prayer to Jamiro, Elano, Matheus, Feliz, Neymar, Amarildo and Caique as they whisk warm milk and blend it with coffee to create a golden brown foam — in other words, the perfect crema on top of a freshly brewed espresso. Our Seven are usually happy to help. Their feast days are spread across the year: February 17 (Elano), February 18 (Feliz), June 8 (Jamiro), October 6 (Matheus) and December 27 (Neymar). August 12 is reserved for Amarildo and Caique, who share the same birthday.

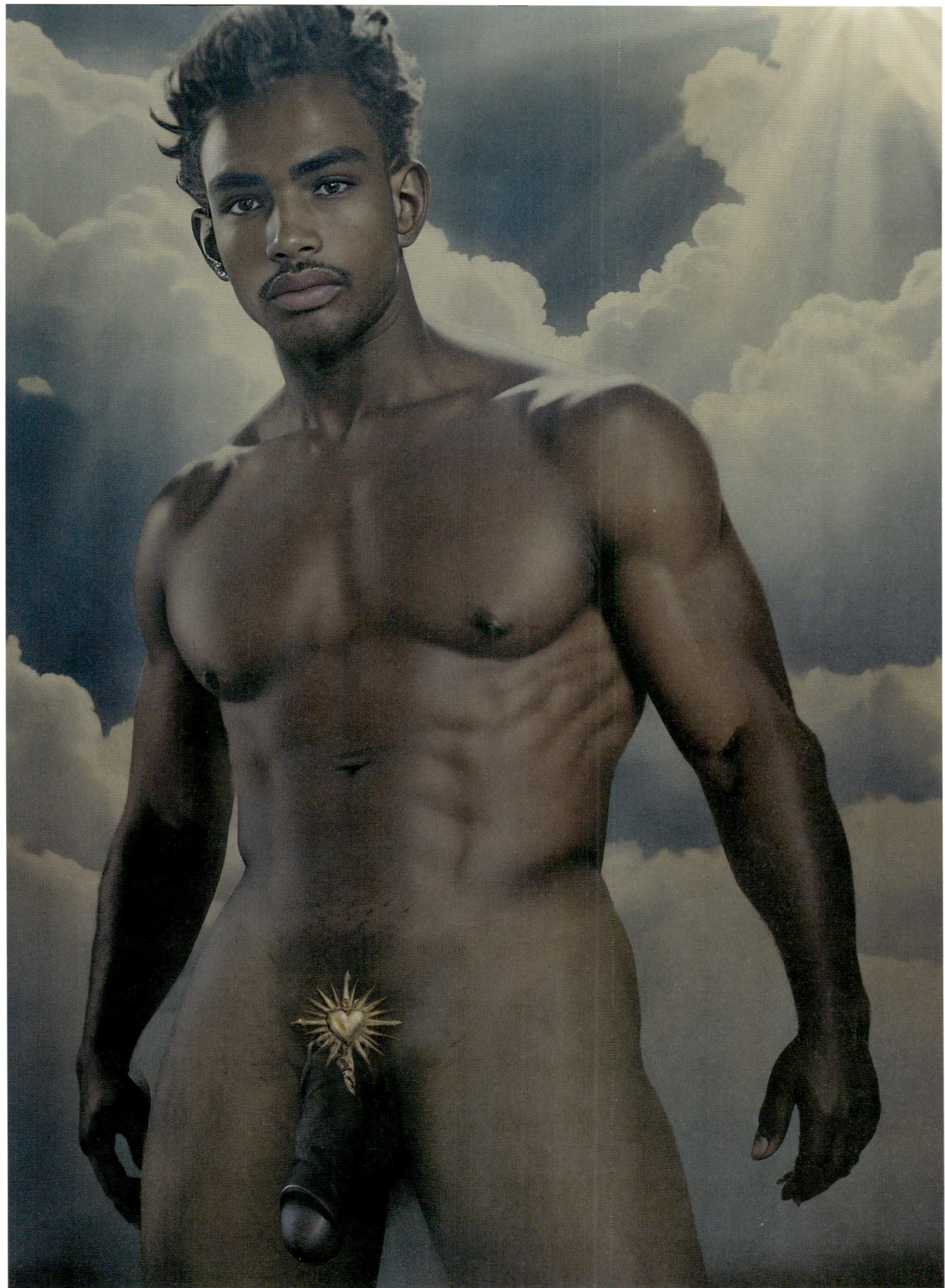

FELIZ

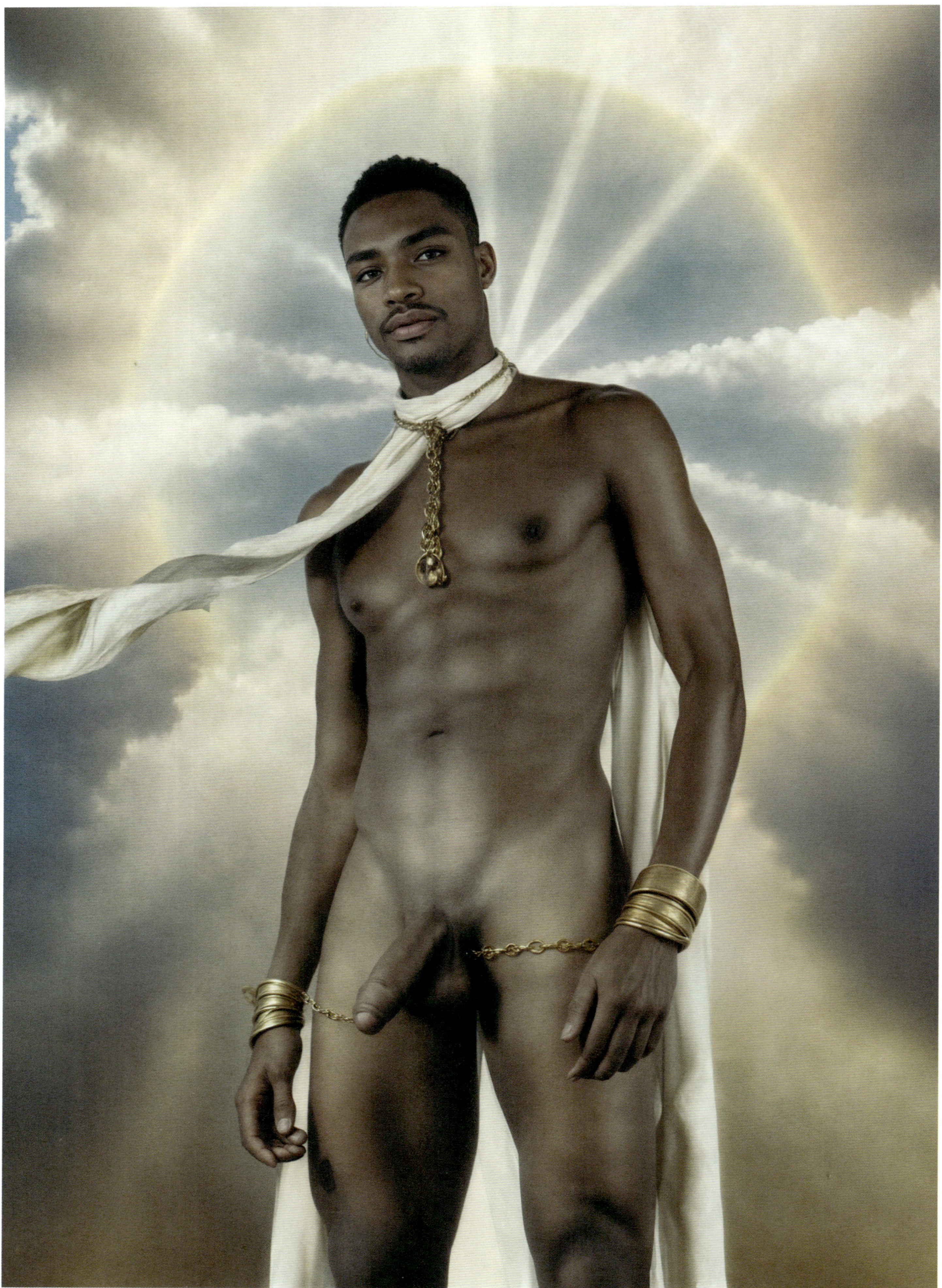

NEYMAR

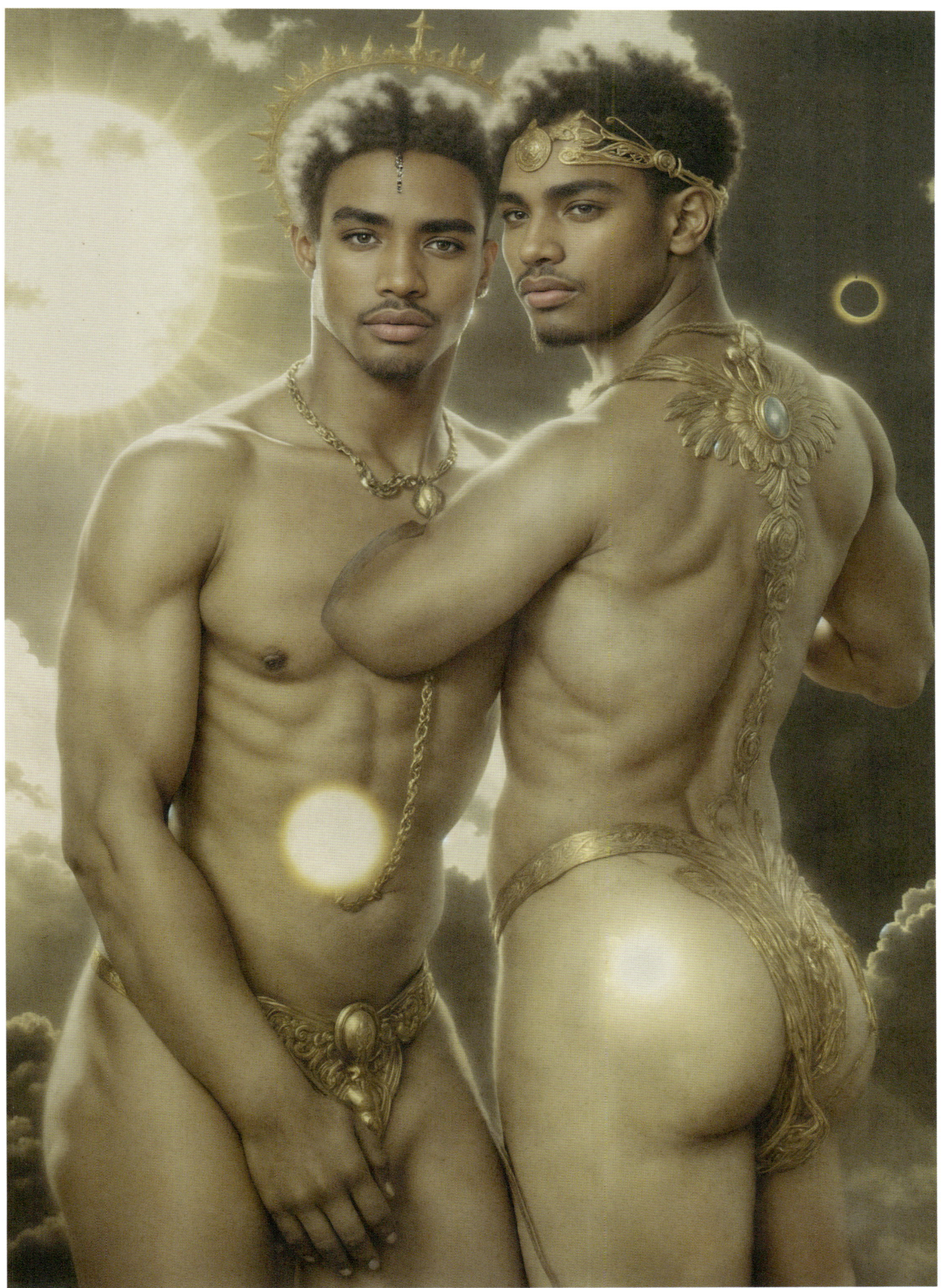

AMARILDO & CAIQUE

JAN SPECKENBÜTTEL

Jan Speckenbüttel wurde 1758 im Hessischen Korbach geboren und 1776 von seinem Landesherren als Söldner an die Briten verkauft. Wie 20.000 weitere Männer aus Hessen sollte er im Amerikanischen Unabhängigkeitskrieg für die Briten kämpfen. Als er in Lehe (gehört heute zu Bremerhaven) aufs Schiff in die Neue Welt gehen sollte, glückte ihm die Flucht. Seinem Freund Peter gelang sie jedoch leider nicht, also reiste Jan ihm kurzentschlossen hinterher. In Boston schloss er sich den *Sons of Liberty*, einer Gruppe freiheitsliebender Patrioten an. Auf breiter Front und mit sehr überzeugenden Argumenten organisierte er den Widerstand gegen die Briten, gründete die *Gay Liberation Army* und prägte den Schlachtruf „Give us liberty, or give us death". Tief in seinem Herzen hatte er dabei natürlich nur eines im Sinn: Peters Befreiung — die nach ein paar spektakulären Erfolgen im Kampf schließlich am 19. Oktober 1781 bei Yorktown gelang. Fünf Jahre nach ihrer Trennung konnte Jan seinen Peter endlich wieder in die Arme schließen. Die beiden gingen nach New York und eröffneten ein Geschäft für Herrenmode. Nach seiner Vereidigung am 30. April 1789 wollte George Washington seinen Freund Speckenbüttel für einen Posten im Kabinett gewinnen, doch Jan lehnte dankend ab. Stattdessen konnte er den angehenden Präsidenten davon überzeugen, bei der Vereidigung eine Speckenbüttel-Kreation zu tragen. Die Folge ist, dass viele modische Highlights aus Peters und Jans Produktion bis heute auf historischen Abbildungen verewigt sind. Das prominenteste Beispiel sind wohl Washingtons Stehkragen und Rüschenschal auf dem Ein-Dollar-Schein.

Jan Speckenbüttel zieht Männer an, bleibt aber lieber im Hintergrund. Seiner wird am 11. März gehuldigt.

JAN SPECKENBÜTTEL

Jan Speckenbüttel was born in Korbach in Hesse in 1758 and sold to the British as a mercenary by the Hessian ruler in 1776. He was supposed to fight for the British in the American War of Independence, along with 20,000 other Hessian men. But just as he was about to board a ship to the New World in Lehe (now part of Bremerhaven), he managed to escape. His boyfriend Peter unfortunately didn't make it off the ship, and so Jan decided to follow him. Upon arriving in Boston, he joined the *Sons of Liberty*, a group of freedom-loving patriots. Armed with very convincing arguments, he organized a broad campaign of resistance against the British, founded the *Gay Liberation Army* and coined the battle cry "Give us liberty, or give us death." Deep down, of course, he only wanted one thing: to free Peter. Finally, in Yorktown on October 19, 1781, after a few spectacular successes in battle and after five years of separation, Jan finally held Peter in his arms again. The two of them went to New York and opened a menswear store. Following his inauguration on April 30, 1789, George Washington hoped to persuade his friend Speckenbüttel to take a position in the cabinet, but Jan declined. Instead, he persuaded the future president to wear a Speckenbüttel creation at the inauguration ceremony. Many fashion highlights from Peter and Jan's production line are still immortalized in historical illustrations to this day as a result. Washington's stock collar and frilled cravat, pictured on the one-dollar bill, are probably the most prominent example.

Jan Speckenbüttel attracts men but prefers to remain in the background. He is honored on March 11.

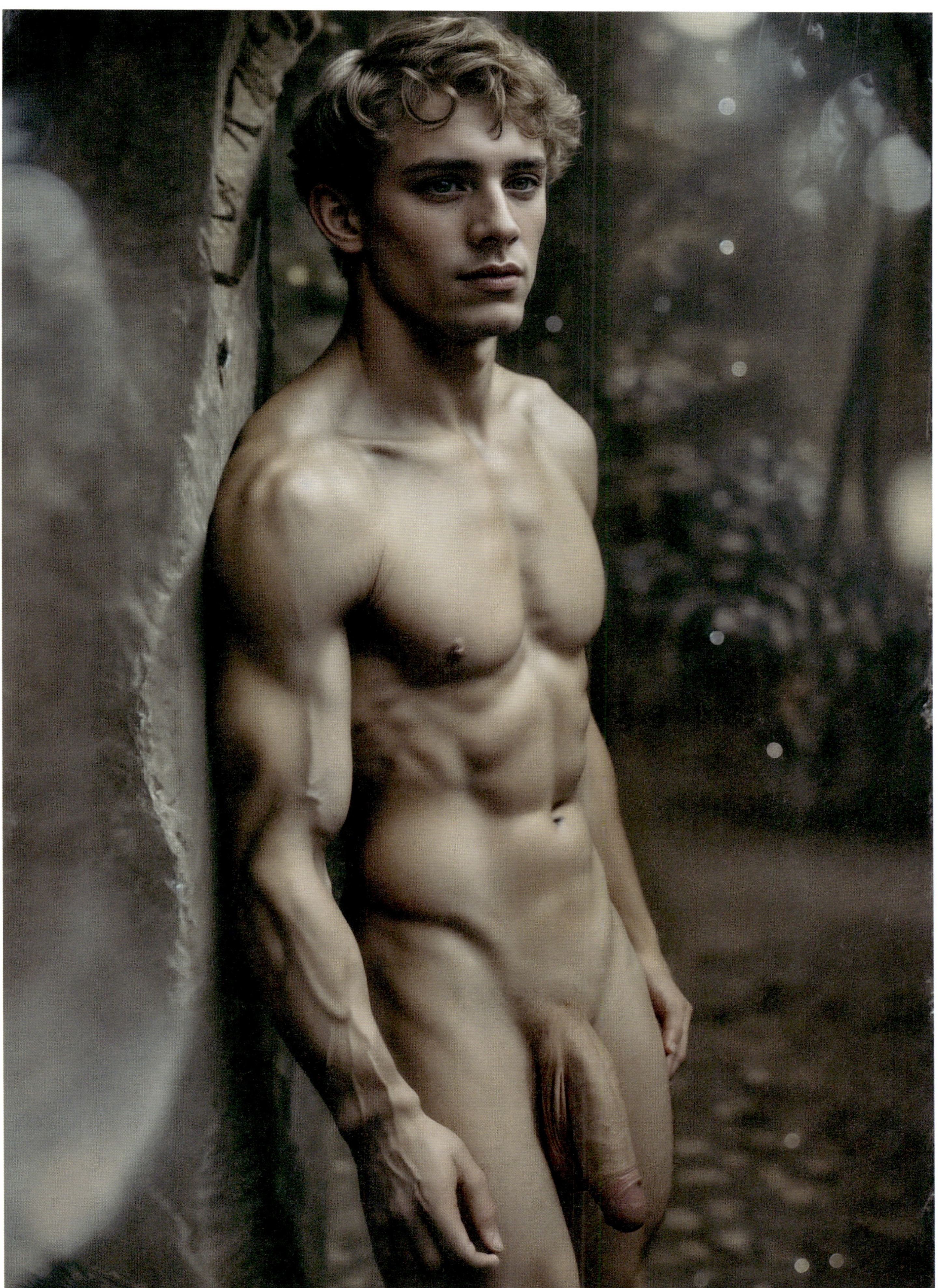

JAN SPECKENBÜTTEL

DER HEILIGE STELLARIO AUS NOTO

Stellario wurde 1672 in den Hybläischen Bergen nahe dem kleinen Dorf Lenzevacche in der Nähe des heutigen Noto Antica auf Sizilien geboren. Am späten Abend — um 21 Uhr — des 9. Januar 1693, während die meisten anderen Stadtbewohner tief und fest schliefen, war Stellario hellwach und hatte fröhlichen Sex mit einem Ziegenhirten in dessen Unterstand unterhalb des *Castello Reale di Don Pietro d'Aragona*. Das legendäre Erdbeben jenes Tages überraschte ihn also nicht im Schlaf, aber in ziemlich abgelenktem Zustand. Genauer gesagt exakt in dem Moment, in dem er seinen Orgasmus hatte. Im selben Augenblick hatte er eine Vision, nämlich dass sich dieser Vorgang wiederholen würde. Und zwar sehr bald. Er erzählte allen Stadtbewohnern Notos von seiner Vorahnung und konnte tatsächlich viele davon überzeugen, die kommenden Nächte lieber unter freiem Himmel als in festen Gebäuden zu verbringen. Allerdings nicht alle, denn viele folgten dem Aufruf des örtlichen Bischofs und versammelten sich in der Kirche *Chiesa Maggiore di San Nicolò*, um zu beten. Diese frommen Menschen hatten das Nachsehen, als wenig später erneut ein Inferno losbrach. Nach einem leichten Vorbeben um 17 Uhr am Nachmittag des 11. Januar 1693 wurde um 21 Uhr die volle Stärke von VIII bis IX auf der *Mercalli-Cancani-Sieberg-Skala* erreicht. Die *Chiesa Maggiore di San Nicolò* stürzte dabei, wie viele andere Gebäude, ein und begrub hunderte von Menschen unter ihren Trümmern. Die Leute hingegen, die Stellarios Ruf ins Freie gefolgt waren, überlebten. Er selbst soll auch diesmal zum Zeitpunkt des Hauptbebens einen Orgasmus gehabt haben — diesmal beim Sex mit einem Bäckerburschen –, aber das ist nicht historisch belegt. Stellarios entscheidender Beitrag zu Notos Wiederaufbau ab 1703 ist dagegen unstrittig. Gemäß seiner beim Schachspiel erworbenen Maxime „Erst denken und dann handeln" veranlasste er die Verlegung der Stadt in den Südosten ihres alten Standortes und initiierte einen modernen Wiederaufbau im Schachbrettmuster mit breiten gepflasterten Straßen, schönen Treppenanlagen, Bäumen und Parkbänken, die sich hervorragend für Flirts und die Kontaktaufnahme unter freiem Himmel eigneten. Folglich trug die Hauptverkehrsstraße der Stadt auch den Namen *Corso Stellario*. Dort stand auch Stellarios Wohnhaus, in dem er eine Bar mit angeschlossener Schachschule betrieb. Er starb 1751. Der Schachbegriff *Sizilianische Verteidigung*, den der italienische Schachverband 1804 zu Ehren Stellarios einführte, zeugt bis heute von den großen Verdiensten dieses Heiligen. Der *Corso Stellario* dagegen wurde 1878 in *Corso Vittorio Emanuele III*. umbenannt.

Das Mitführen eines Stellario-Heiligenbildes erhöht (vor allem außerhalb von festen Gebäuden) die Gewinnchancen beim Schachspiel und schützt (egal bei welcher Tätigkeit) vor Erdbeben. Warum der heilige Stellario nicht am 11. Januar, sondern am 4. April gefeiert wird, verstehen wir auch nicht so richtig.

SAINT STELLARIO OF NOTO

Stellario was born in 1672 near the small village of Lenzevacche in the Hyblaean Mountains, not far from present-day Noto Antica in Sicily. One evening — around 9 p.m. — on January 9, 1693, when most of the other townspeople were fast asleep, Stellario was wide awake and cheerfully having sex with a goatherd in his lean-to below the *Castello Reale di Don Pietro d'Aragona*, and so the famous earthquake did not surprise him in his sleep, but in a rather distracted state: right in the middle of an orgasm. In the same instant, he had a vision, namely that this would happen again. Very soon. He told all the residents of Noto about his premonition and was actually able to convince many of them to spend the coming nights out in the open rather than inside their houses. Not everyone, however: many people followed the call of the local bishop and assembled in the *Chiesa Maggiore di San Nicolò* to pray. These pious people were at a disadvantage when another inferno broke out a little later. After a gentle early tremor at 5 pm on the afternoon of January 11, 1693, the earthquake reached its full magnitude of VIII to IX on the *Mercalli-Cancani-Sieberg scale* at 9 pm. Like many other buildings, the *Chiesa Maggiore di San Nicolò* collapsed, burying hundreds of people under the rubble. The people who had listened to Stellario and spent the night outside, however, survived. He himself is also said to have had another orgasm when the main earthquake struck — this time while having sex with a baker's boy — but this is not historically proven. Stellario's key contribution to the reconstruction of Noto from 1703 onwards, however, is undisputed. In keeping with the maxim "Think before you act," which he had learned while playing chess, he had the city relocated to the southeast of its former position and initiated a modern reconstruction in a chessboard pattern with wide cobbled streets, attractive stairways, trees and park benches, which were ideal for flirting and socializing in the open air. The city's main thoroughfare was accordingly named the *Corso Stellario*. This was also where Stellario built his house, where he ran a bar with an adjoining chess school. He died in 1751. The chess term *Sicilian defense*, which was introduced by the Italian Chess Federation in 1804 in honor of Stellario, still bears witness to this saint's tremendous achievements. The *Corso Stellario*, on the other hand, was renamed *Corso Vittorio Emanuele III* in 1878.

Carrying a holy image of Stellario with you increases your chances of winning at chess (especially outdoors) and protects you from earthquakes (regardless of what you may be doing at the time). St. Stellario is not celebrated on January 11, but on April 4 — no, we don't know why either.

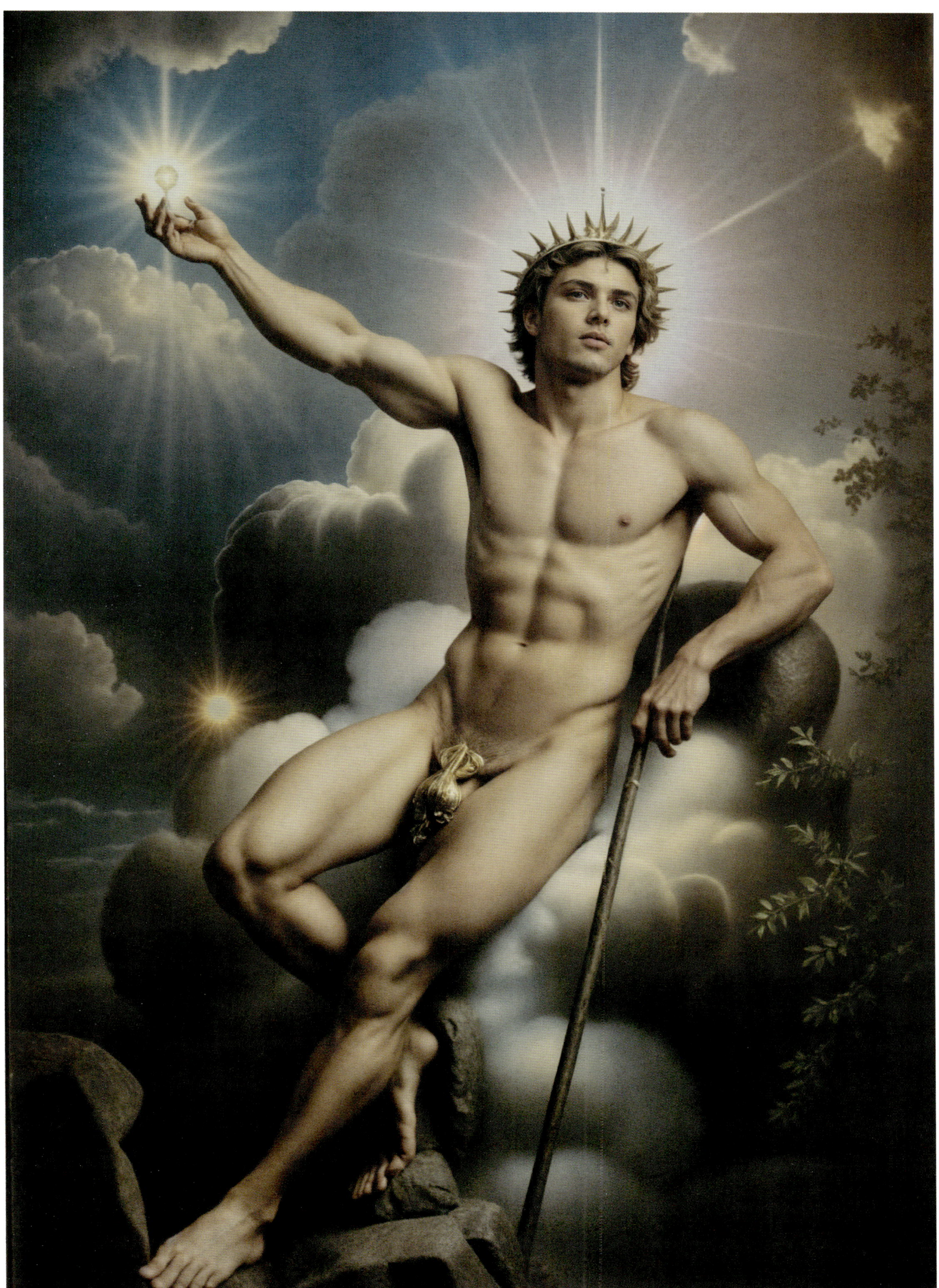

DER HEILIGE STELLARIO AUS NOTO · SAINT STELLARIO OF NOTO

DER HEILIGE TADDEO

Taddeo wurde anno 62 in Neapel geboren, war Mitglied einer Straßengang und hauste im Schatten der Stadtmauer (gut erkennbar auf unserer Darstellung). Gelegentlich half er den Fischern und Marktleuten aus, das meiste Geld verdiente er aber, indem er Jobs in den Villen von Posillipo ergatterte. Er lebte hauptsächlich von Prostitution. Einmal nahm ihn ein reicher Römer auch mit ins benachbarte Pompei, wo er für eine pornographische Wandmalerei Modell stand (*Taddeo beim Abspritzen*, heute unter Verschluss im Archäologischen Nationalmuseum). Bei Sonnenuntergang träumte Taddeo vom nahegelegenen Capri, dem früheren Wohnort von Kaiser Tiberius, dessen legendäre Partys der Insel zu einem verheißungsvollen Ruf verholfen hatten. Als im Jahr 79 der Vesuv ausbrach, beziehungsweise mittels plinianischer Eruptionen die ganze Region mit gewaltigen Aschefällen und Kubikkilometern von Magma überzog, kam Taddeos große Stunde. Selbstlos organisierte er in Neapel die Hilfe für die Überlebenden, schenkte allen sein großes Herz, teilte mit ihnen das Wenige, was er besaß, und gab wortwörtlich sein letztes Höschen. Damit steht er am Anfang einer langen Ahnenreihe von Sexarbeitern, die alles, aber auch wirklich alles geben. In der römischen Gesellschaft wurde er deshalb als „Liebling des Menschengeschlechts“ *(amor ac deliciae generis humani)* gepriesen. In unserer künstlerisch sehr ausgefeilten Abbildung ist Taddeo selbstverständlich nackt dargestellt (er hatte ja alles gegeben). Zudem zeigt das Bild die bereits erwähnte Stadtmauer und eine durch den Vulkanausbruch verdunkelte Sonne. In der einen Hand hält Taddeo sein Herz, in der anderen Hand das Licht, beziehungsweise die Weltkugel, die bei sehr genauem Hinschauen die Züge eines Emoticons offenbart. Das soll uns sagen, dass auf schlechte stets bessere Tage folgen, also auch auf (Asche-)Regen irgendwann Sonnenschein folgt. Taddeos Geschlechtsorgan wird hier in einer zensierten Form gezeigt. Wie die Ausgrabungen von Pompei bewiesen haben, war sein tatsächliches Gemächt deutlich länger. Über mehrere Jahrhunderte trug Neapels heutiger Stadtteil Santa Lucia den Namen Taddeos, bis frühe Feministinnen seine Umbenennung nach einer Jungfrau aus dem sizilianischen Syrakus erzwangen.

Der heilige Taddeo war das Vorbild vieler Heiliger, bleibt aber in seinem radikalen Altruismus unübertroffen. Sein Gedenktag ist der 28. August.

SAINT TADDEO

Taddeo was born in Naples in 62. He was a member of a street gang and lived in the shadow of the city walls (as you can clearly see from our illustration). He sometimes did odd jobs for fishermen and market traders but earned most of his money working in the villas of Posillipo. His main source of income was prostitution. A rich Roman once took him to nearby Pompei, where he posed for a pornographic mural (*Taddeo ejaculating*, now sealed away in the National Archaeological Museum). At sundown, Taddeo dreamed of nearby Capri, the former home of Emperor Tiberius, whose legendary parties had earned the island its bewitching reputation. Taddeo's big moment was in 79, when Mount Vesuvius covered the entire region with huge amounts of ash and cubic kilometers of magma with its Plinian eruptions. He selflessly organized emergency aid for the survivors in Naples, sharing his big heart and what little else he had with everyone, and literally giving away his last pair of underpants. This makes him the first in a long line of sex workers who give everything, and we do mean everything. As a result, he was celebrated in Roman society as the "darling of the human race" *(amor ac deliciae generis humani)*. In our highly sophisticated illustration, Taddeo is of course depicted naked (after all, he had given away everything). The picture also shows the aforementioned city wall and the sun, which is partly obscured by the volcanic eruption. In one hand Taddeo holds his heart, in the other hand the light, or rather the world, which, if you look very closely, bears the features of an emoticon. This is meant to tell us that every bad day is always followed by a better one, meaning that even a rain of ashes will eventually be followed by sunshine. Taddeo's genitals have been censored. As the excavations at Pompeii have shown, they were actually much larger. For several centuries, the present-day district of Santa Lucia in Naples was called Taddeo, until early feminists demanded that it be renamed after a virgin from Syracuse.

St. Taddeo has served as a role model for many saints, but his radical altruism remains unsurpassed. His feast day is August 28.

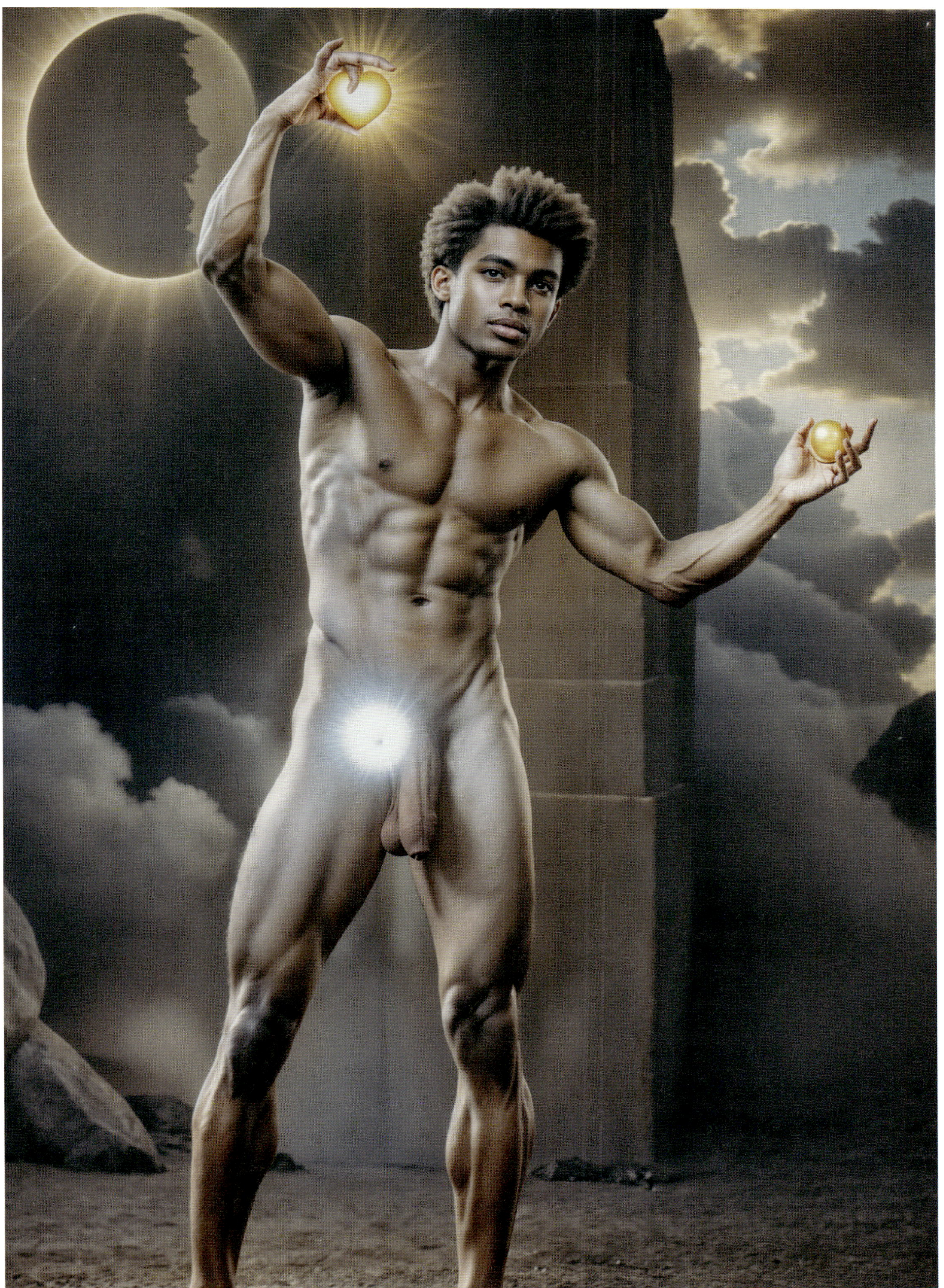

DER HEILIGE TADDEO · SAINT TADDEO

DIE HEILIGEN TEKLE UND MENELEK

Der Ritus der Adelphopoiesis (*Schwurbruderschaft*, slawisch *Pobratimstvo*) war in der orthodoxen Kirche weit verbreitet. Auch Tekle und Menelek aus Aksum, Hauptstadt des aksumitischen Reichs (heute im nördlichen Äthiopien gelegen), wählten im Jahr 316 diesen Weg, um ihrer Liebe Ausdruck zu verleihen. Bei der Adelphopoiesis (wörtlich *Bruder machen*) wird die Beziehung zweier Menschen des gleichen Geschlechts von der Kirche besiegelt. Dabei werden die zukünftigen Brüder zum Altar geführt, wobei der ältere auf der rechten und der jüngere auf der linken Seite geht. Es folgen Gebete, dass die beiden auf ewig in Liebe vereint sein mögen. Dann werden ihre Hände mit einem Gürtel aneinandergebunden und das Paar wird um den Altar herumgeführt, während die Gemeinde singt: „Herr, schau vom Himmel und sieh." Dann kommt endlich der Kuss, zu dem die Gemeinde trällert: „Seht doch, wie gut und schön ist es, wenn Brüder miteinander in Eintracht wohnen." Danach sind alle ganz gerührt und weinen lauthals, und irgendwann werden die Hände dann wieder vom Gürtel befreit, aber zu welchem Zeitpunkt genau, entzieht sich unserer Kenntnis. Auch, warum Tekle und Menelek sich für dieses kitschige Ritual entschieden haben, wissen wir nicht. Ging es ihnen um Steuervorteile? Oder um bevorzugte Behandlung beim Adoptionsrecht? Auf jeden Fall hielt ihre Ehe, Verzeihung, ihre Adelphopoiesis, bis dass der Tod sie schied, was bei den damaligen (und heutigen) Scheidungsraten ja wirklich ein kleines Wunder ist. Besonders in der Äthiopisch-Orthodoxen Tewahedo-Kirche (amharisch የኢትዮጵያ ኦርቶዶክስ ተዋሕዶ ቤተ ክርስቲያን) werden sie dafür dementsprechend frenetisch gefeiert.

Tekle und Menelek werden bei der Gründung von Kleinfamilien (*Ehe für alle*) in der Hoffnung angerufen, dass sie das Geheimnis einer langen Beziehung preisgeben. Der Tekle-Menelek-Gedenktag ist der 10. Oktober.

SAINT TEKLE AND MENELEK

The practice of adelphopoiesis (*sworn brotherhood*, *pobratimstvo* in Slavic) was widespread in the Orthodox Church. Tekle and Menelek of Aksum, the capital of the Aksumite Empire (located in present-day northern Ethiopia), also chose this path in 316 as a way of declaring their love. Adelphopoiesis (literally *to make brothers*) is a ritual by which the relationship between two people of the same sex is confirmed by the church. The brothers-to-be are led to the altar, with the older one on the right and the younger one on the left. This is followed by prayers that the two may be eternally united in love. Then their hands are tied together with a belt and the couple is led around the altar while the congregation sings: "Lord, look down from heaven and see." Then they finally kiss, and the congregation sings: "Behold, how good and beautiful it is when brothers live together in unity." Afterwards, everyone is very moved and there is a lot of noisy weeping, and at some point the couple's hands are untied again, but we don't know exactly when. Nor do we know why Tekle and Menelek chose to perform this cheesy ritual. Was it for the tax benefits? Preferential treatment under adoption law? In any case, their marriage — sorry, their adelphopoiesis — lasted until death did them part, which is truly a small miracle given the divorce rates of the time (and today). They are celebrated enthusiastically, especially in the Ethiopian Orthodox Tewahedo Church (Amharic: የኢትዮጵያ ኦርቶዶክስ ተዋሕዶ ቤተ ክርስቲያን) for this reason.

Tekle and Menelek are invoked by those who wish to start a nuclear family (*marriage rights for everyone*) in the hope that they will reveal the secret of a long-term relationship. The feast day of Tekle and Menelek is October 10.

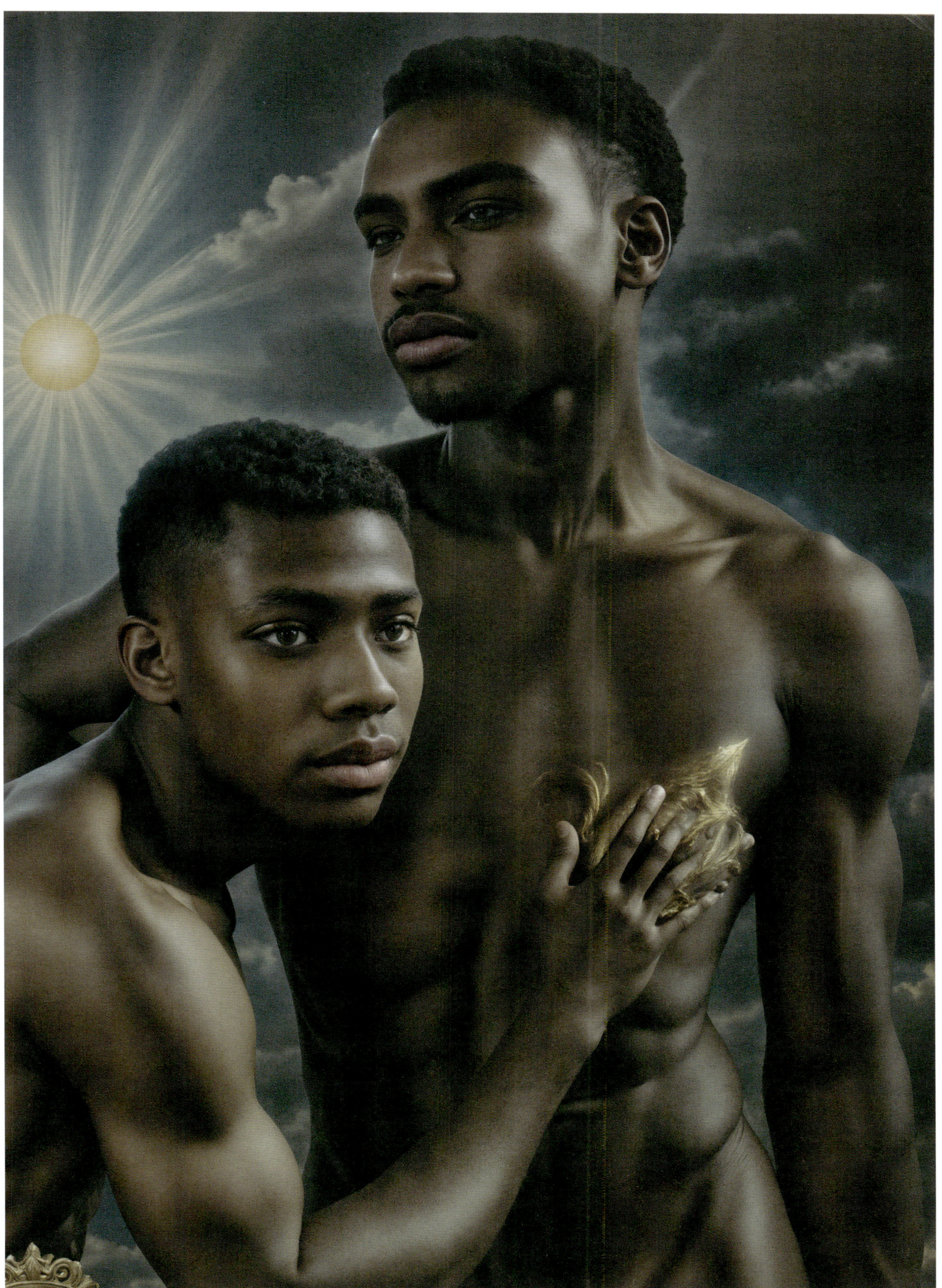

DIE HEILIGEN TEKLE UND MENELEK · SAINT TEKLE AND MENELEK

DER HEILIGE URSLI VON EINSIEDELN

In der katholischen Kirche werden hunderte, wenn nicht sogar tausende von *Schwarzen Madonnen* verehrt, was ein untrügliches Zeichen dafür ist, wie *liberal, aufgeschlossen* und *tolerant* diese Glaubensgemeinschaft ist. Selbstverständlich hatten viele dieser Madonnen Kinder, darunter rein statistisch 51% Jungs und 49% Mädchen, von denen wiederum 7% schwul, lesbisch oder irgendwie nicht-heteronormativ tickten. Die *Schwarze Madonna von Einsiedeln* oder auch *Maria Einsiedeln* ist 117 cm groß und wohnt seit Mitte des 15. Jahrhunderts in der *Gnadenkapelle der Wallfahrts- und Klosterkirche des Klosters Einsiedeln* im Kanton Schwyz. In ihrer rechten Hand hält sie ein Zepter und in der linken, etwas von sich weggestreckt, das nackte Jesuskind. Moderne Mütter und Väter wissen, dass man ein Baby auf keinen Fall auf diese Weise tragen sollte, schließlich muss eine Hand immer den Kopf stützen, aber das ist ein anderes Thema. Madonnensohn Ursli, der spätere heilige Ursli von Einsiedeln, hat die fahrlässige Behandlung zum Glück unbeschadet überstanden und den Strapazen zum Trotz ein äußerst sonniges Gemüt entwickelt. Schon als Kind probierte er gerne die über dreißig verschiedenen Kleider seiner Mutter an und spielte mit ihrem Schmuck und Firlefanz. Darüber hinaus gilt Ursli von Einsiedeln als Erfinder des Wintersports und des modernen Schweiz-Tourismus. Hintergrund war, dass die Pilger, die seine Mutter besuchten, sehr geizig waren, in der Regel nur im Sommer nach Einsiedeln reisten und generell nie genug Geld in der Stadt ließen, um sie zu Wohlstand zu bringen. Diesen prekären Umständen setzte Ursli ein Ende, indem er das Après-Ski erfand. Er organisierte winterliche Besäufnisse mit schlechter Musik, die so unwiderstehlich waren, dass sie einerseits die Touristen glücklich machten und andererseits die Kassen der Einheimischen klingeln ließen. Seine Affinität zu auffälliger Kleidung und übertriebenem Schmuck wusste Ursli dabei geschicht einzusetzen. Diese Gabe muss er wohl von seiner Mutter gehabt haben. Nach den ersten Après-Ski-Erfolgen kam die Katholische Kirche auf den Geschmack und investierte im großen Stil in der Schweiz. In diesem Zusammenhang verwundert die Heiligsprechung des Ursli von Einsiedeln ebenso wenig wie die Tatsache, dass er besonders von Casino-Kapitalisten und Croupiers verehrt wird. Die Heiligenbiografie des Ursli von Einsiedeln wäre natürlich nicht komplett, wenn Ursli nicht mit dem Erreichen des vierzigsten Lebensjahres den Ausstieg gewagt und sich auf eine einsame Almhütte zurückgezogen hätte. Dort lebte er glücklich und zufrieden mit seinem etwas jüngeren Freund Peter und ein paar Ziegen und betätigte sich in der Käseproduktion. Die Schriftstellerin Johanna Spyri griff die Geschichte der beiden 1879 in ihrem Buch *Heidis Lehr- und Wanderjahre* auf, verfälschte sie dabei aber so sehr, dass sie am Ende kaum noch zu erkennen war. Mit dem 1881 erschienenen Folgeband *Heidi kann brauchen, was es gelernt hat* ging die Geschichtsklitterung weiter. Historisch völlig unkorrekt. Im Gegensatz zu unserer formvollendeten Darstellung des heiligen Ursli von Einsiedeln.

Ursli kann angerufen werden, wenn beim Après-Ski der Alkohol ausgeht oder die Musikanlage ausfällt. Aber natürlich auch an seinem Gedenktag, dem 4. Mai, wenn auf der Alm der Frühling beginnt.

SAINT URSLI OF EINSIEDELN

Hundreds, if not thousands, of *Black Madonnas* are worshipped in the Catholic Church, which is an unmistakable sign of how *liberal, open-minded* and *tolerant* this religious community is. Of course, many of these Madonnas had children, of whom statistically 51% were boys and 49% girls, and 7% of these were gay, lesbian or otherwise non-heteronormative. The *Black Madonna of Einsiedeln*, or *Maria Einsiedeln*, is 117 cm tall and has lived in the *Chapel of Grace of the pilgrimage and monastery church of Einsiedeln Abbey* in the canton of Schwyz since the mid-15th century. She holds a scepter in her right hand and the naked baby Jesus, held at a slight distance, in her left. Today's mothers and fathers know that you should never carry a baby like this, as one hand needs to support the head at all times, but that's another topic. The son of the Madonna, Ursli, who later became St. Ursli of Einsiedeln, fortunately survived this negligent handling unscathed and developed an extremely sunny disposition despite his ordeal. Even as a child, he loved trying on the more than thirty different dresses belonging to his mother and playing with her jewelry and trinkets. Ursli von Einsiedeln is also regarded as the inventor of winter sports and modern Swiss tourism. The story behind this was that the pilgrims who visited his mother were usually quite tight-fisted, only traveling to Einsiedeln in the summer and generally never spending enough money in the town to make it prosperous. Ursli put an end to these precarious circumstances by inventing après-ski. He organized winter drinks parties with bad music that were so irresistible that they made the tourists happy and helped fill the local coffers. Ursli knew how to use his penchant for flashy clothing and over-the-top jewelry to attract attention. He probably inherited this talent from his mother. After the success of the first après-ski parties, the Catholic Church acquired a taste for them and began making large-scale investments in Switzerland. They soon enjoyed excellent returns and super-safe investments, which steadily grew more attractive and valuable over the centuries. In this context, the canonization of Ursli von Einsiedeln comes as no surprise, nor does the fact that he is particularly revered by casino capitalists and croupiers. The biography of Ursli von Einsiedeln would of course not be complete without mentioning that Ursli decided to leave the business and retire to a lonely mountain hut at the age of forty. There he lived happily and contentedly with his slightly younger boyfriend Peter and a couple of goats and took up cheesemaking. The writer Johanna Spyri used their story in her 1879 novel *Heidi: Her Years of Wandering and Learning* but changed it so much that it was barely recognizable at the end. She continued along this path of bowdlerization in her follow-up novel *Heidi: How She Used What She Learned*, which was published in 1881. Completely historically incorrect. Unlike our perfectly crafted depiction of St. Ursli of Einsiedeln.

Ursli is invoked at après-ski parties whenever the alcohol runs out or the stereo breaks down. But of course also on his feast day, May 4, when spring arrives on the mountain pastures.

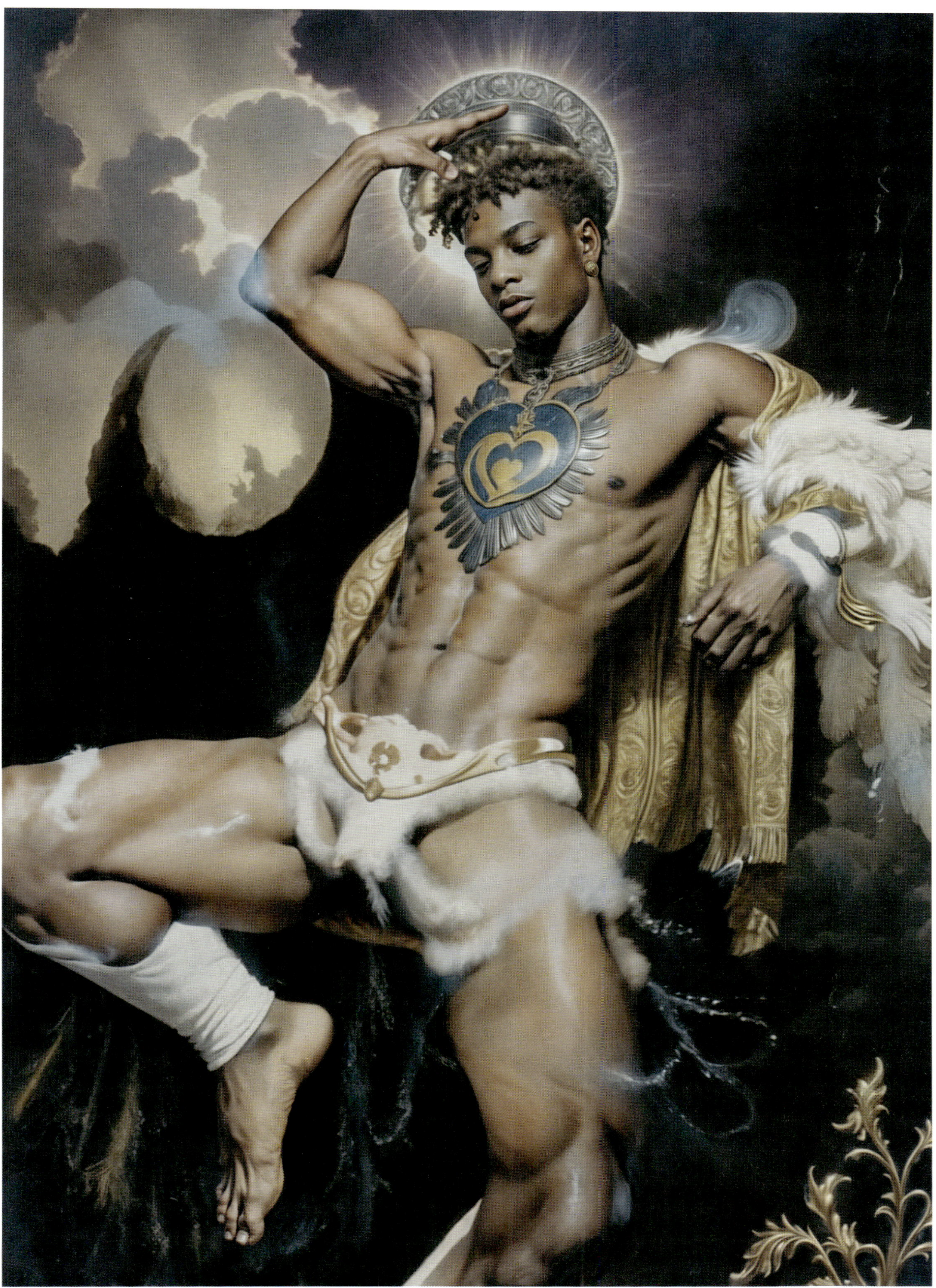

DER HEILIGE URSLI VON EINSIEDELN · SAINT URSLI OF EINSIEDELN

DER HEILIGE VINOD UND DACIA

Vinod, dessen Name sich aus dem Indischen und Pakistanischen mit *Freude* übersetzen lässt, lebte von 324 bis 401 in Bengaluru. Er entwickelte das Dualsystem, auch Zweiersystem oder Binärsystem genannt, bei dem zur Darstellung von Zahlen nur zwei verschiedene Ziffern oder Buchstaben benutzt werden. Interessanterweise benutzte er hierfür nicht die 0 und die 1, sondern die Buchstaben A und P. Sowas nennt sich wohl *positive Logik*. *Negative Logik* wäre dementsprechend P und A, und A und A oder P und P wären einfach nur *unlogisch*. Solches Wissen benötigt man wohl, um einen Computer zum Laufen zu bringen. An dieser Stelle konzentrieren wir uns aber lieber auf die kunsthistorische Besonderheit, dass der heilige Vinod sowohl von vorne als auch von hinten dargestellt wurde, wobei sein modisches Tuch jeweils genau richtig sitzt. Das passt ja auch. Denn genau wie der Name der Stadt Bengaluru im Jahr 2014 heutigen sprachlichen Gepflogenheiten entsprechend in Kannada ಬೆಂಗಳೂರು geändert wurde, entspricht ja irgendwie auch der doppelseitige Vinod heutigen *nichtbinären*, *non-binären* oder *genderqueeren* Gepflogenheiten, oder? Dankenswerterweise fand sich in den Archiven zusätzlich eine Abbildung von Dacia, Vinods Freund, der ursprünglich aus *Colonia Ulpia Traiana Augusta Dacica Sarmizegetusa* (altgriechisch Ζαρμιζεγέθουσα, heute im rumänischen Siebenbürgen gelegen) stammte und um das Jahr 344 nach Bengaluru kam. Reisen nach Indien waren in der späten Antike sehr beliebt — wegen der schönen Männer, wegen der Hoffnung auf spirituelle Erleuchtung, wegen des preiswerten Haschisch. Als Dacia zum ersten Mal auf Vinod traf, war er sofort von positiver Logik erfüllt. Die beiden ergänzten sich hervorragend. Das fand auch Vinods Mutter. Sie war es, die Dacia den im Bild sehr hübsch getroffenen *Koh-i-Noor* schenkte, einen Diamanten von 186 Karat. Er trug ihn stolz auf der Brust. Wäre es nach Vinod und Dacia gegangen, wäre der Edelstein für immer in Indien verblieben, um das Glück schwuler Männer zu schmücken. Doch leider: 1850 fiel er der *Britischen Ostindien-Kompanie* in die Hände und gelangte von dort in den Besitz von Königin Viktoria. Danach kam auf einmal das Gerücht auf, der Stein würde Unglück bringen, wenn er von Männern getragen wird. Eine haltlose Behauptung, die von den späteren Besitzerinnen Queen Mary, Elisabeth I. und Elisabeth II. aber wohl bewusst kultiviert wurde. Wenn man bedenkt, dass das britische Empire keine hundert Jahre, nachdem der *Koh-i-Noor* in Viktorias Besitz gekommen war, in Trümmern lag, könnte man eher auf die Idee kommen, dass er Frauen Unglück bringt. Aber über derlei binären Humbug könnte der heilige Vinod mit Sicherheit nur laut lachen.

Der heilige Vinod kümmert sich um das Funktionieren von Computern, Dacia um glücksbringende schöne Dinge des Lebens. Vinod feiern wir am 21. April, Dacia am 11. Oktober.

SAINT VINOD AND DACIA

Vinod, whose name in Hindi means *Delight*, lived in Bengaluru from 324 to 401. He developed the base-2 or binary numeral system, which uses only two different digits or letters to represent numbers. Interestingly, he did not use 0 and 1 for this, but the letters A and P. This is called *positive logic*. *Negative logic* would be P and A, and A and A or P and P would simply be *illogical*. This is the kind of knowledge you need to operate a computer. At this juncture, however, we will focus on the unusual artistic detail that St. Vinod was depicted from both the front and the back, with his fashionable wrap positioned in exactly the right spot either way. Fittingly enough. Because just as the city of Bengaluru changed its name to Kannada ಬೆಂಗಳೂರು in 2014 in line with modern linguistic conventions, the ambiguous Vinod also somehow corresponds to modern *non-binary*, *genderfluid* and *genderqueer* conventions. Thankfully, the archives also contained a picture of Vinod's boyfriend Dacia, who originally came from *Colonia Ulpia Traiana Augusta Dacica Sarmizegetusa* (ancient Greek Ζαρμιζεγέθουσα, located in present-day Transylvania, Romania) and arrived in Bengaluru around the year 344. Travel to India was very popular in late antiquity — because of the beautiful men, the hope of spiritual enlightenment, and the promise of cheap hashish. From the moment Dacia first met Vinod, he was immediately consumed with positive logic. The two complemented each other beautifully. Vinod's mother obviously thought so too, for it was she who gave Dacia the *Koh-i-Noor*, a 186-carat diamond, which is beautifully captured in our illustration. He wore it around his neck. If it had been up to Vinod and Dacia, the jewel would have remained in India forever to adorn the union of gay men. In 1850, however, it fell into the hands of the *British East India Company* and from there came into the possession of Queen Victoria. It was then suddenly rumored that the stone would bring bad luck if it was worn by men. A completely unfounded claim, but one that was deliberately cultivated by its later owners Queen Mary, Elizabeth I and Elizabeth II. Given the fact that the British Empire was in ruins less than a hundred years after the *Koh-i-Noor* came into Victoria's possession, one might be forgiven for thinking that it brings bad luck to women. But St. Vinod would surely laugh at this kind of binary hokum.

St. Vinod is responsible for ensuring the functionality of computers, while Dacia looks after the beautiful things in life that bring good luck. We celebrate Vinod on April 21, and Dacia on October 11.

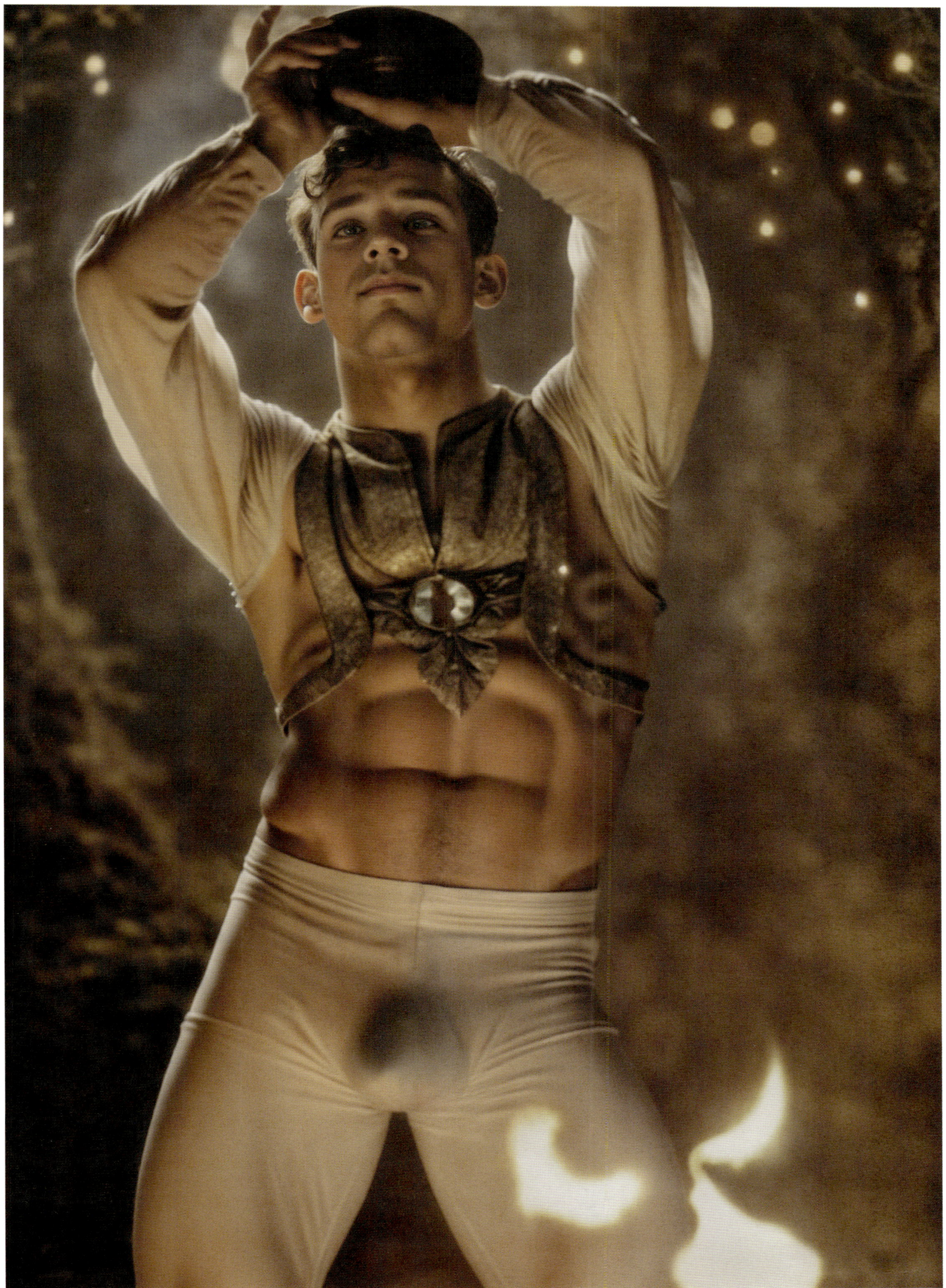

DACIA

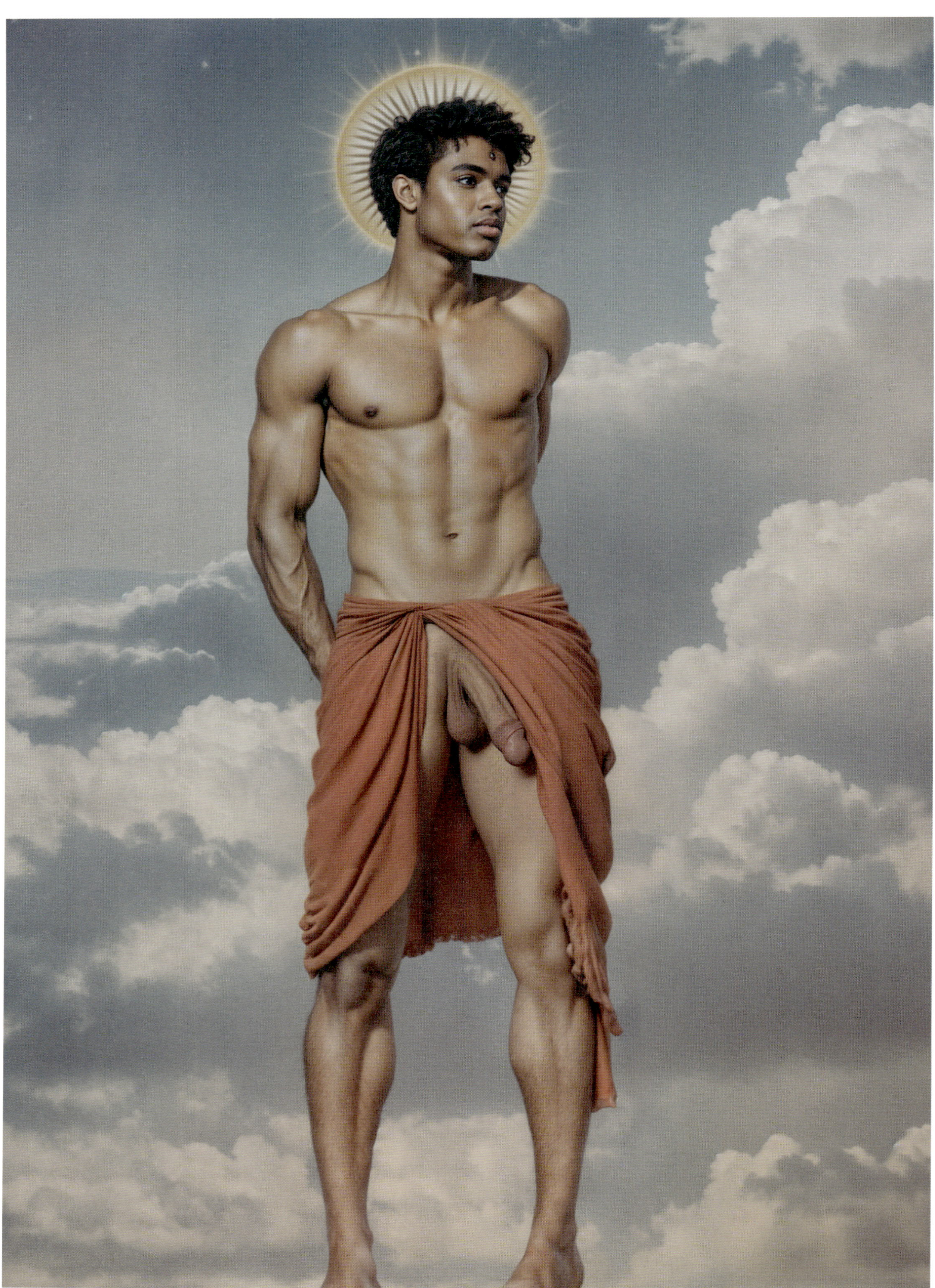

DER HEILIGE VINOD · SAINT VINOD

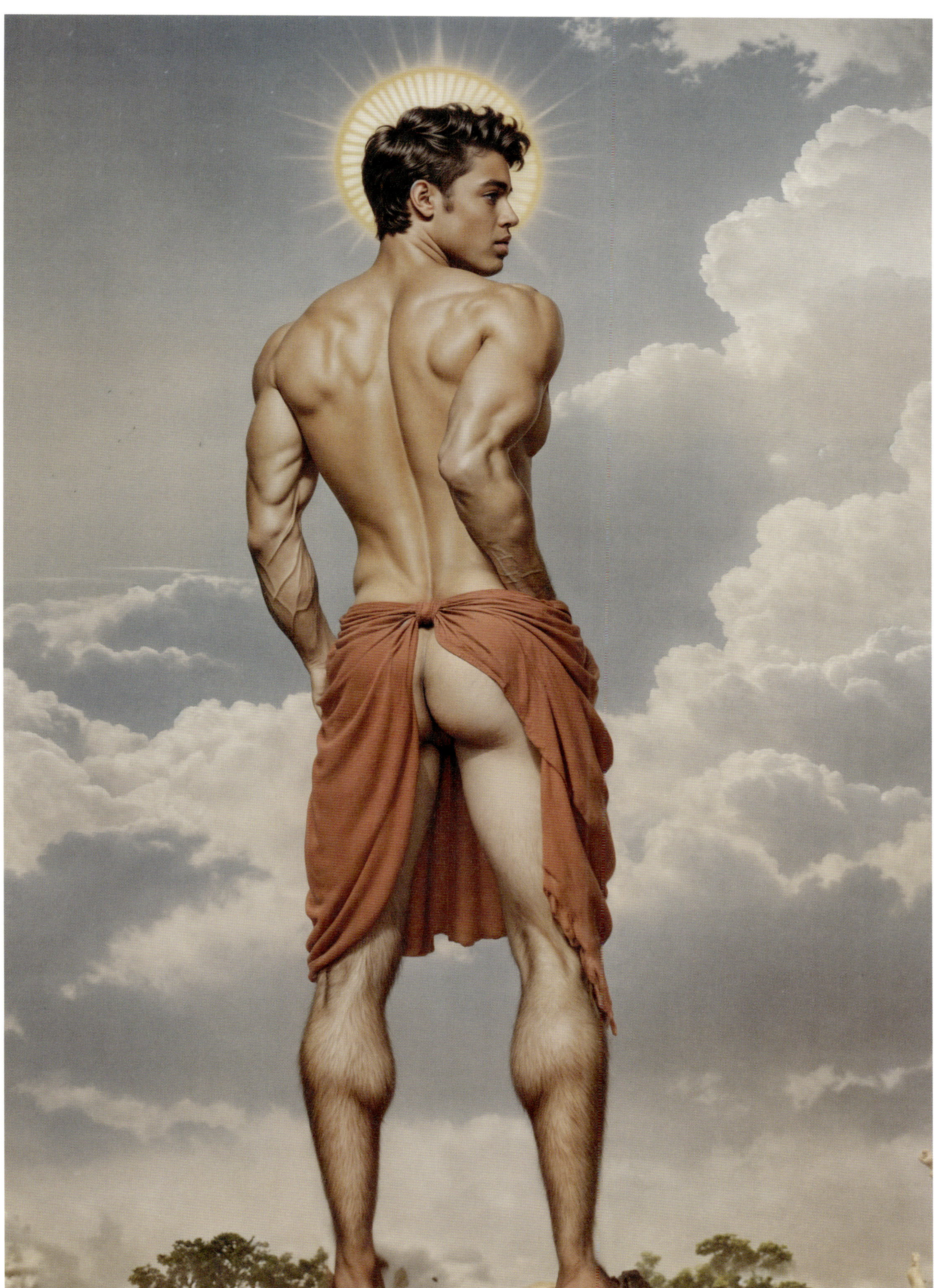

DER HEILIGE VINOD · SAINT VINOD

DER HEILIGE WILBUR

Wilbur lebte als Frauenarzt in vielen Ländern, vielen Kulturen und vielen Epochen. Er ist sozusagen ein Wiedergänger. Seine Darstellung erfolgt meist in Weiß, der bevorzugten Farbe von Ärzten und Pflegern, wird allerdings stets mit düster-stürmischen Gewitterhintergründen kontrastiert, die die Dummheit und Borniertheit vieler Männer symbolisieren. Wilbur grämte sich nämlich sehr darüber, dass viele seiner Geschlechtsgenossen nicht kapieren wollten, dass die Entscheidung über einen Schwangerschaftsabbruch die alleinige Angelegenheit der Frau ist. Kunstgeschichtlich steht die Düsternis natürlich auch für die vielen Regeln, mit denen Menschen sich das Leben gegenseitig schwer machen. Eine wichtige literarische Bearbeitung dieses Themas lieferte John Irving 1985 mit seinem Roman *Gottes Werk und Teufels Beitrag*. Darin spricht Homer Wells, der spätere Dr. Fuzzy Stone, den Grundsatz aus: „Regeln, die für uns gelten sollen, machen wir selbst!" Dieser Spruch hätte auch von Wilbur stammen können. Er und seine Wiedergänger hätten ihn wohl allerdings vor allem auf sexuelle Praktiken bezogen, um die es bei Irving nicht ging, auch wenn man bei der Verfilmung des Romans dank Homer-Darsteller Tobias Vincent „Tobey" Maguire durchaus eindeutige Fantasien entwickeln könnte. Aber ob mit oder ohne Sex: Die vielen Wilburs stehen dafür, dass jeder Mensch der Held seines eigenen Lebens werden kann.

„Gute Nacht, ihr Prinzen von Maine, ihr Könige von Neuengland!" Diesen Gruß am 29. Mai, dem Gedenktag des heiligen Wilbur, auszusprechen, wirkt Wunder — in welchem Kontext auch immer.

SAINT WILBUR

Wilbur was a gynecologist who lived in many countries, many cultures and many eras. He is essentially a revenant. He is usually depicted wearing white, the preferred color of doctors and nurses, but is always juxtaposed against dark, stormy backgrounds that symbolize the stupidity and narrow-mindedness of many men. For Wilbur resented the fact that many of his peers did not understand that the decision to terminate a pregnancy was the sole prerogative of the woman. In terms of art history, darkness of course also symbolizes the many rules that people use to make life difficult for each other. John Irving produced an important literary take on this topic in 1985 with his novel *The Cider House Rules*. In it, the protagonist Homer Wells, who would later become Dr. Fuzzy Stone, states: "We make the rules that apply to us!" Wilbur would have agreed. However, he and his various incarnations would probably have related it primarily to sexual practices, which were not the subject of Irving's novel, even if the film adaptation and especially the actor Tobias Vincent "Tobey" Maguire, who plays Homer, does trigger the occasional explicit fantasy. But with or without sex: the many Wilburs symbolize the belief that everyone can become the hero of their own life.

"Goodnight, you princes of Maine, kings of New England!" Saying this on May 29, the feast day of St. Wilbur, can work miracles — whatever the context.

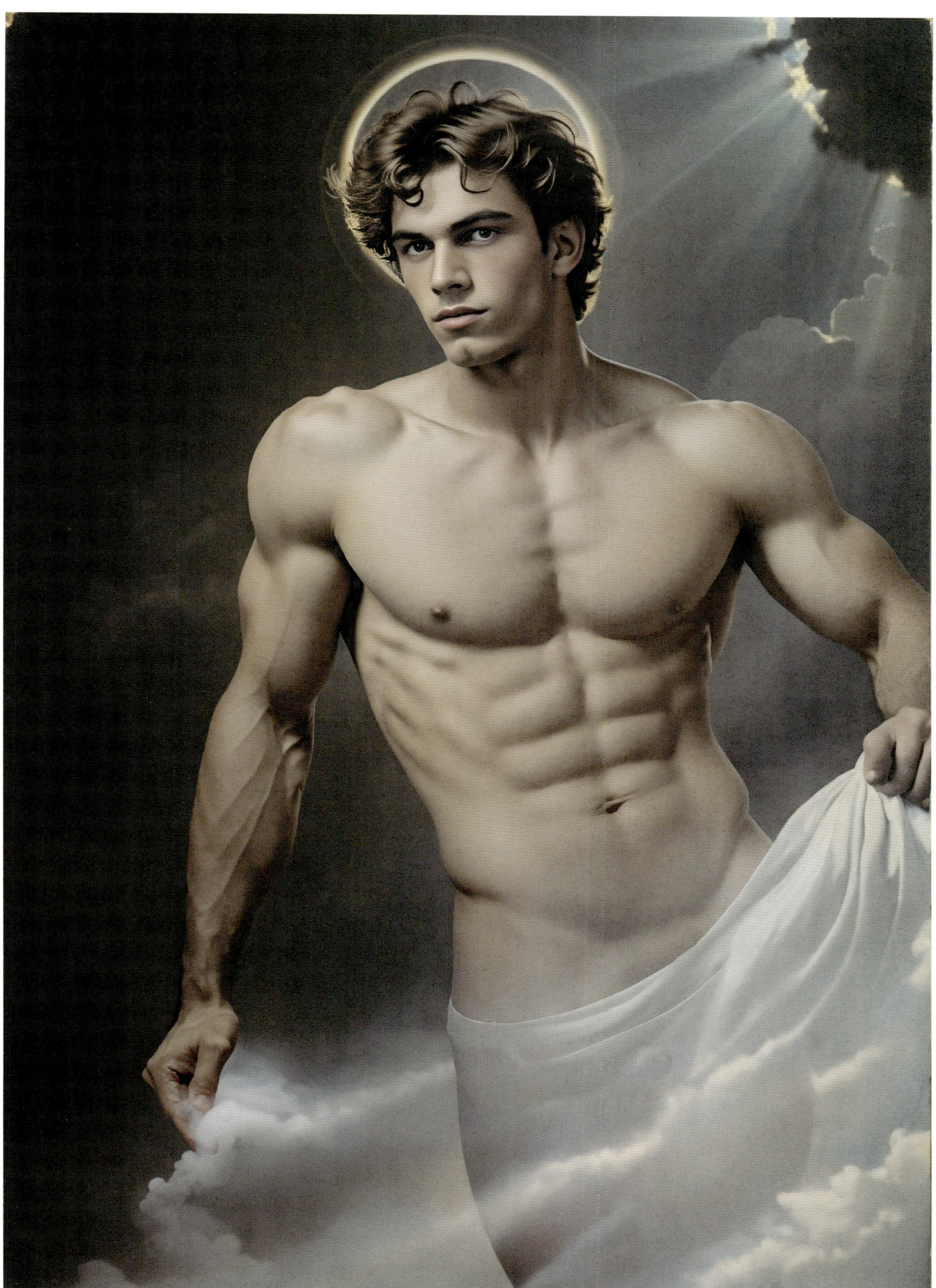

DER HEILIGE WILBUR · SAINT WILBUR

DER HEILIGE XAVIER

Xavier (* 13. März 1769 in Etxaberri; † 3. Mai 1845 in Paris) stammte aus dem spanischen Teil des Baskenlandes, wo er eine Bäckerlehre absolvierte. Mit 17 Jahren ging er nach Paris. In jener Zeit backte man in der französischen Metropole noch ausschließlich Kugelbrote (französisch *boules*, daher auch französisch *boulangerie* für die Bäckerei). Xavier wohnte im Marais und hatte trotz der ziemlich miserablen Lebensumstände, die kurz vor der Revolution in der Stadt herrschten, viel Spaß. Seine nächtlichen Erfahrungen mit den französischen Jungs ließ er in seine Arbeit einfließen. So entfernte er sich von der Kugelform und produzierte die ersten *baguettes*, was sich in etwa mit *kleiner Stock* oder *Stab* übersetzen lässt. Ob das Attribut *klein* zu einer *Stange* mit einer Durchschnittslänge von etwa 55 bis 70 Zentimetern und einem Querschnitt von etwa fünf Zentimetern passt, möge jeder selbst entscheiden, Fakt ist aber, dass Xaviers *baguettes* ein Riesenerfolg waren. Er entwickelte dann noch die *Flûte (Flöte)*, die mit gleichem Gewicht aber doppelter Länge und halbem Umfang eines *Baguettes* daherkam, die *Ficelle (Faden* — gleiches Gewicht, aber ebenfalls länger und dünner) und den *Bâtard (Bastard)*, der Form und Größe eines Rugby-Balls und ca. 30 Zentimeter Durchmesser aufwies. Eigentlich ging es Xavier immer nur um das Eine, aber als die Franzosen ihn einfach so vereinnahmen wollten und das *Baguette* zu einem französischen Nationalheiligtum erklärten (dabei war er doch stolzer Baske!), hat er zäh verhandelt: 1791 wurde Homosexualität in Frankreich legalisiert. So leben Schwule in Frankreich dank dem heiligen Xavier seit 1791 straffrei. Ein weiteres Politikum konnte Xavier dagegen leider nicht lösen. Bis heute ist die französische Regierung nicht bereit, den Angehörigen der baskischen Minderheit die sprachlichen und kulturellen Rechte zu gewähren, die ihnen zustehen.

Der heilige Xavier ist der Schutzpatron aller Bäcker und mahnt uns auch abseits der Backstuben dazu, den Teig schonend zu kneten und zu bearbeiten. Sein Gedenktag ist der 13. März, an dem Sie in der *Boulangerie* Ihres Vertrauens auf attraktive Sonderrabatte hoffen dürfen.

SAINT XAVIER

Xavier (* March 13, 1769 in Etxaberri; † May 3, 1845 in Paris) hailed from the Spanish part of the Basque Country, where he completed an apprenticeship as a baker. At the age of seventeen, he traveled to Paris. In those days, bakers in the French metropolis were still only baking spherical loaves (French *boules*, hence the French term *boulangerie* for bakery). Xavier lived in the Marais and had a great time despite the deplorable living conditions in the city shortly before the revolution. He incorporated his nocturnal experiences with French studs into his work. Abandoning the spherical loaf, he began to produce the first *baguettes*, which roughly translates to *small stick* or *rod*. Whether the adjective *small* is appropriate for a *stick* with an average length of around twenty-two to twenty-eight inches and a diameter of around two inches is for each individual to decide, but one thing is certain: Xavier's *baguettes* were a huge success. He then developed the *flûte (flute)*, which was the same weight but twice the length and half the circumference of a *baguette*, the *ficelle (thread* — same weight but also longer and thinner) and the *bâtard (bastard)*, which was the shape and size of a rugby ball with a diameter of around twelve inches. Xavier was only ever really interested in one thing, but when the French tried to appropriate him and declare the *baguette* a French national treasure (even though he was a proud Basque!), he drove a hard bargain with them and won: homosexuality was legalized in France in 1791. Thanks to St. Xavier, gays in France have lived a life of impunity since 1791. Unfortunately, Xavier was unable to resolve a second political conflict. To this day, the French government refuses to grant the members of the Basque minority the linguistic and cultural rights that are their due.

St. Xavier is the patron saint of all bakers and reminds us to knead and work the dough gently, both inside and outside the bakery. His feast day is March 13, when you can look forward to special discounts at your favorite *boulangerie*.

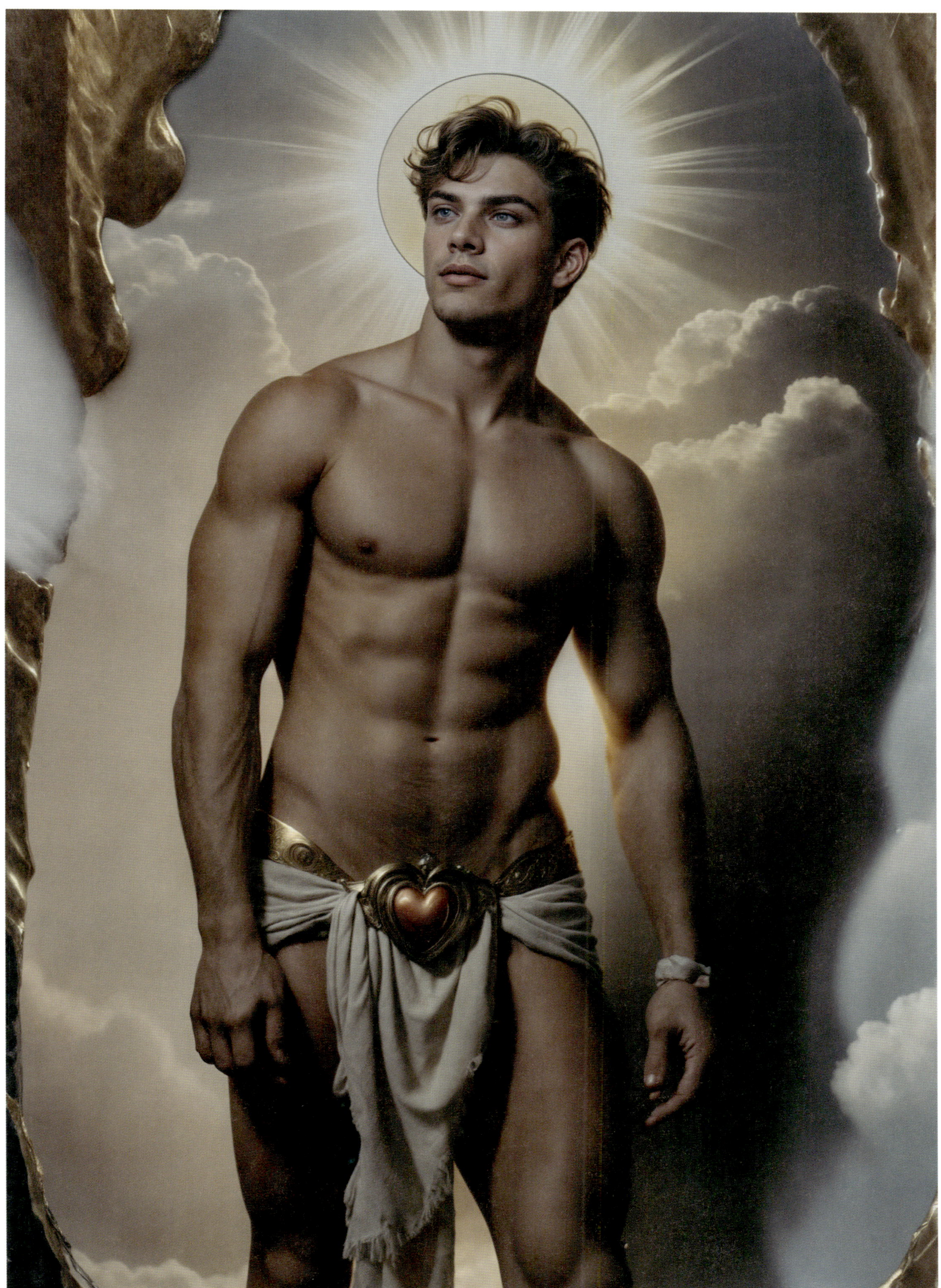

DER HEILIGE XAVIER · SAINT XAVIER

DER HEILIGE ZEBEDÄUS

Zebedäus (altgriechisch Ζεβεδαίος Zebedaíos) ist die griechische Form des hebräischen Namens זְבַדְיָה *Sebadja (zevadjāh)*, was sich sinngemäß mit *Beschenkt von Gott* übersetzen lässt. Im *Neuen Testament* gibt es einen Zebedäus, der Vater von Jakobus und Johannes war und dessen Frau wohl bei der Kreuzigung Jesu dabei war, aber um ihn geht es hier nicht. Unser Zebedäus lebte später. Er war Fischer in Tiberias am Westufer des Sees Genezareth. Seine Arbeit verrichtete er schon als kleiner Junge ganz unbefangen nackt (Kinder- und Jugendarbeit war damals ja noch üblich). Als er heranwuchs, lernte Zebedäus von den anderen Jungs im Gebüsch am See viele spannende Dinge, die ihm großen Spaß machten, wurde aber auch häufig wegen seines kleinen Penis gehänselt. So beschloss er, seinen Schritt mit einer Muschel zu bedecken, um indiskrete Blicke abzuwehren. Bei den Spielereien im Gebüsch legte er die Muschel natürlich wieder ab, um sie anschließend durch eine neue zu ersetzen. Und siehe da: Jedes Mal, wenn er sich seiner Muschel entledigte, verwandelte sie sich in pures Gold. Ein Geschenk des Himmels? Oder ein Zeichen? Zebedäus tippte auf Letzteres. Statt durch das Tragen immer neuer Muscheln großen Reichtum anzuhäufen, besann er sich auf seine alte Unbefangenheit zurück. Fortan lief er wieder nackt und stolz herum. Die Episode hatte ihn daran erinnert, dass sein Penis ungeachtet seiner Größe Gold wert war — ob mit oder ohne Muschel.

☙ Zebedäus erinnert uns daran, dass jeder Körper ein Geschenk ist. Er wird besonders von Nudisten und sonstigen Freunden der Wahrheit verehrt und schützt die Jugend vor Gemeinheiten — insbesondere an seinem Heiligentag, dem 10. November. ❧

SAINT ZEBEDEE

Zebedee (ancient Greek Ζεβεδαίος Zebedaíos) is the Greek form of the Hebrew name זְבַדְיָה or *Sebadja (zevadjāh)*, which can be translated as *The Lord has bestowed*. There is a Zebedee in the *New Testament* who was the father of James and John and whose wife was probably present at the crucifixion of Jesus, but this is not about him. Our Zebedee was born later. He was a fisherman in Tiberias on the western shore of the Sea of Galilee. Even as a young boy, he carried out his work (child labor was still common at the time) completely and unabashedly naked. Growing up, Zebedee learned many exciting things from the other boys in the bushes by the lake, which he really enjoyed, but was also often teased because of his small penis. So he decided to cover his crotch with a seashell to fend off intrusive stares. Of course, he took the shell off while playing in the bushes and replaced it with another one afterwards. And lo! Every time he removed his shell, it turned into pure gold. A gift from heaven? Or a sign? Zebedee went for the second option. Instead of amassing an enormous fortune by wearing more and more shells, he returned to his old lack of inhibition. From then on, he proudly walked around naked again. The incident had reminded him that his penis was worth its weight in gold, regardless of its size — with or without a shell.

☙ Zebedee reminds us that each body is a gift. He is particularly revered by nudists and other truth lovers and protects young people from bullying — especially on his saint's day, November 10. ❧

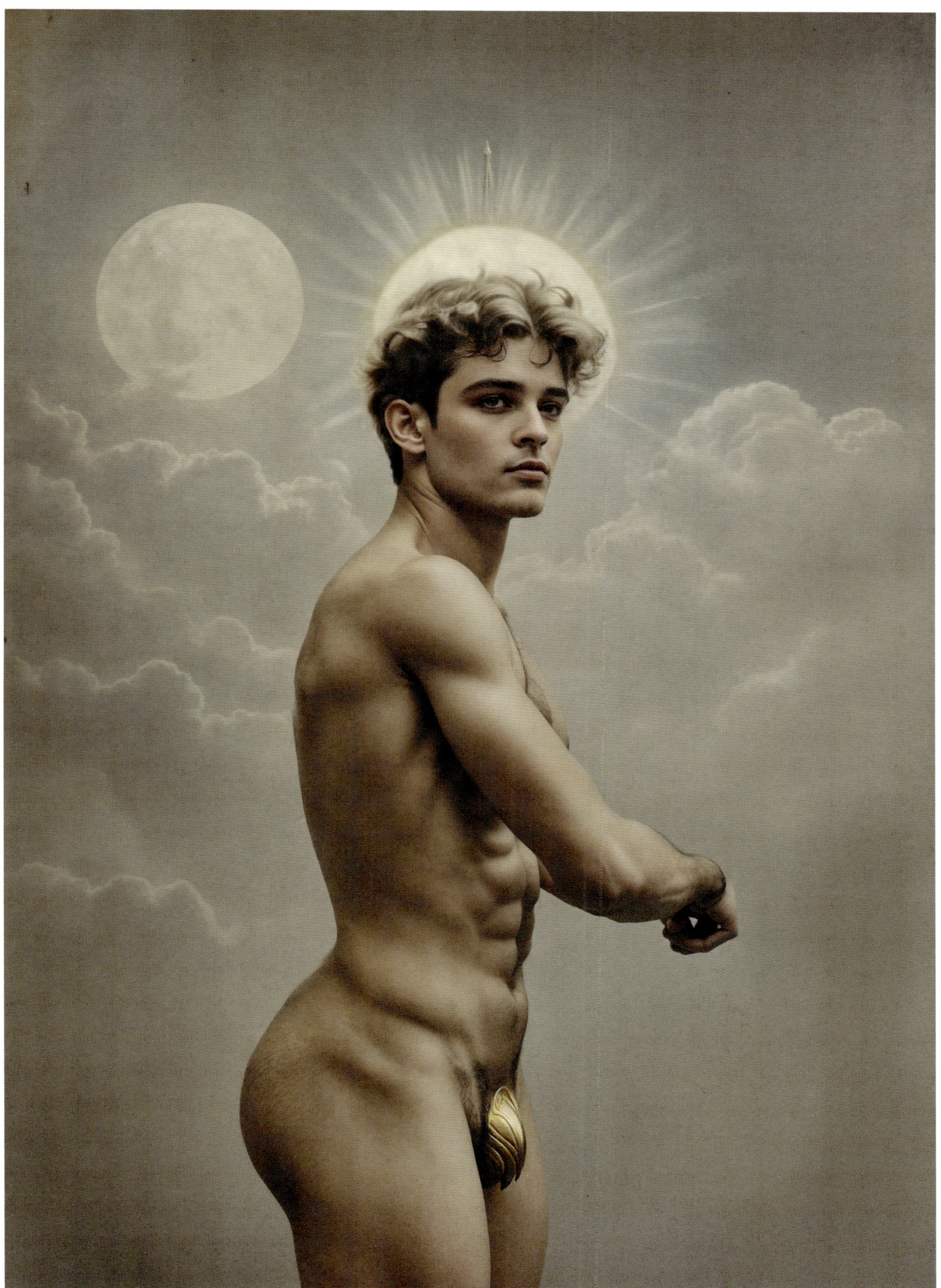

DER HEILIGE ZEBEDÄUS · SAINT ZEBEDEE

DER HEILIGE ŽIVKO

Živko wurde 1720 in Grocka (serbisch Гроцка, gesprochen: *Grotzka*) geboren und verstarb 1799 in Den Haag. Heutzutage ist das an der Donau gelegene Grocka ein Vorstadtbezirk von Belgrad. Zu Živkos Lebzeiten wurde es zum Schauplatz des *Russisch-Österreichischen Türkenkriegs* (1736–1739); wahlweise auch *4. Russischer Türkenkrieg* oder *7. Österreichischer Türkenkrieg.* Zur Einordnung: Zwischen 1423 und 1878 wurden acht *Venezianische*, vier *Polnische*, zehn *Russische* und acht *Österreichische Türkenkriege* geführt. An der Schlacht von Grocka am 22. Juli 1739 musste auch Živko teilnehmen. Am Vorabend hielt er noch eine bewegende und vielbeachtete Rede mit dem Motto „Die Waffen nieder!", in der er die Schrecken des Krieges aus der Sicht eines schwulen Mannes beschrieb. Damit traf er den Nerv der friedliebenden serbischen Bevölkerung, die damals wie heute vorbildlich in Friedens- und Frauen- und Emanzipationsfragen war. Nachdem die Österreicher die Schlacht verloren hatten, zog Živko nach Den Haag, um dort eine Friedenskonferenz vorzubereiten. Seine Vision war, alle Angelegenheiten der nationalen und internationalen Sicherheit, der Abrüstung und des länderübergreifenden Zusammenlebens in Frieden durch ein internationales Schiedsgericht zu klären. Dafür trat er bis zum Schluss seines Lebens ein, erlebte die Konferenz aber nicht mehr persönlich. Als sie 1899 endlich stattfand, wurden Živkos Gedanken von einer neuen Generation Friedenskämpfer vertreten, insbesondere von *Bertha von Suttner*, die dafür sechs Jahre später als erste Frau mit dem Friedensnobelpreis ausgezeichnet wurde. Živko ist derweil das geblieben, was er schon zu Lebzeiten war: eine Symbolfigur der Friedensliebe des serbischen Volks.

☙ Beim Anblick des Halsbands, das Živko in unserer Abbildung trägt, könnte man annehmen, er sei ein osmanischer Sklave gewesen. In Wahrheit trug unser Heiliger diesen Schmuck aber nur, weil er ihm gefiel — und zwar immer, nicht nur an seinem Gedenktag, dem 21. Juli. ❧

SAINT ŽIVKO

Živko was born in Grocka (Serbian Гроцка, pronounced *Grotzka*) in 1720 and died in The Hague in 1799. Today, Grocka, which lies on the Danube, is a suburban district of Belgrade. While Živko was alive, it became the scene of the *Russo-Austrian Turkish War* (1736-1739); also known as the *fourth Russian Turkish War* or the *seventh Austrian Turkish War.* To put this in context: eight *Venetian*, four *Polish*, ten *Russian* and eight *Austrian Turkish wars* were fought between 1423 and 1878. Živko was forced to fight in the Battle of Grocka on July 22, 1739. On the eve of the battle, he held a moving and highly acclaimed speech under the heading "Lay down your arms!" in which he described the horrors of war from the perspective of a gay man. This struck a chord with the peace-loving Serbian people, who were, and still are, champions of peace, women's rights and emancipation. After the Austrians had lost the battle, Živko went to The Hague to prepare a peace conference. He hoped to resolve all matters relating to national and international security, disarmament, and peaceful coexistence between nations through an international court of arbitration. He continued to advocate for this until the end of his life, but did not live to witness the conference in person. When it finally took place in 1899, Živko's ideas were championed by a new generation of peace activists, in particular *Bertha von Suttner*, who six years later became the first woman to be awarded the Nobel Peace Prize. Živko has remained the same figure he was during his lifetime: a symbol of the Serbian people's love of peace.

☙ The necklace Živko is wearing in our illustration could lead one to assume that he was an Ottoman slave. In reality, however, our saint wore this piece of jewelry simply because he liked it — all the time, and not just on his feast day, July 21. ❧

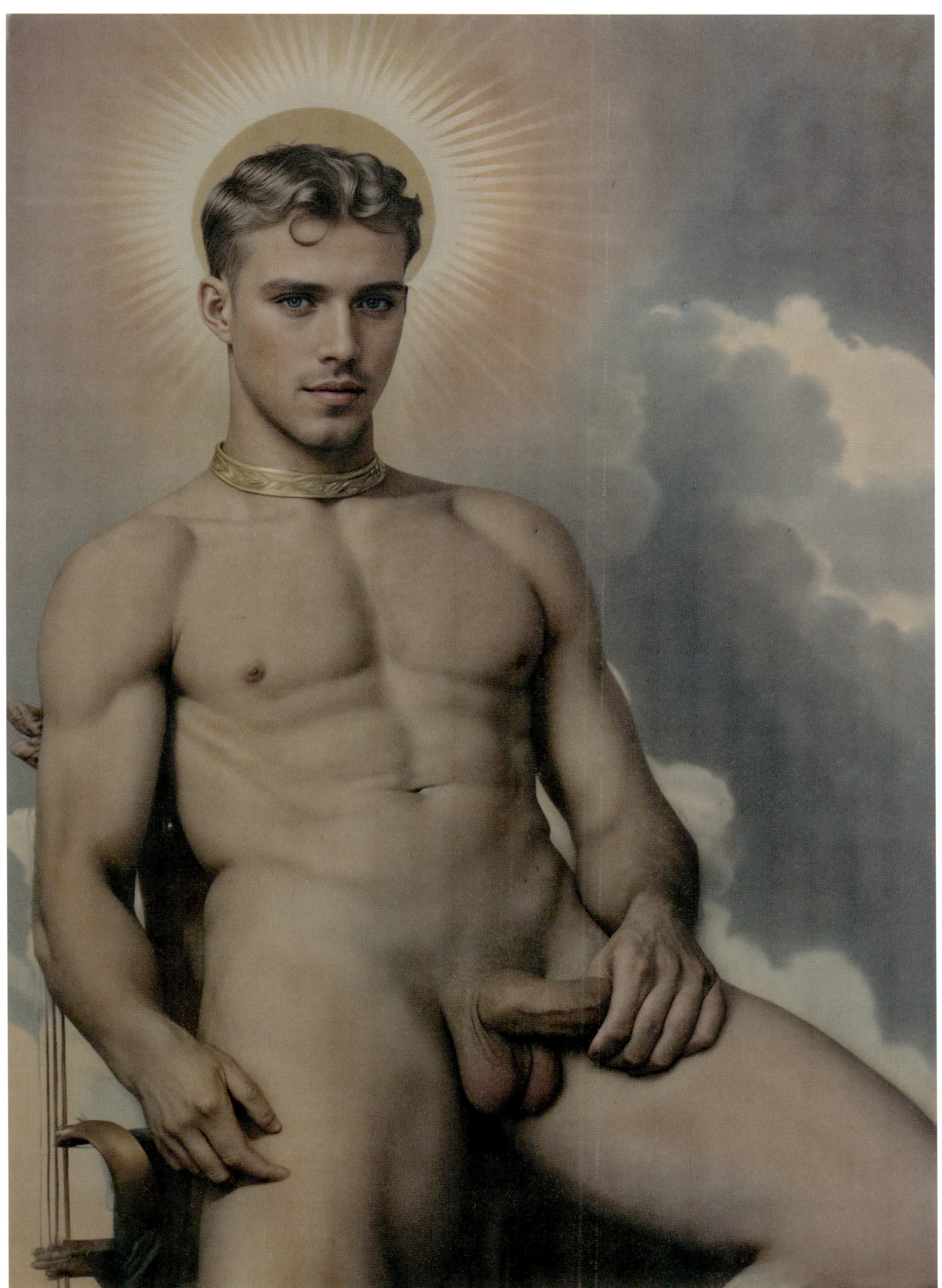

DER HEILIGE ŽIVKO · SAINT ŽIVKO

INDEX SANCTORUM MASCULORUM CONCUBITORUM
MARTYROLOGIUM SODOMITARUM

HEILIG DURCH DAS JAHR
SANCTI PER ANNUM

F.G. BORGHI · BJÖRN KOLL
UNHOLY – AN ALMOST COMPLETE HAGIOGRAPHY OF GAY SAINTS

Salzgeber Buchverlage GmbH

Wilhelmine-Gemberg-Weg 6 / K
10179 Berlin · Germany

support@salzgeber.de · www.salzgeber.de

Texts: Björn Koll
Translated from German by Nicola Heine

Created and designed by Björn Koll and Johann Peter Werth

Paper: Arctic Volume
Printing/Binding: DH PrintingHouse, Riga
Printed in Latvia

First Edition 2025

ISBN 978-3-95985-713-0